Story & Art by

Chitose Yagami

Shojo Beat

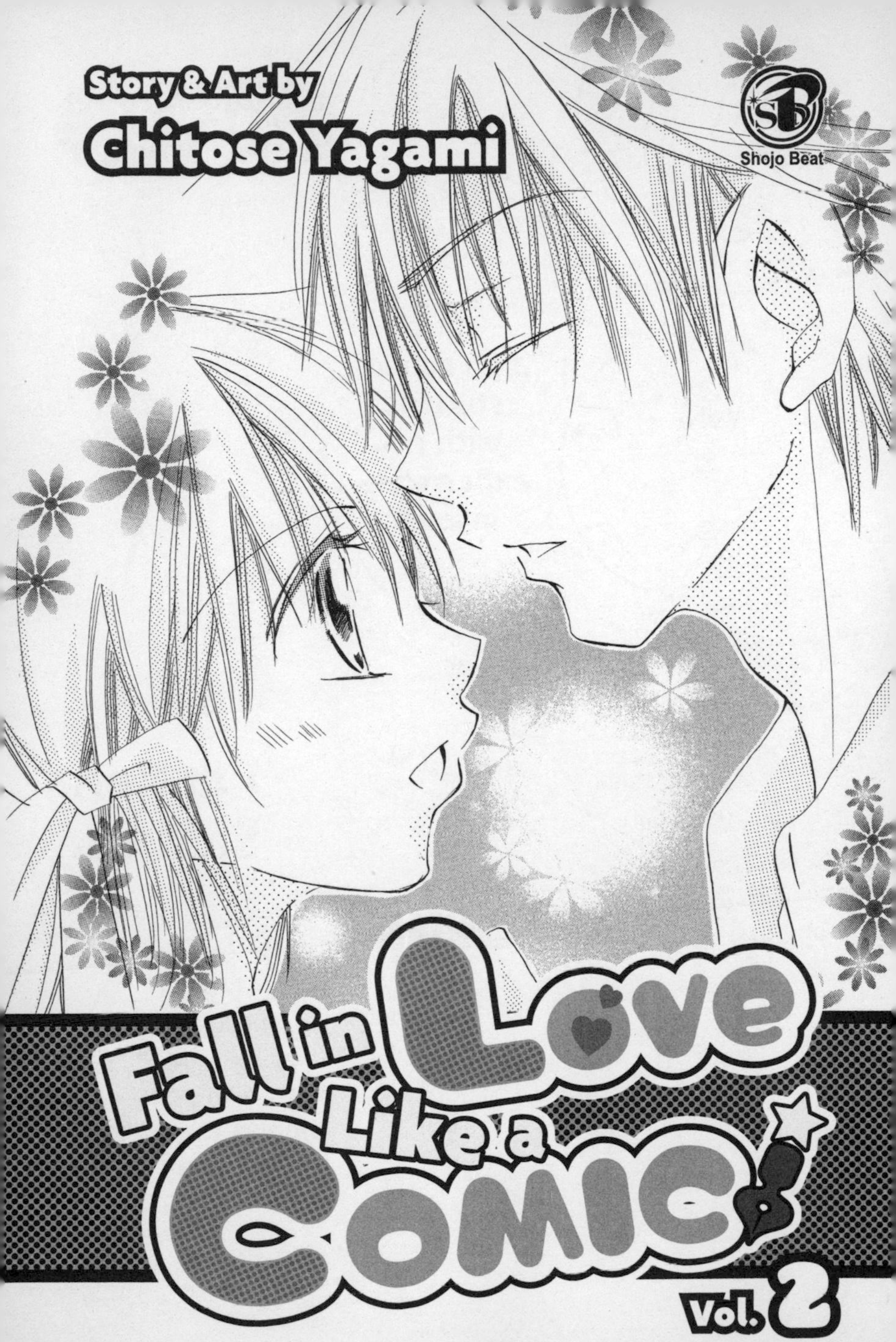

Fall in Love Like a Comic

Vol. 2

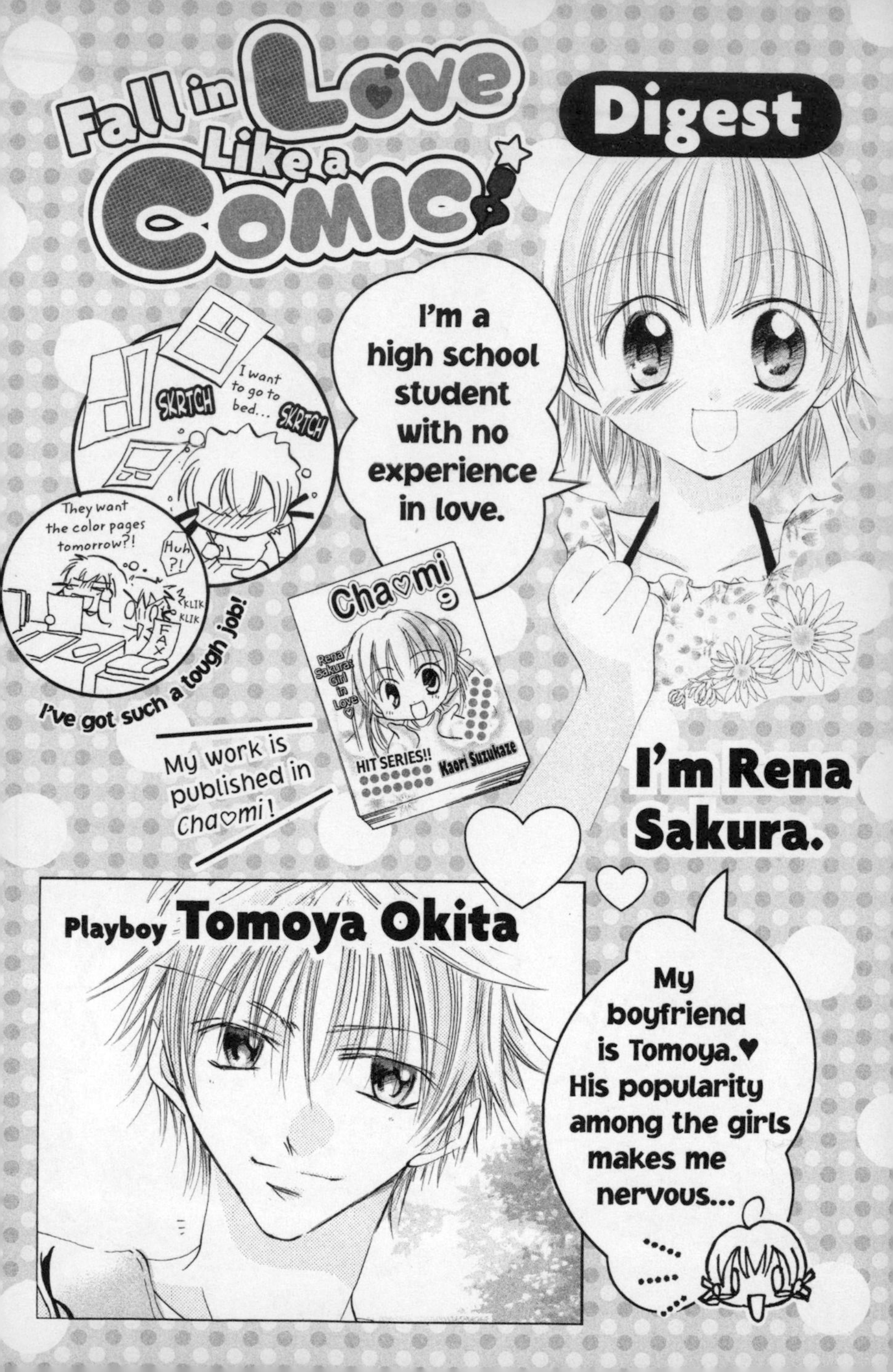
Fall in Love Like a Comic!
Digest
I'm a high school student with no experience in love.
I'm Rena Sakura.
I want to go to bed...
SKRTCH
SKRTCH
They want the color pages tomorrow?!
Huh?!
KLIK KLIK
FAX
I've got such a tough job!
Cha♡mi 9
Rena Sakura: Girl in Love ♡
HIT SERIES!!
Kaori Suzukaze
My work is published in Cha♡mi!
My boyfriend is Tomoya.♥ His popularity among the girls makes me nervous...
.....
.....
.....
Playboy Tomoya Okita

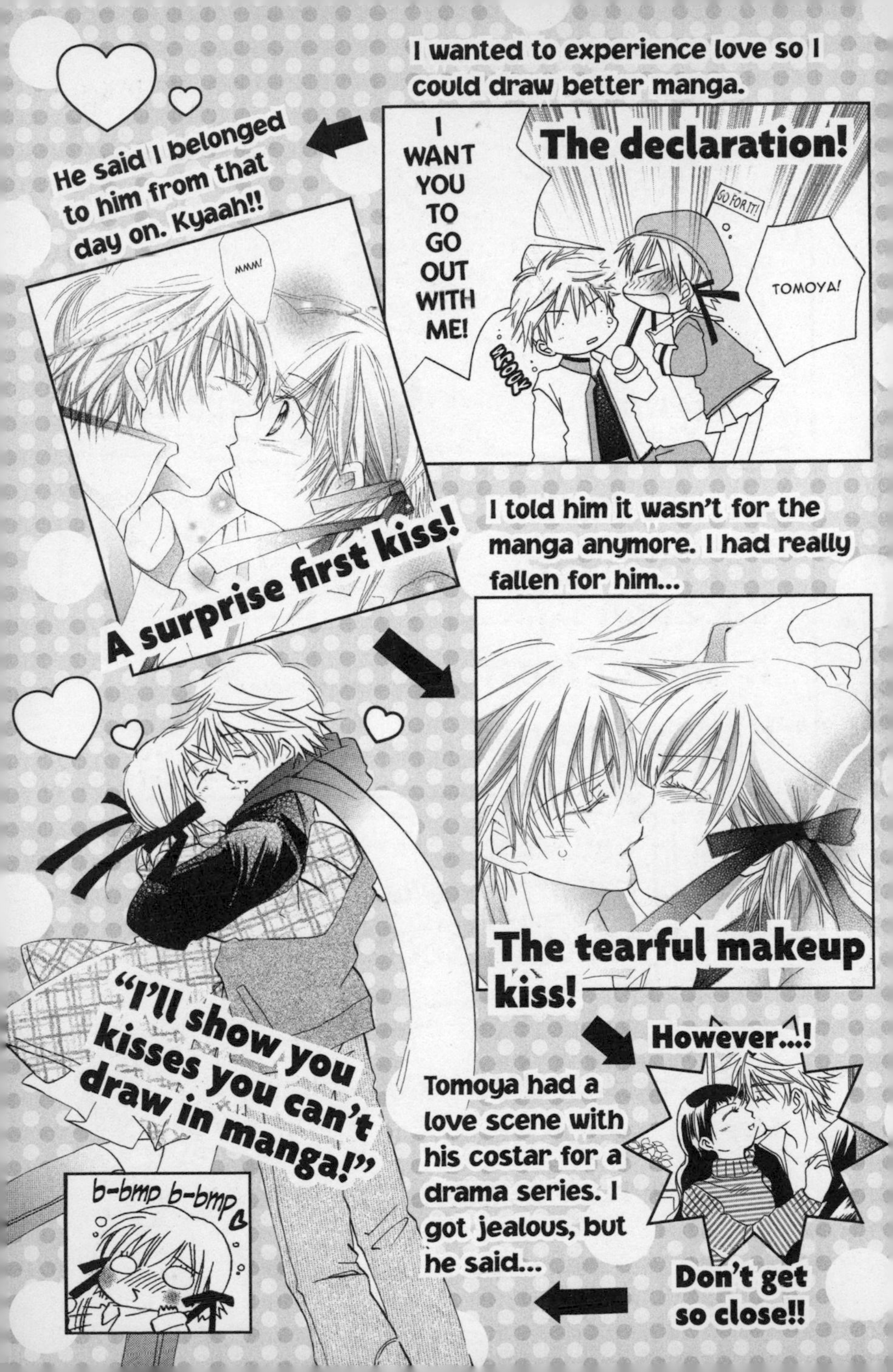

I wanted to experience love so I could draw better manga.
The declaration!
I WANT YOU TO GO OUT WITH ME!
GO FOR IT!
TOMOYA!
He said I belonged to him from that day on. Kyaah!!
MMM!
A surprise first kiss!
I told him it wasn't for the manga anymore. I had really fallen for him...
The tearful makeup kiss!
However...!
Tomoya had a love scene with his costar for a drama series. I got jealous, but he said...
Don't get so close!!
"I'll show you kisses you can't draw in manga!"
b-bmp b-bmp

Fall in Love Like a Comic!

CHITOSE YAGAMI

Contents

Vol. 2

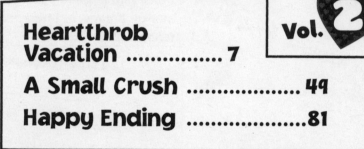

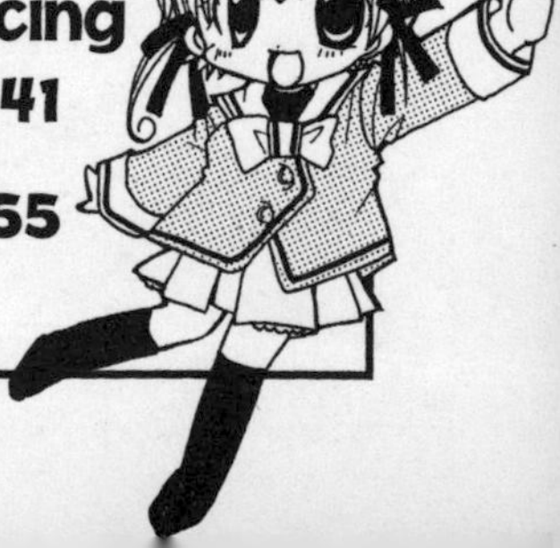

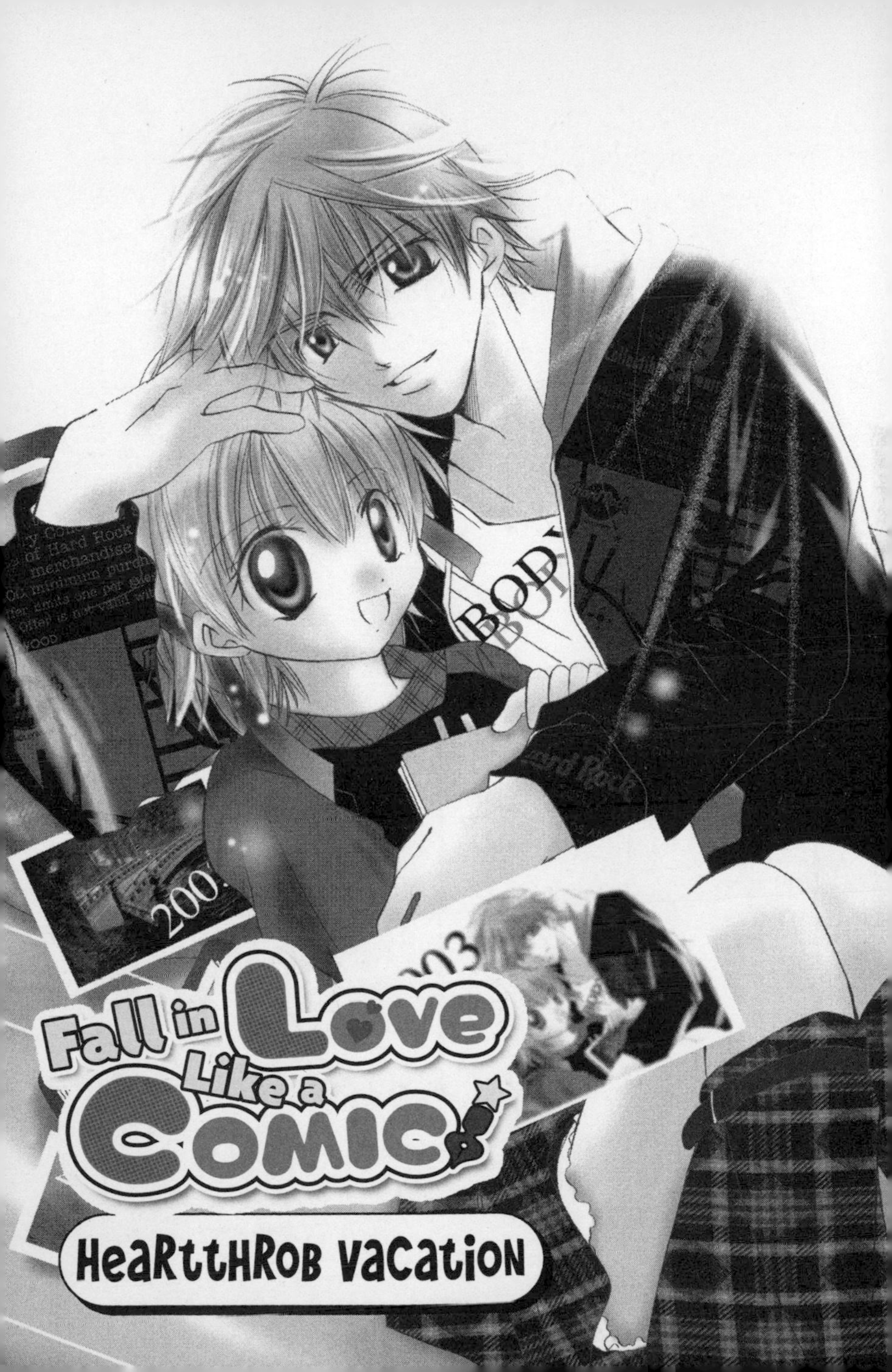
Fall in Love Like a Comic!
Heartthrob Vacation

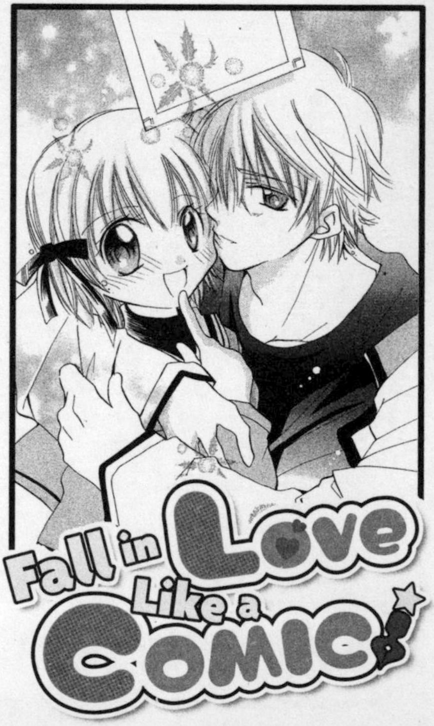
Fall in Love Like a Comic!

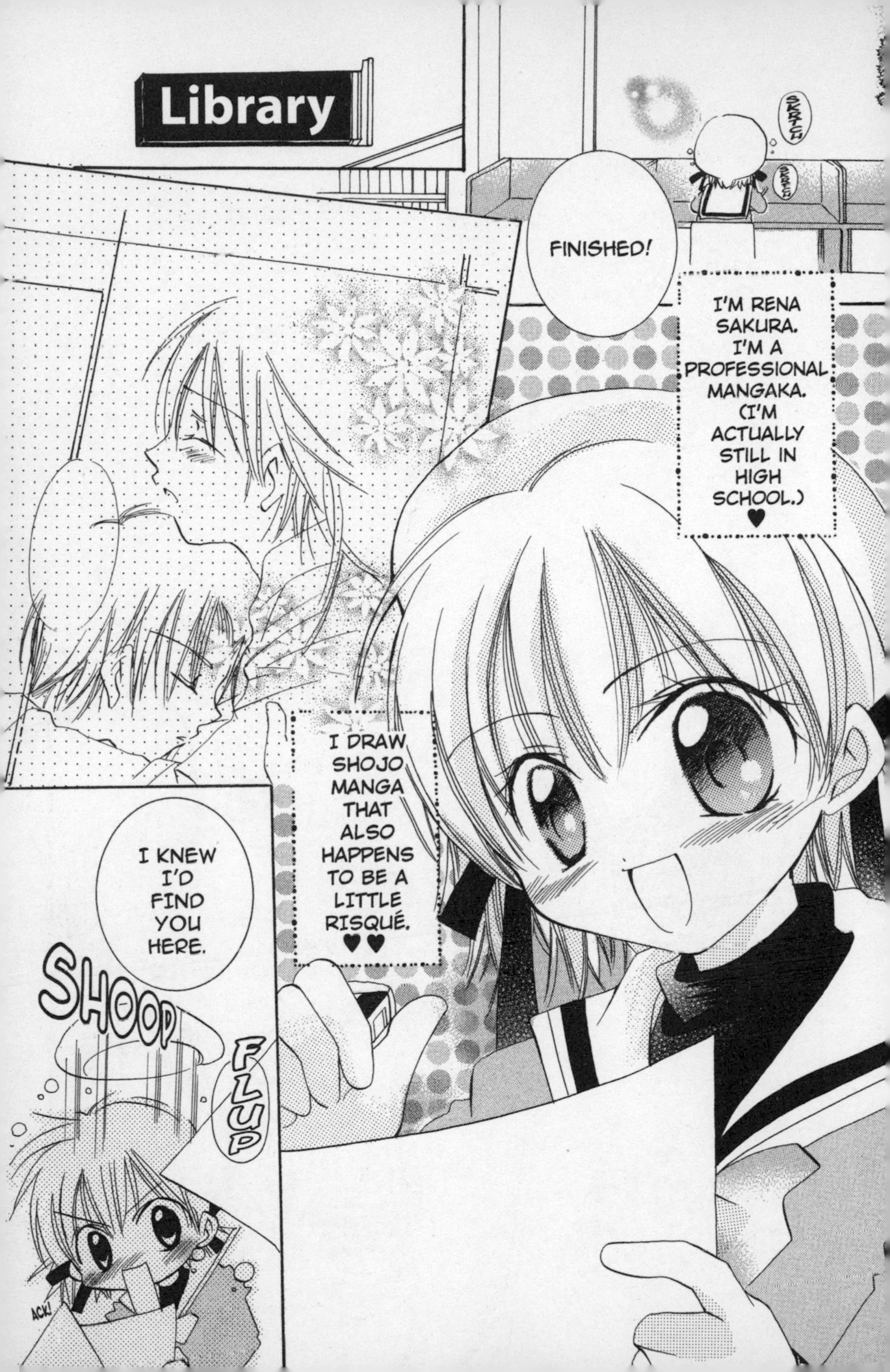
Library
SKRTCH
SKRTCH
FINISHED!
I'M RENA SAKURA. I'M A PROFESSIONAL MANGAKA. (I'M ACTUALLY STILL IN HIGH SCHOOL.) ♥
I DRAW SHOJO MANGA THAT ALSO HAPPENS TO BE A LITTLE RISQUÉ. ♥♥
I KNEW I'D FIND YOU HERE.
SHOOP
FLUP
ACK!

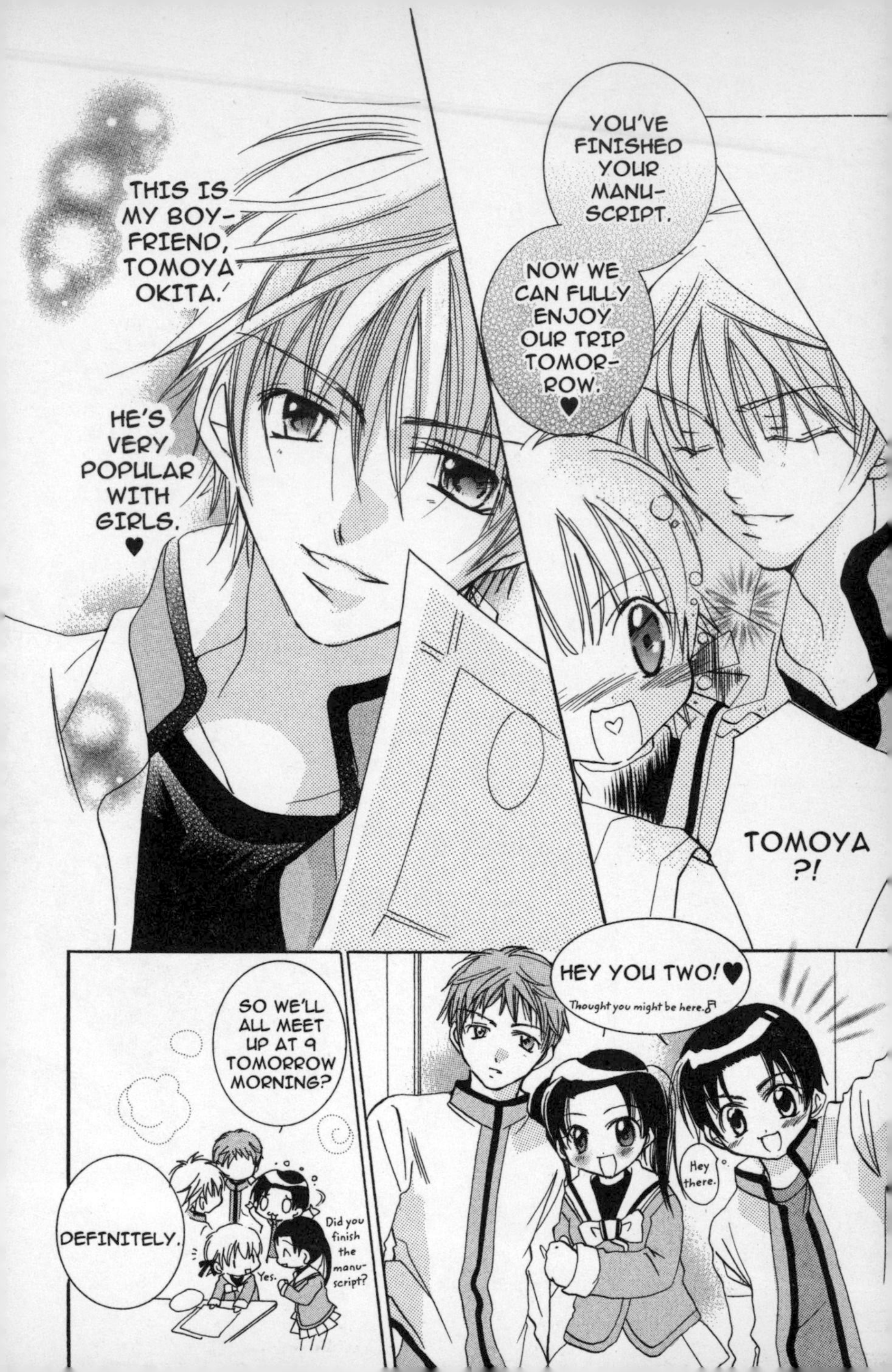
YOU'VE FINISHED YOUR MANU-SCRIPT.
NOW WE CAN FULLY ENJOY OUR TRIP TOMOR-ROW. ♥
TOMOYA ?!
THIS IS MY BOY-FRIEND, TOMOYA OKITA.
HE'S VERY POPULAR WITH GIRLS. ♥
HEY YOU TWO! ♥
Thought you might be here.♫
Hey there.
SO WE'LL ALL MEET UP AT 9 TOMORROW MORNING?
Did you finish the manu-script?
Yes.
DEFINITELY.

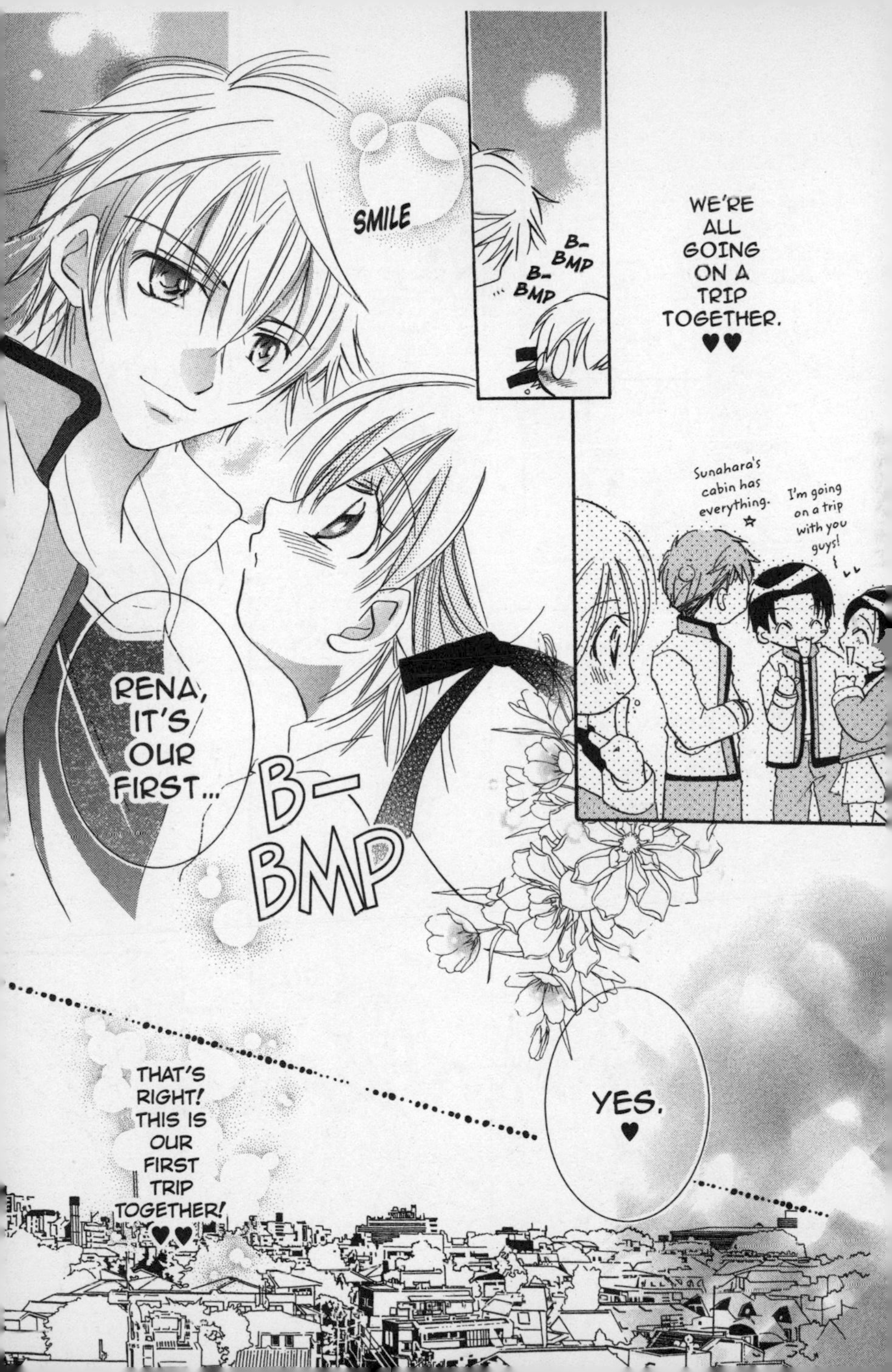

WE'RE ALL GOING ON A TRIP TOGETHER. ♥♥
B-BMP
B-BMP
Sunahara's cabin has everything. ☆
I'm going on a trip with you guys!
SMILE
RENA, IT'S OUR FIRST...
B-BMP
YES. ♥
THAT'S RIGHT! THIS IS OUR FIRST TRIP TOGETHER! ♥♥

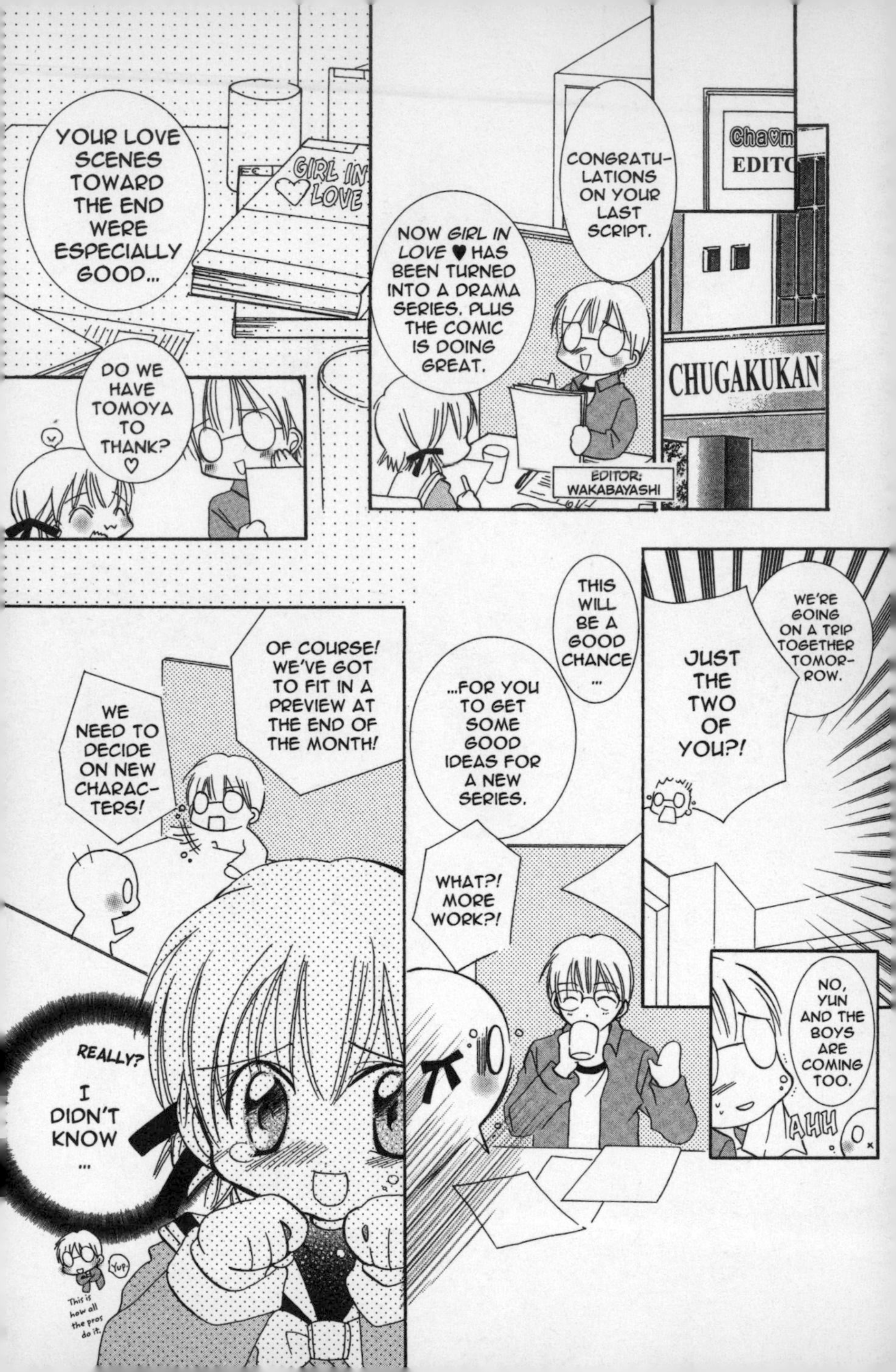
Cha♥m
EDITO
CHUGAKUKAN
CONGRATULATIONS ON YOUR LAST SCRIPT.
NOW GIRL IN LOVE♥ HAS BEEN TURNED INTO A DRAMA SERIES. PLUS THE COMIC IS DOING GREAT.
EDITOR: WAKABAYASHI
YOUR LOVE SCENES TOWARD THE END WERE ESPECIALLY GOOD...
GIRL IN ♥ LOVE
DO WE HAVE TOMOYA TO THANK? ♡
WE'RE GOING ON A TRIP TOGETHER TOMORROW.
JUST THE TWO OF YOU?!
NO, YUN AND THE BOYS ARE COMING TOO.
AHH
THIS WILL BE A GOOD CHANCE...
...FOR YOU TO GET SOME GOOD IDEAS FOR A NEW SERIES.
WHAT?! MORE WORK?!
OF COURSE! WE'VE GOT TO FIT IN A PREVIEW AT THE END OF THE MONTH!
WE NEED TO DECIDE ON NEW CHARACTERS!
REALLY?
I DIDN'T KNOW...
Yup.
This is how all the pros do it.

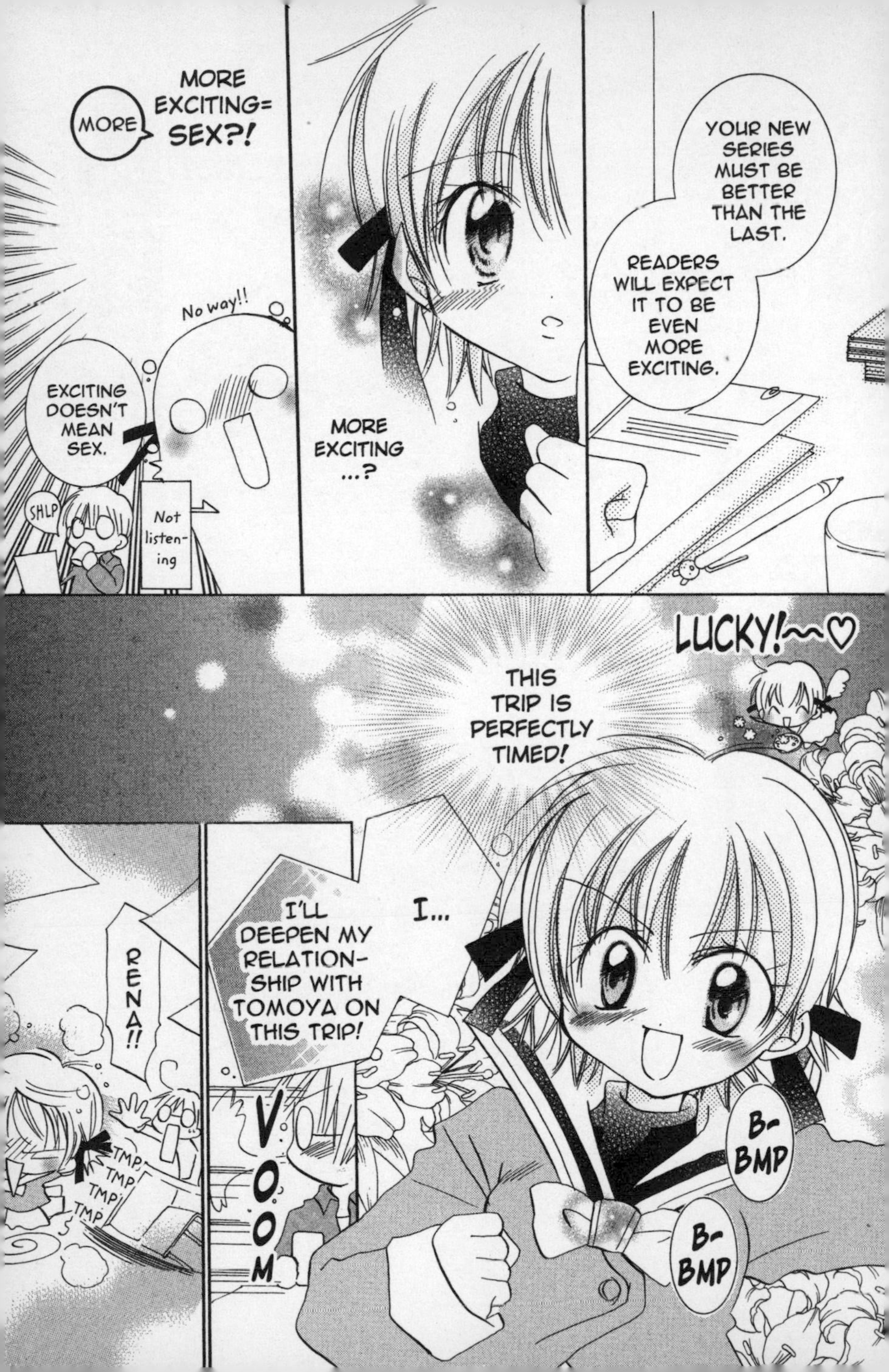
YOUR NEW SERIES MUST BE BETTER THAN THE LAST.
READERS WILL EXPECT IT TO BE EVEN MORE EXCITING.
MORE EXCITING ...?
MORE EXCITING= SEX?!
MORE
No way!!
EXCITING DOESN'T MEAN SEX.
SHLP
Not listen-ing
LUCKY!~~♡
THIS TRIP IS PERFECTLY TIMED!
I...
I'LL DEEPEN MY RELATION-SHIP WITH TOMOYA ON THIS TRIP!
B-BMP
B-BMP
VOOM
RENA!!
TMP TMP TMP TMP

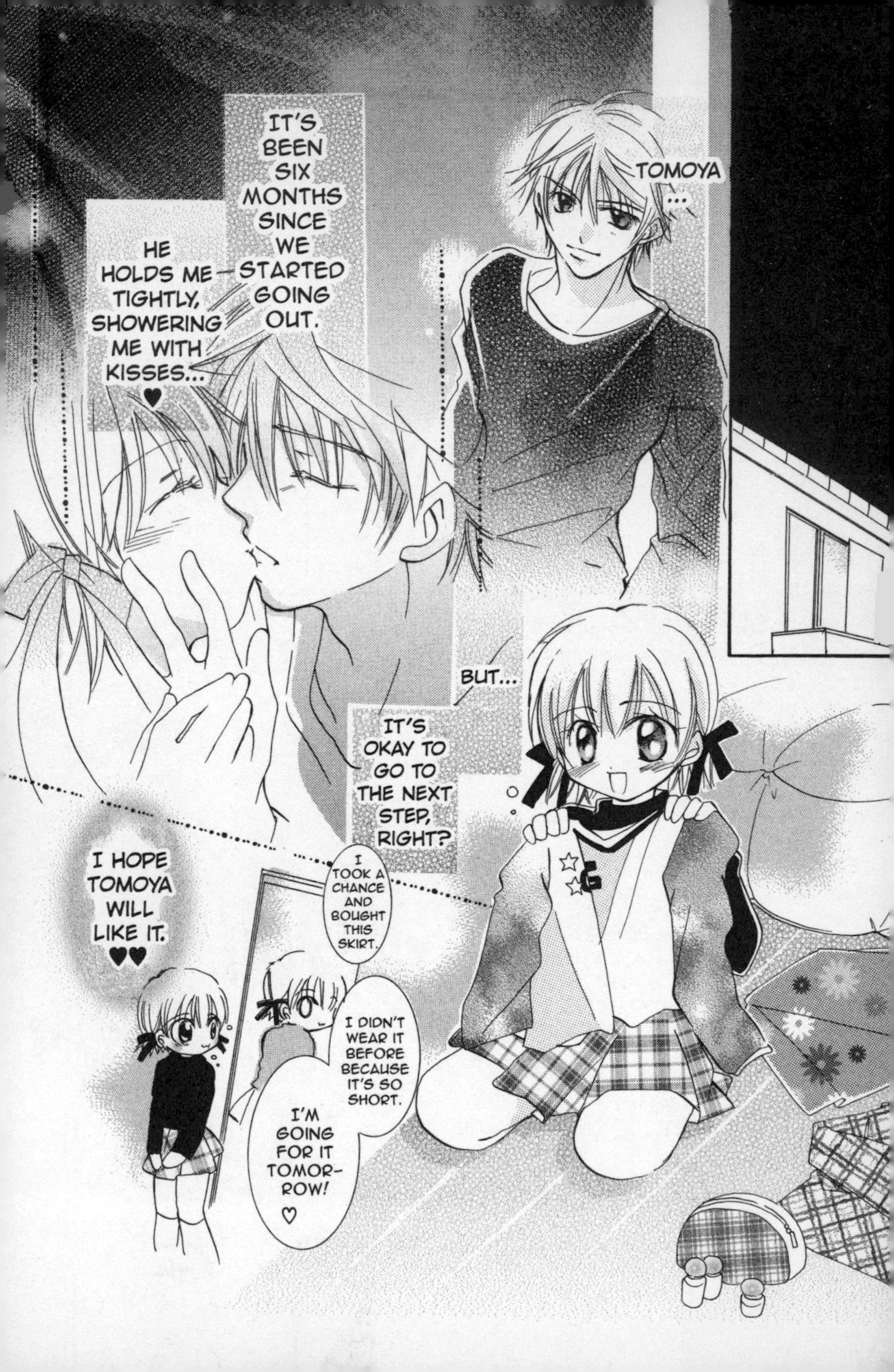

TOMOYA...
IT'S BEEN SIX MONTHS SINCE WE STARTED GOING OUT.
HE HOLDS ME TIGHTLY, SHOWERING ME WITH KISSES... ♥
BUT...
IT'S OKAY TO GO TO THE NEXT STEP, RIGHT?
I TOOK A CHANCE AND BOUGHT THIS SKIRT.
I DIDN'T WEAR IT BEFORE BECAUSE IT'S SO SHORT.
I'M GOING FOR IT TOMORROW! ♡
I HOPE TOMOYA WILL LIKE IT. ♥♥

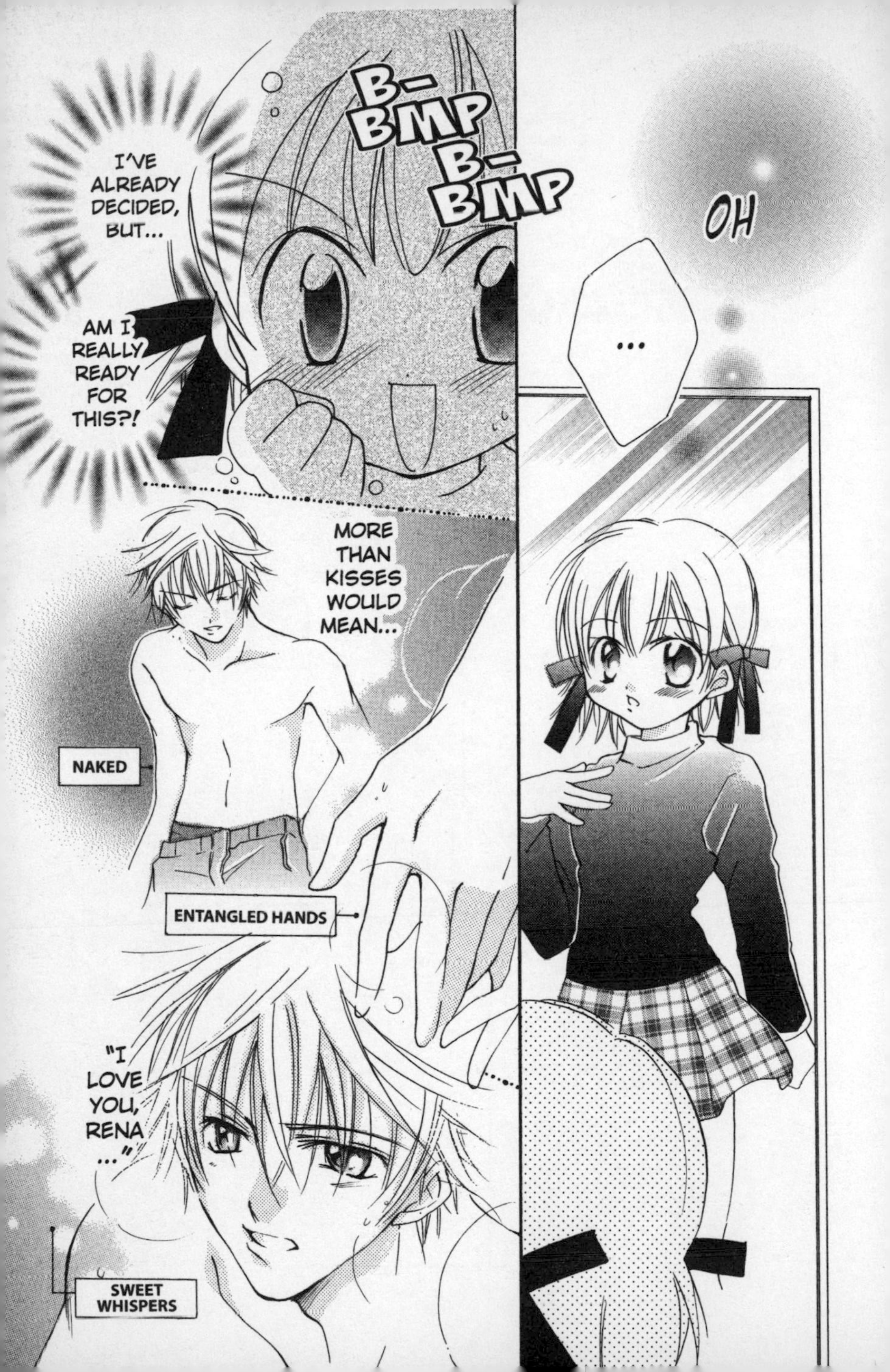
OH
...
B-BMP B-BMP
I'VE ALREADY DECIDED, BUT...
AM I REALLY READY FOR THIS?!
MORE THAN KISSES WOULD MEAN...
NAKED
ENTANGLED HANDS
"I LOVE YOU, RENA..."
SWEET WHISPERS

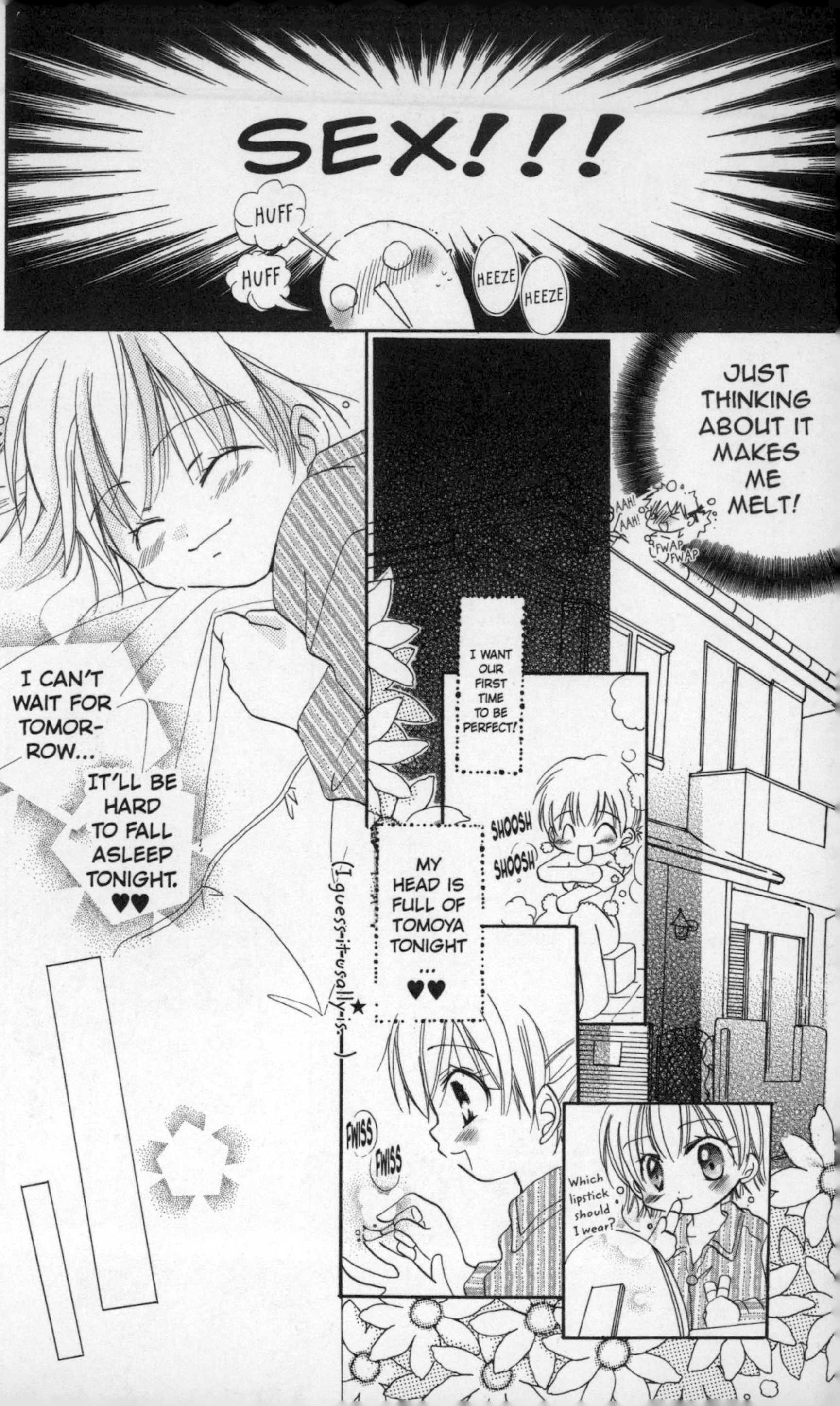
SEX!!!
HUFF
HUFF
HEEZE
HEEZE
JUST THINKING ABOUT IT MAKES ME MELT!
AAH! AAH!
FWAP FWAP
I WANT OUR FIRST TIME TO BE PERFECT!
SHOOSH SHOOSH
MY HEAD IS FULL OF TOMOYA TONIGHT... ♥♥
Which lipstick should I wear?
FWISS FWISS
I CAN'T WAIT FOR TOMORROW...
IT'LL BE HARD TO FALL ASLEEP TONIGHT. ♥♥
(I guess it usually is.)★

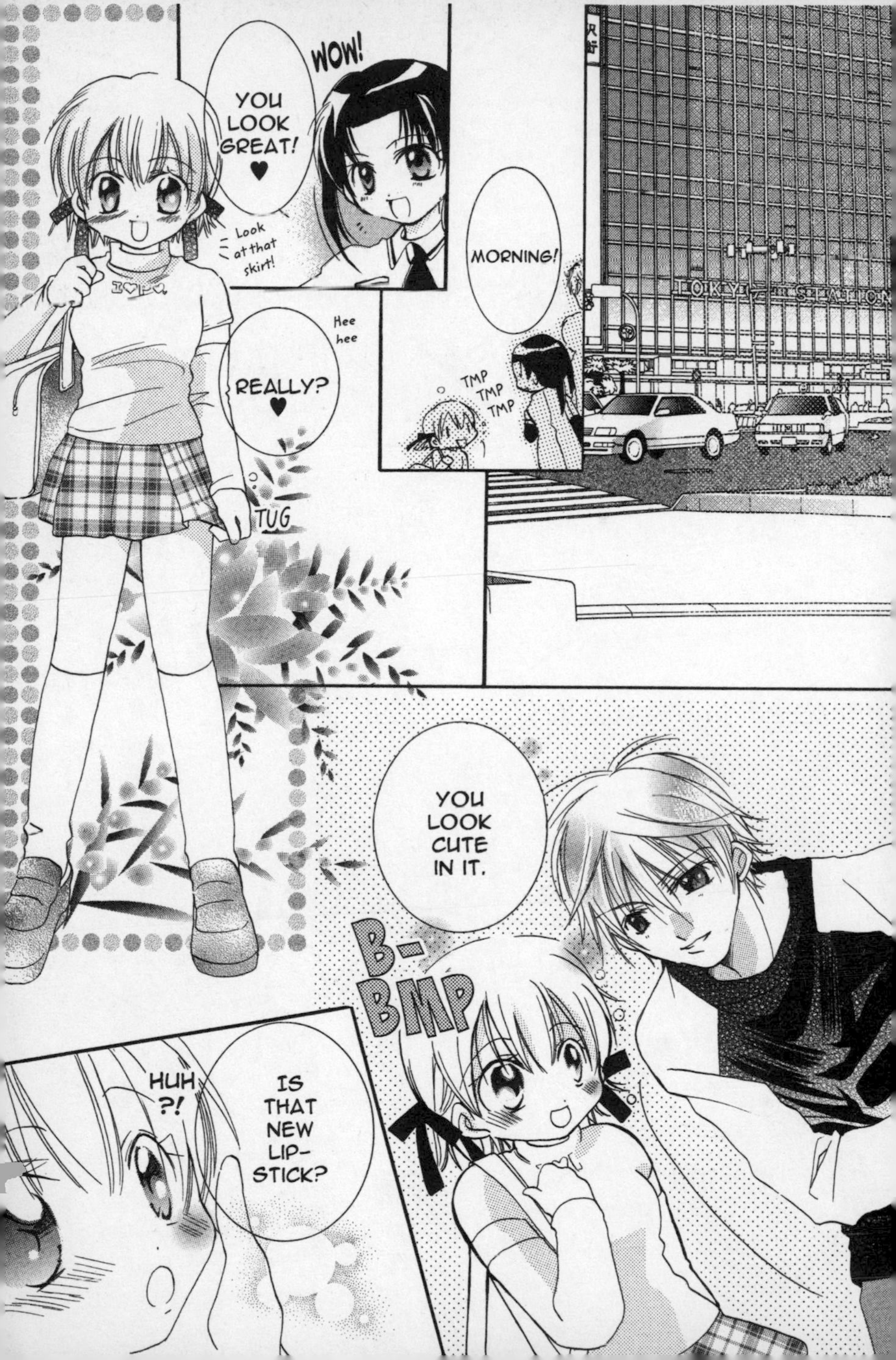
MORNING!
TMP TMP TMP
WOW!
YOU LOOK GREAT! ♥
Look at that skirt!
REALLY? ♥
Hee hee
TUG
YOU LOOK CUTE IN IT.
B-BMP
IS THAT NEW LIP-STICK?
HUH?!

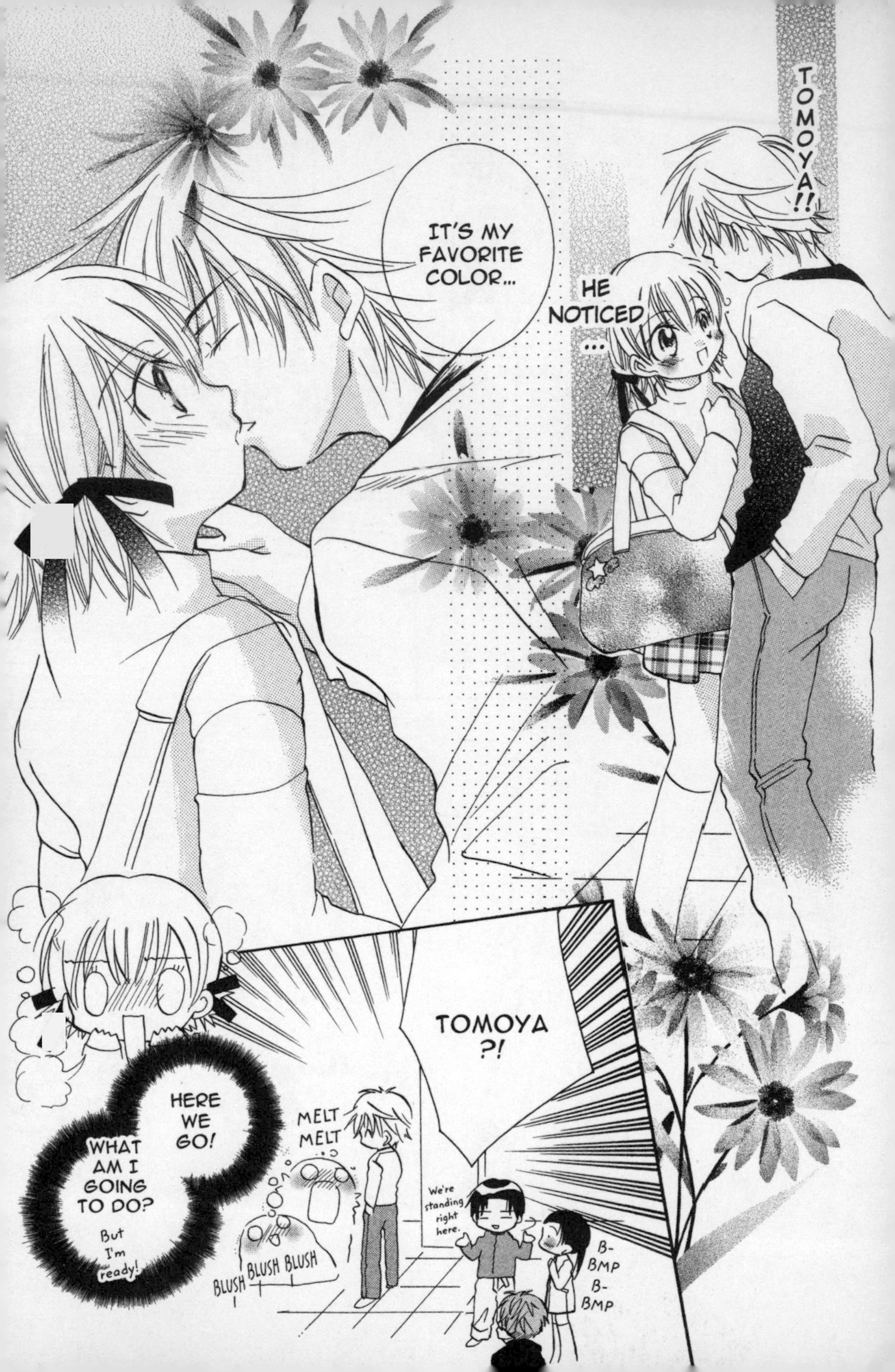
TOMOYA!!
HE NOTICED...
IT'S MY FAVORITE COLOR...
TOMOYA ?!
B-BMP B-BMP
We're standing right here.
MELT MELT
BLUSH BLUSH BLUSH
HERE WE GO!
WHAT AM I GOING TO DO?
But I'm ready!

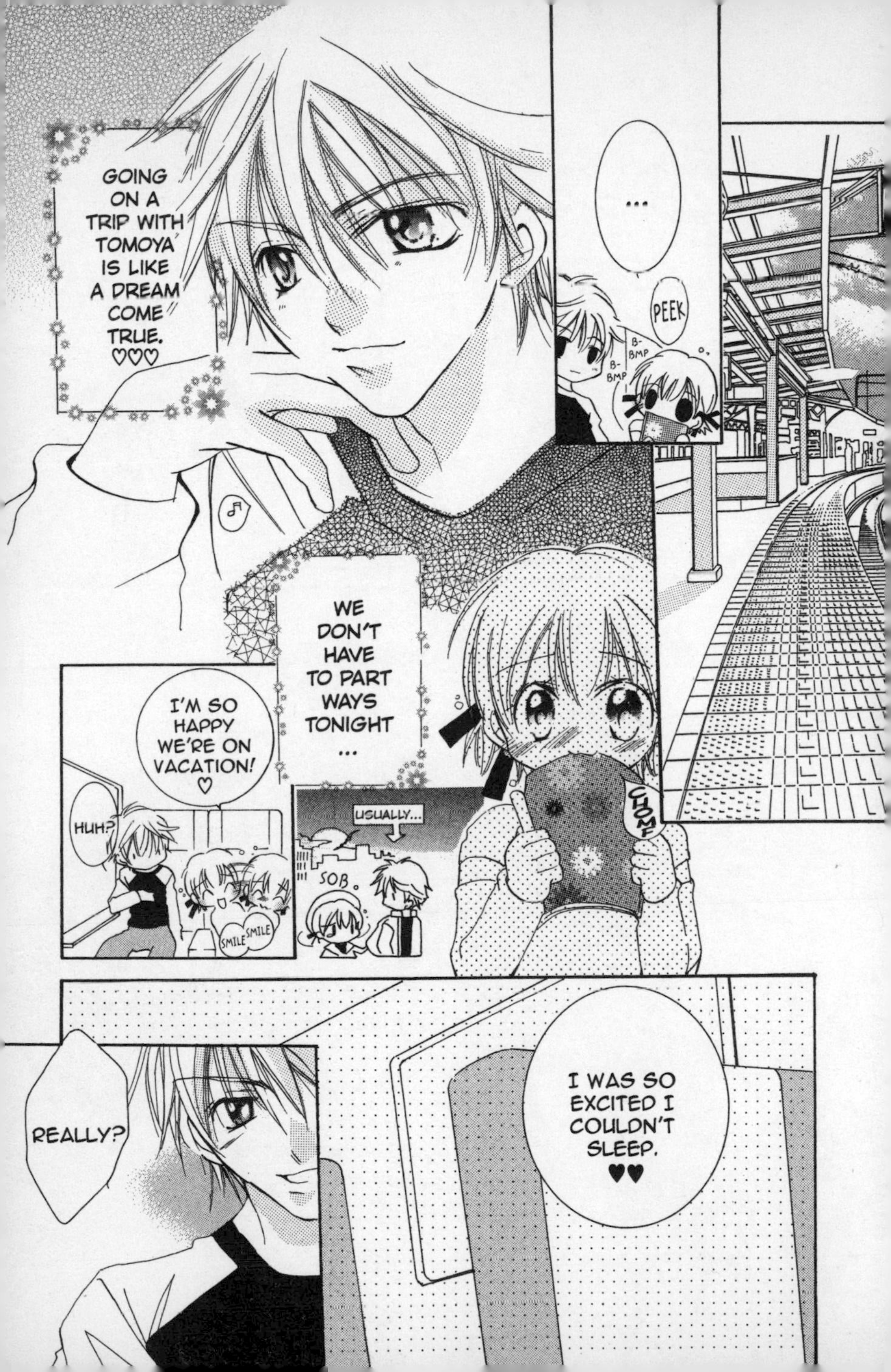
...
PEEK
B-BMP B-BMP
GOING ON A TRIP WITH TOMOYA IS LIKE A DREAM COME TRUE. ♡♡♡
♪
CHOMP
WE DON'T HAVE TO PART WAYS TONIGHT ...
USUALLY...
SOB
I'M SO HAPPY WE'RE ON VACATION! ♡
HUH?
SMILE SMILE
I WAS SO EXCITED I COULDN'T SLEEP. ♥♥
REALLY?

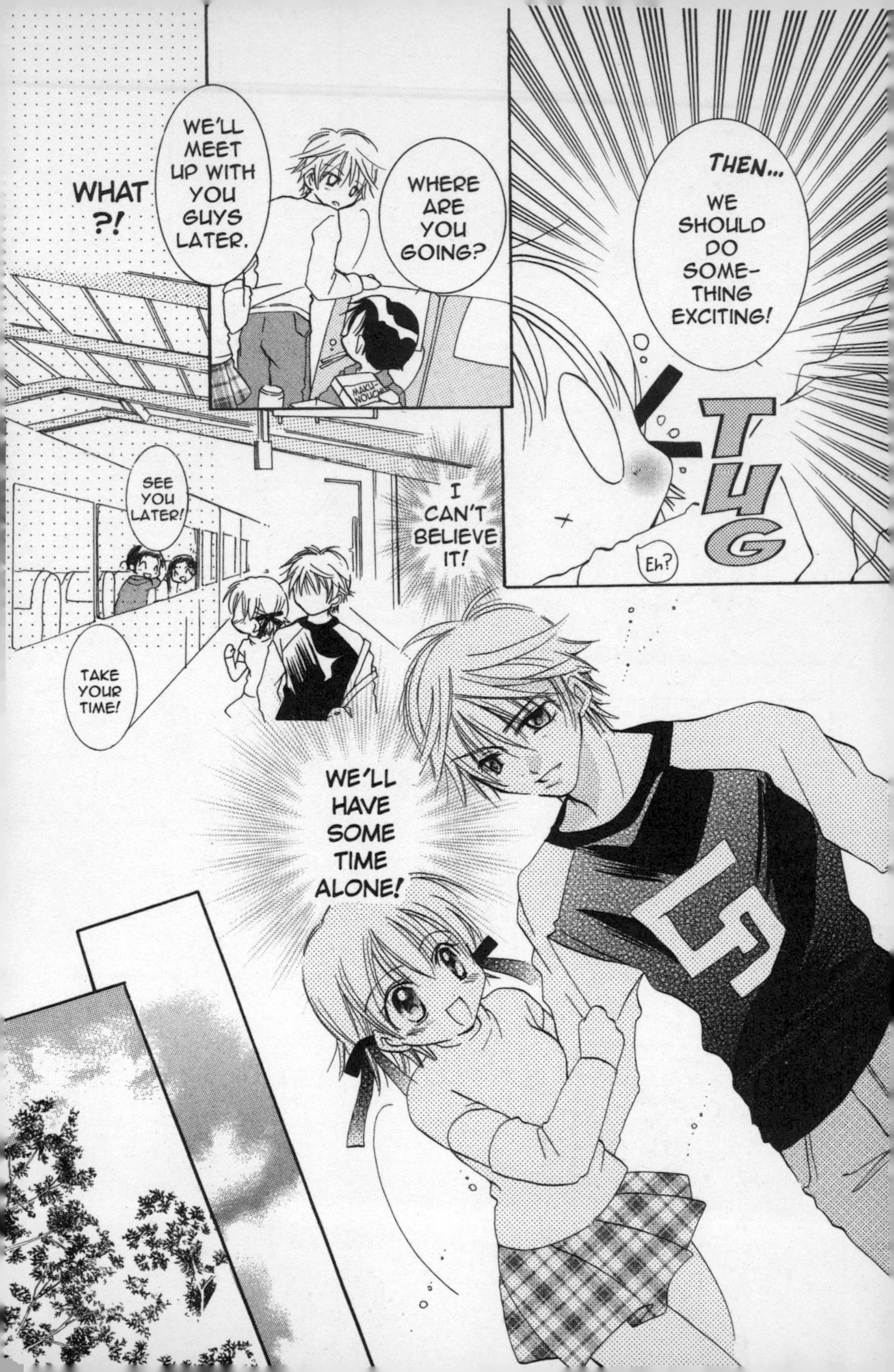
THEN... WE SHOULD DO SOMETHING EXCITING!
TUG
Eh?
WHERE ARE YOU GOING?
WE'LL MEET UP WITH YOU GUYS LATER.
MAKU-NOUCHI
WHAT?!
I CAN'T BELIEVE IT!
SEE YOU LATER!
TAKE YOUR TIME!
WE'LL HAVE SOME TIME ALONE!

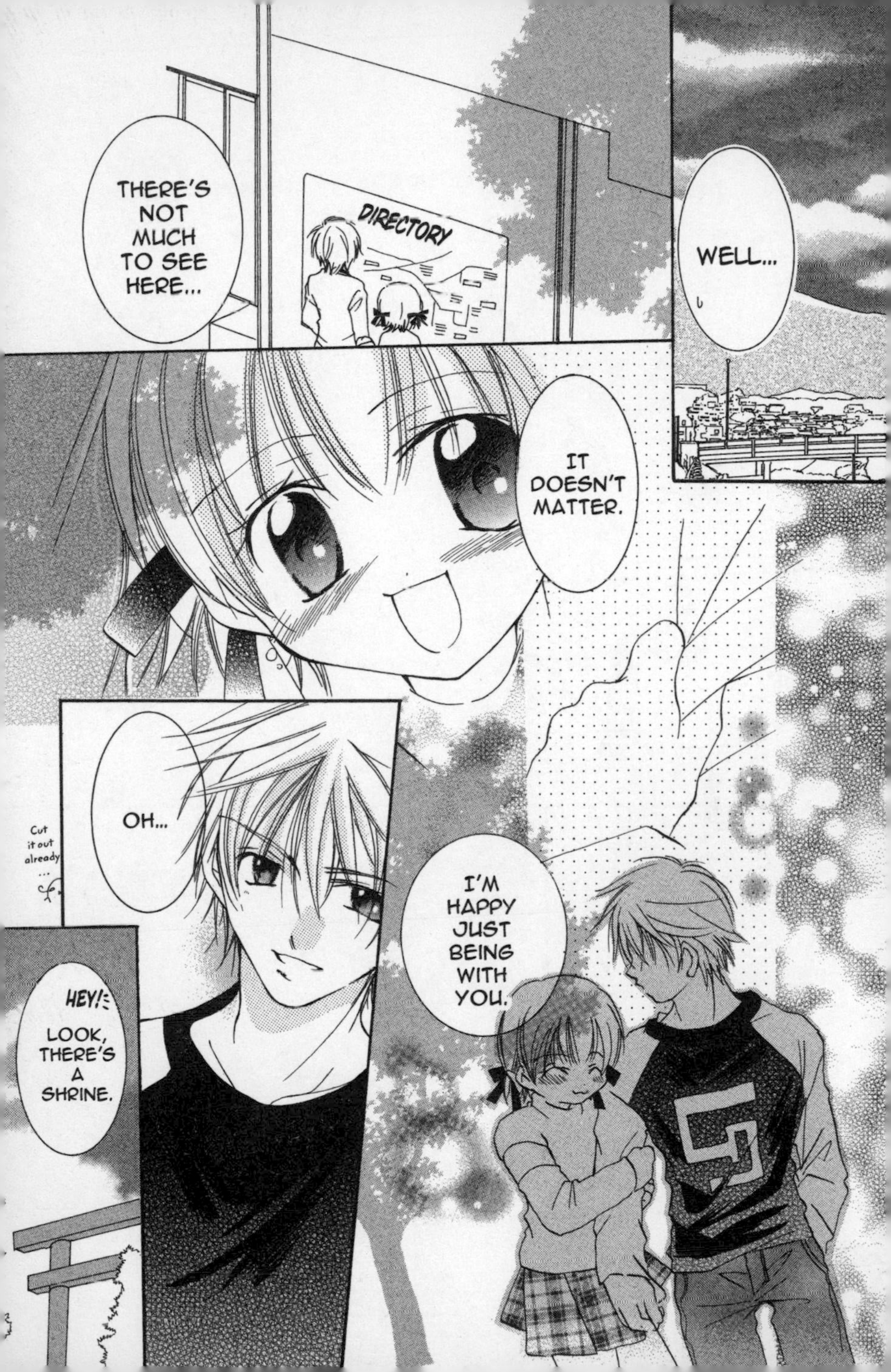
WELL...
DIRECTORY
THERE'S NOT MUCH TO SEE HERE...
IT DOESN'T MATTER.
I'M HAPPY JUST BEING WITH YOU.
OH...
Cut it out already...
HEY!
LOOK, THERE'S A SHRINE.

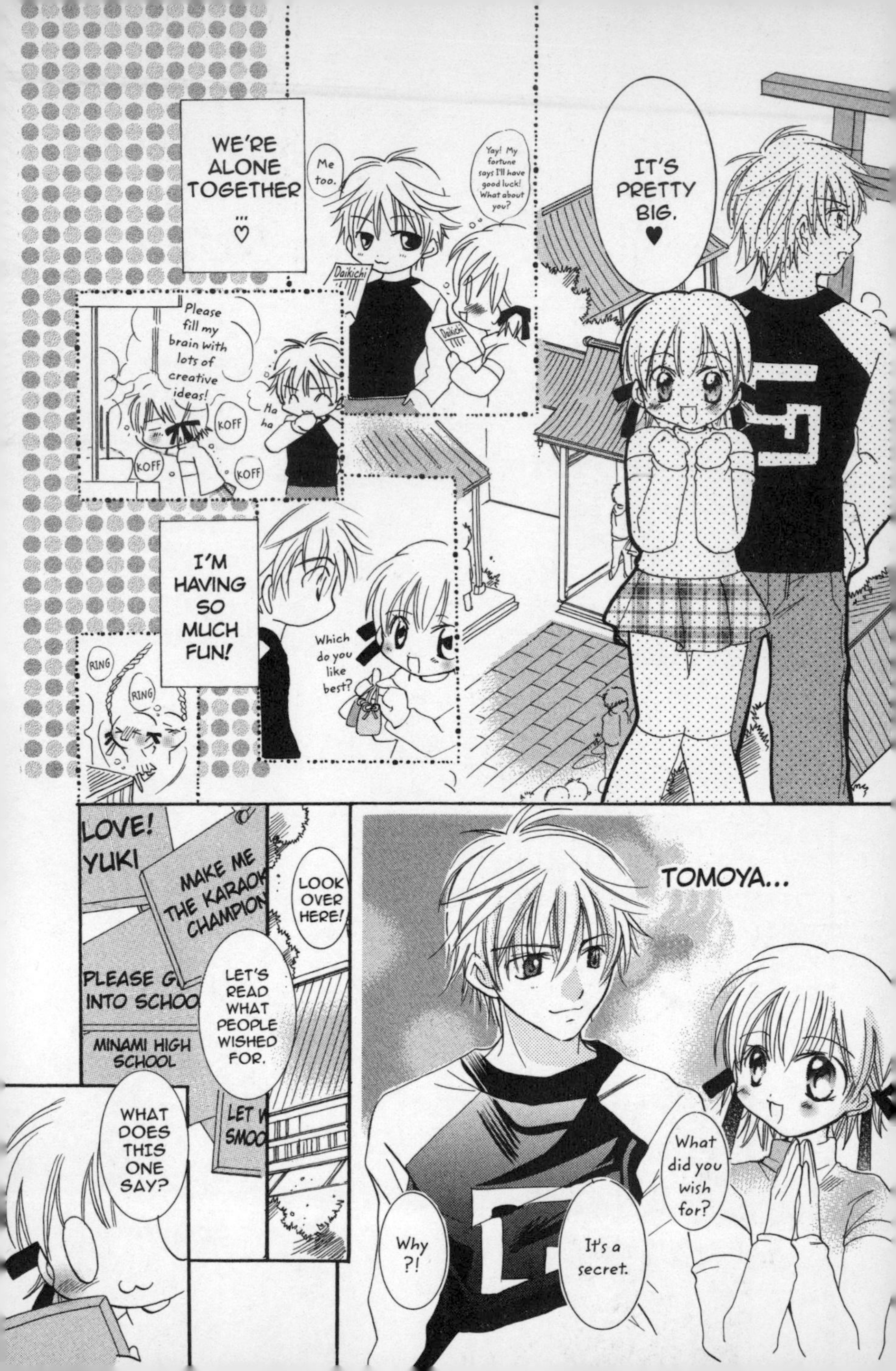
IT'S PRETTY BIG. ♥
WE'RE ALONE TOGETHER... ♡
Yay! My fortune says I'll have good luck! What about you?
Daikichi
Me too.
Daikichi
Please fill my brain with lots of creative ideas!
Ha ha
KOFF
KOFF
KOFF
I'M HAVING SO MUCH FUN!
Which do you like best?
RING
RING
TOMOYA...
What did you wish for?
It's a secret.
Why?!
LOOK OVER HERE!
LOVE! YUKI
MAKE ME THE KARAOK CHAMPION
PLEASE G INTO SCHOO
MINAMI HIGH SCHOOL
LET W SMOO
LET'S READ WHAT PEOPLE WISHED FOR.
WHAT DOES THIS ONE SAY?

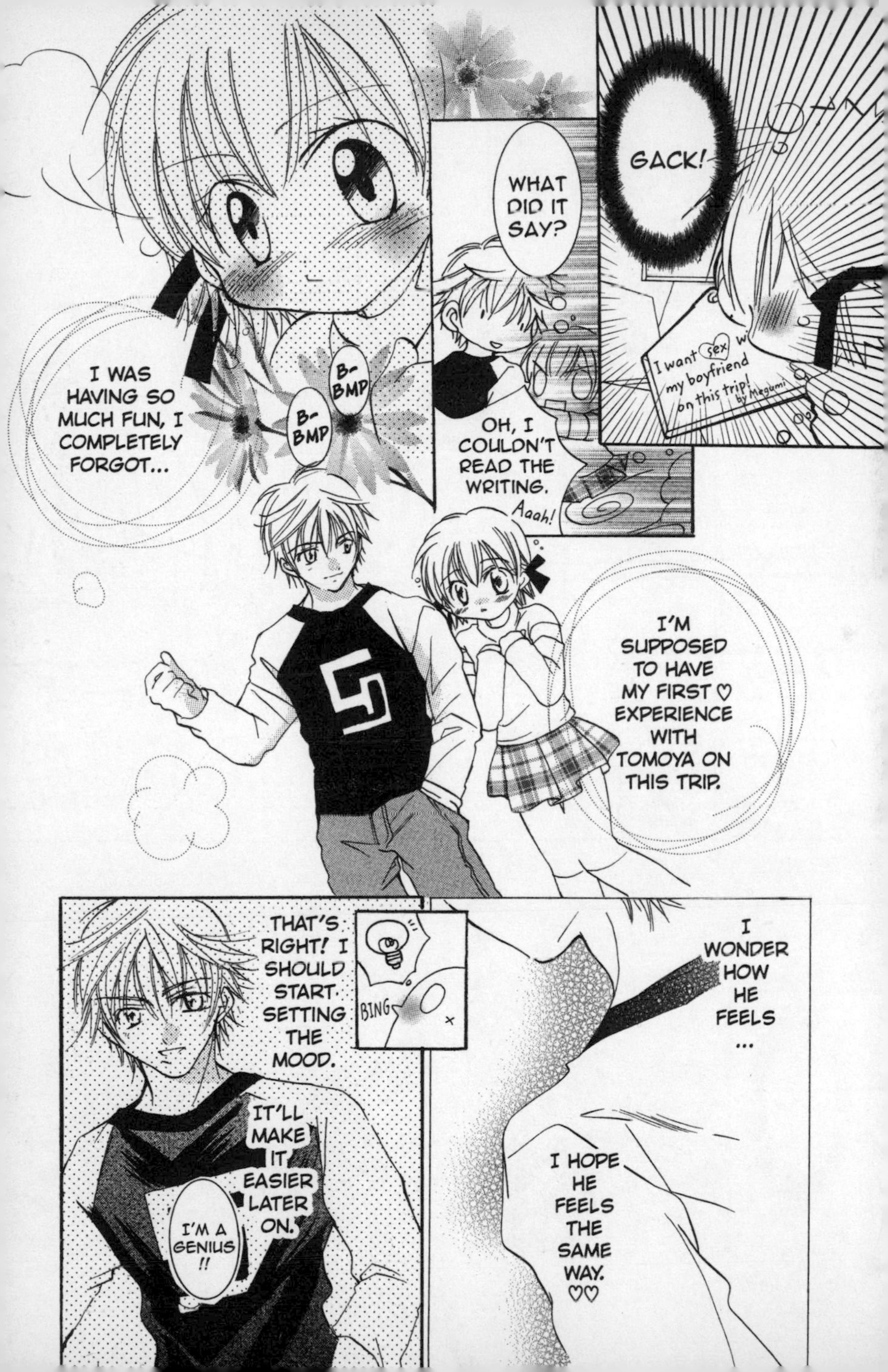
GACK!
I want sex w
my boyfriend
on this trip!
by Megumi
WHAT DID IT SAY?
OH, I COULDN'T READ THE WRITING.
Aaah!
I WAS HAVING SO MUCH FUN, I COMPLETELY FORGOT...
B-BMP
B-BMP
I'M SUPPOSED TO HAVE MY FIRST ♡ EXPERIENCE WITH TOMOYA ON THIS TRIP.
I WONDER HOW HE FEELS ...
I HOPE HE FEELS THE SAME WAY. ♡♡
BING
THAT'S RIGHT! I SHOULD START SETTING THE MOOD.
IT'LL MAKE IT EASIER LATER ON.
I'M A GENIUS !!

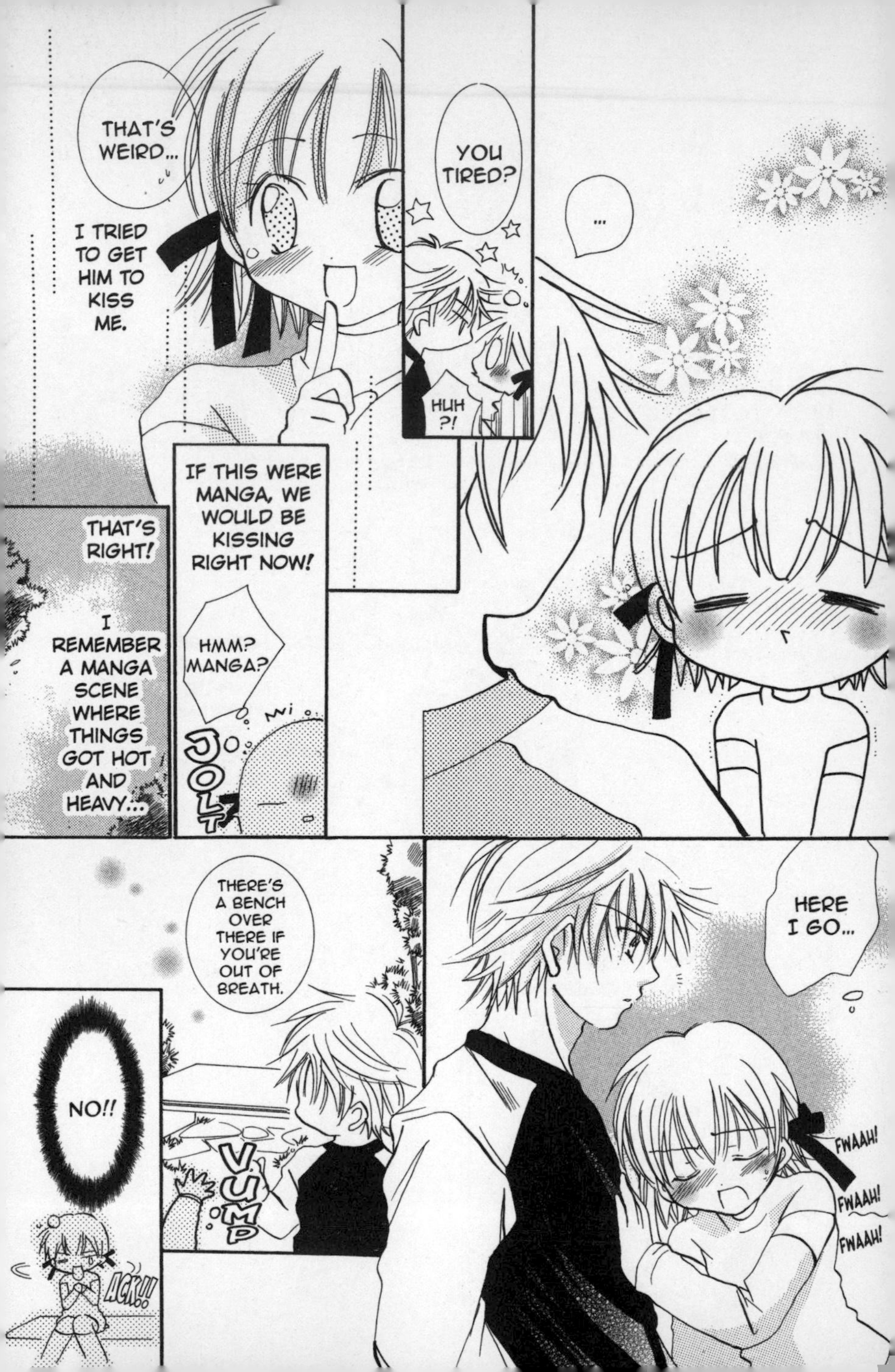
...
YOU TIRED?
HUH ?!
THAT'S WEIRD...
I TRIED TO GET HIM TO KISS ME.
IF THIS WERE MANGA, WE WOULD BE KISSING RIGHT NOW!
HMM? MANGA?
JOLT
THAT'S RIGHT!
I REMEMBER A MANGA SCENE WHERE THINGS GOT HOT AND HEAVY...
HERE I GO...
FWAAH!
FWAAH!
FWAAH!
THERE'S A BENCH OVER THERE IF YOU'RE OUT OF BREATH.
VUMP
NO!!
ACK!!

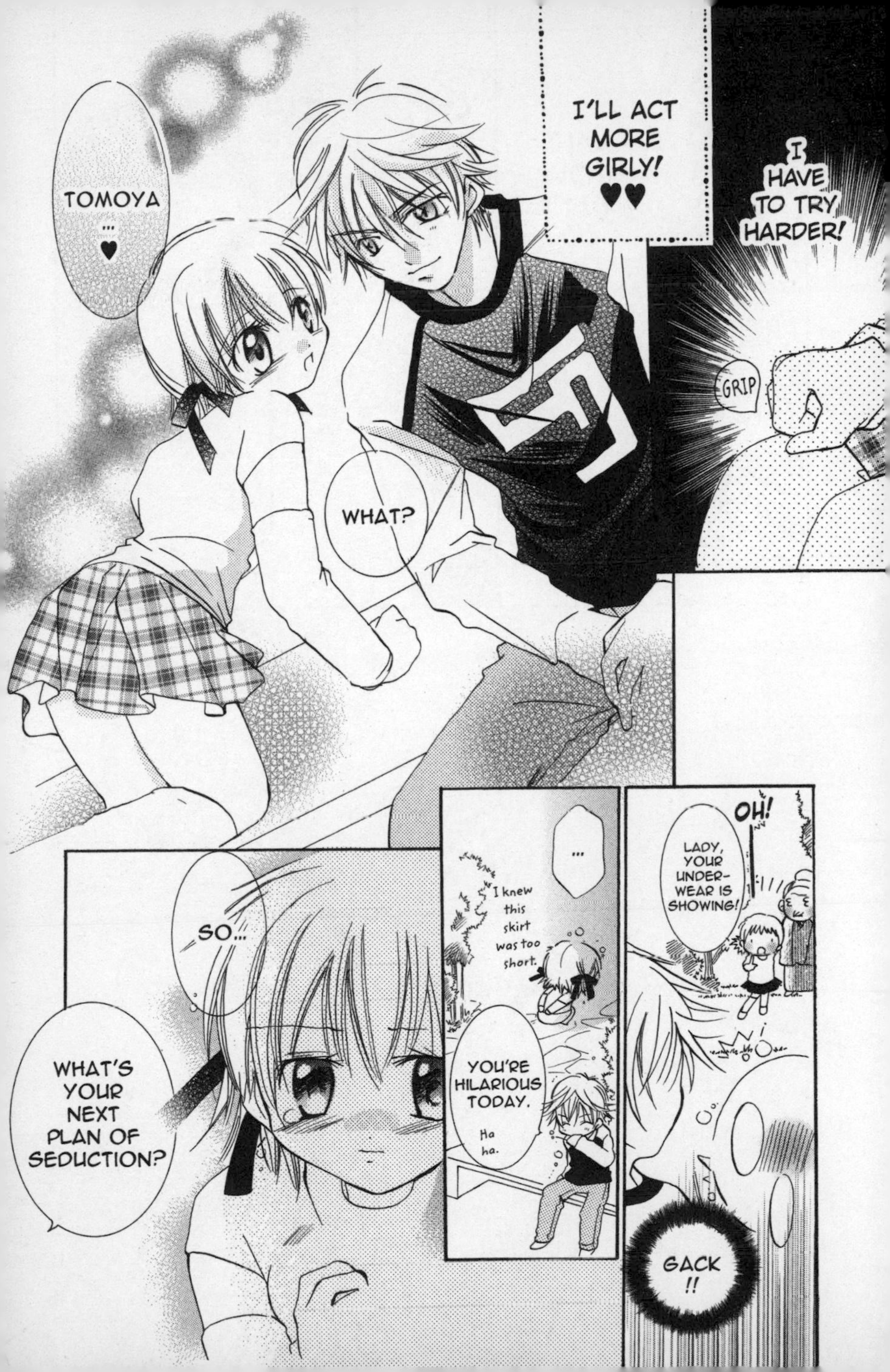
I HAVE TO TRY HARDER!
I'LL ACT MORE GIRLY! ♥♥
GRIP
TOMOYA ... ♥
WHAT?
OH!
LADY, YOUR UNDER-WEAR IS SHOWING!
GACK !!
...
I knew this skirt was too short.
YOU'RE HILARIOUS TODAY.
Ha ha.
SO...
WHAT'S YOUR NEXT PLAN OF SEDUCTION?

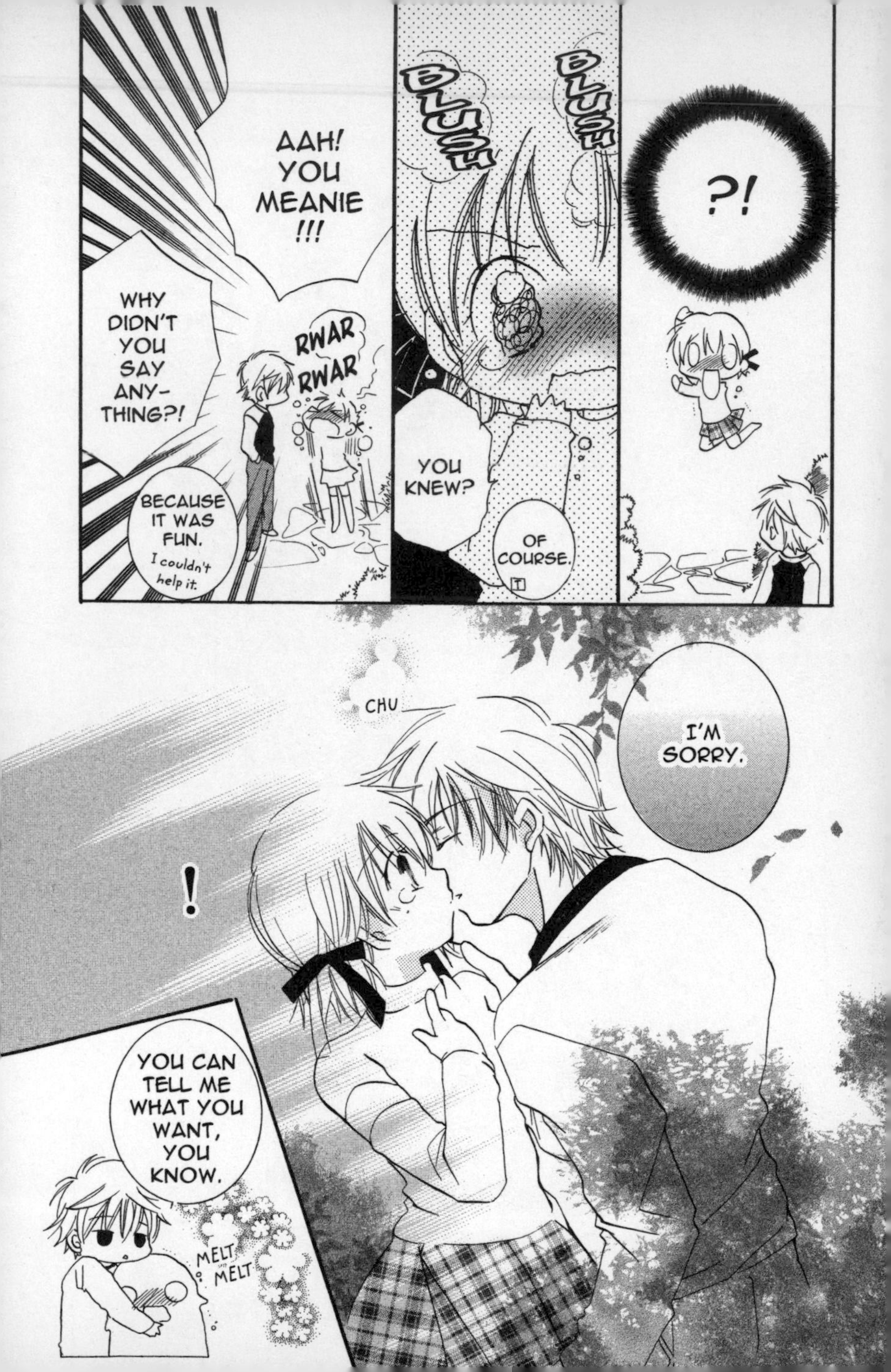
?!
BLUSH
BLUSH
YOU KNEW?
OF COURSE.
AAH! YOU MEANIE!!!
WHY DIDN'T YOU SAY ANY-THING?!
RWAR RWAR
BECAUSE IT WAS FUN.
I couldn't help it.
I'M SORRY.
CHU
!
YOU CAN TELL ME WHAT YOU WANT, YOU KNOW.
MELT MELT

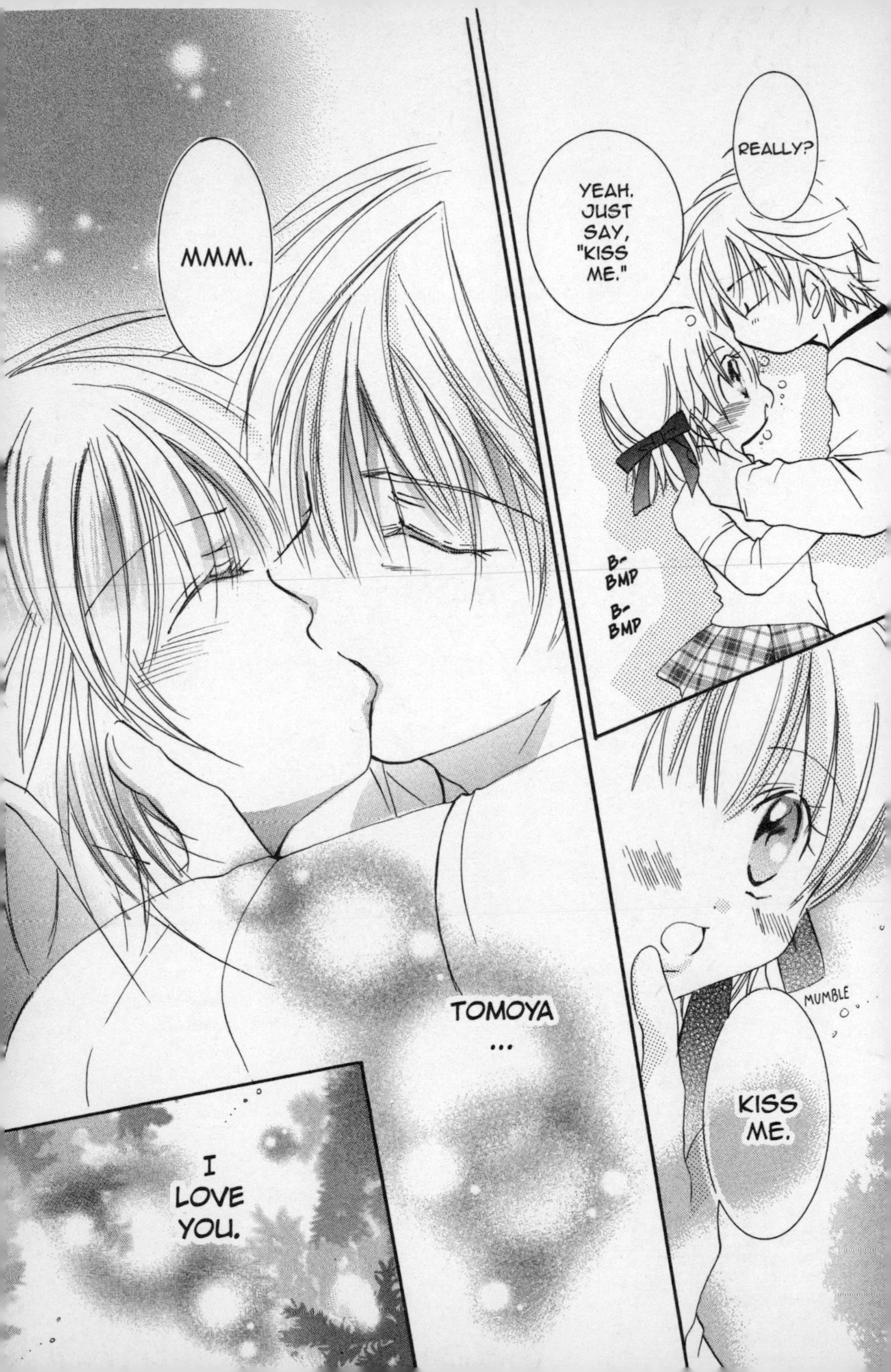
REALLY?
YEAH. JUST SAY, "KISS ME."
B-BMP
B-BMP
MUMBLE
KISS ME.
MMM.
TOMOYA ...
I LOVE YOU.

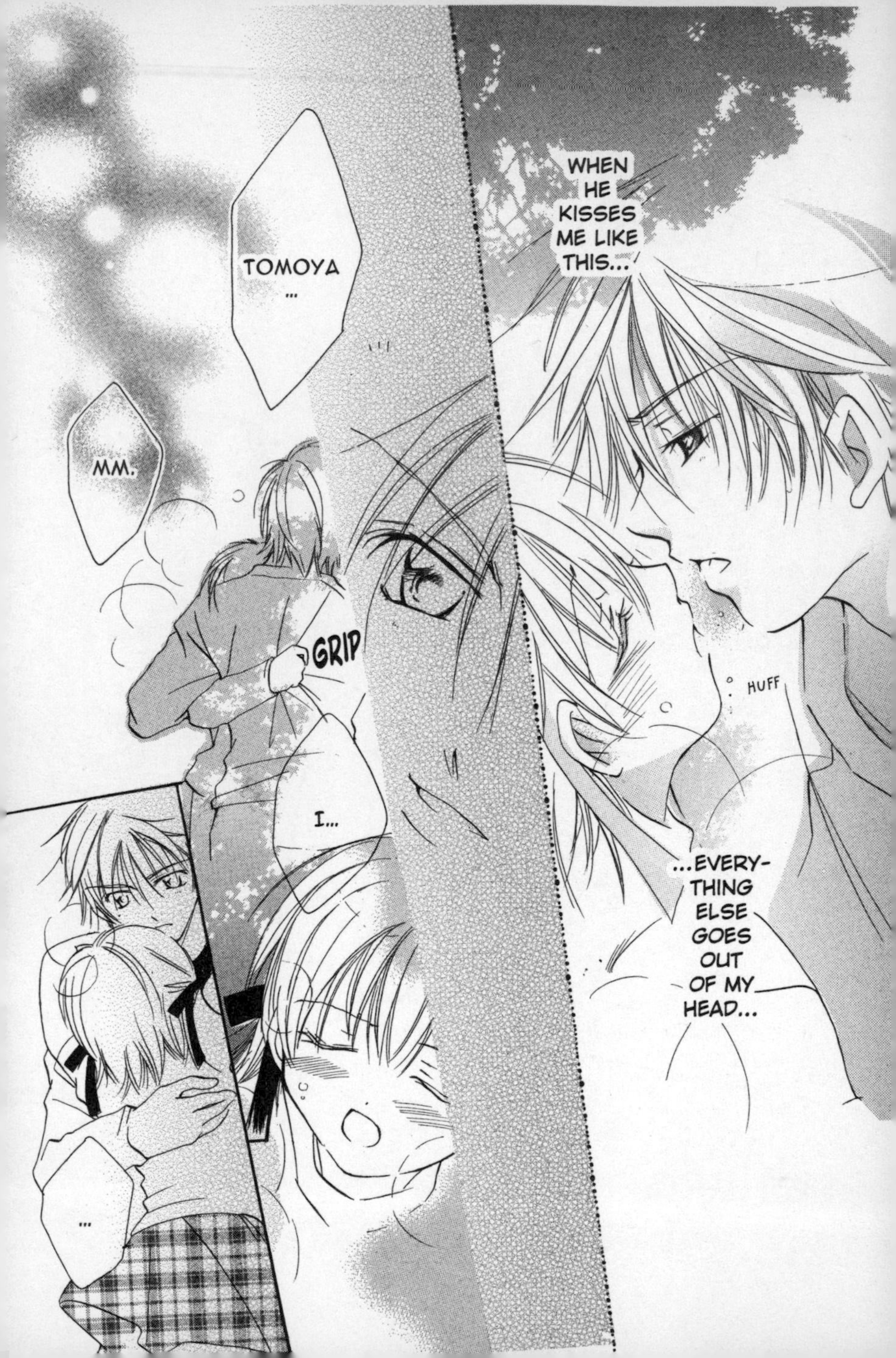
WHEN HE KISSES ME LIKE THIS...
HUFF
...EVERY-THING ELSE GOES OUT OF MY HEAD...
TOMOYA ...
MM.
GRIP
I...
...

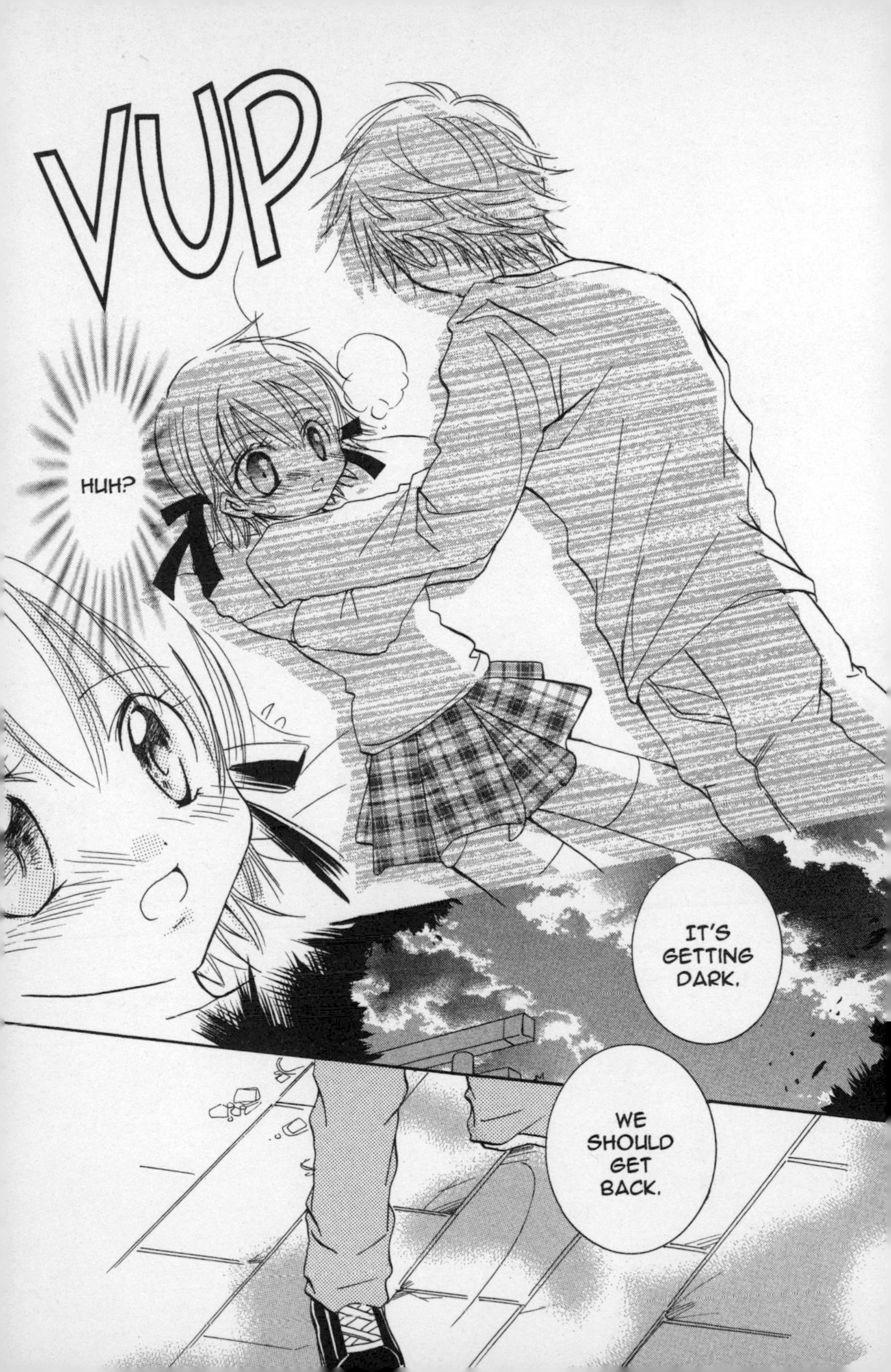
VUP
HUH?
IT'S GETTING DARK.
WE SHOULD GET BACK.

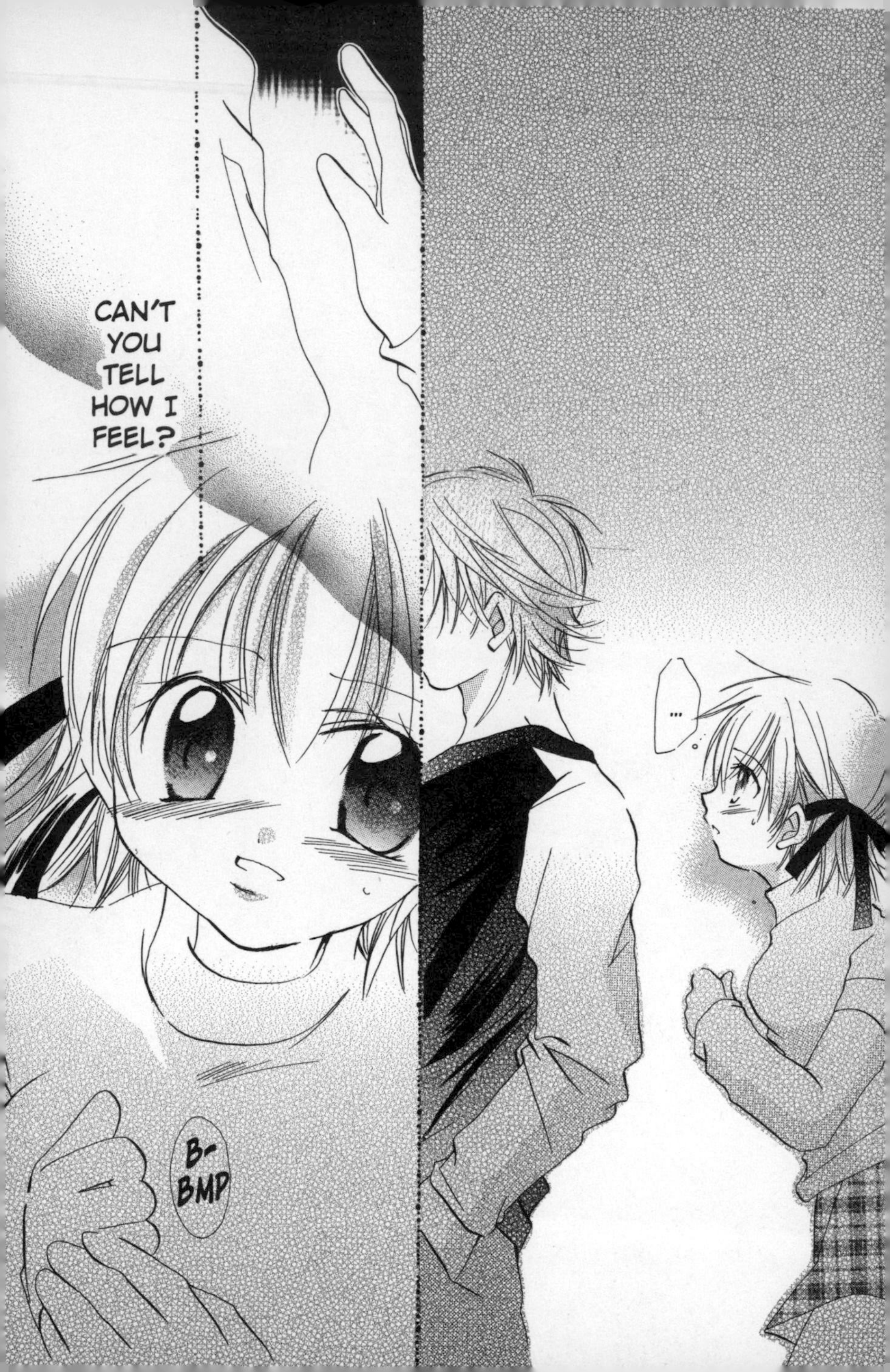
...
CAN'T YOU TELL HOW I FEEL?
B-BMP

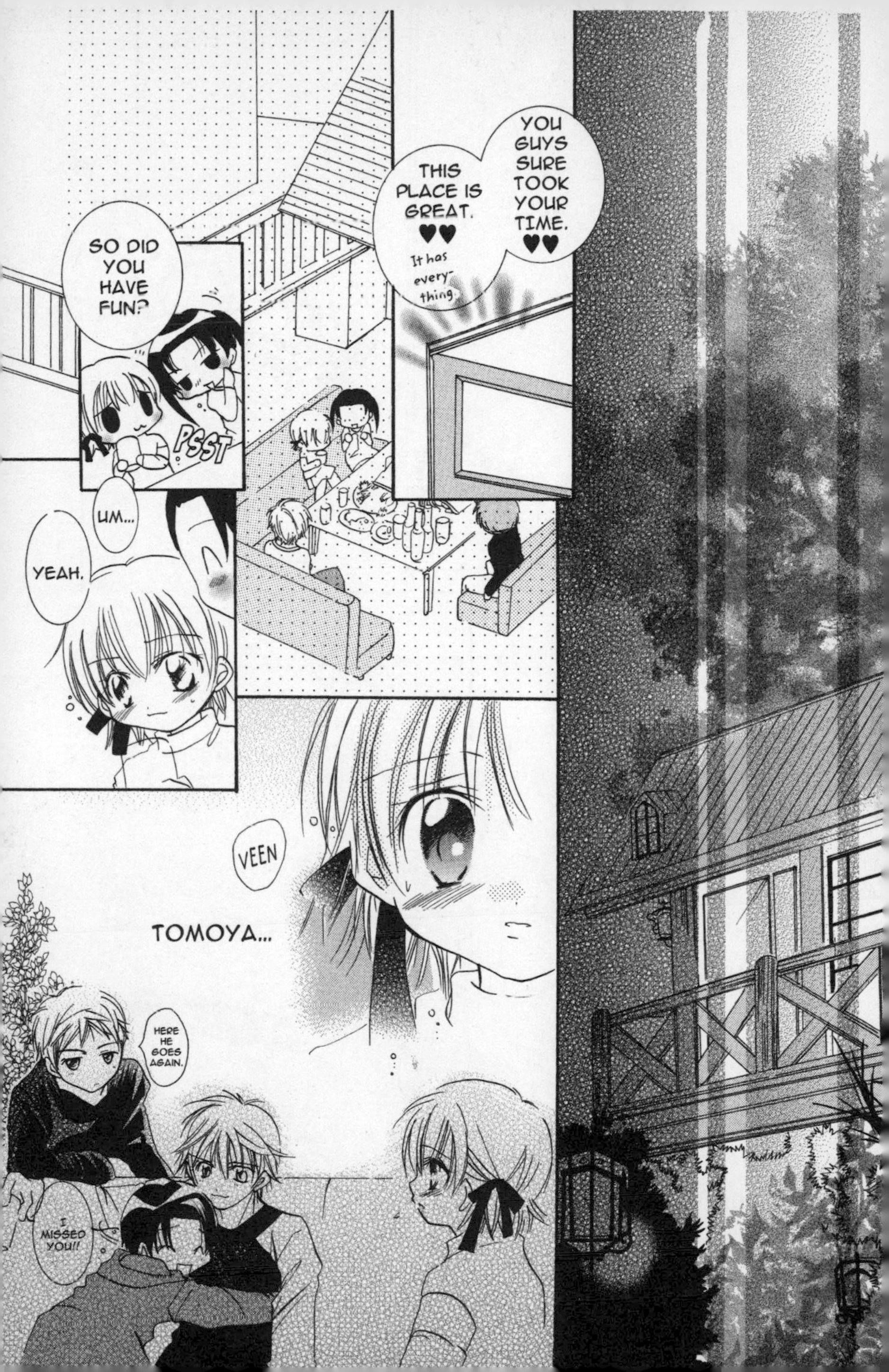
YOU GUYS SURE TOOK YOUR TIME. ♥♥
THIS PLACE IS GREAT. ♥♥
It has every-thing.
SO DID YOU HAVE FUN?
PSST
UM...
YEAH.
VEEN
TOMOYA...
HERE HE GOES AGAIN.
I MISSED YOU!!!

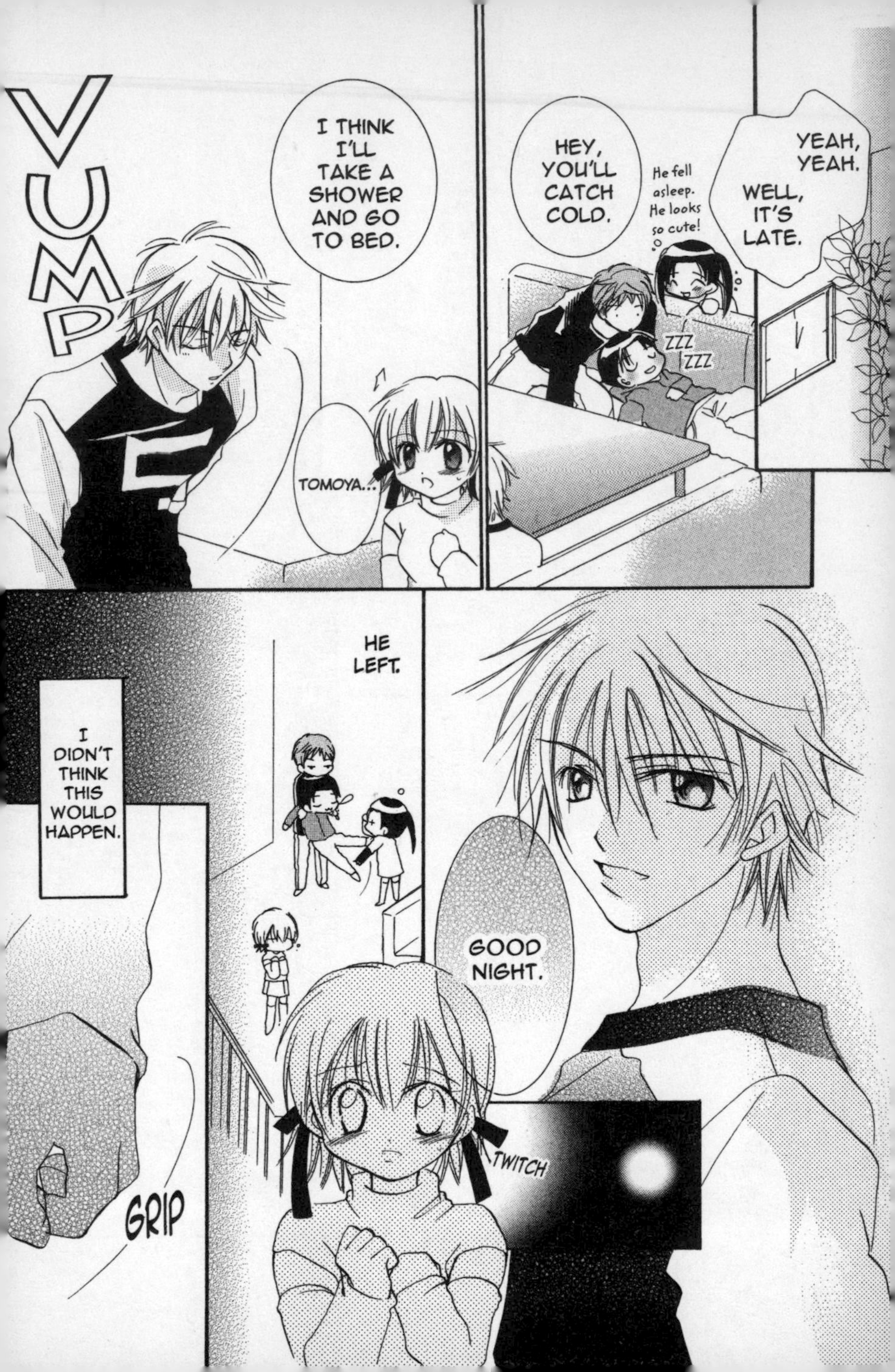

YEAH, YEAH.
WELL, IT'S LATE.
HEY, YOU'LL CATCH COLD.
He fell asleep. He looks so cute!
ZZZ ZZZ
I THINK I'LL TAKE A SHOWER AND GO TO BED.
TOMOYA...
VUMP
GOOD NIGHT.
TWITCH
HE LEFT.
I DIDN'T THINK THIS WOULD HAPPEN.
GRIP

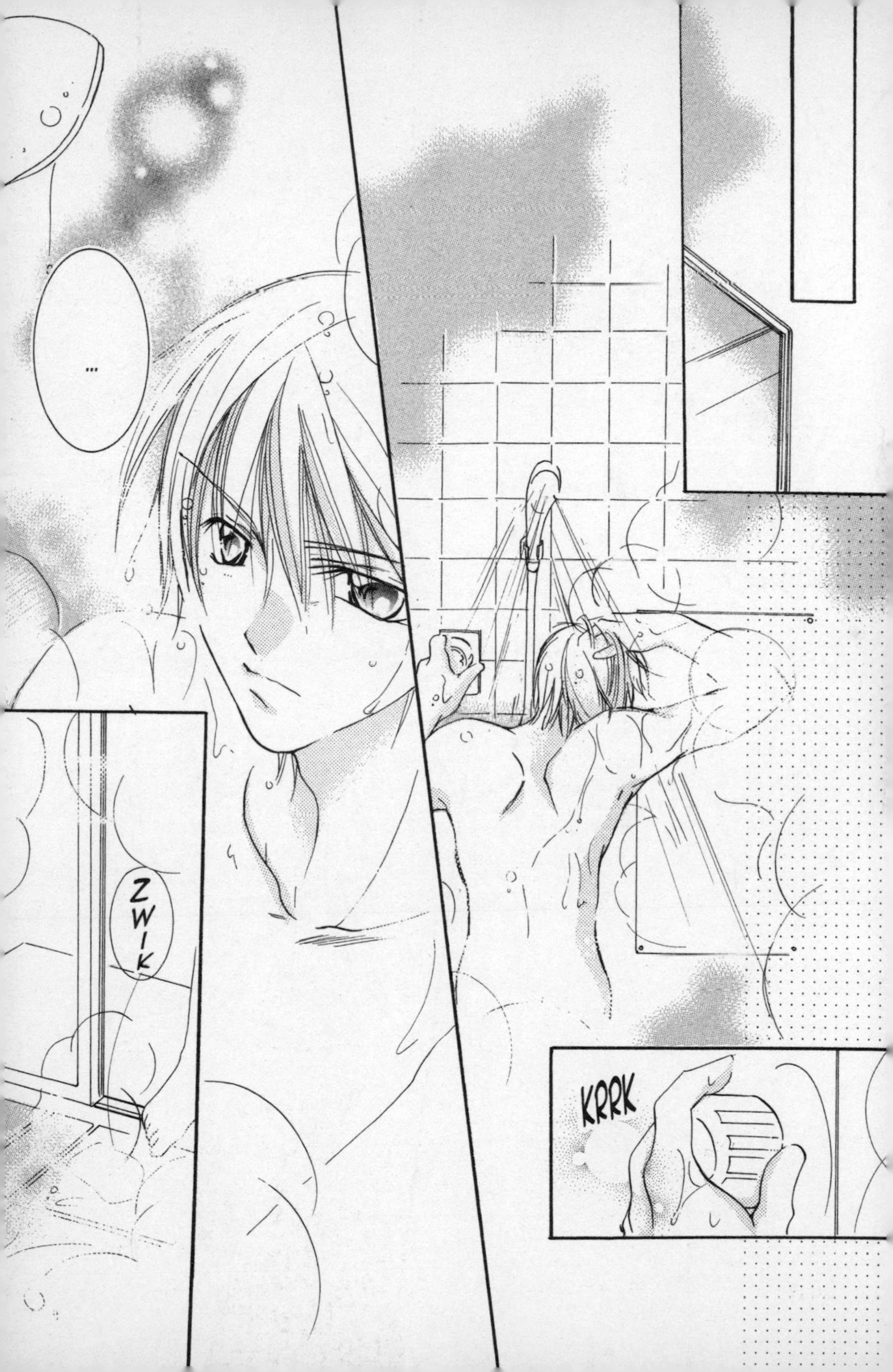
KRRK
...
ZWIK

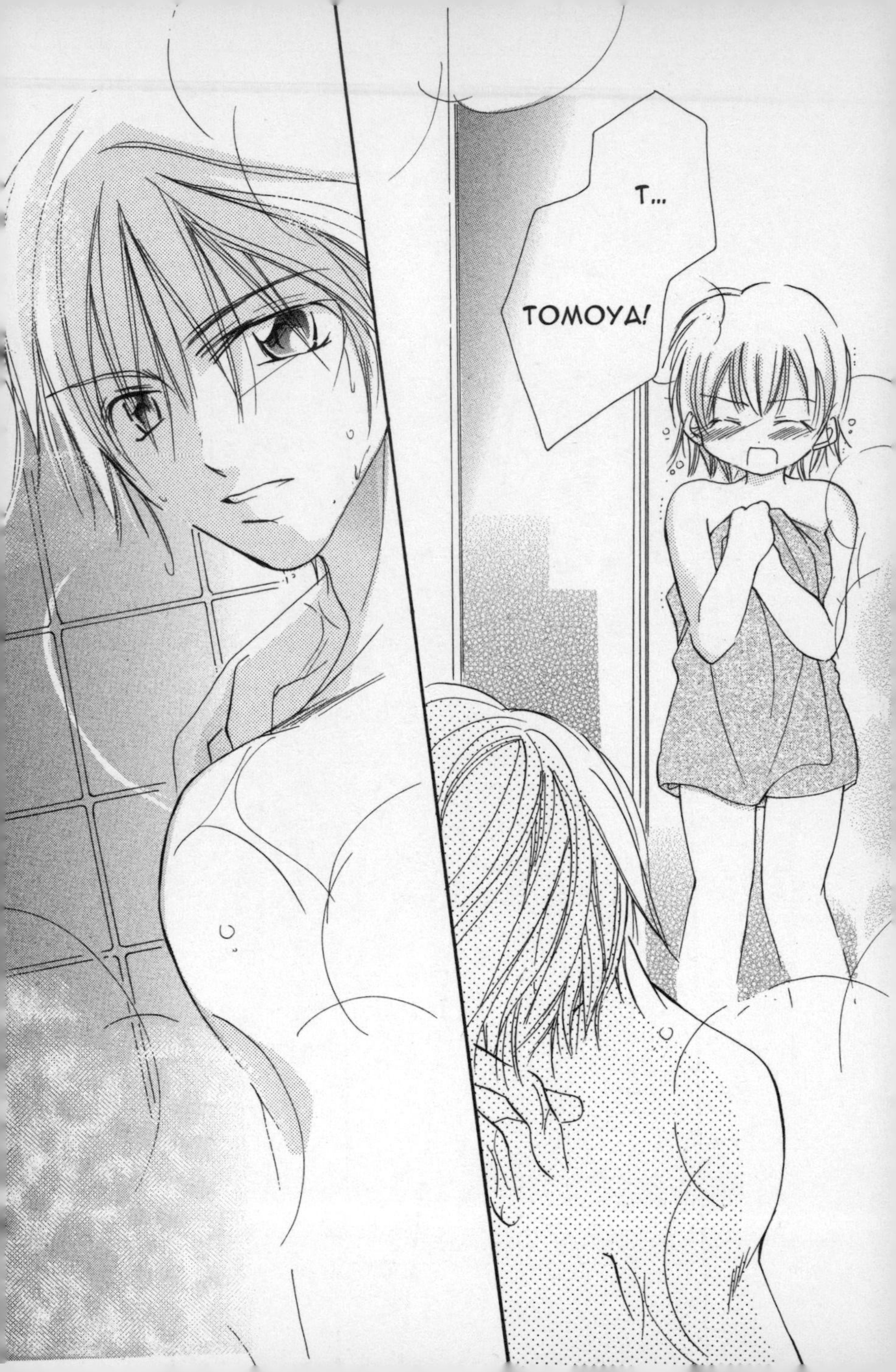
T...
TOMOYA!

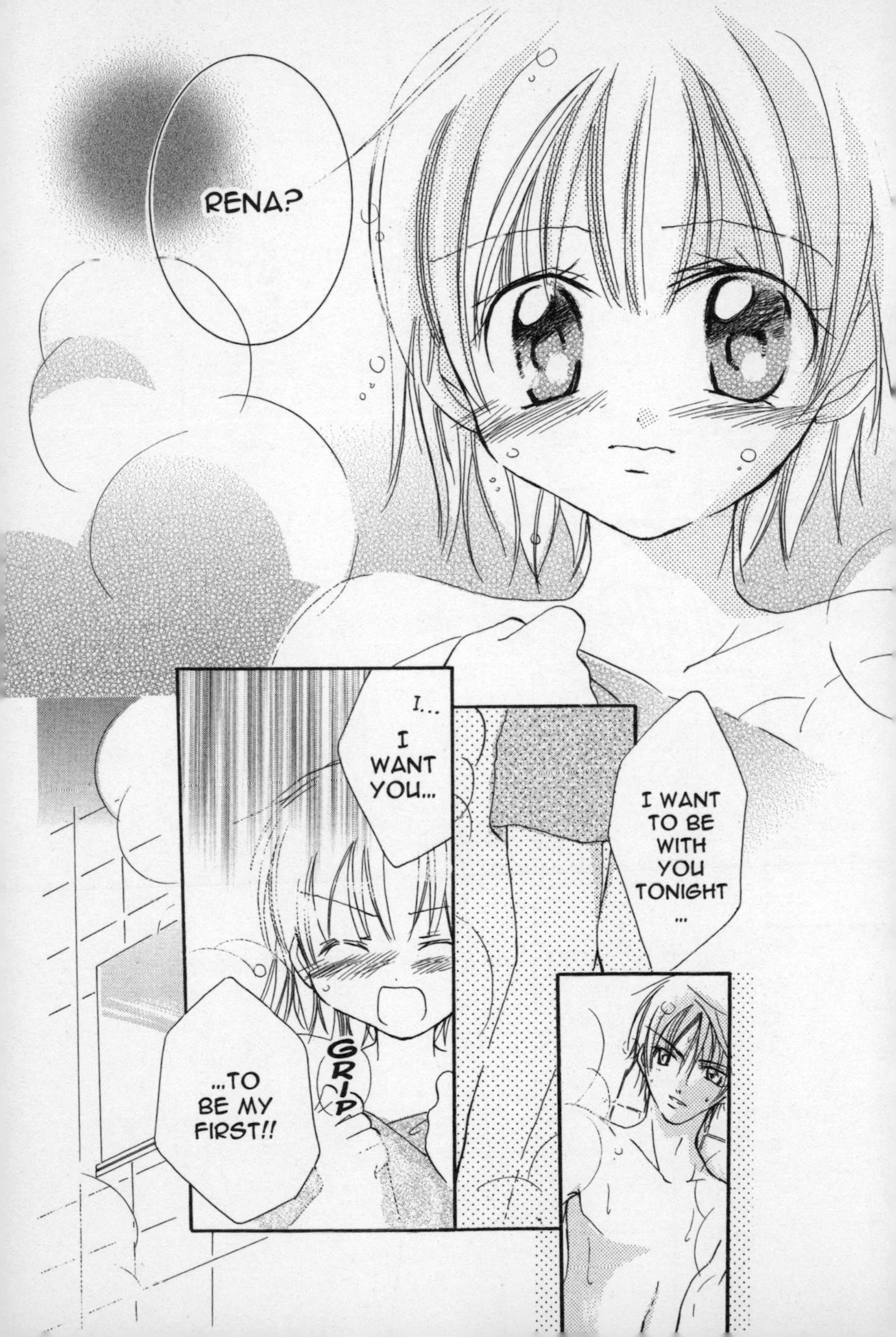

RENA?
I WANT TO BE WITH YOU TONIGHT ...
I...
I WANT YOU...
GRIP
...TO BE MY FIRST!!

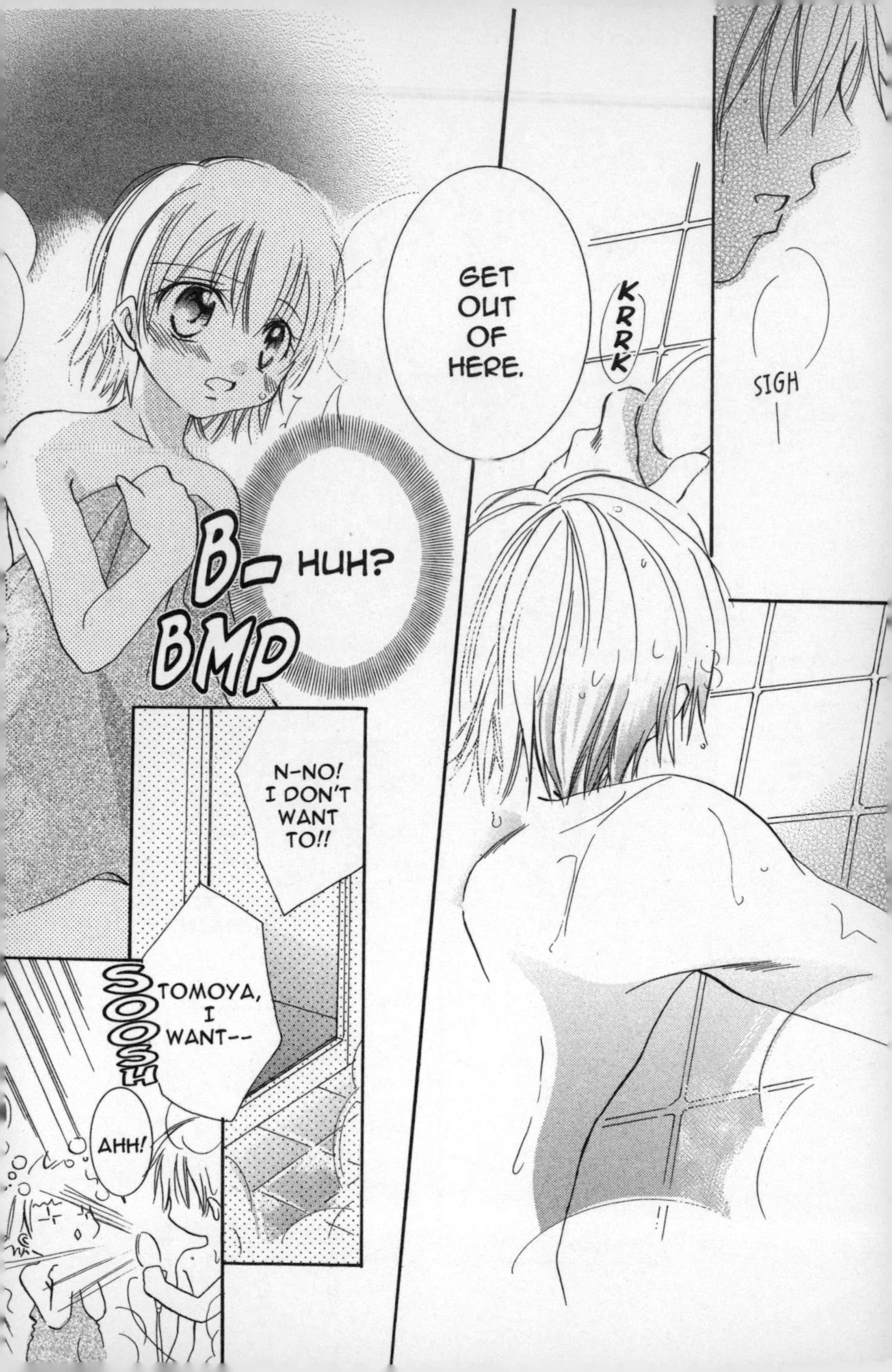
SIGH
GET OUT OF HERE.
KRRK
B-BMP
HUH?
N-NO! I DON'T WANT TO!!
TOMOYA, I WANT--
SOOSH
AHH!

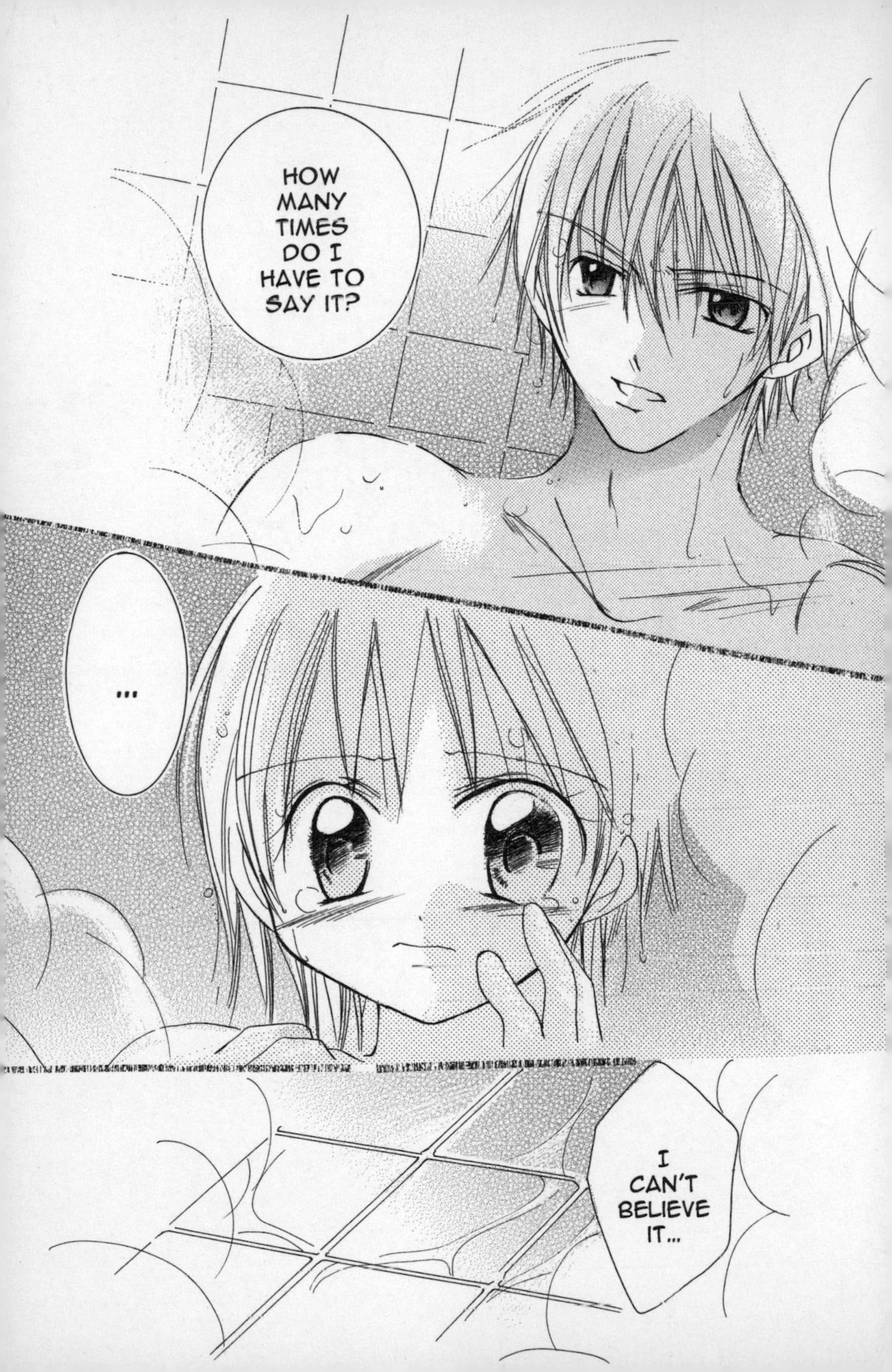
HOW MANY TIMES DO I HAVE TO SAY IT?
...
I CAN'T BELIEVE IT...

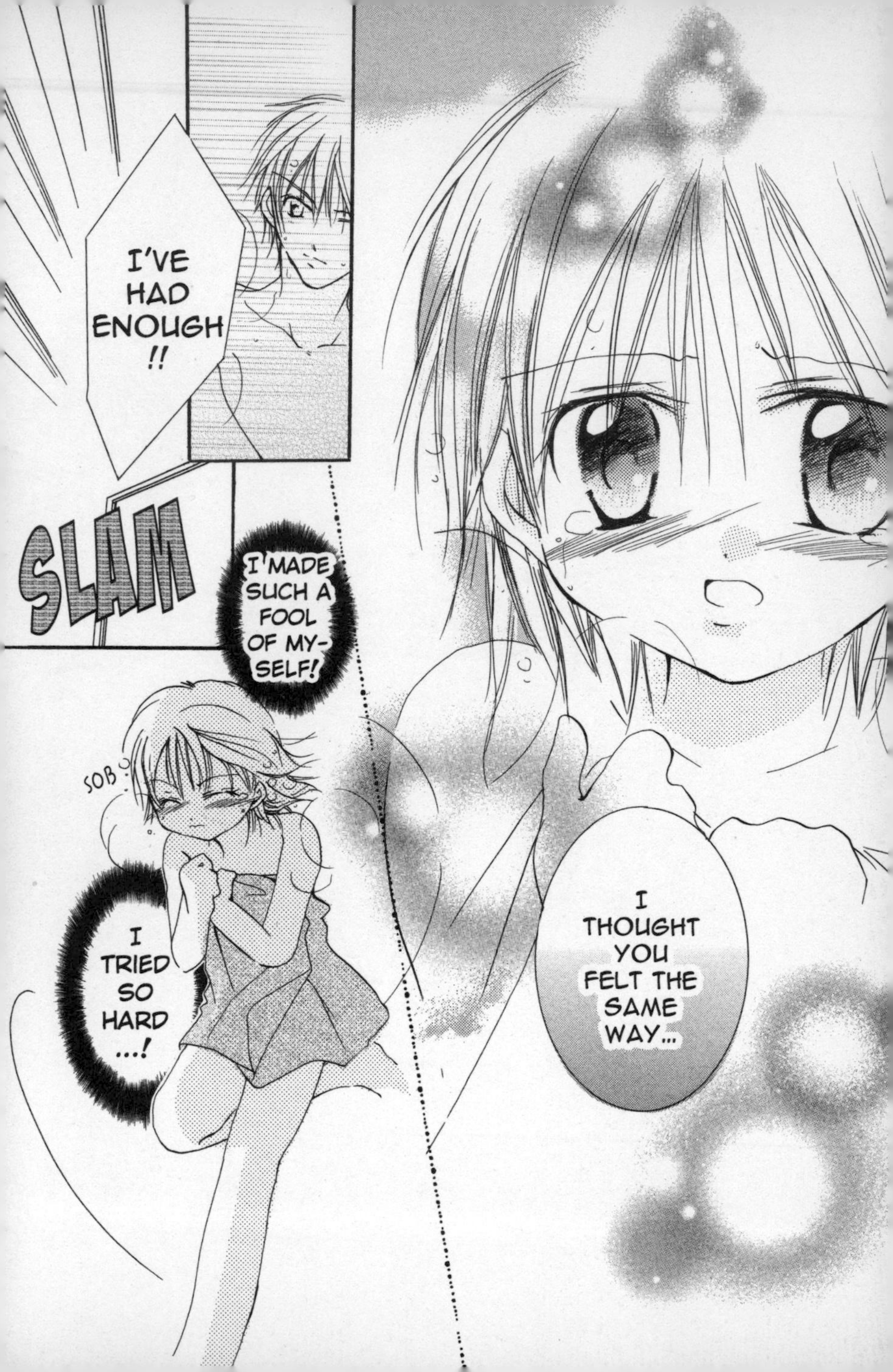
I THOUGHT YOU FELT THE SAME WAY...
I'VE HAD ENOUGH!!
SLAM
I MADE SUCH A FOOL OF MY-SELF!
SOB
I TRIED SO HARD...!

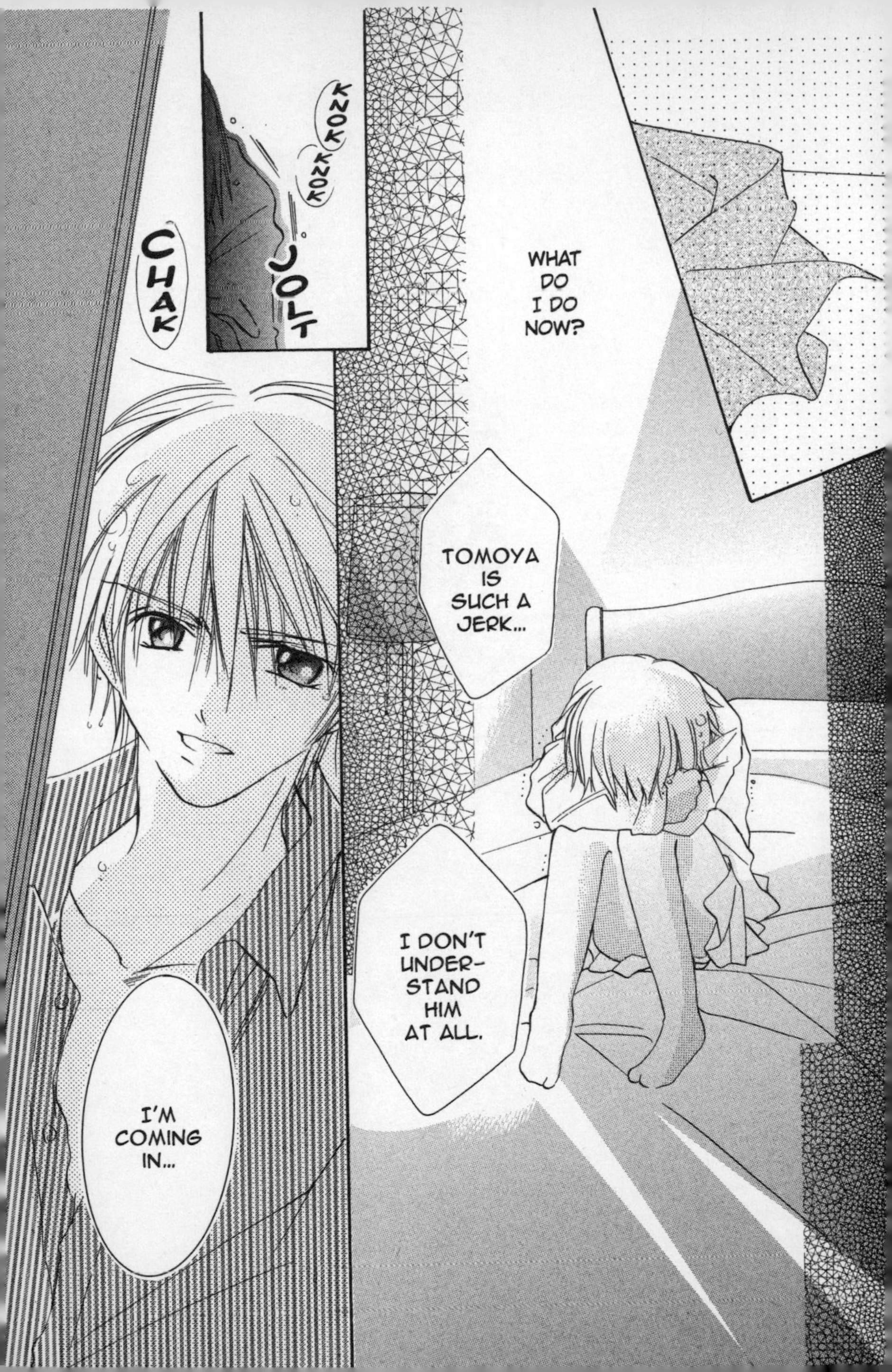
WHAT DO I DO NOW?
TOMOYA IS SUCH A JERK...
I DON'T UNDER-STAND HIM AT ALL.
KNOK KNOK
JOLT
CHAK
I'M COMING IN...

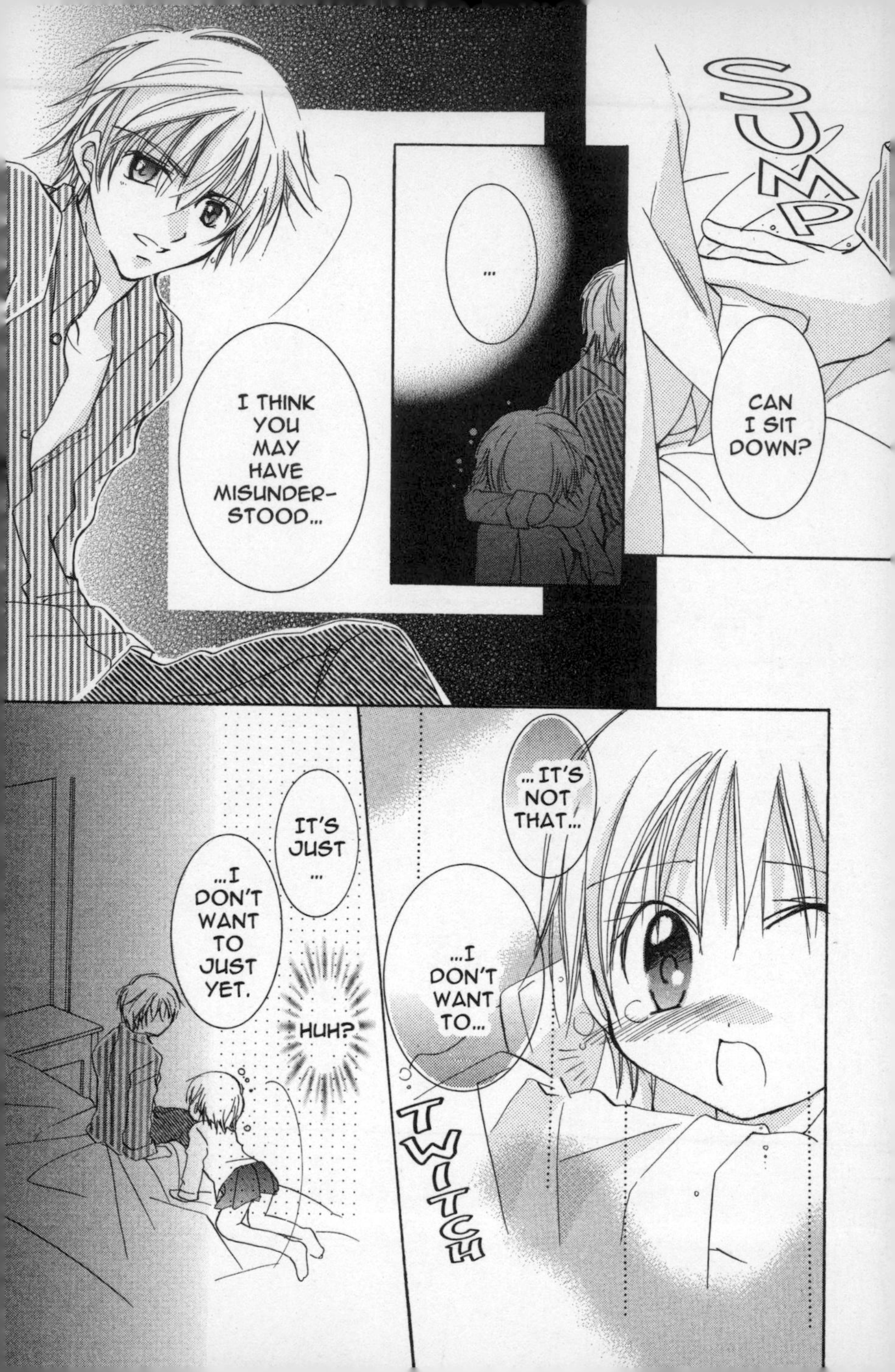
SUMP
CAN I SIT DOWN?
...
I THINK YOU MAY HAVE MISUNDERSTOOD...
...IT'S NOT THAT...
...I DON'T WANT TO...
TWITCH
IT'S JUST...
...I DON'T WANT TO JUST YET.
HUH?

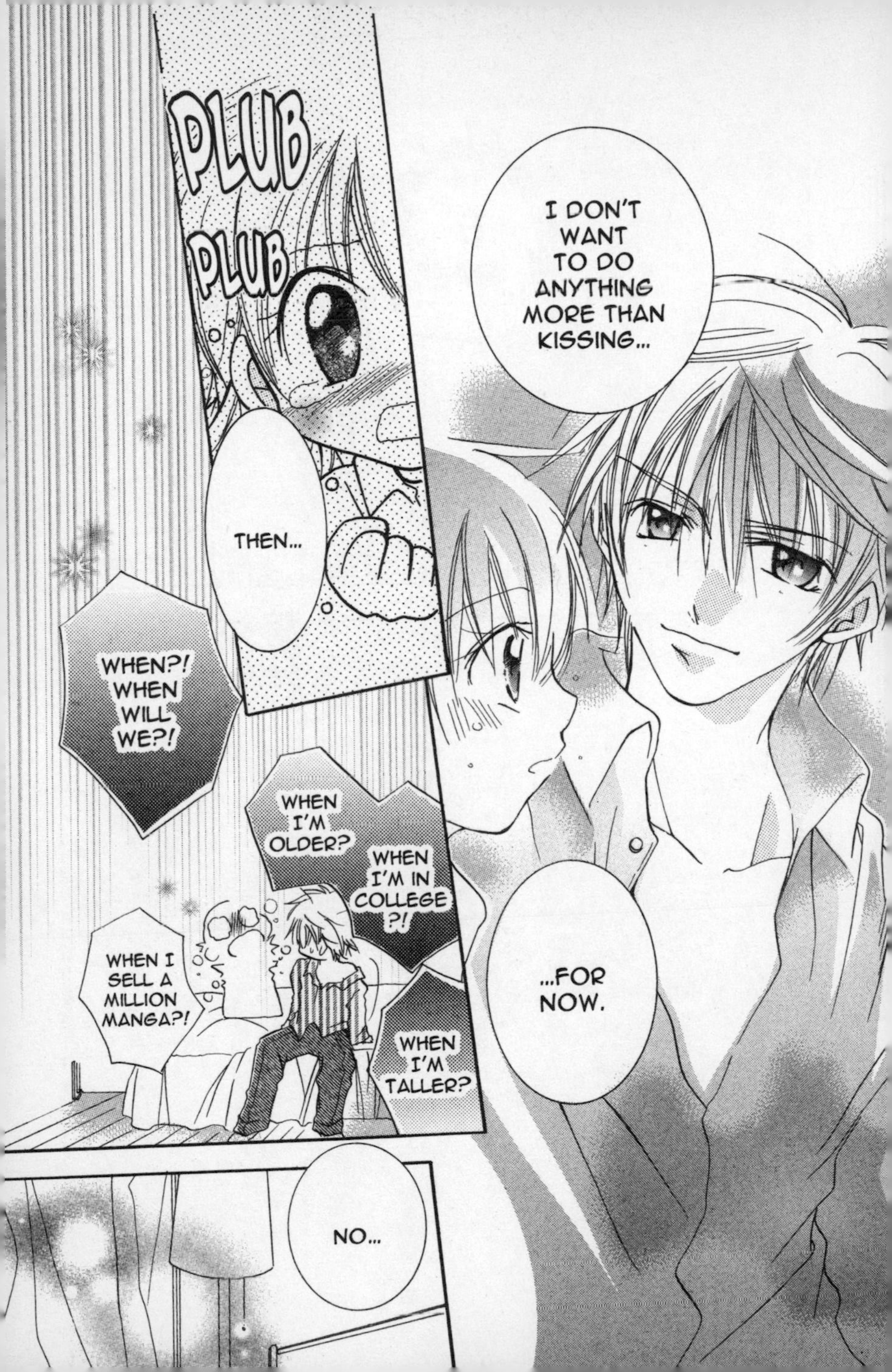
I DON'T WANT TO DO ANYTHING MORE THAN KISSING...
...FOR NOW.
PLUB
PLUB
THEN...
WHEN?! WHEN WILL WE?!
WHEN I'M OLDER?
WHEN I'M IN COLLEGE?!
WHEN I'M TALLER?
WHEN I SELL A MILLION MANGA?!
NO...

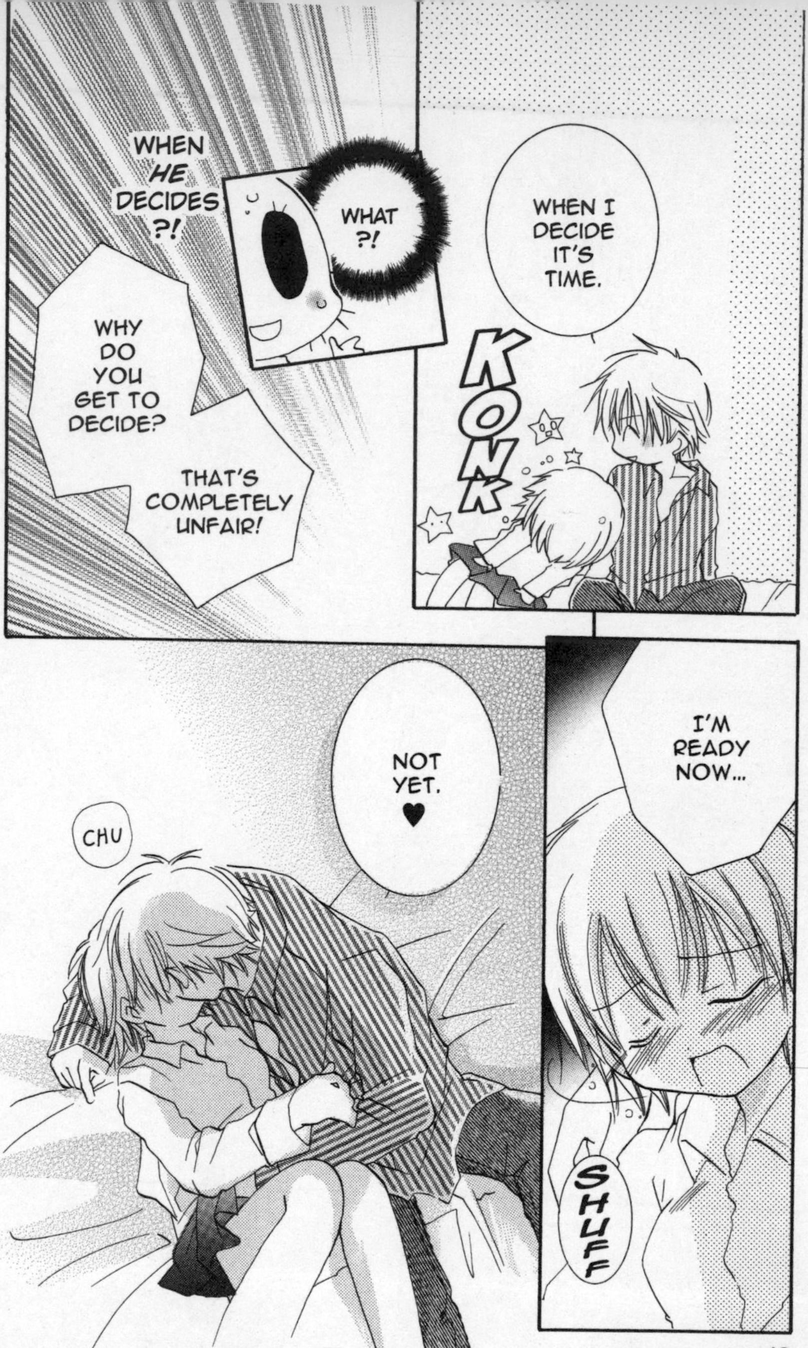
WHEN I DECIDE IT'S TIME.
KONK
WHAT ?!
WHEN HE DECIDES ?!
WHY DO YOU GET TO DECIDE?
THAT'S COMPLETELY UNFAIR!
I'M READY NOW...
SHUFF
NOT YET. ♥
CHU

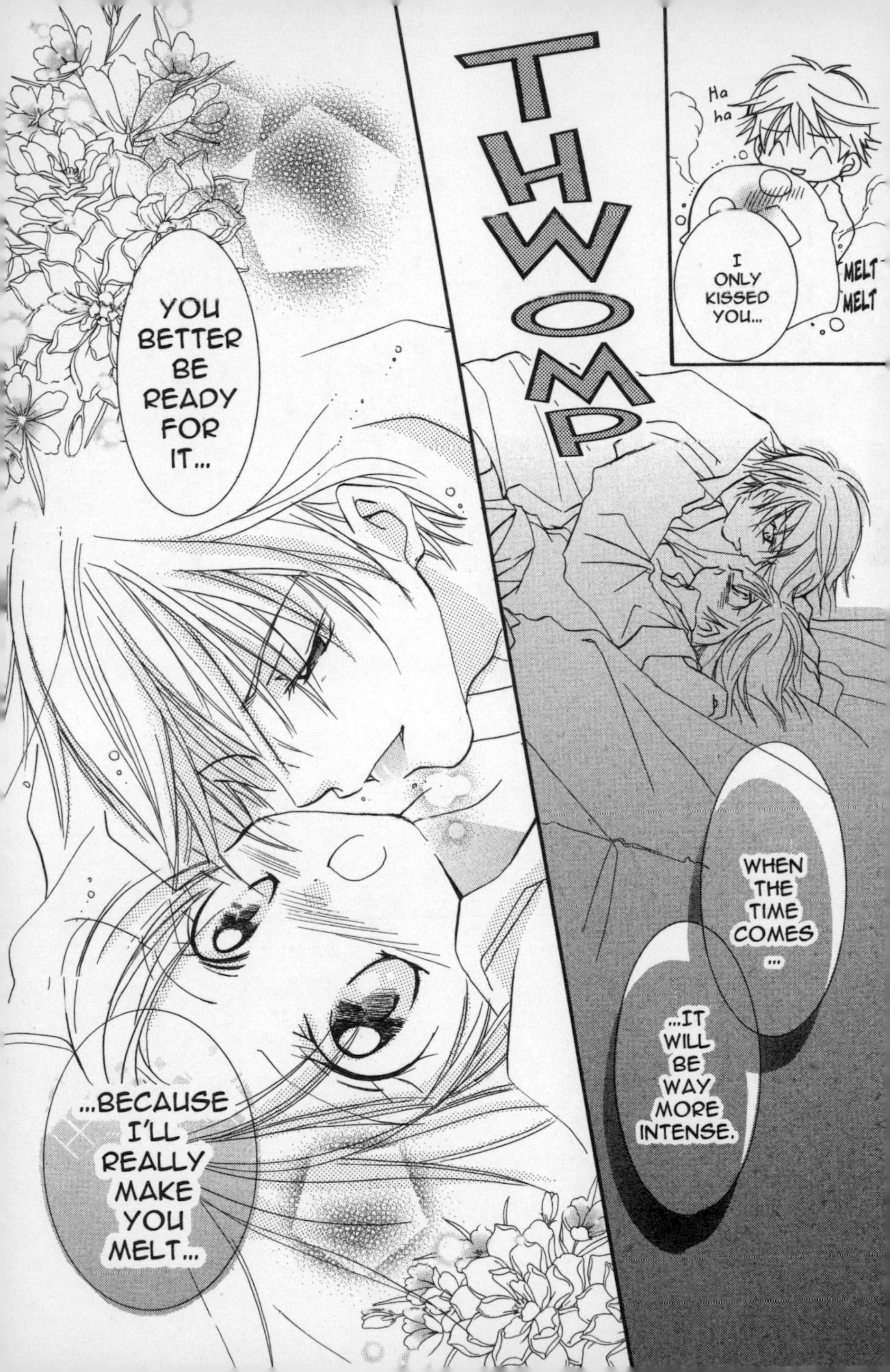
Ha ha
I ONLY KISSED YOU...
MELT MELT
THWOMP
WHEN THE TIME COMES...
...IT WILL BE WAY MORE INTENSE.
YOU BETTER BE READY FOR IT...
...BECAUSE I'LL REALLY MAKE YOU MELT...

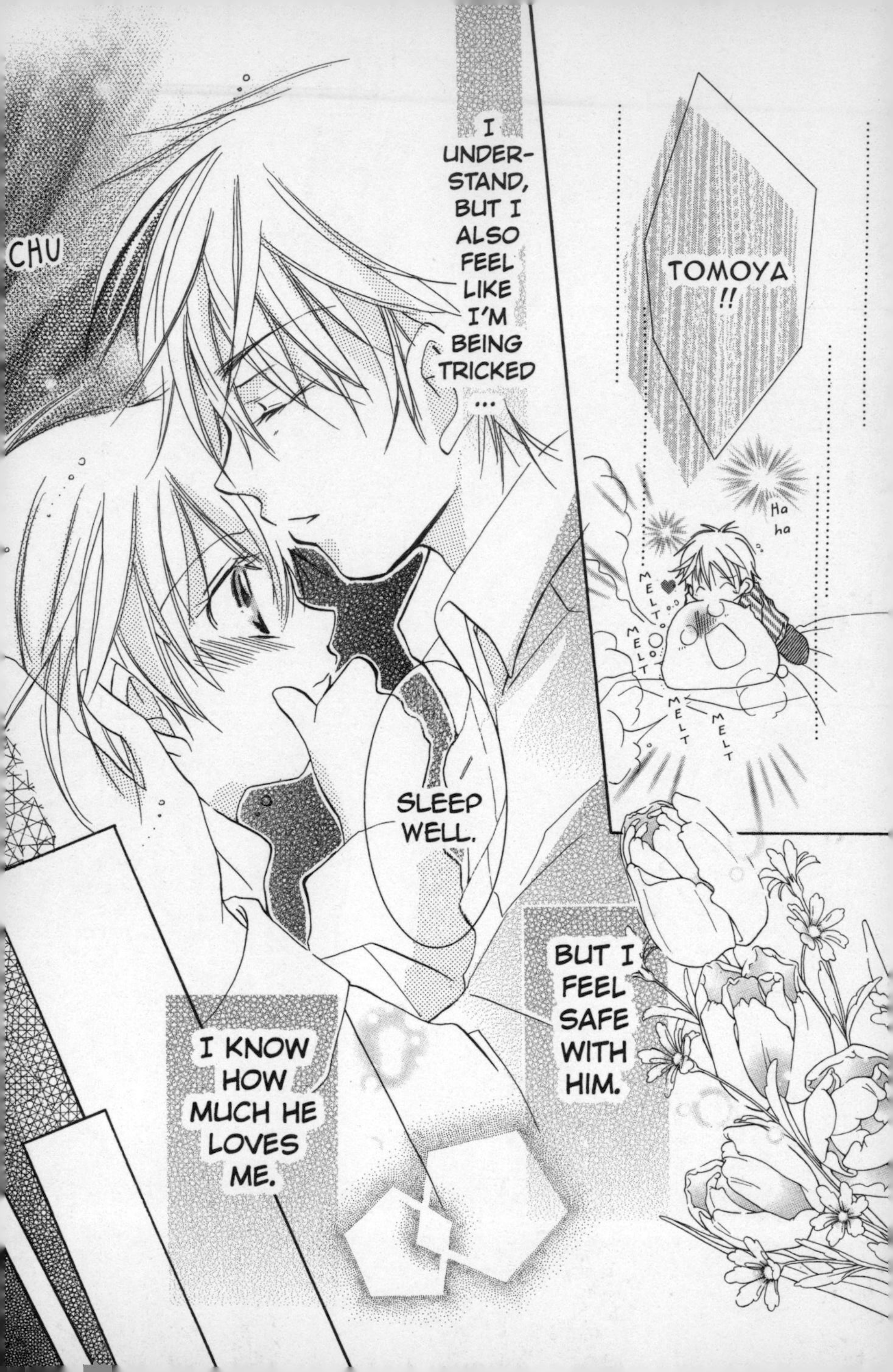
TOMOYA!!
Ha ha
MELT
MELT
MELT
MELT
I UNDERSTAND, BUT I ALSO FEEL LIKE I'M BEING TRICKED...
CHU
SLEEP WELL.
BUT I FEEL SAFE WITH HIM.
I KNOW HOW MUCH HE LOVES ME.

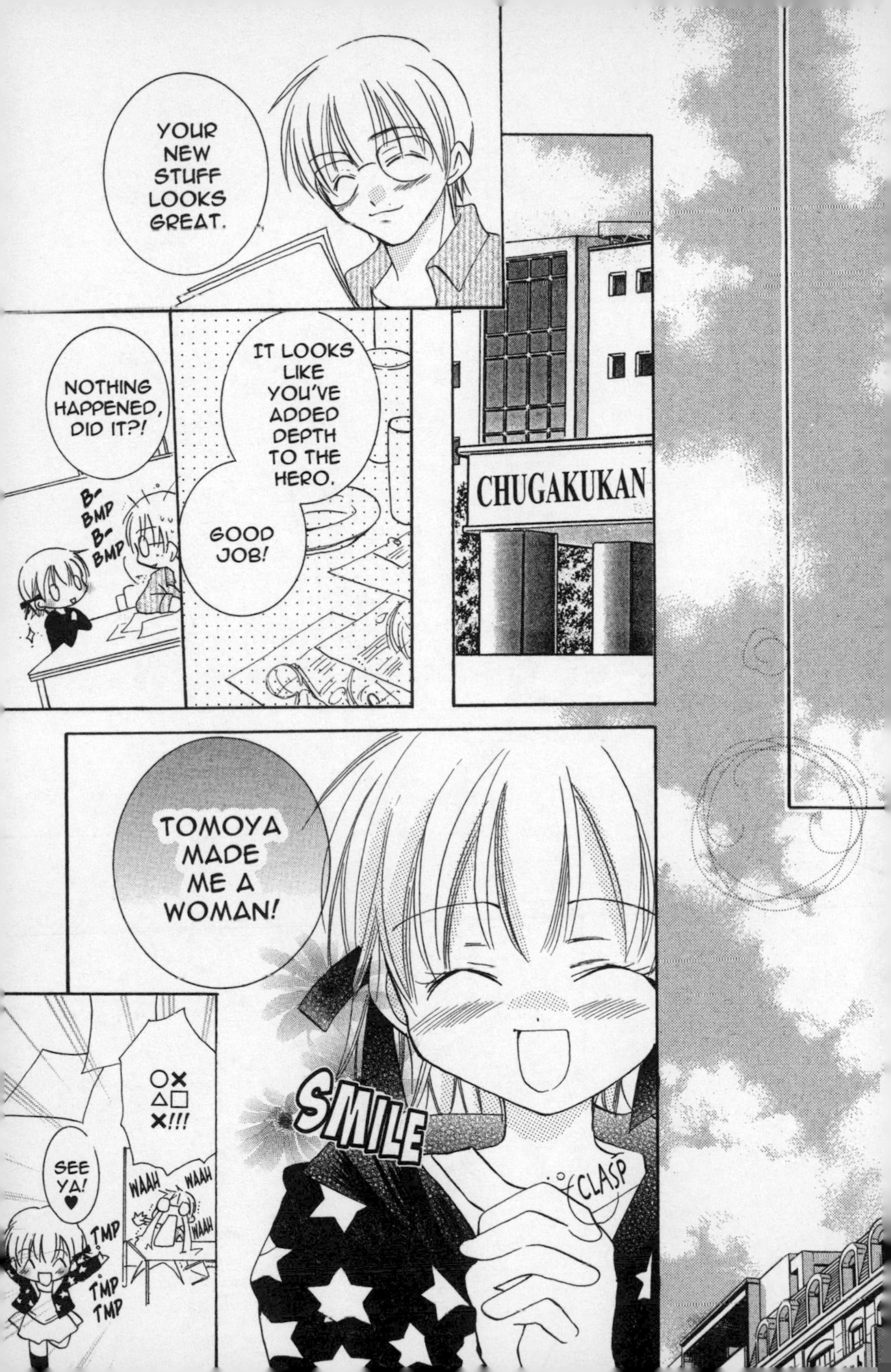
CHUGAKUKAN
YOUR NEW STUFF LOOKS GREAT.
IT LOOKS LIKE YOU'VE ADDED DEPTH TO THE HERO.
GOOD JOB!
NOTHING HAPPENED, DID IT?!
B-BMP B-BMP
TOMOYA MADE ME A WOMAN!
SMILE
CLASP
○×△□×!!!
WAAH WAAH WAAH WAAH
SEE YA! ♥
TMP TMP TMP

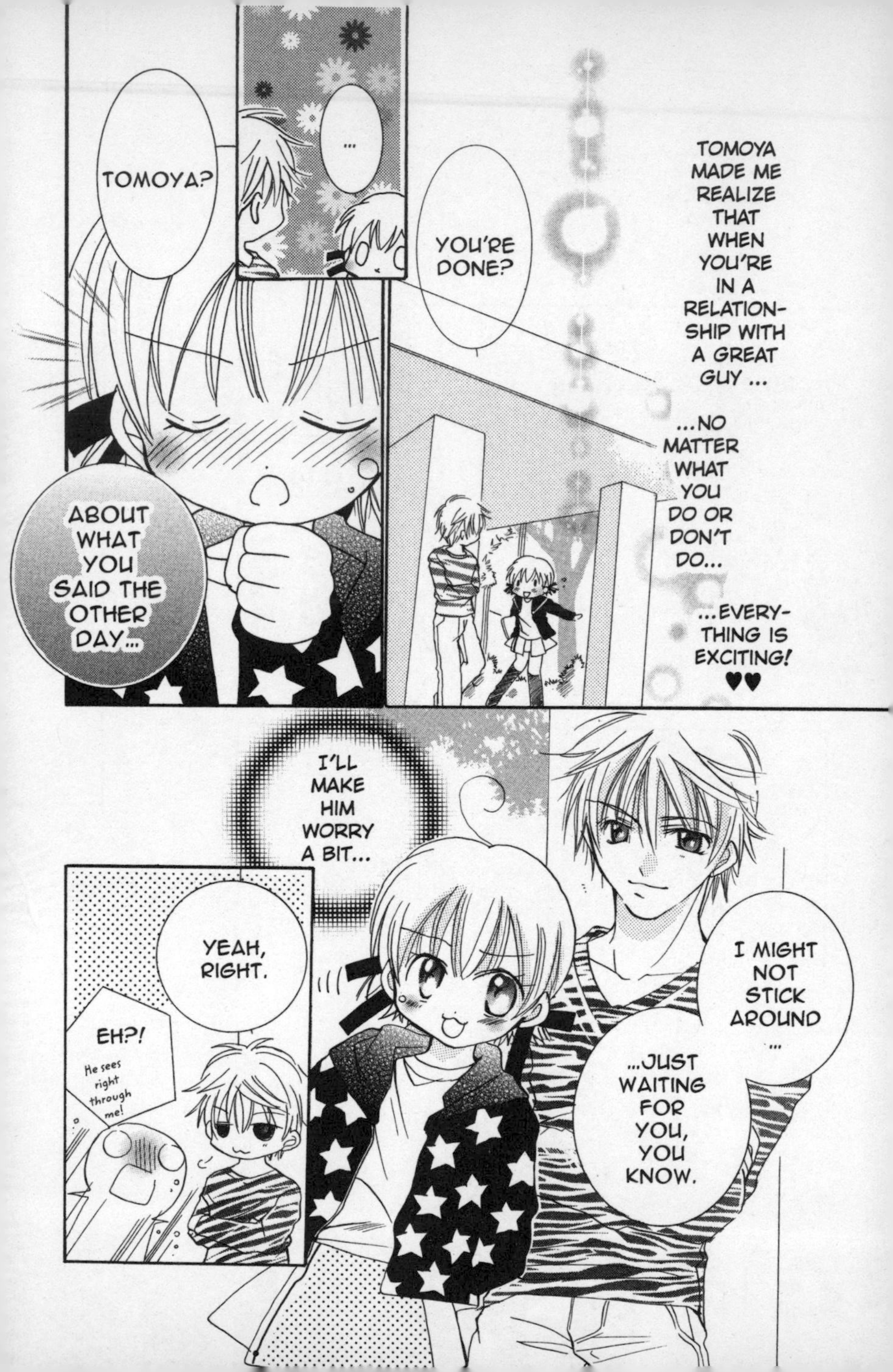
TOMOYA MADE ME REALIZE THAT WHEN YOU'RE IN A RELATIONSHIP WITH A GREAT GUY ...
YOU'RE DONE?
...NO MATTER WHAT YOU DO OR DON'T DO...
...EVERYTHING IS EXCITING! ♥♥
...
TOMOYA?
ABOUT WHAT YOU SAID THE OTHER DAY...
I'LL MAKE HIM WORRY A BIT...
I MIGHT NOT STICK AROUND ...
...JUST WAITING FOR YOU, YOU KNOW.
YEAH, RIGHT.
EH?!
He sees right through me!

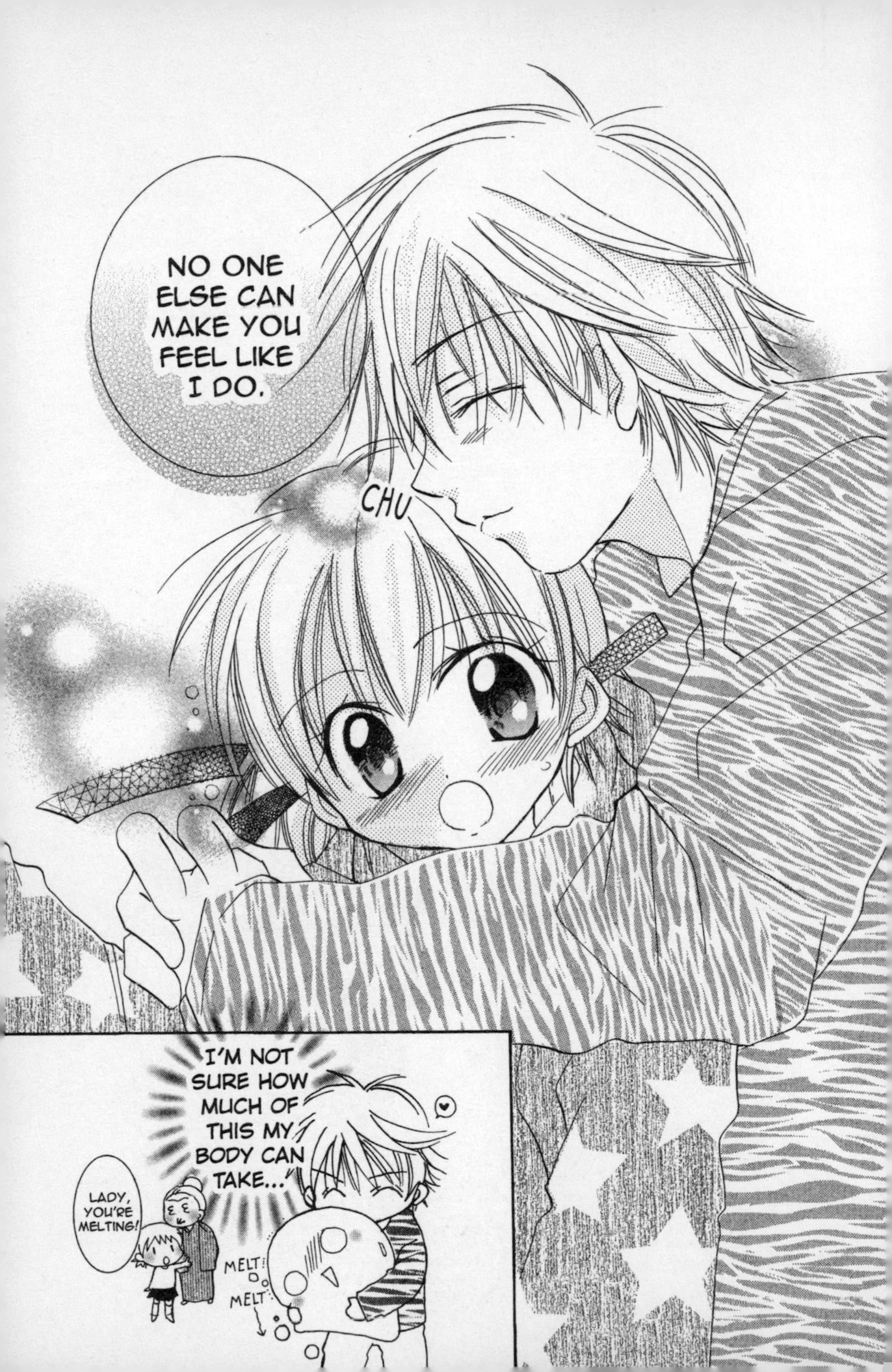
NO ONE ELSE CAN MAKE YOU FEEL LIKE I DO.
CHU
I'M NOT SURE HOW MUCH OF THIS MY BODY CAN TAKE...
MELT
MELT
LADY, YOU'RE MELTING!

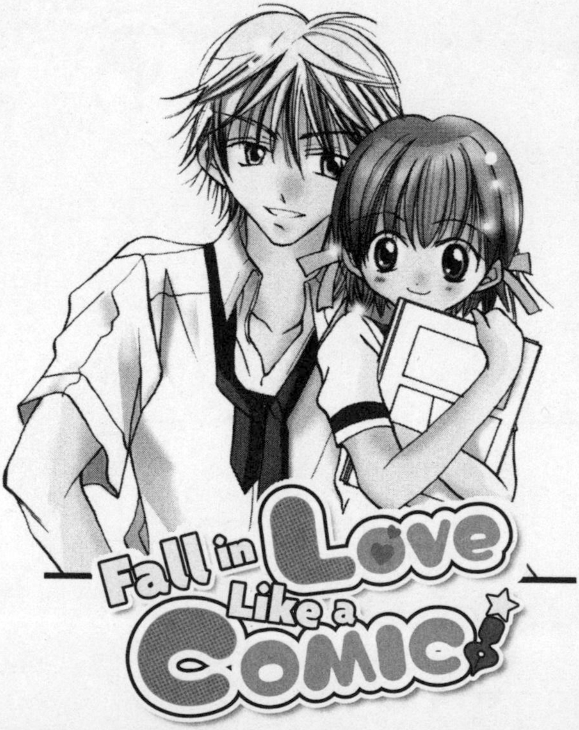
Fall in Love Like a Comic

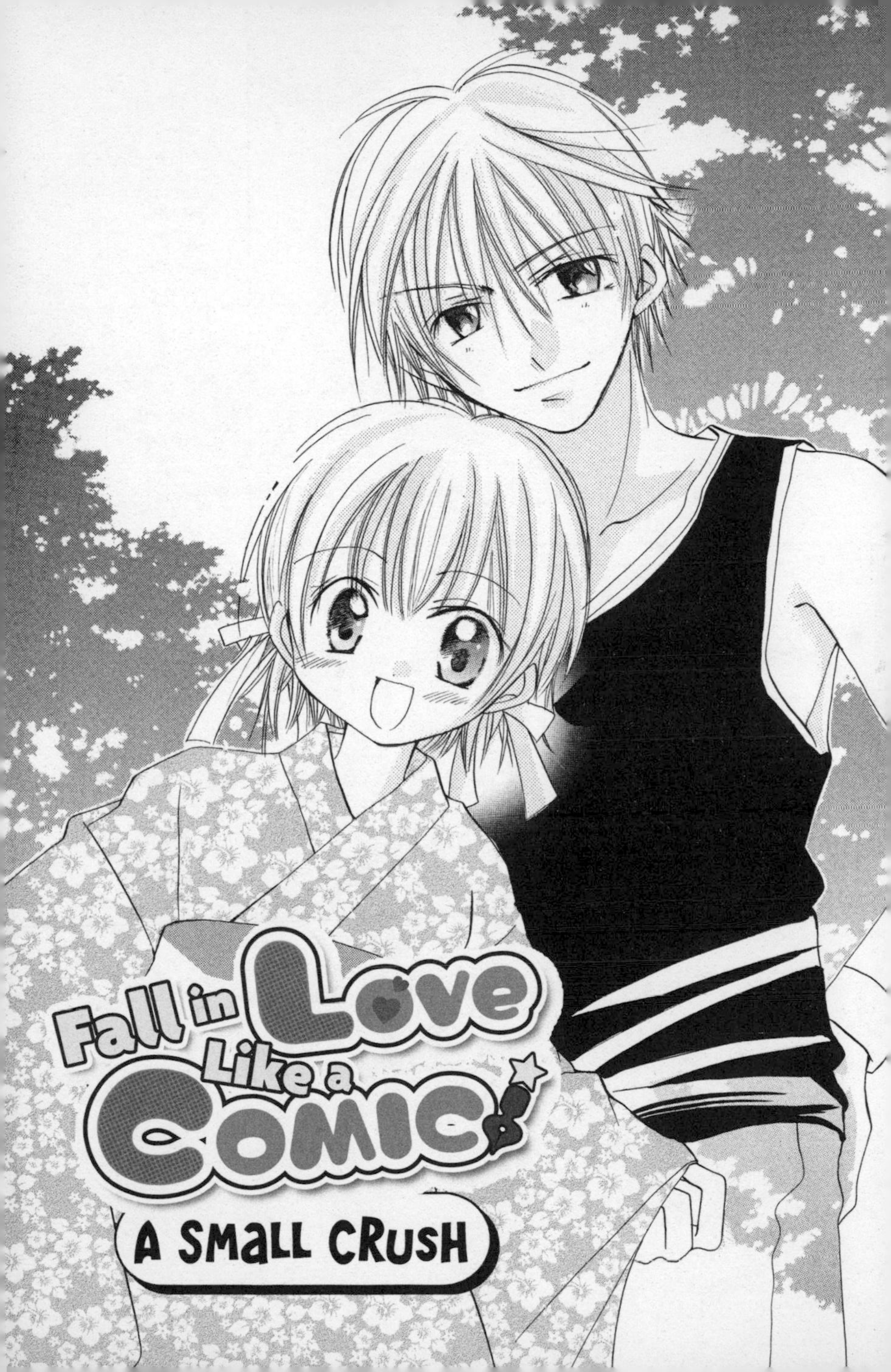
Fall in Love Like a Comic
A SMALL CRUSH

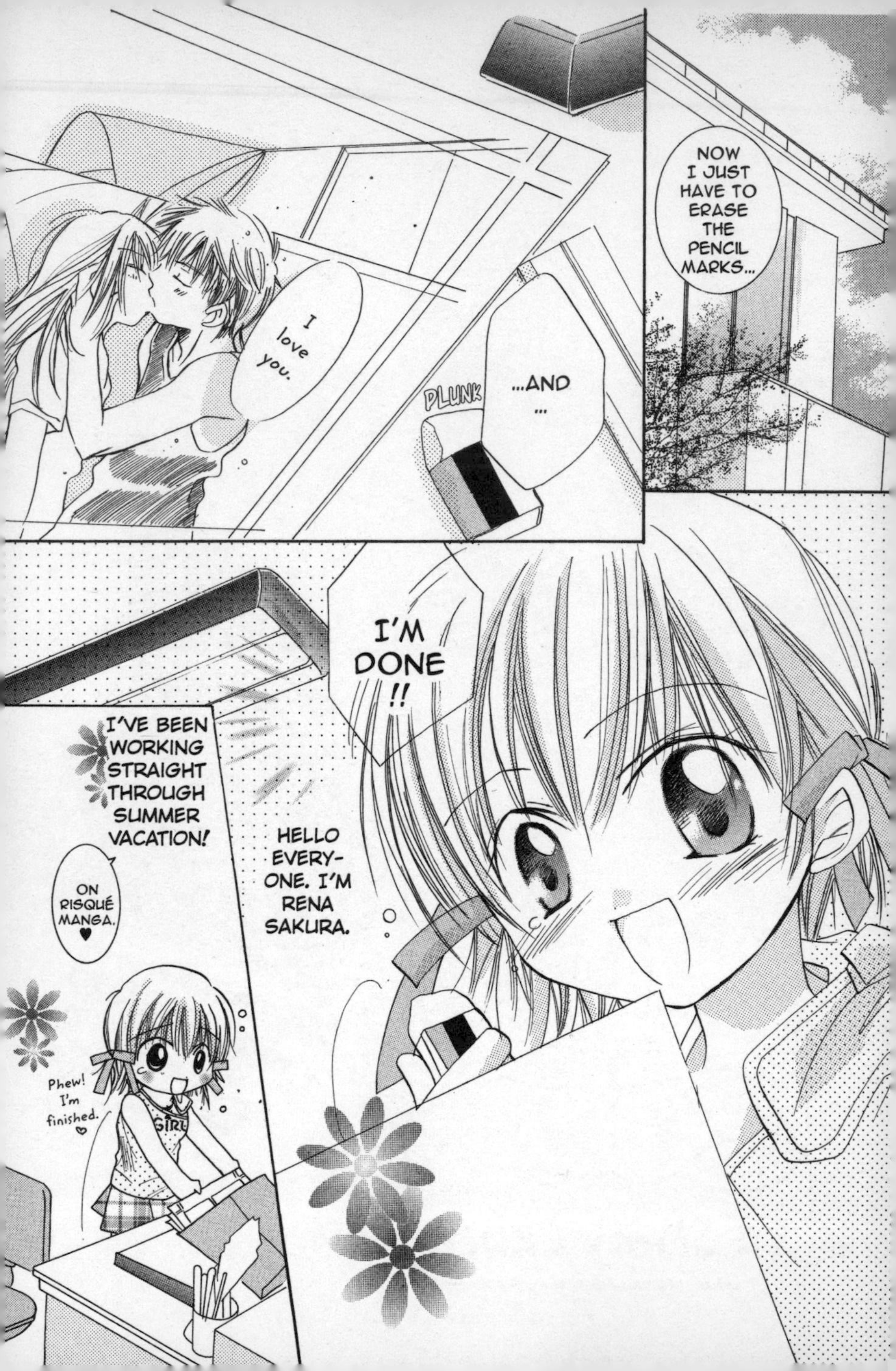
NOW I JUST HAVE TO ERASE THE PENCIL MARKS...
...AND ...
PLUNK
I love you.
I'M DONE !!
HELLO EVERYONE. I'M RENA SAKURA.
I'VE BEEN WORKING STRAIGHT THROUGH SUMMER VACATION!
ON RISQUÉ MANGA. ♥
Phew! I'm finished. ♥

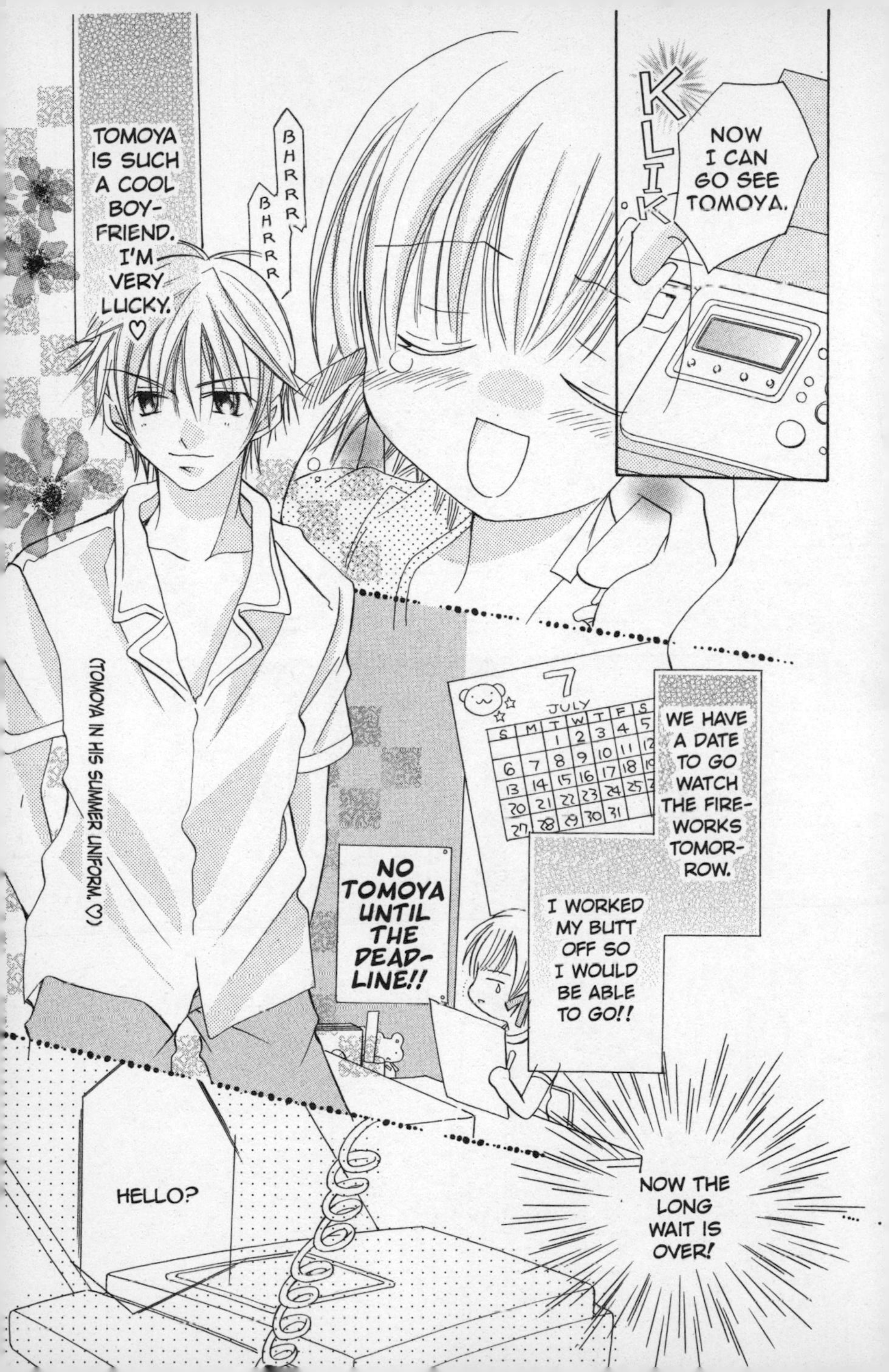
KLIK
NOW I CAN GO SEE TOMOYA.
BHRRR
BHRRR
TOMOYA IS SUCH A COOL BOY-FRIEND. I'M VERY LUCKY. ♡
7
JULY
WE HAVE A DATE TO GO WATCH THE FIRE-WORKS TOMOR-ROW.
I WORKED MY BUTT OFF SO I WOULD BE ABLE TO GO!!
NO TOMOYA UNTIL THE DEAD-LINE!!
(TOMOYA IN HIS SUMMER UNIFORM. ♡)
NOW THE LONG WAIT IS OVER!
HELLO?

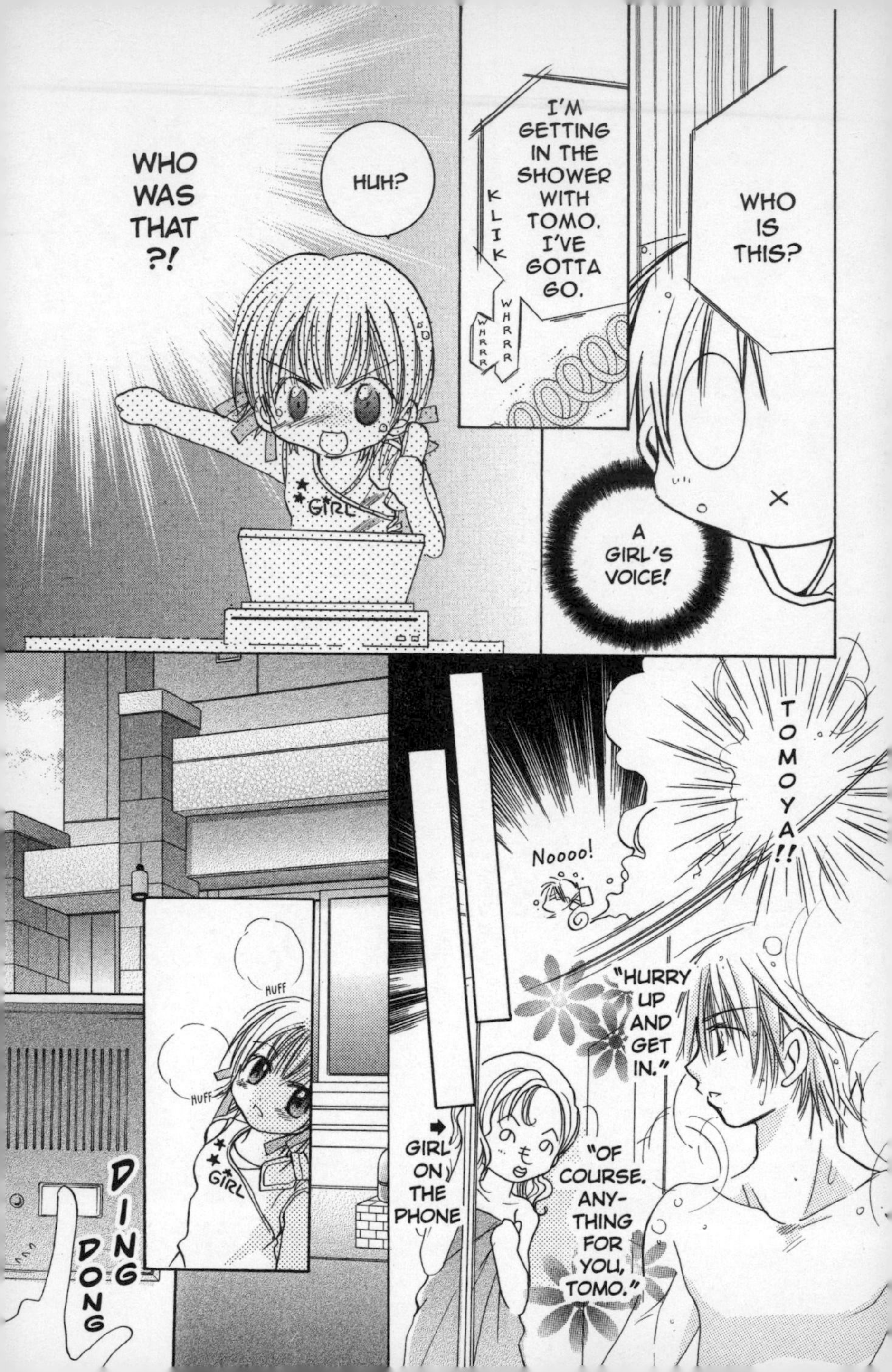
WHO IS THIS?
A GIRL'S VOICE!
I'M GETTING IN THE SHOWER WITH TOMO. I'VE GOTTA GO.
KLIK
WHRRR
WHRRR
HUH?
WHO WAS THAT?!
TOMOYA!!
Noooo!
"HURRY UP AND GET IN."
"OF COURSE. ANYTHING FOR YOU, TOMO."
GIRL ON THE PHONE
HUFF
HUFF
DING DONG

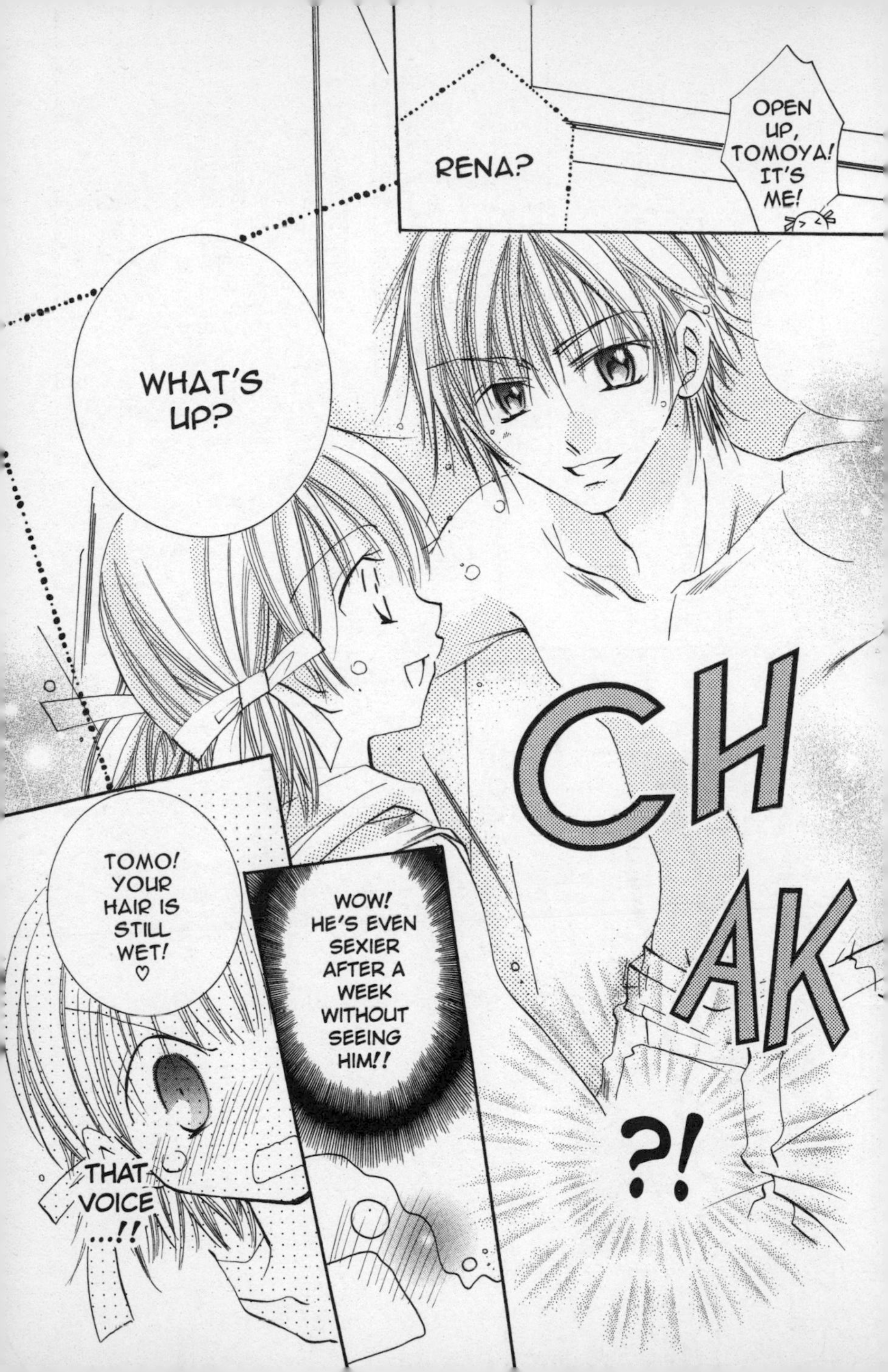
OPEN UP, TOMOYA! IT'S ME!
RENA?
WHAT'S UP?
CHAK
?!
WOW! HE'S EVEN SEXIER AFTER A WEEK WITHOUT SEEING HIM!!
TOMO! YOUR HAIR IS STILL WET! ♡
THAT VOICE ...!!

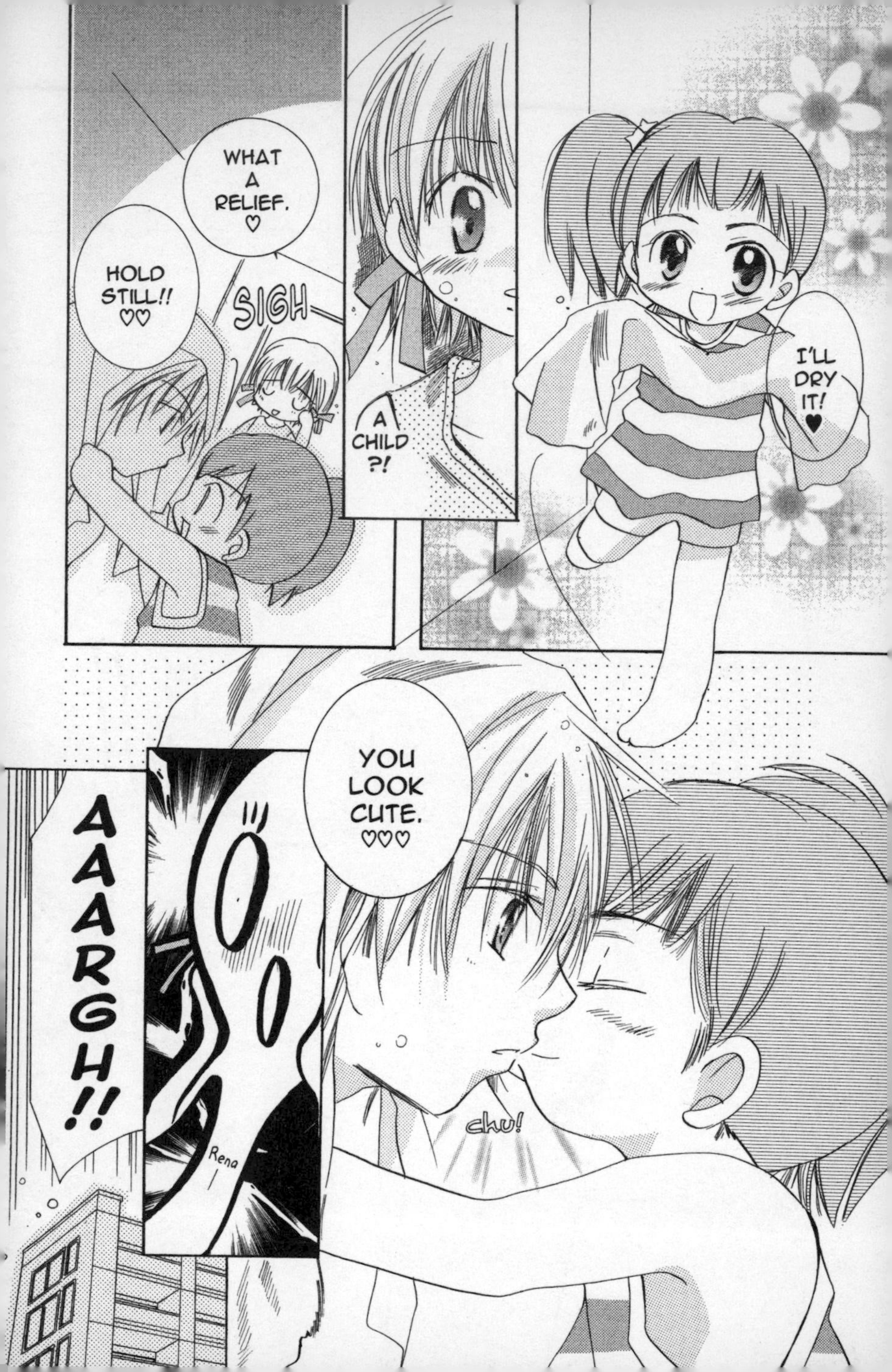
I'LL DRY IT! ♥
A CHILD ?!
WHAT A RELIEF. ♡
SIGH
HOLD STILL!! ♡♡
YOU LOOK CUTE. ♡♡♡
chu!
Rena
AAARGH!!

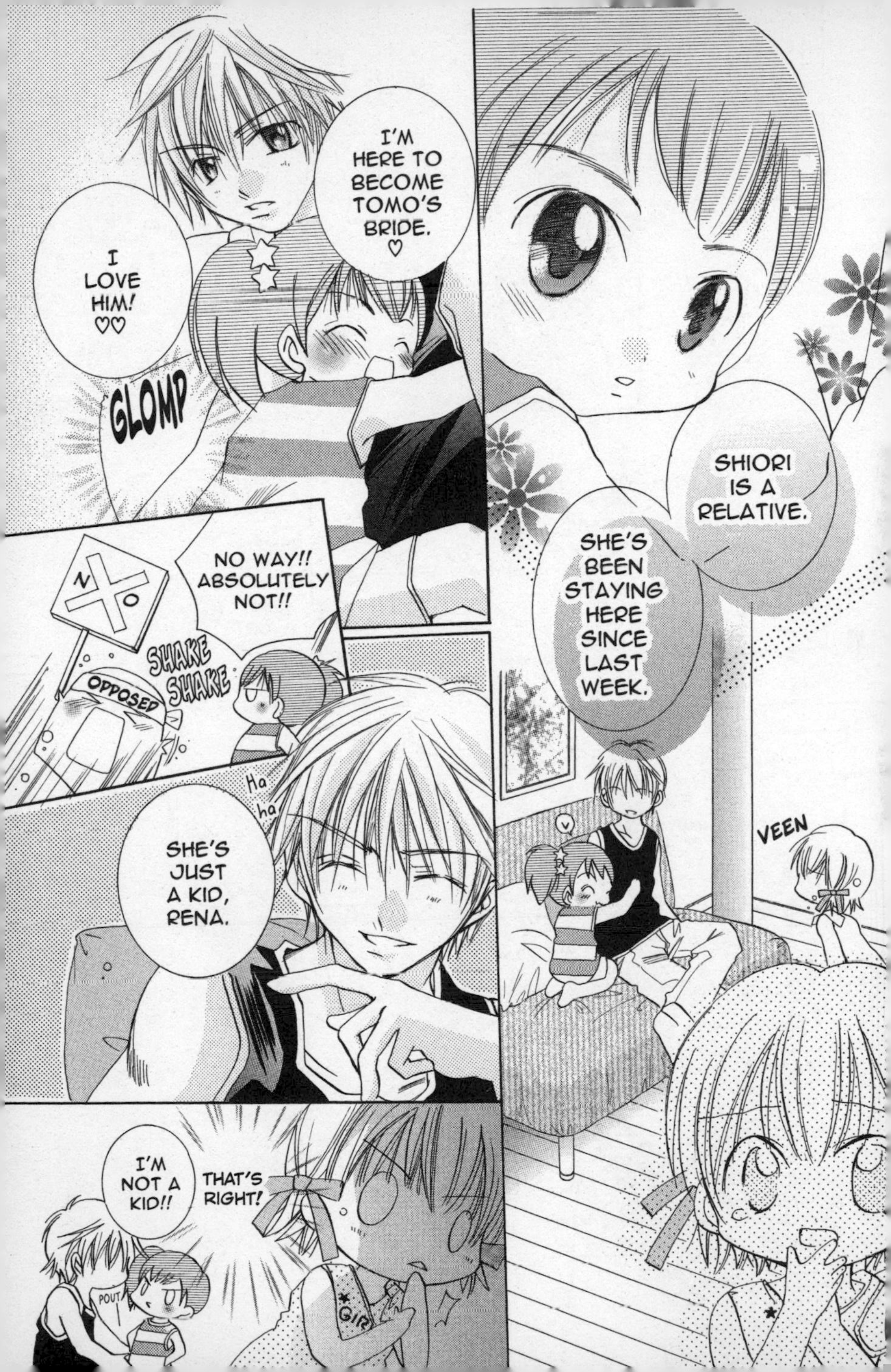

SHIORI IS A RELATIVE.
SHE'S BEEN STAYING HERE SINCE LAST WEEK.
VEEN
I'M HERE TO BECOME TOMO'S BRIDE. ♡
I LOVE HIM! ♡♡
GLOMP
NO WAY!! ABSOLUTELY NOT!!
N O
SHAKE SHAKE
OPPOSED
Ha ha
SHE'S JUST A KID, RENA.
THAT'S RIGHT!
I'M NOT A KID!!
POUT

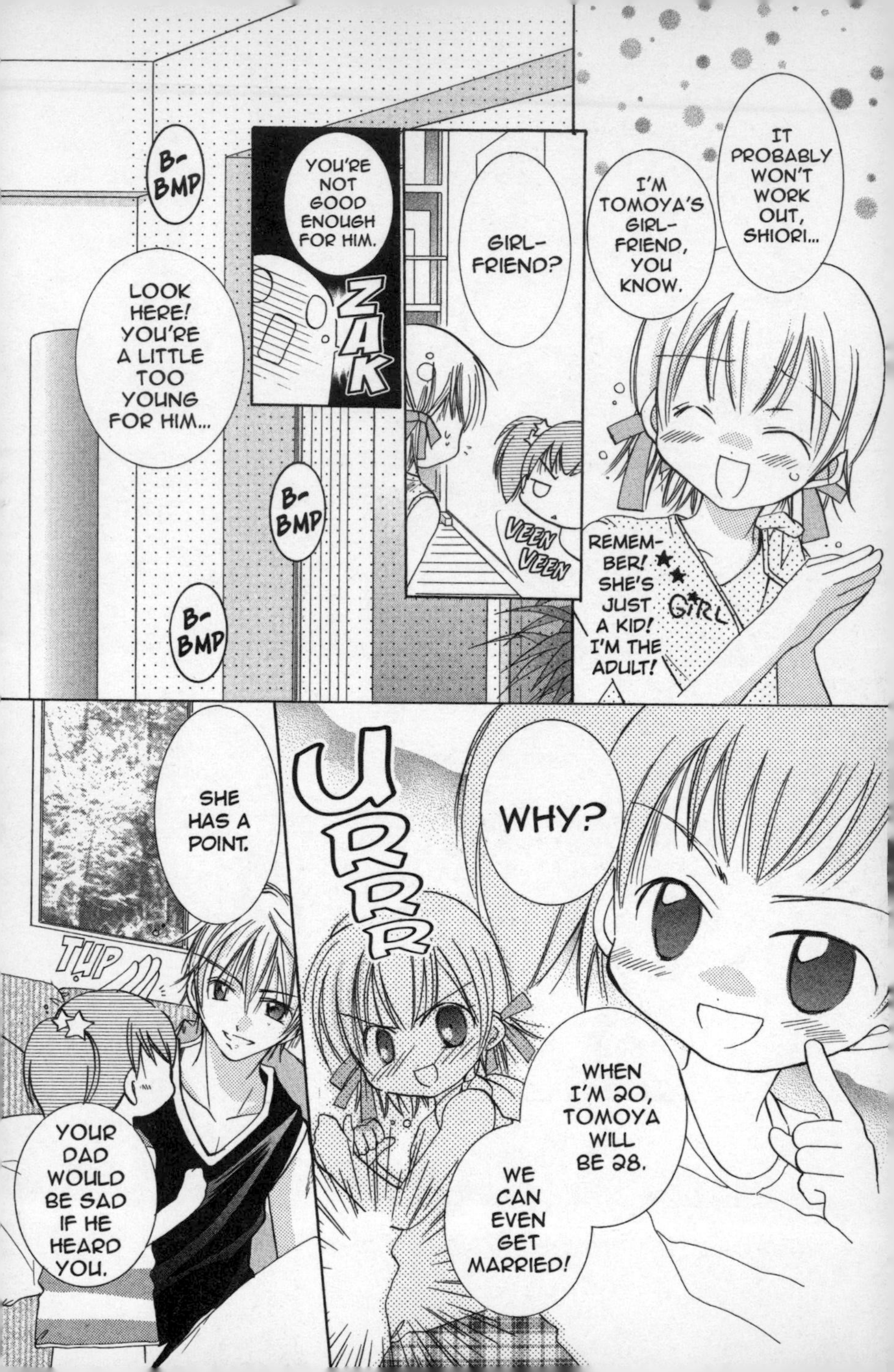
IT PROBABLY WON'T WORK OUT, SHIORI...
I'M TOMOYA'S GIRL-FRIEND, YOU KNOW.
REMEMBER! SHE'S JUST A KID! I'M THE ADULT!
GIRL
GIRL-FRIEND?
VEEN VEEN
YOU'RE NOT GOOD ENOUGH FOR HIM.
ZAK
LOOK HERE! YOU'RE A LITTLE TOO YOUNG FOR HIM...
B-BMP
B-BMP
B-BMP
WHY?
WHEN I'M 20, TOMOYA WILL BE 28.
WE CAN EVEN GET MARRIED!
URRR
SHE HAS A POINT.
TUP
YOUR DAD WOULD BE SAD IF HE HEARD YOU.

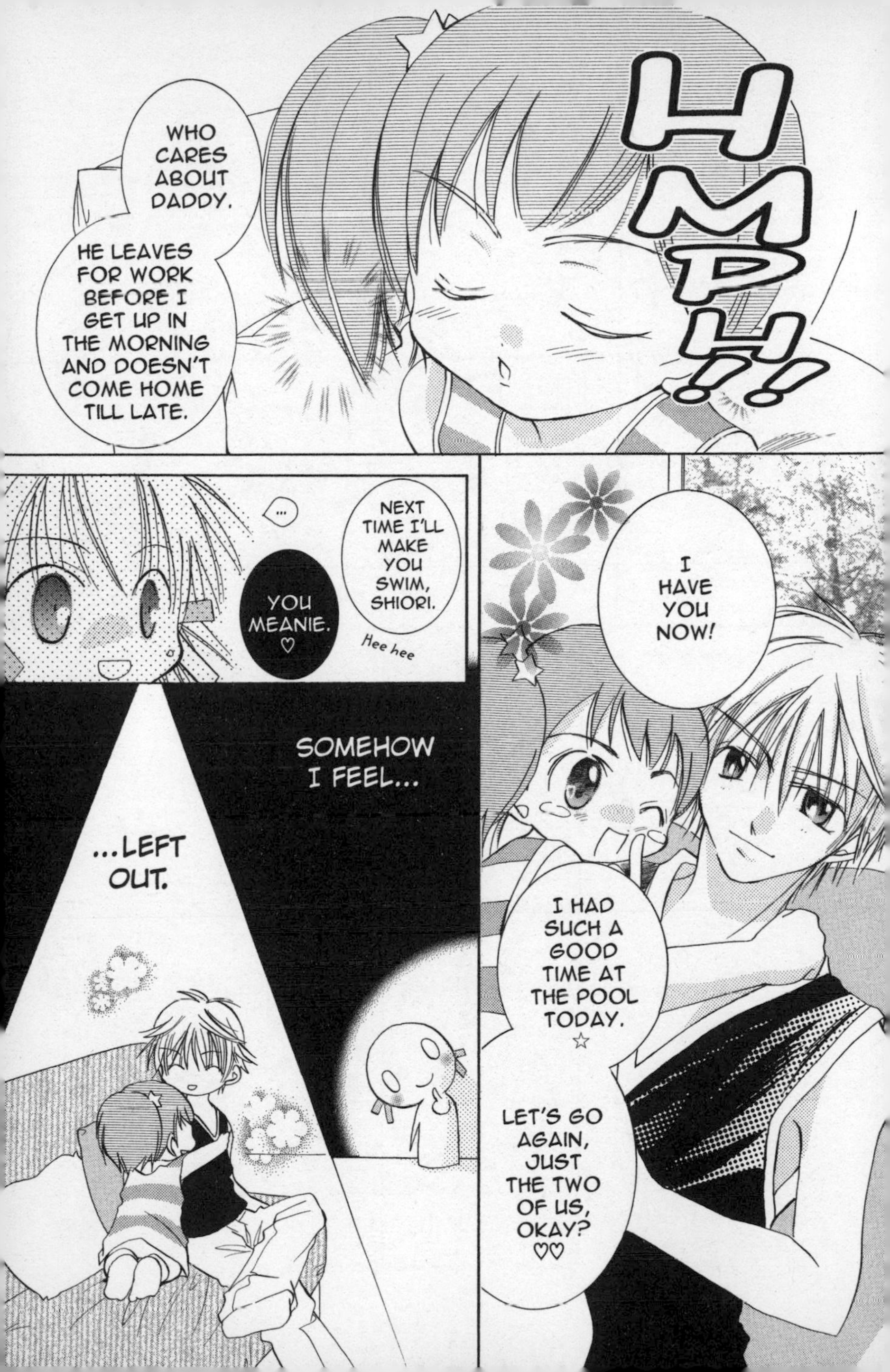
HMPH!!
WHO CARES ABOUT DADDY.
HE LEAVES FOR WORK BEFORE I GET UP IN THE MORNING AND DOESN'T COME HOME TILL LATE.
I HAVE YOU NOW!
I HAD SUCH A GOOD TIME AT THE POOL TODAY. ☆
LET'S GO AGAIN, JUST THE TWO OF US, OKAY? ♡♡
NEXT TIME I'LL MAKE YOU SWIM, SHIORI.
YOU MEANIE. ♡
...
Hee hee
SOMEHOW I FEEL...
...LEFT OUT.

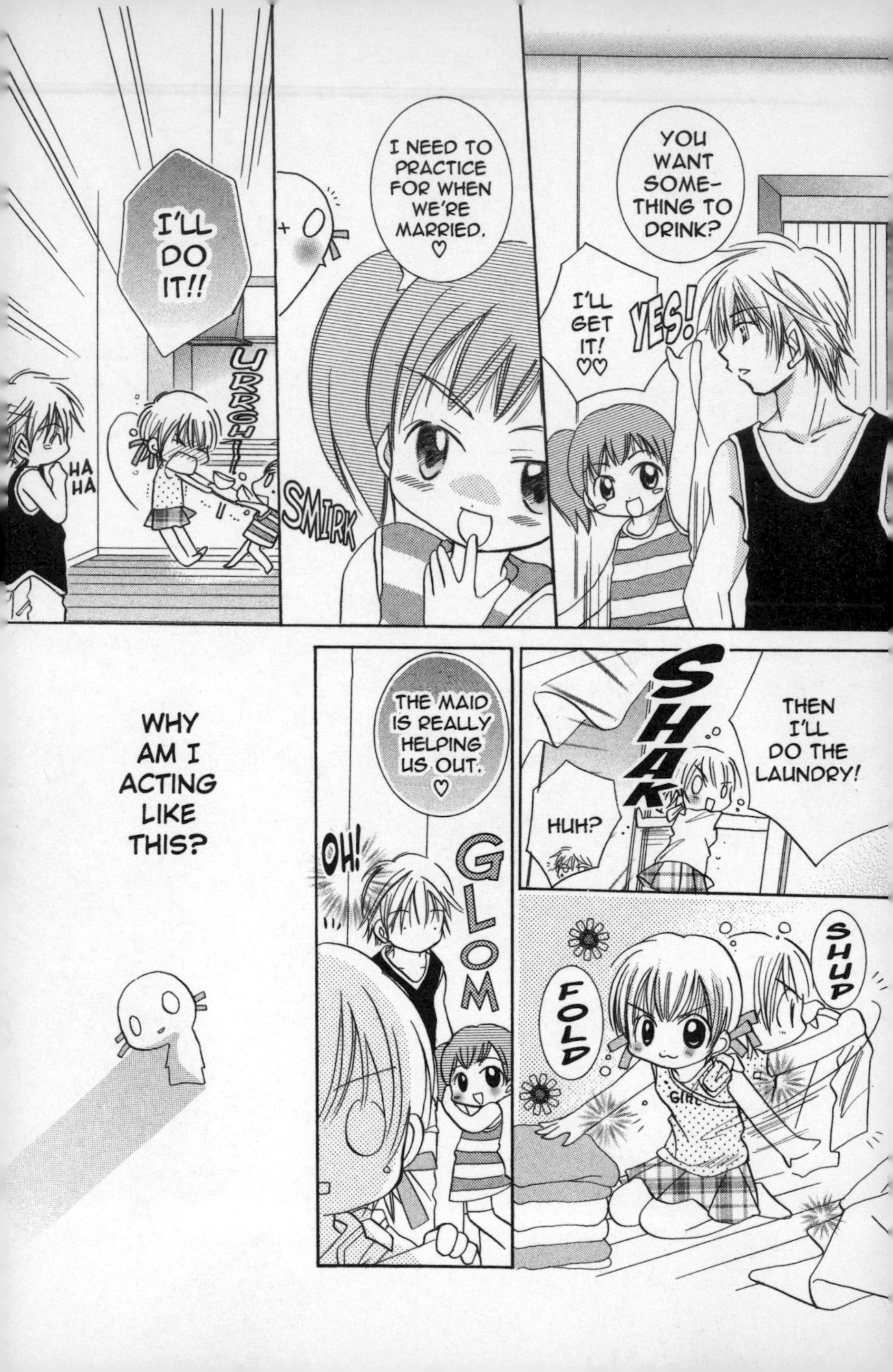
YOU WANT SOME- THING TO DRINK?
YES!
I'LL GET IT! ♡♡
I NEED TO PRACTICE FOR WHEN WE'RE MARRIED. ♡
SMIRK
I'LL DO IT!!
URRGH!
HA HA
SHAK
THEN I'LL DO THE LAUNDRY!
HUH?
SHUP
FOLD
THE MAID IS REALLY HELPING US OUT. ♡
OH!
GLOM
WHY AM I ACTING LIKE THIS?

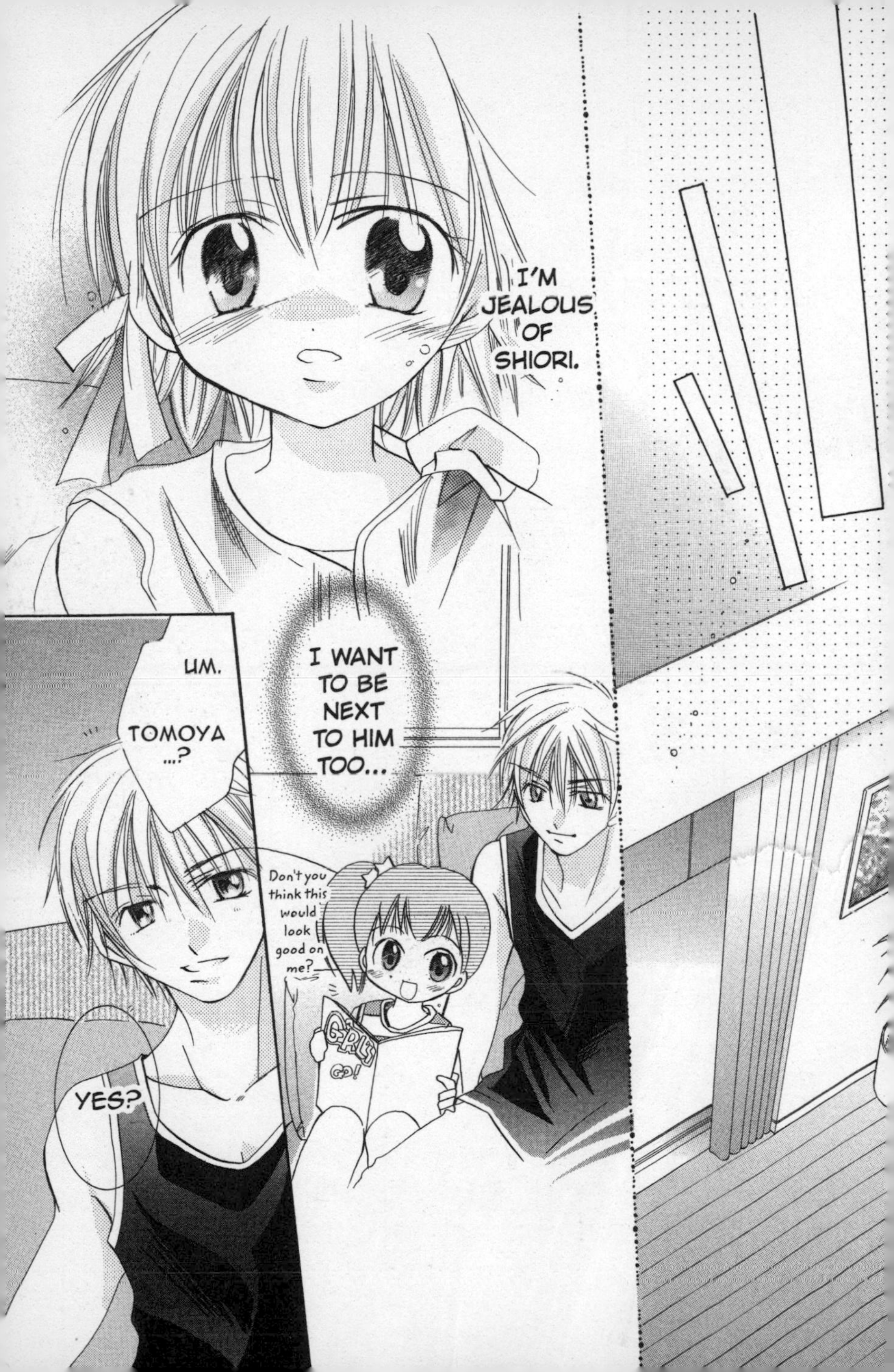
I'M JEALOUS OF SHIORI.
I WANT TO BE NEXT TO HIM TOO...
Don't you think this would look good on me?
UM.
TOMOYA ...?
YES?

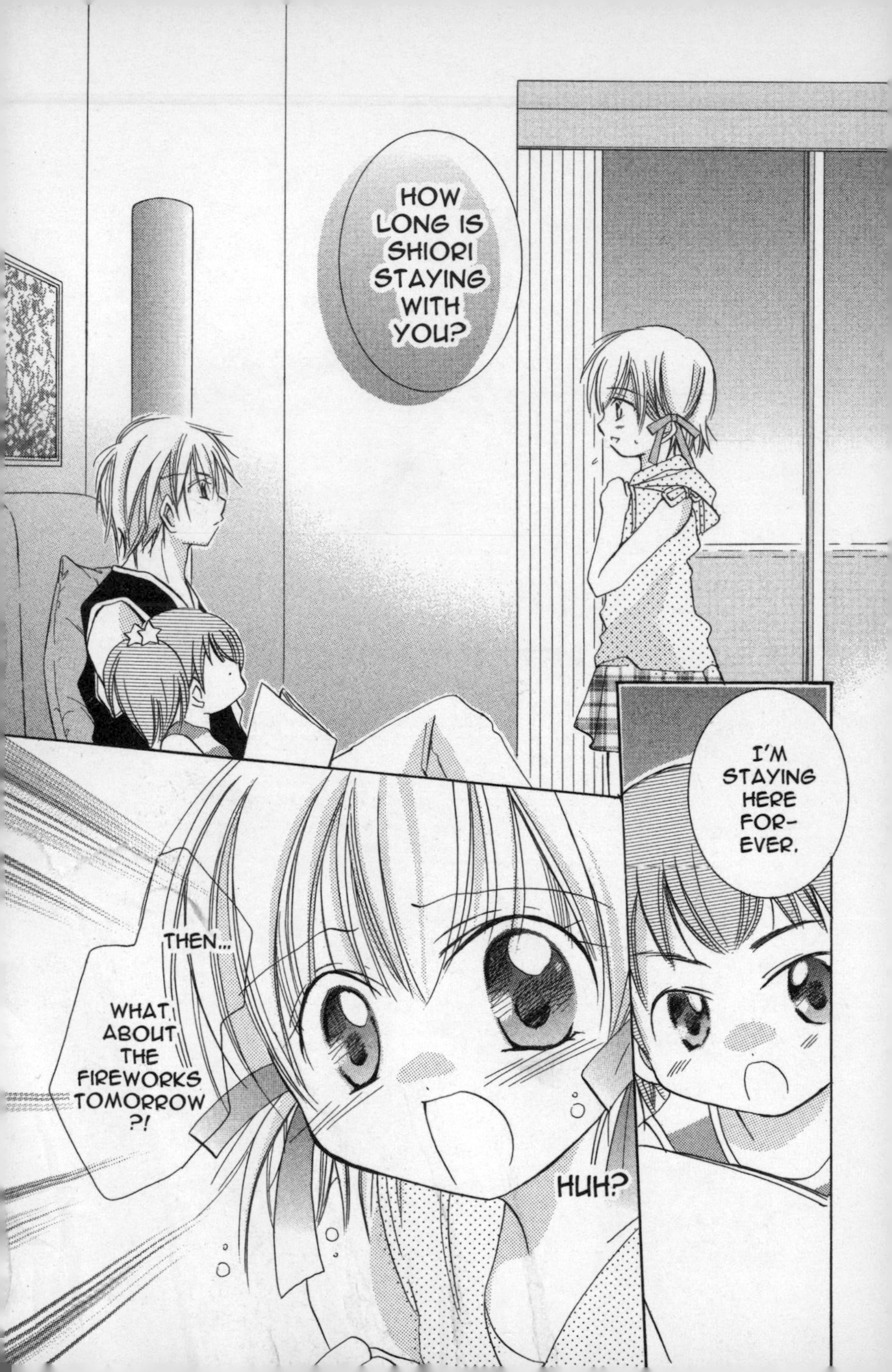
HOW LONG IS SHIORI STAYING WITH YOU?
I'M STAYING HERE FOREVER.
THEN...
WHAT ABOUT THE FIREWORKS TOMORROW?!
HUH?

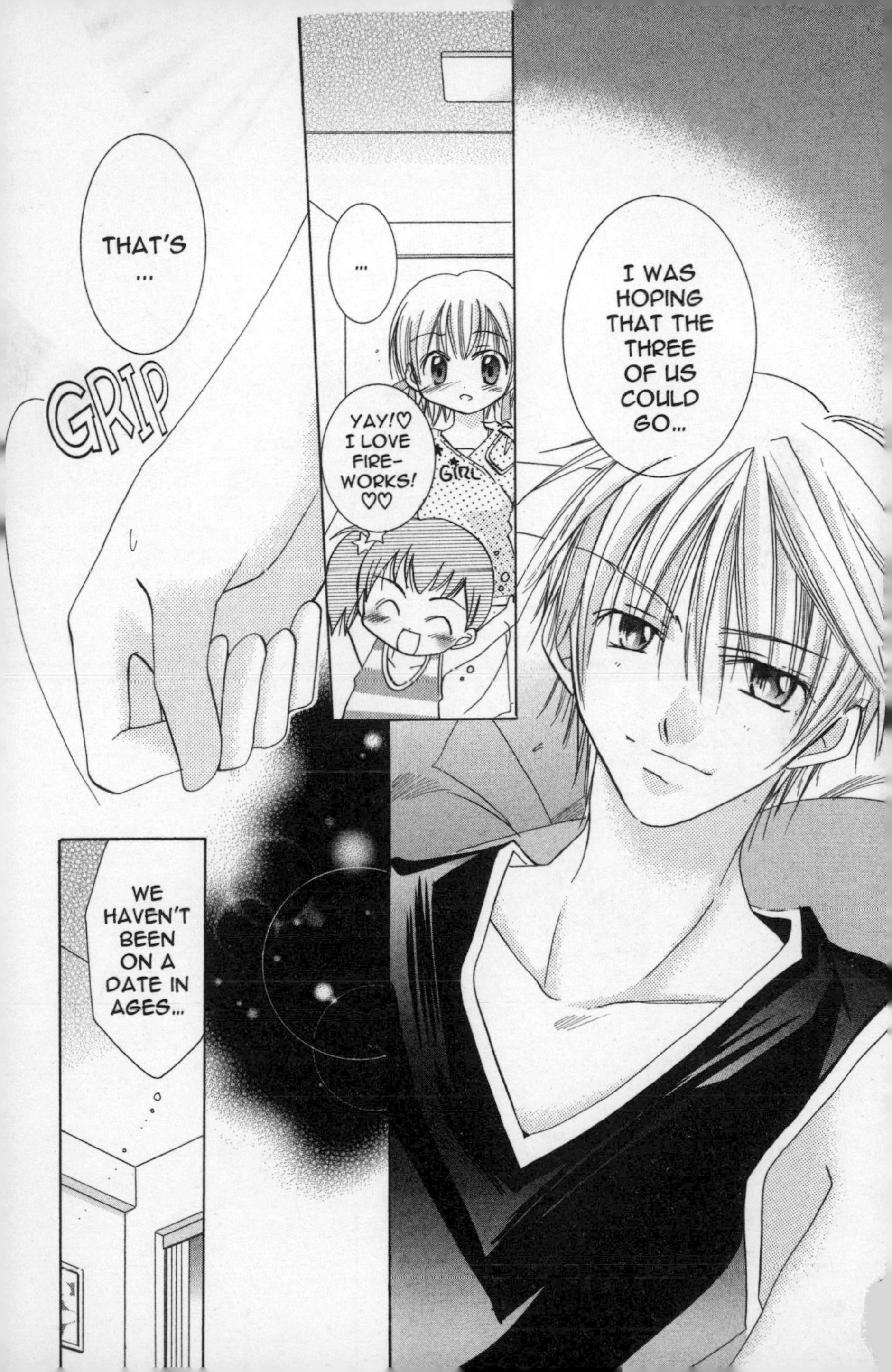
I WAS HOPING THAT THE THREE OF US COULD GO...
...
YAY!♡ I LOVE FIRE-WORKS! ♡♡
GIRL
THAT'S ...
GRIP
WE HAVEN'T BEEN ON A DATE IN AGES...

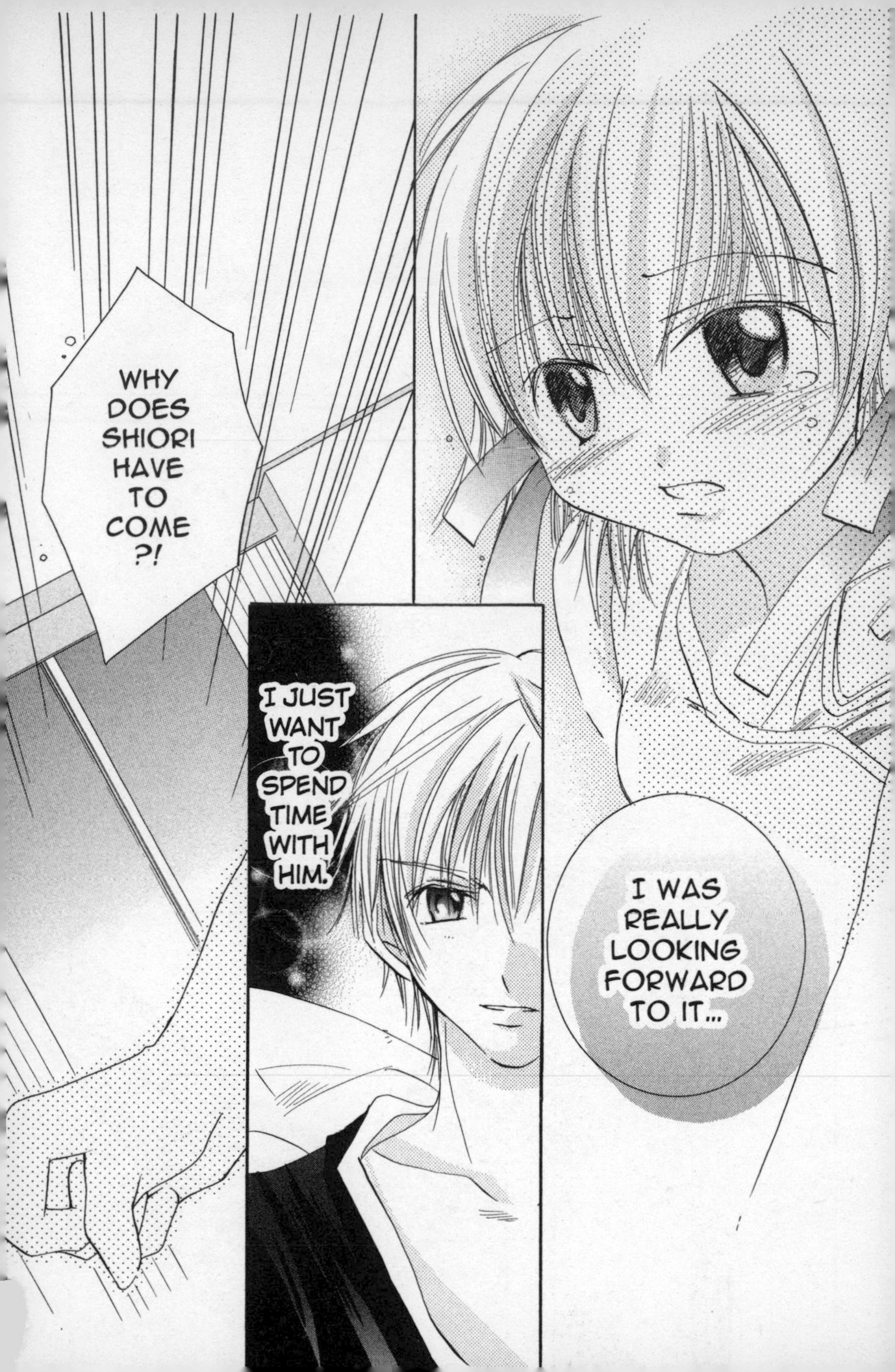
WHY DOES SHIORI HAVE TO COME?!
I WAS REALLY LOOKING FORWARD TO IT...
I JUST WANT TO SPEND TIME WITH HIM.

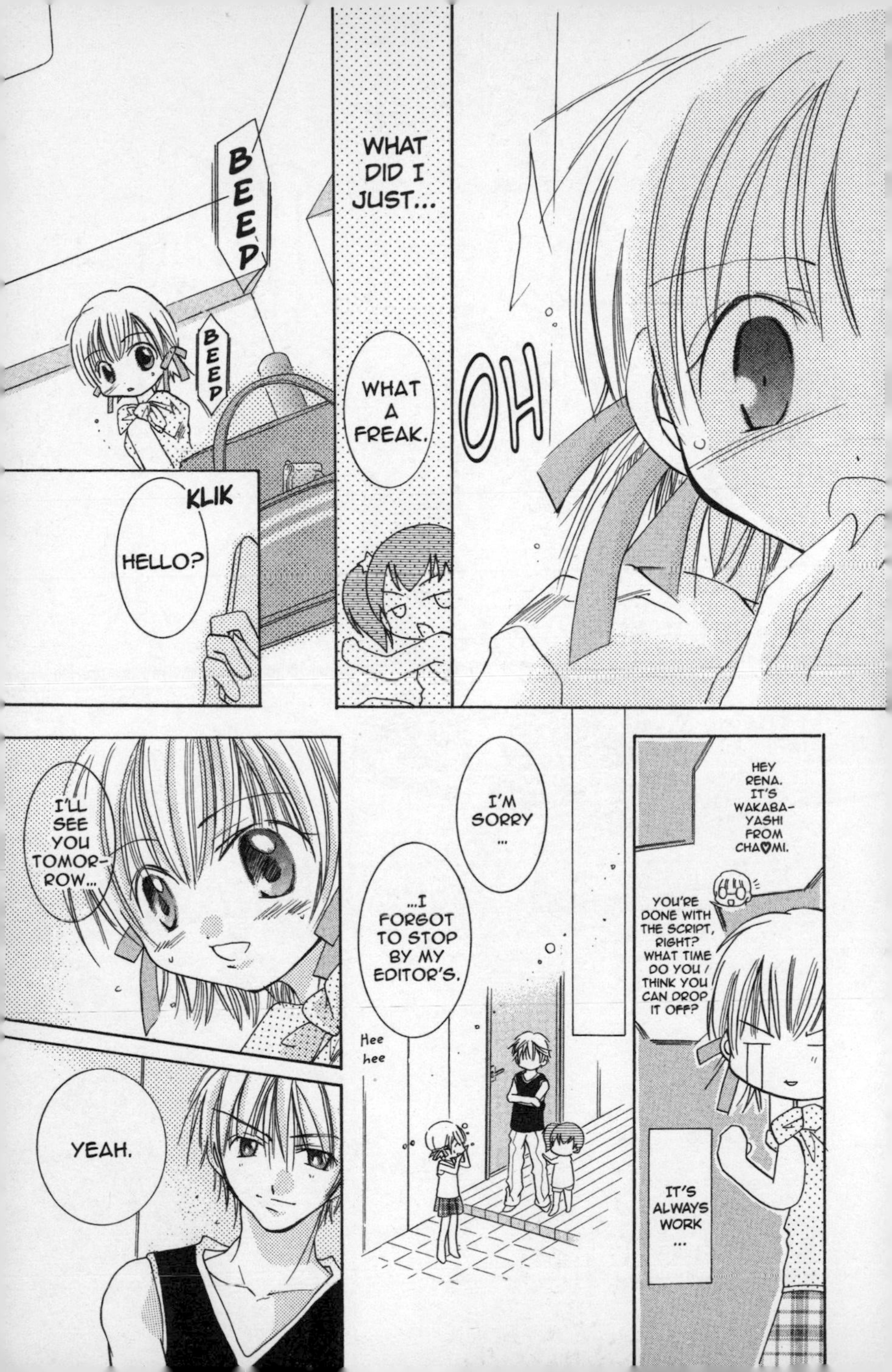
OH
WHAT DID I JUST...
WHAT A FREAK.
BEEP
BEEP
KLIK
HELLO?
HEY RENA. IT'S WAKABA-YASHI FROM CHA♥MI.
YOU'RE DONE WITH THE SCRIPT, RIGHT? WHAT TIME DO YOU / THINK YOU CAN DROP IT OFF?
IT'S ALWAYS WORK...
I'M SORRY...
...I FORGOT TO STOP BY MY EDITOR'S.
Hee hee
I'LL SEE YOU TOMOR-ROW...
YEAH.

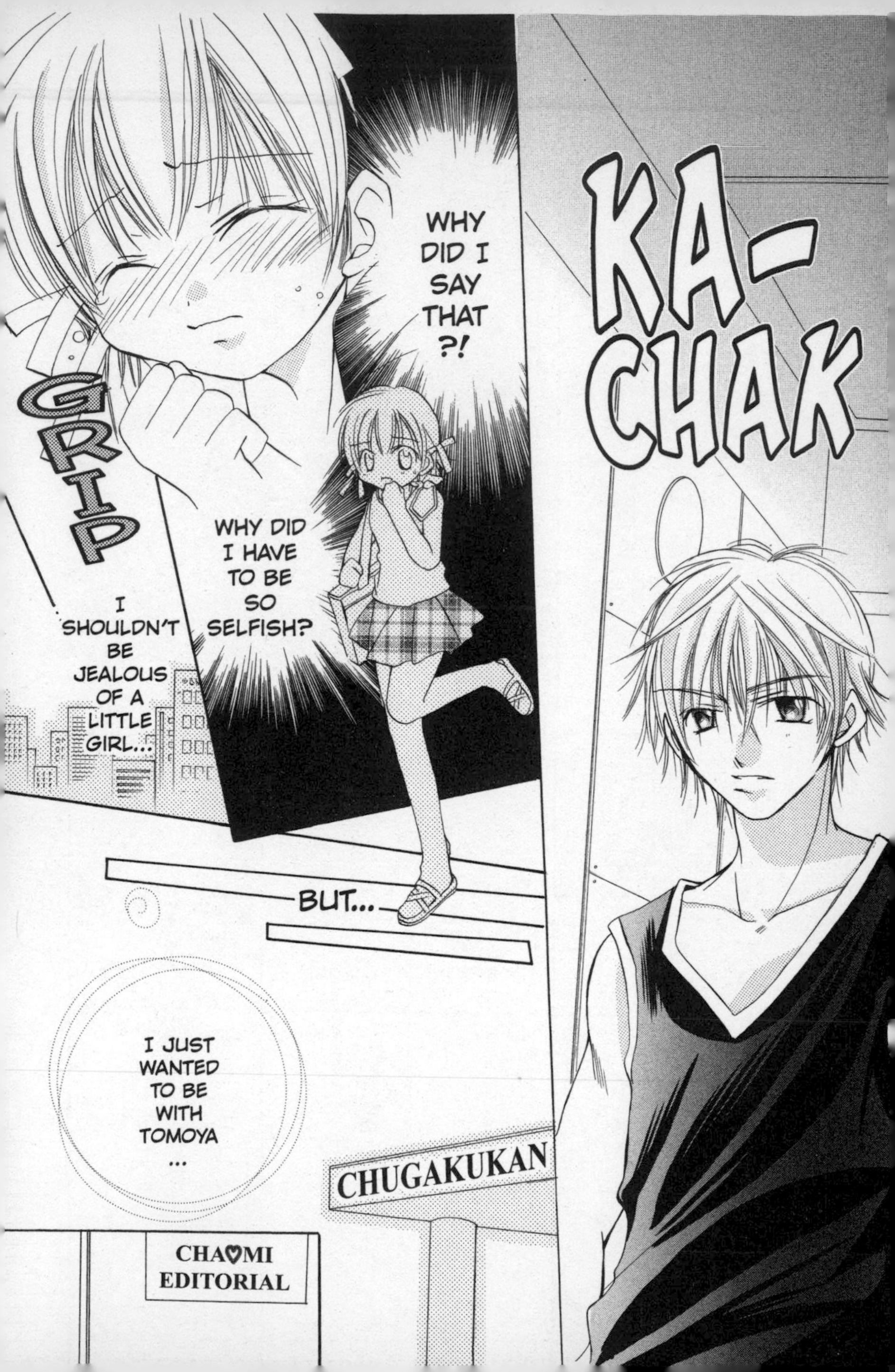
KA-CHAK
WHY DID I SAY THAT?!
GRIP
WHY DID I HAVE TO BE SO SELFISH?
I SHOULDN'T BE JEALOUS OF A LITTLE GIRL...
BUT...
CHUGAKUKAN
I JUST WANTED TO BE WITH TOMOYA ...
CHA♡MI EDITORIAL

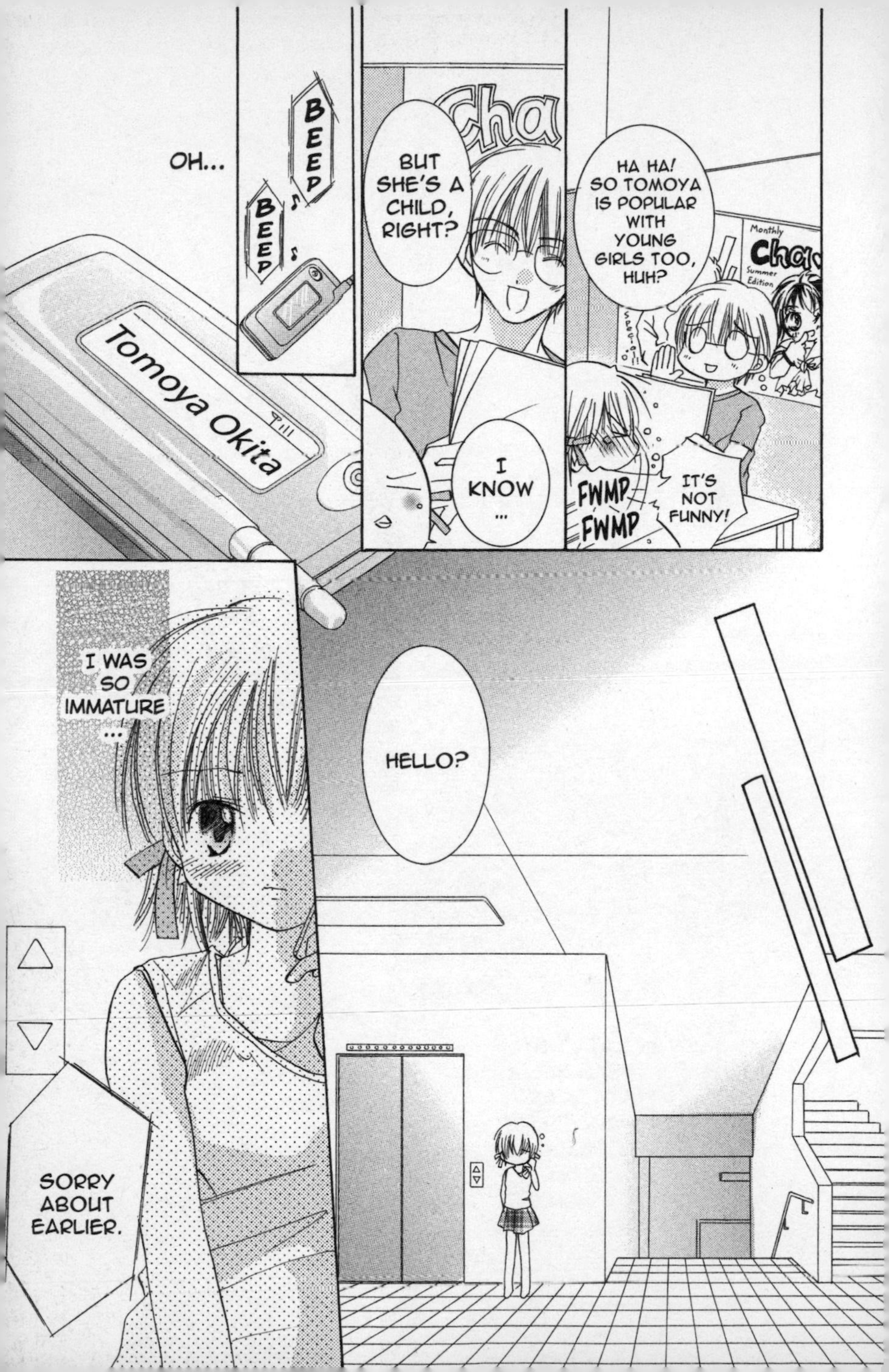
Monthly Cha Summer Edition
HA HA! SO TOMOYA IS POPULAR WITH YOUNG GIRLS TOO, HUH?
IT'S NOT FUNNY!
FWMP FWMP
Cha
BUT SHE'S A CHILD, RIGHT?
I KNOW...
BEEP BEEP
OH...
Tomoya Okita
HELLO?
I WAS SO IMMATURE...
SORRY ABOUT EARLIER.

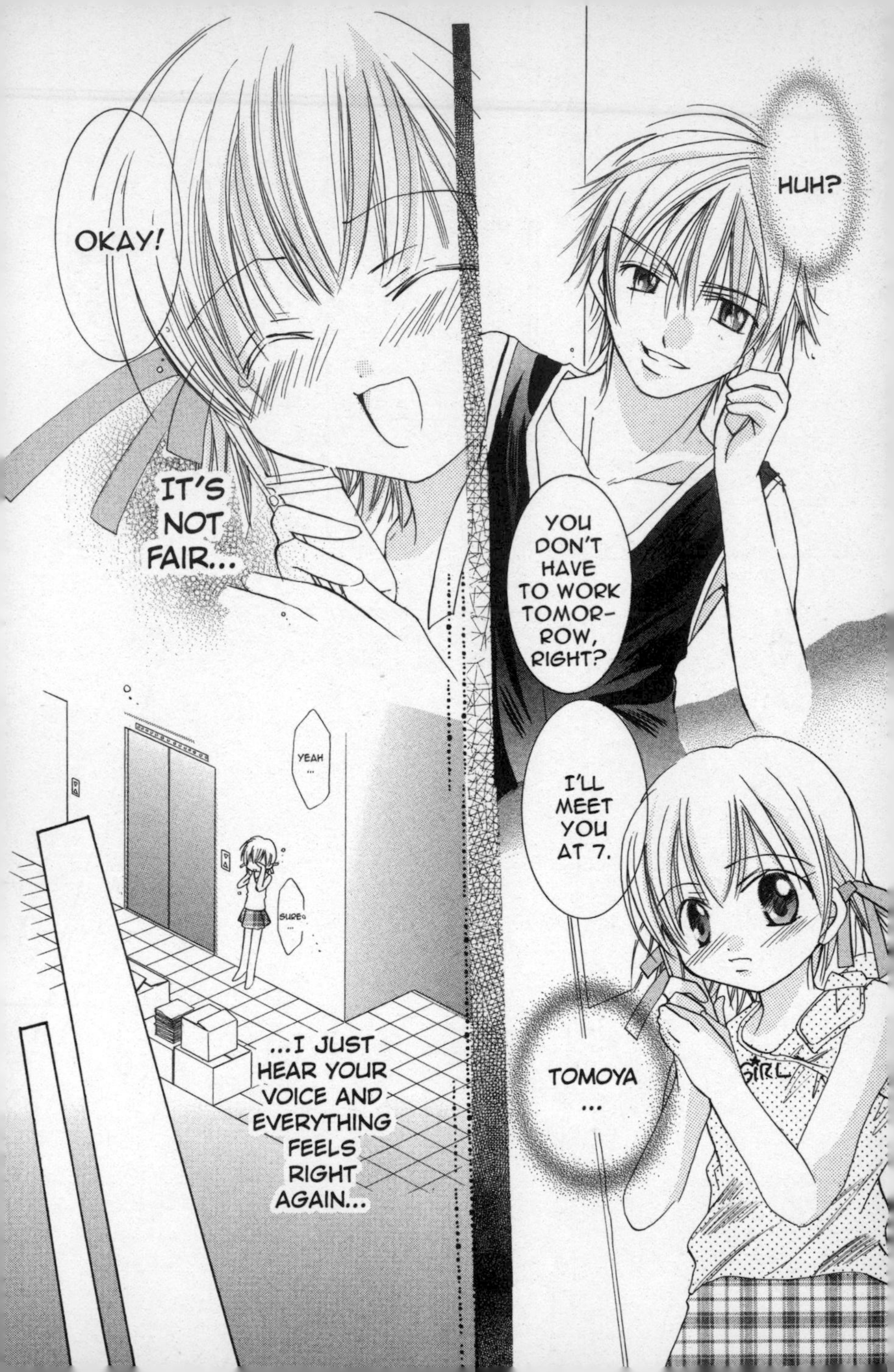
HUH?
YOU DON'T HAVE TO WORK TOMORROW, RIGHT?
I'LL MEET YOU AT 7.
GIRL
TOMOYA ...
OKAY!
IT'S NOT FAIR...
YEAH ...
SURE. ...
...I JUST HEAR YOUR VOICE AND EVERYTHING FEELS RIGHT AGAIN...

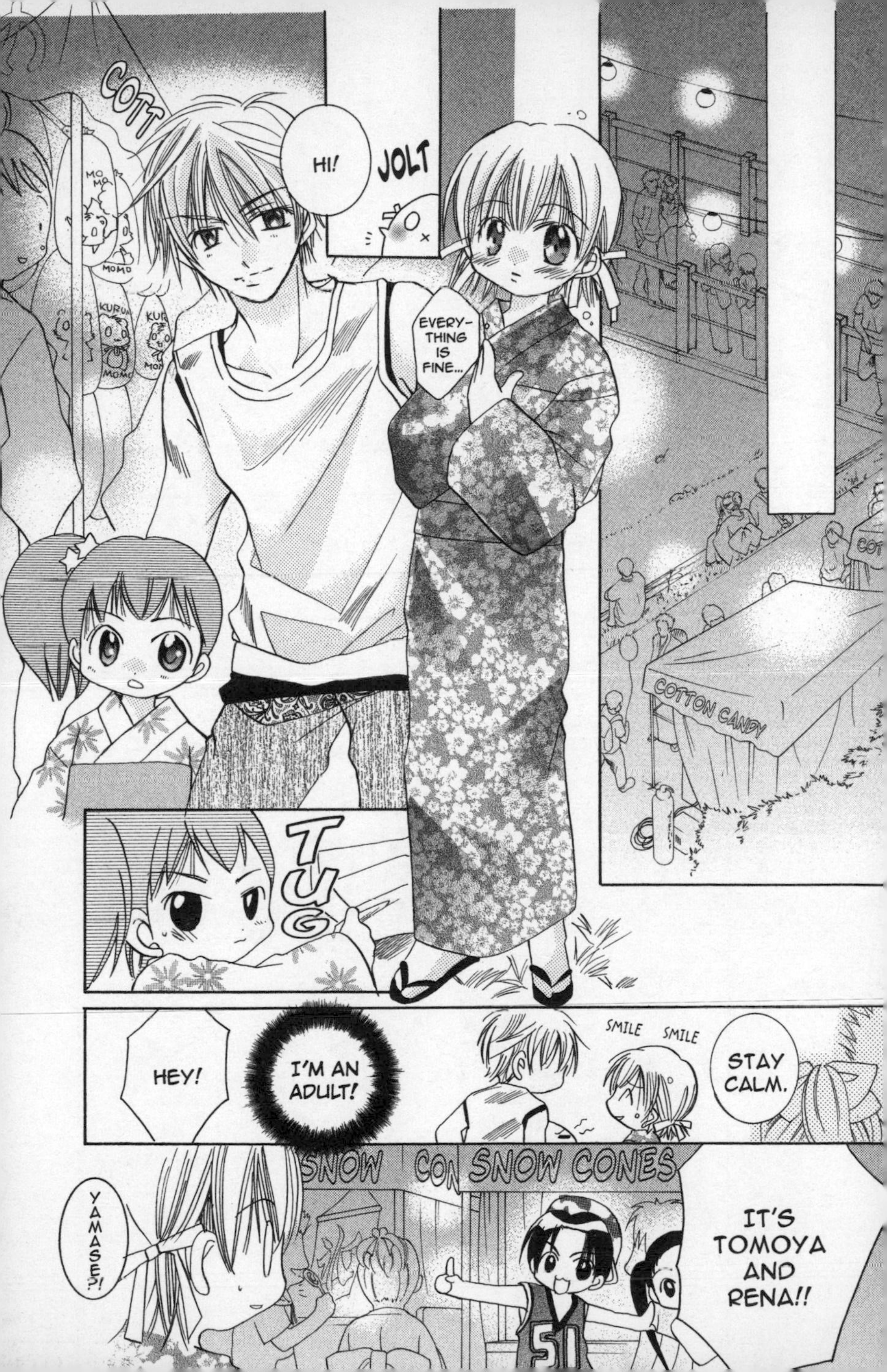
COTTON CANDY
COTT
HI!
JOLT
EVERY-THING IS FINE...
TUG
STAY CALM.
SMILE SMILE
I'M AN ADULT!
HEY!
SNOW CONES
IT'S TOMOYA AND RENA!!
YAMASE?!

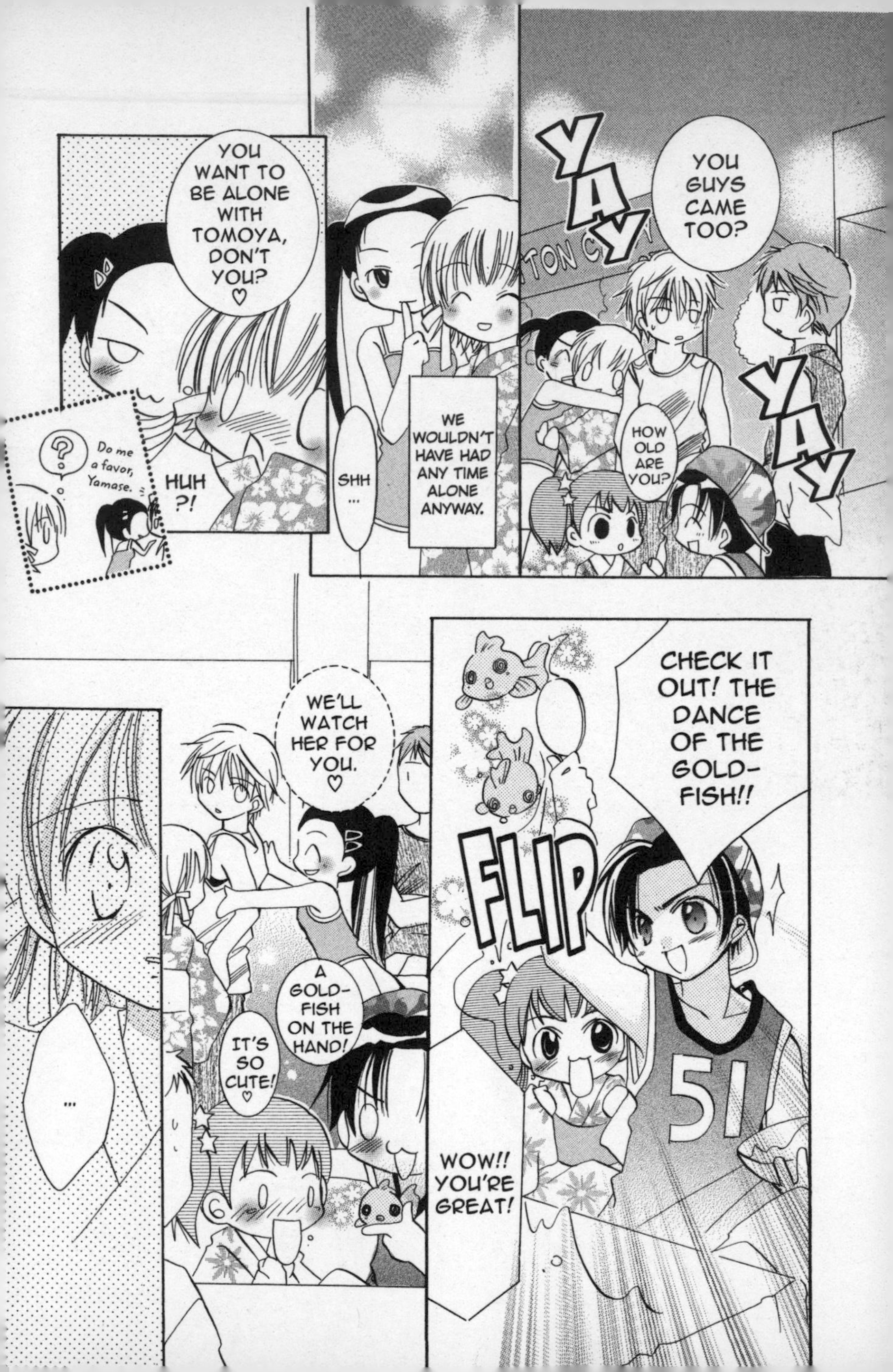
YAY
YOU GUYS CAME TOO?
YAY
HOW OLD ARE YOU?
WE WOULDN'T HAVE HAD ANY TIME ALONE ANYWAY.
SHH...
YOU WANT TO BE ALONE WITH TOMOYA, DON'T YOU? ♡
HUH?!
?
Do me a favor, Yamase.
CHECK IT OUT! THE DANCE OF THE GOLD-FISH!!
FLIP
WOW!! YOU'RE GREAT!
WE'LL WATCH HER FOR YOU. ♡
A GOLD-FISH ON THE HAND!
IT'S SO CUTE! ♡
...

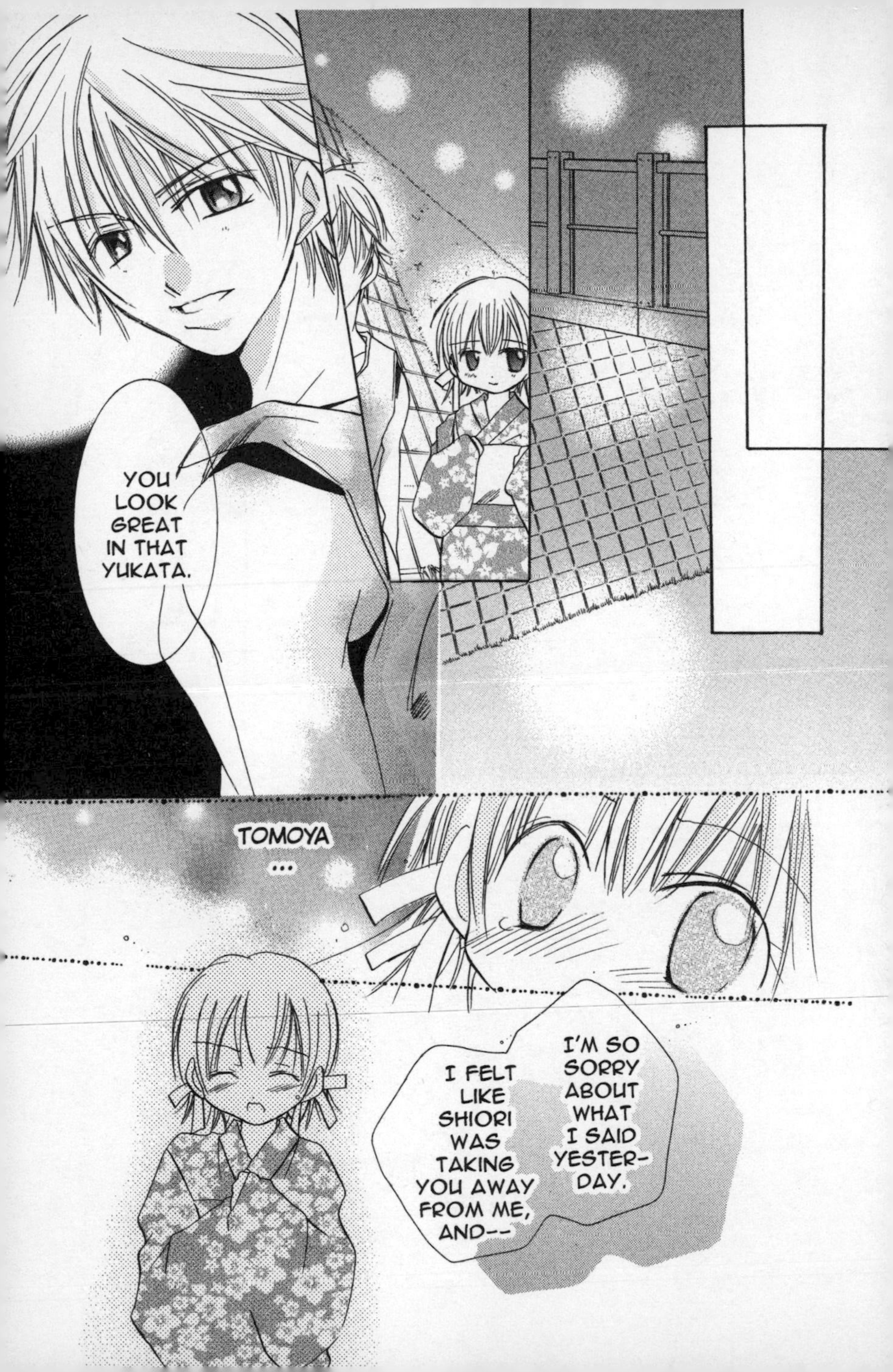
YOU LOOK GREAT IN THAT YUKATA.
TOMOYA ...
I'M SO SORRY ABOUT WHAT I SAID YESTER-DAY.
I FELT LIKE SHIORI WAS TAKING YOU AWAY FROM ME, AND--

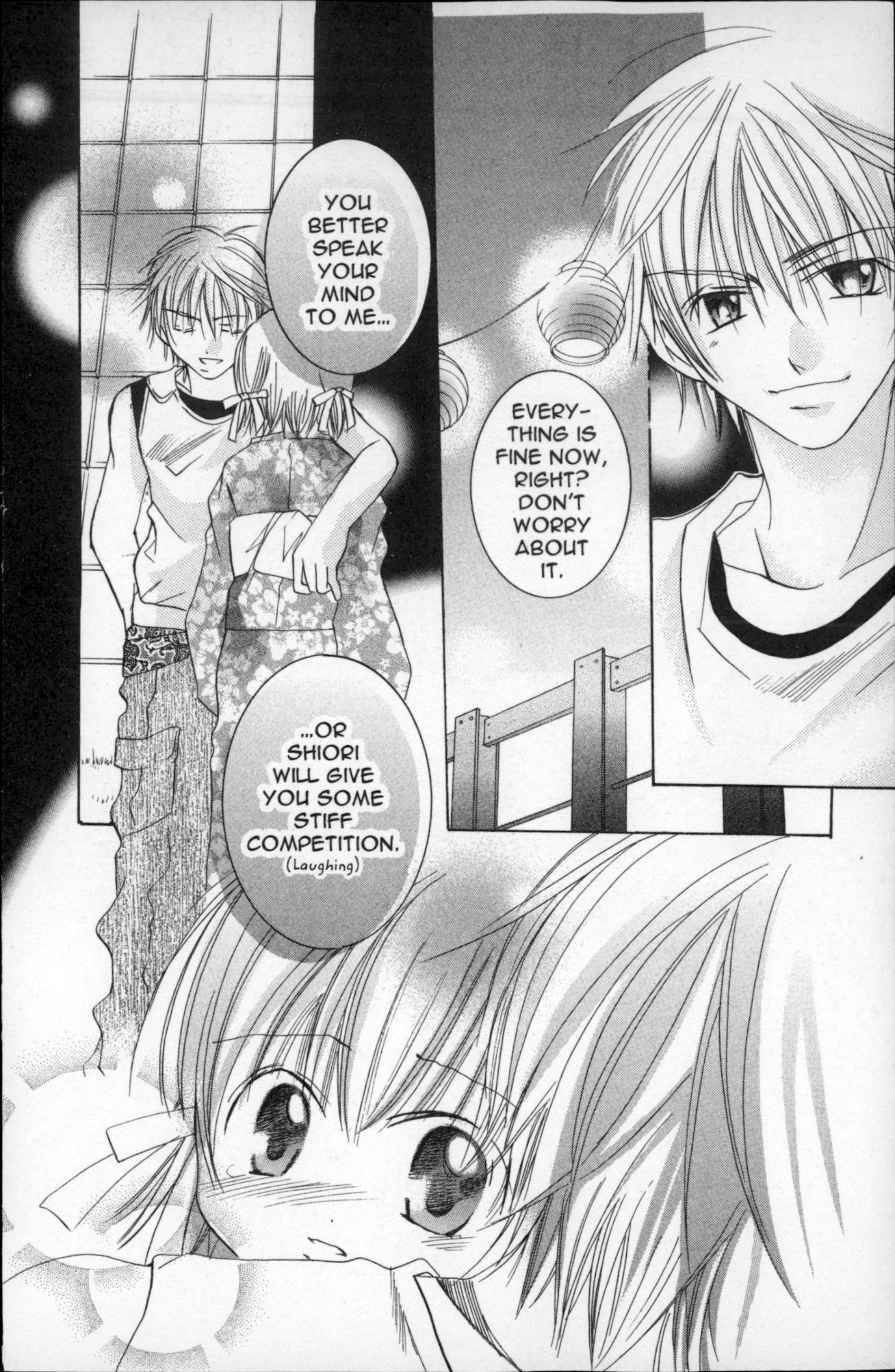
EVERY-THING IS FINE NOW, RIGHT? DON'T WORRY ABOUT IT.
YOU BETTER SPEAK YOUR MIND TO ME...
...OR SHIORI WILL GIVE YOU SOME STIFF COMPETITION.
(Laughing)

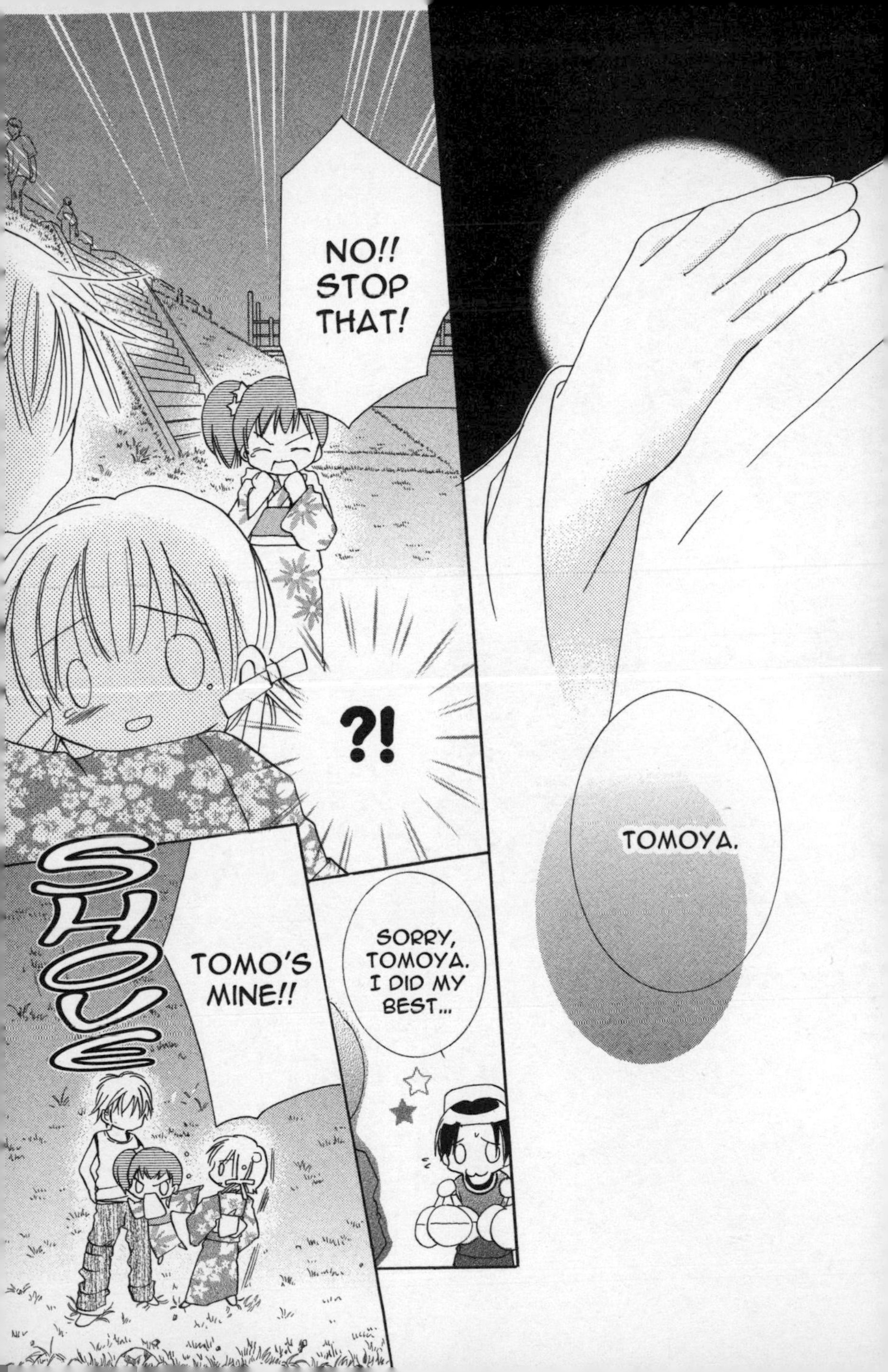
TOMOYA.
NO!! STOP THAT!
?!
SORRY, TOMOYA. I DID MY BEST...
SHOVE
TOMO'S MINE!!

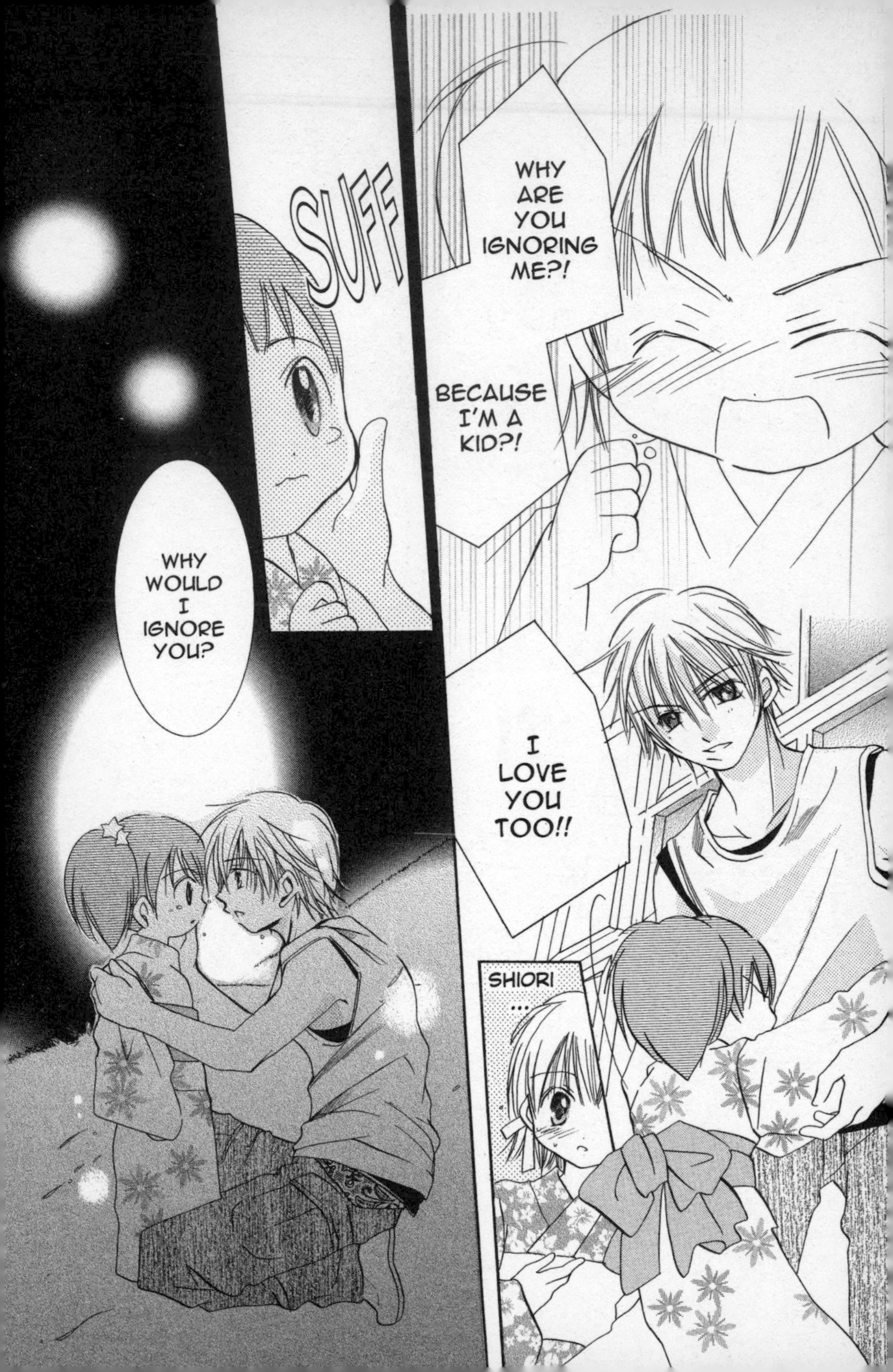
WHY ARE YOU IGNORING ME?!
BECAUSE I'M A KID?!
I LOVE YOU TOO!!
SHIORI ...
SUFF
WHY WOULD I IGNORE YOU?

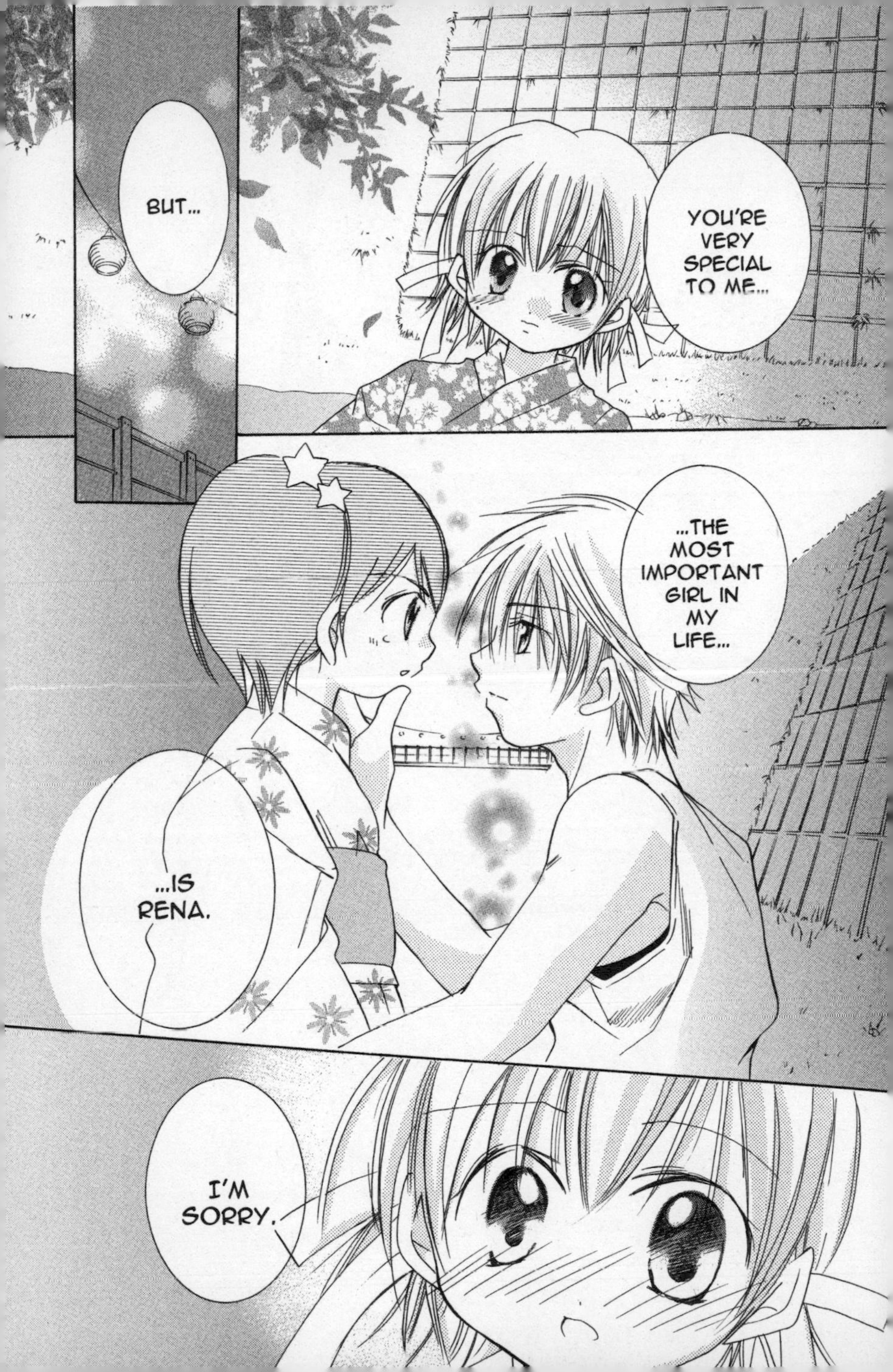
YOU'RE VERY SPECIAL TO ME...
BUT...
...THE MOST IMPORTANT GIRL IN MY LIFE...
...IS RENA.
I'M SORRY.

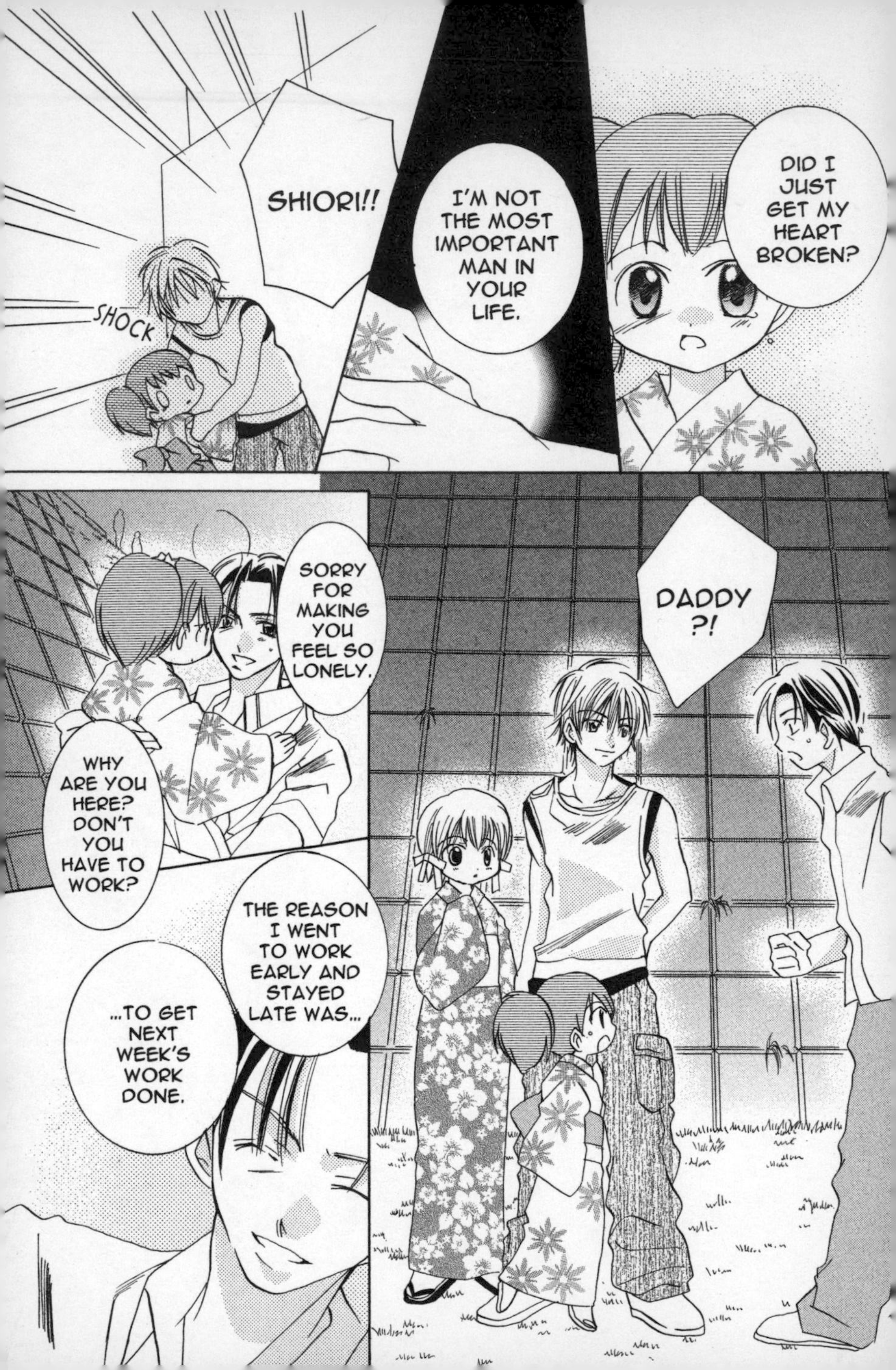
DID I JUST GET MY HEART BROKEN?
I'M NOT THE MOST IMPORTANT MAN IN YOUR LIFE.
SHIORI!!
SHOCK
DADDY ?!
SORRY FOR MAKING YOU FEEL SO LONELY.
WHY ARE YOU HERE? DON'T YOU HAVE TO WORK?
THE REASON I WENT TO WORK EARLY AND STAYED LATE WAS...
...TO GET NEXT WEEK'S WORK DONE.

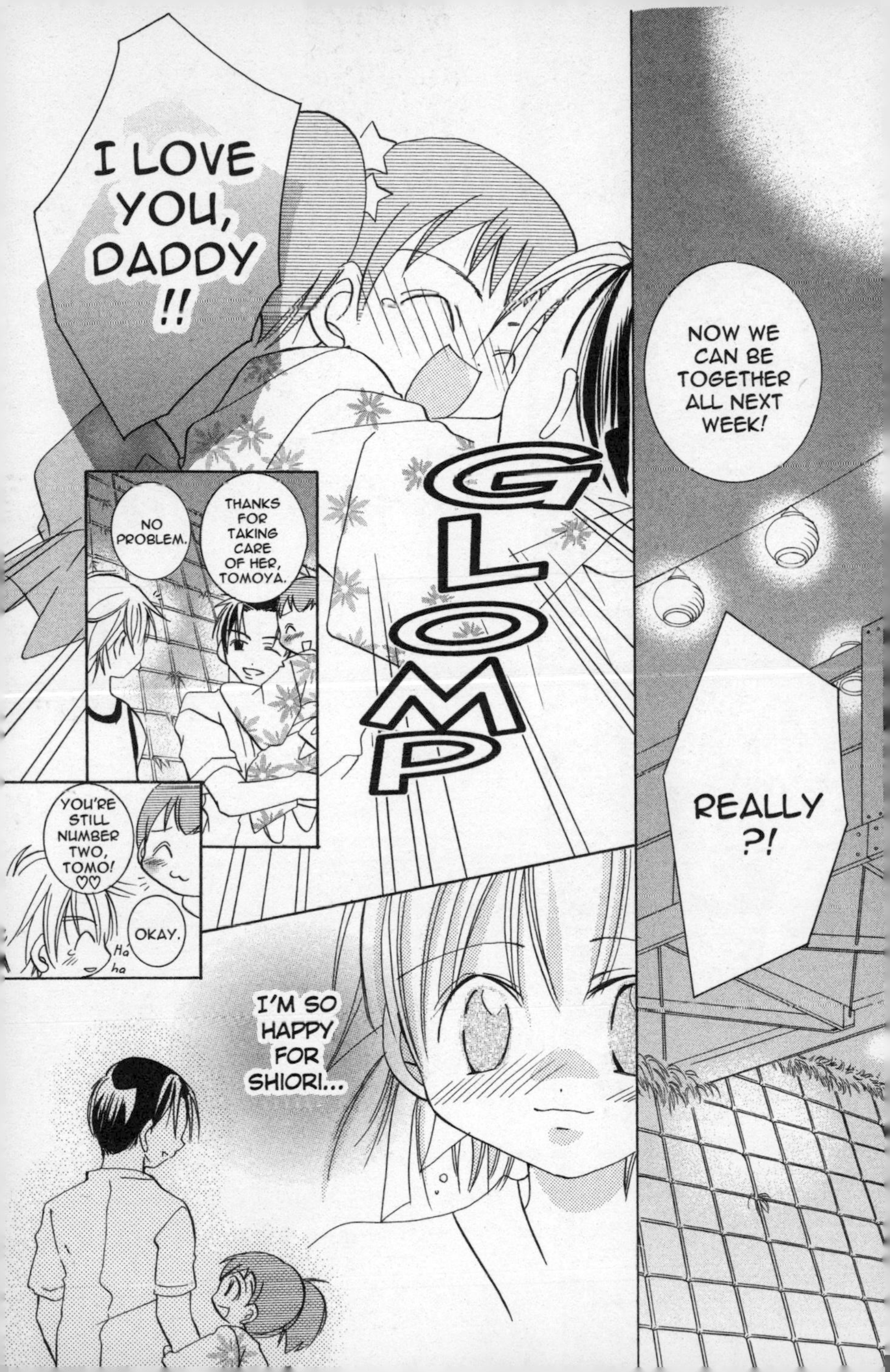
NOW WE CAN BE TOGETHER ALL NEXT WEEK!
REALLY ?!
I LOVE YOU, DADDY !!
GLOMP
THANKS FOR TAKING CARE OF HER, TOMOYA.
NO PROBLEM.
YOU'RE STILL NUMBER TWO, TOMO! ♡♡
OKAY.
Ha ha
I'M SO HAPPY FOR SHIORI...

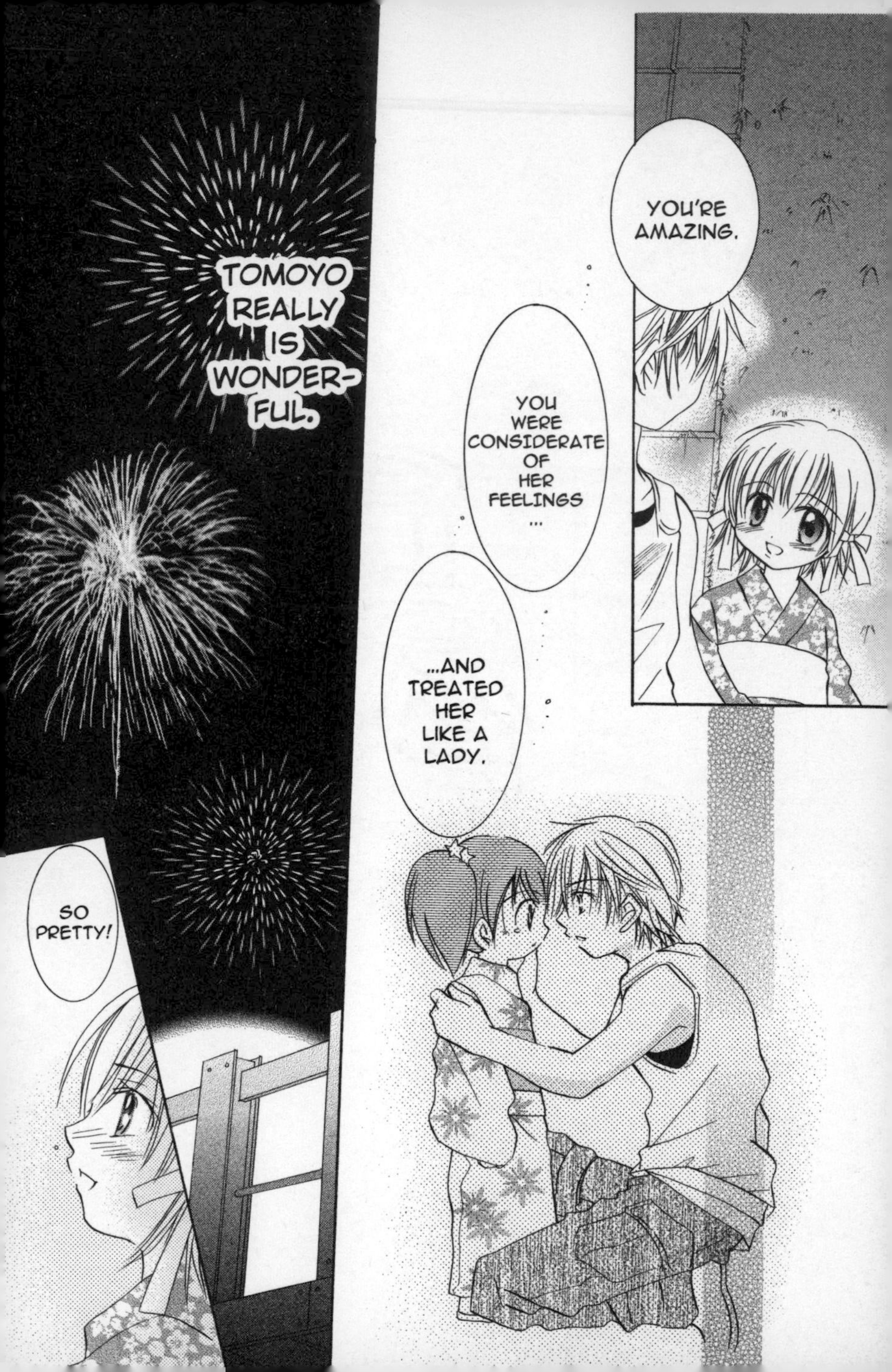
YOU'RE AMAZING.
YOU WERE CONSIDERATE OF HER FEELINGS ...
...AND TREATED HER LIKE A LADY.
TOMOYO REALLY IS WONDER-FUL.
SO PRETTY!

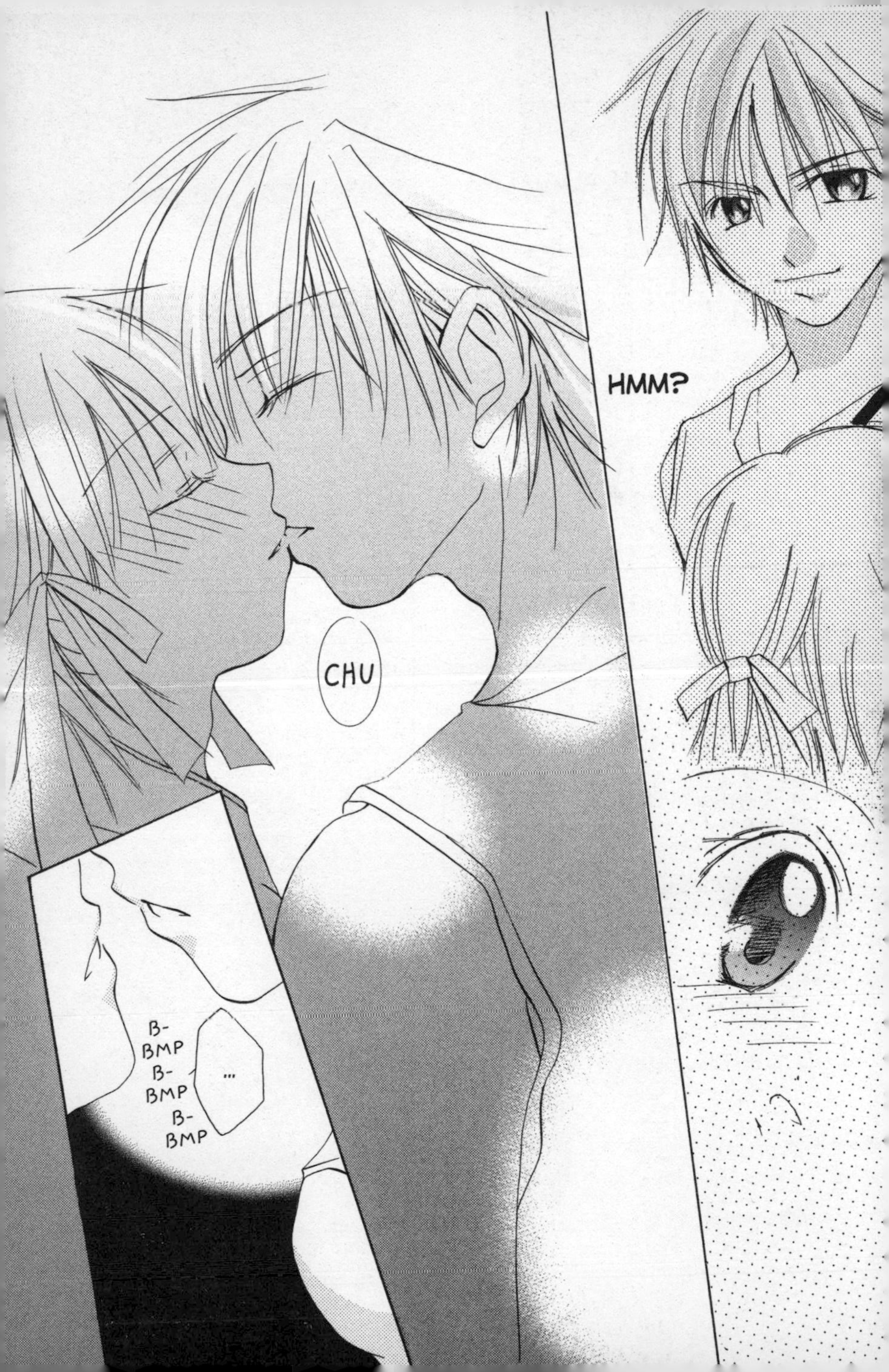
HMM?
CHU
...
B-BMP B-BMP B-BMP

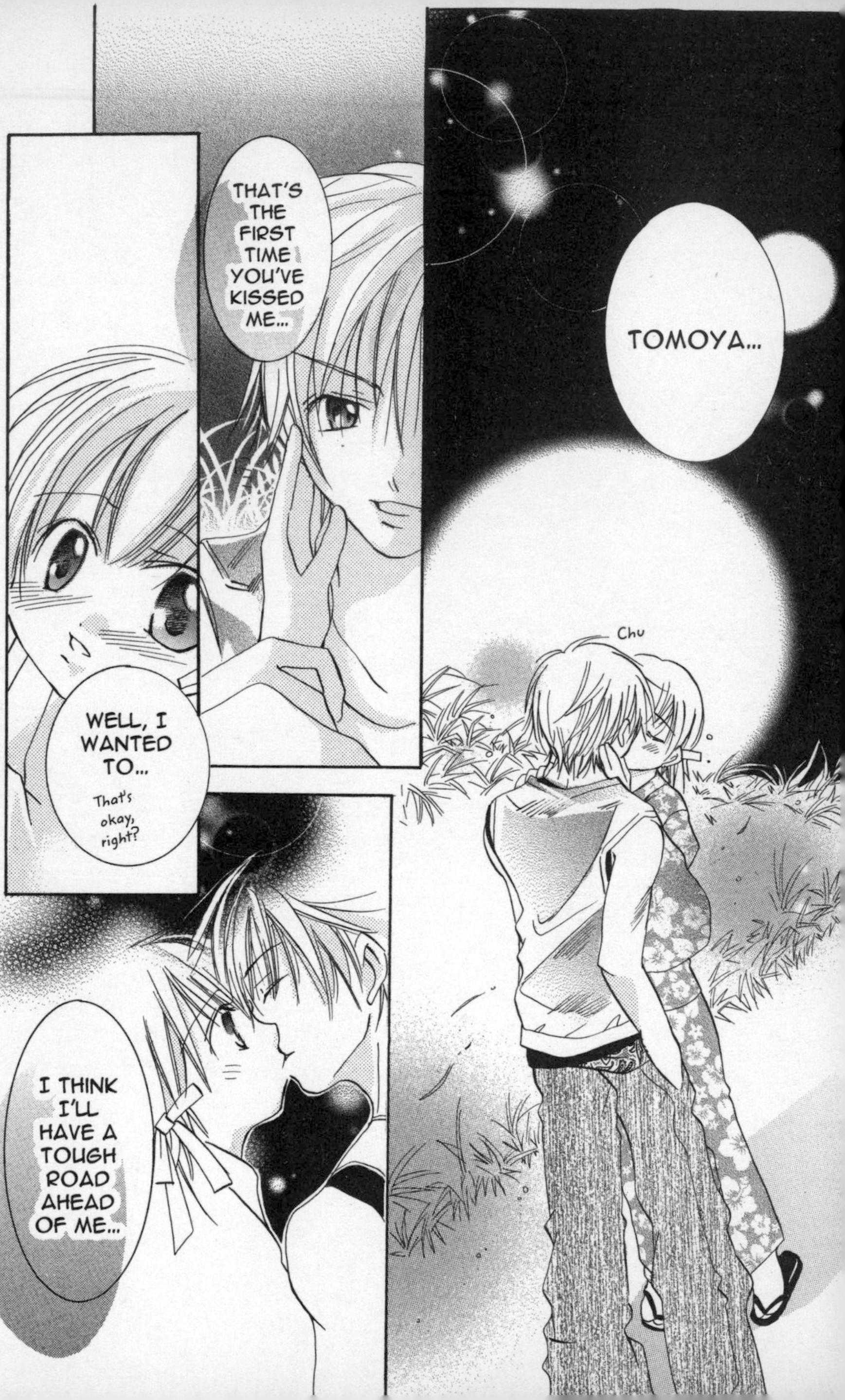
TOMOYA...
Chu
THAT'S THE FIRST TIME YOU'VE KISSED ME...
WELL, I WANTED TO...
That's okay, right?
I THINK I'LL HAVE A TOUGH ROAD AHEAD OF ME...

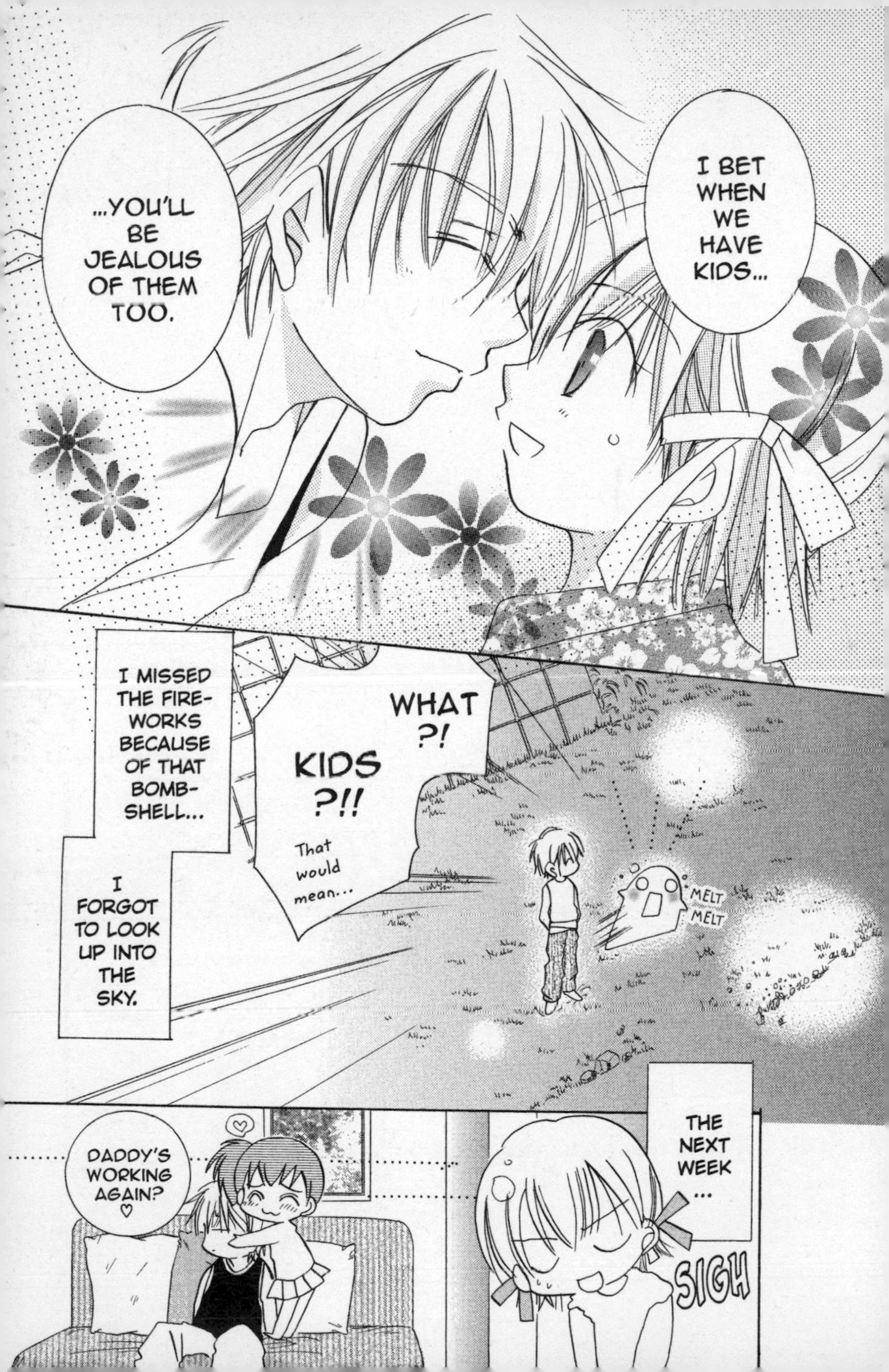
I BET WHEN WE HAVE KIDS...
...YOU'LL BE JEALOUS OF THEM TOO.
WHAT ?!
KIDS ?!!
That would mean...
MELT MELT
I MISSED THE FIRE-WORKS BECAUSE OF THAT BOMB-SHELL...
I FORGOT TO LOOK UP INTO THE SKY.
THE NEXT WEEK ...
SIGH
DADDY'S WORKING AGAIN? ♡

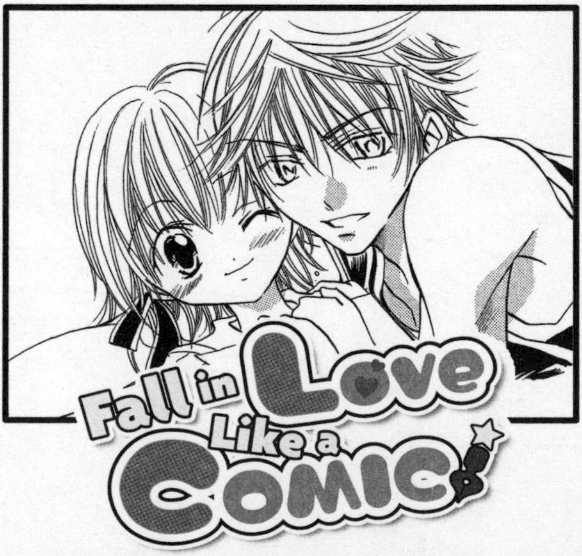
Fall in Love Like a Comic!

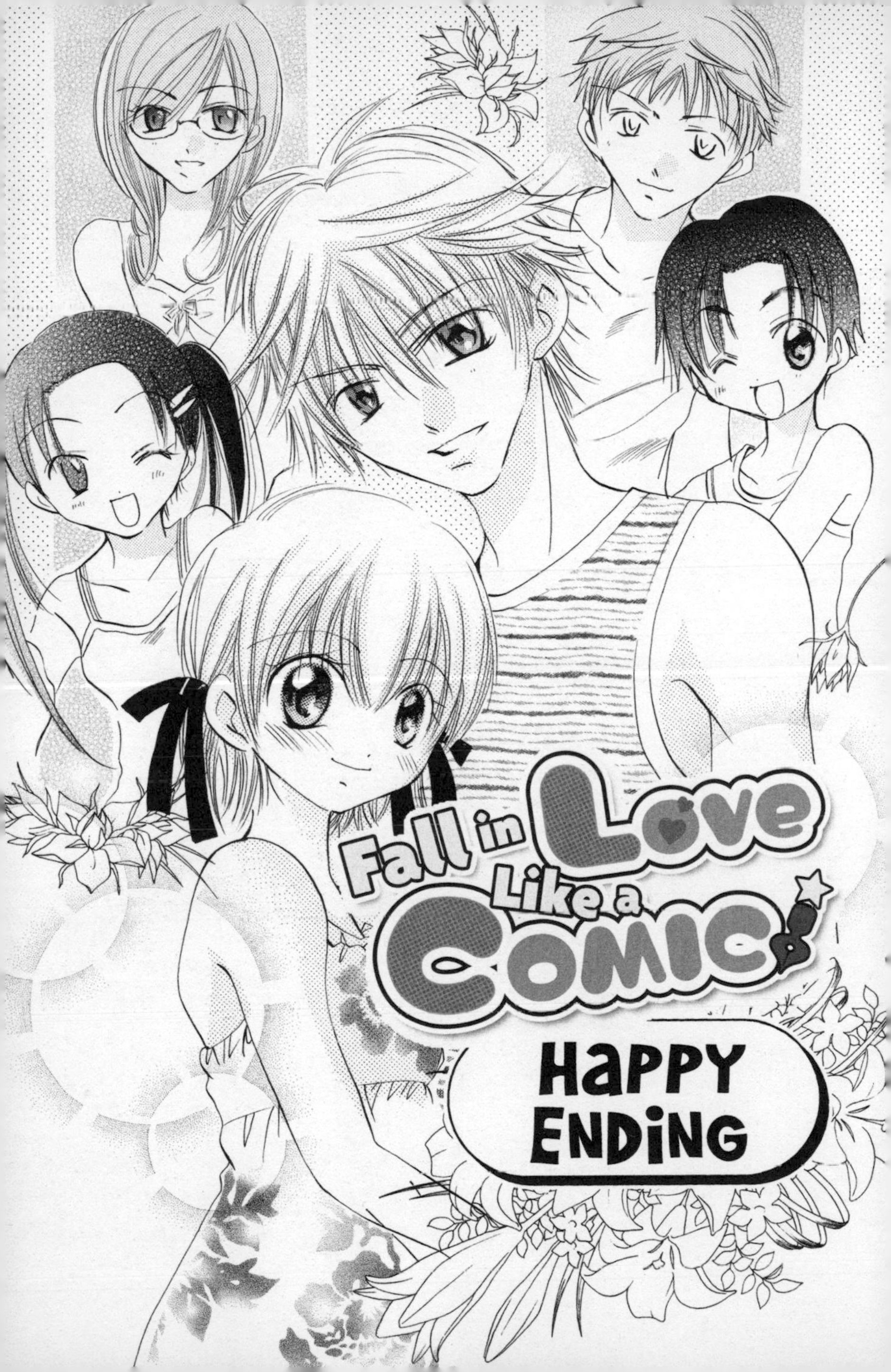
Fall in Love Like a Comic!
HAPPY ENDING

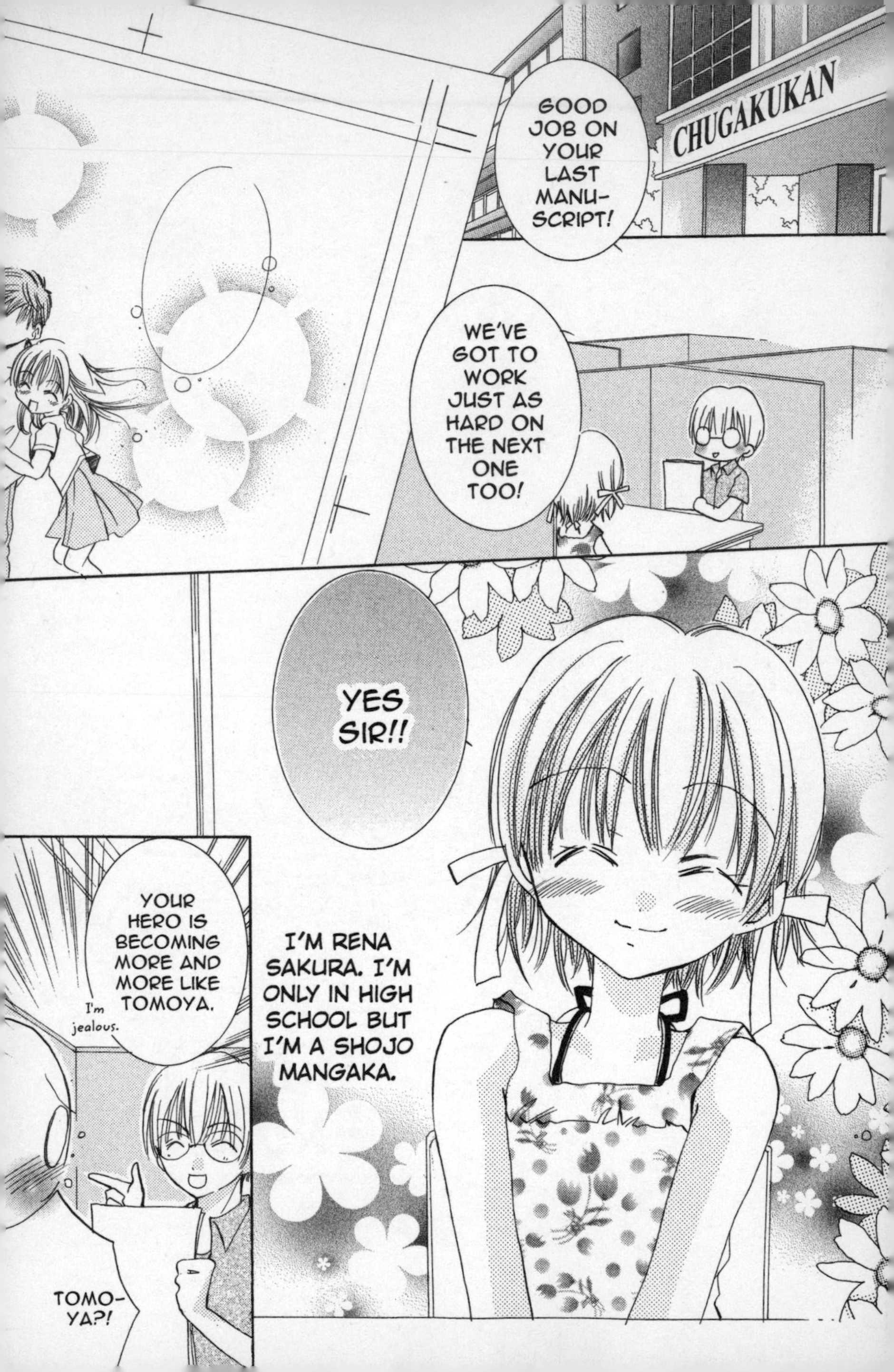
CHUGAKUKAN
GOOD JOB ON YOUR LAST MANU-SCRIPT!
WE'VE GOT TO WORK JUST AS HARD ON THE NEXT ONE TOO!
YES SIR!!
I'M RENA SAKURA. I'M ONLY IN HIGH SCHOOL BUT I'M A SHOJO MANGAKA.
YOUR HERO IS BECOMING MORE AND MORE LIKE TOMOYA.
I'm jealous.
TOMOYA?!

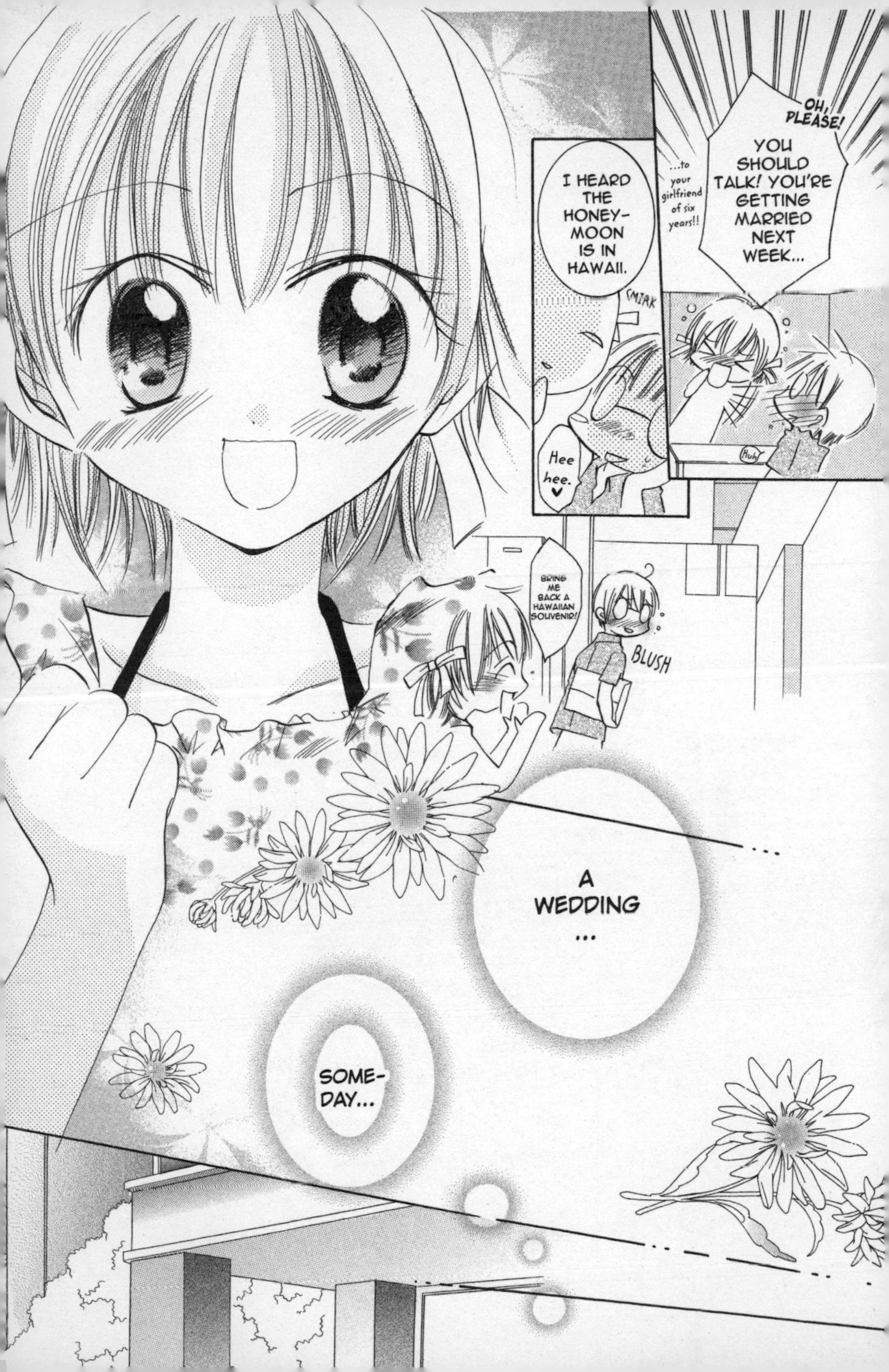
OH, PLEASE!
YOU SHOULD TALK! YOU'RE GETTING MARRIED NEXT WEEK...
...to your girlfriend of six years!!
Huh
I HEARD THE HONEY-MOON IS IN HAWAII.
SMIRK
Hee hee. ♥
BRING ME BACK A HAWAIIAN SOUVENIR!
BLUSH
A WEDDING...
SOME-DAY...

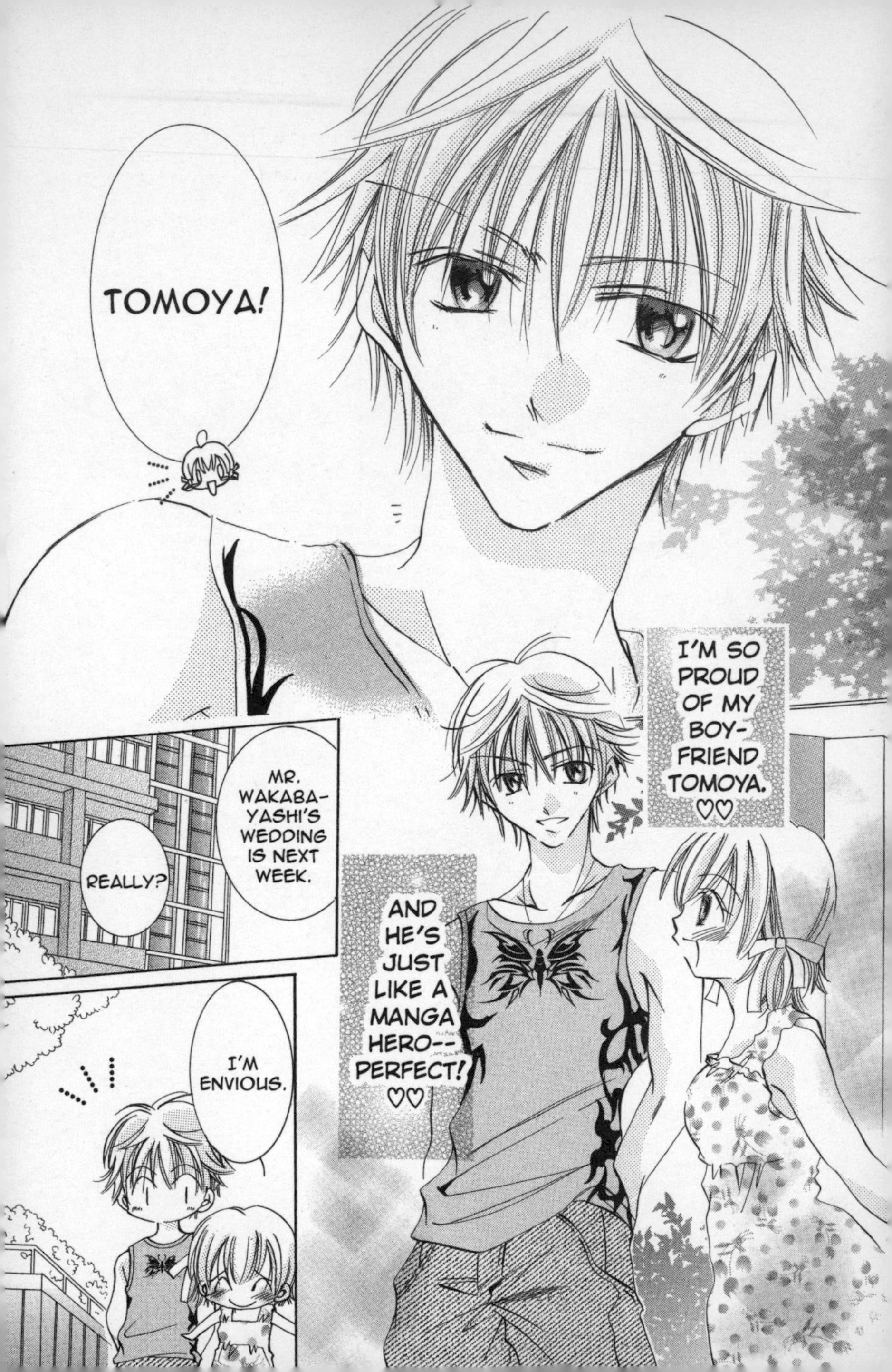
TOMOYA!
I'M SO PROUD OF MY BOY-FRIEND TOMOYA.
AND HE'S JUST LIKE A MANGA HERO--PERFECT!
MR. WAKABA-YASHI'S WEDDING IS NEXT WEEK.
REALLY?
I'M ENVIOUS.

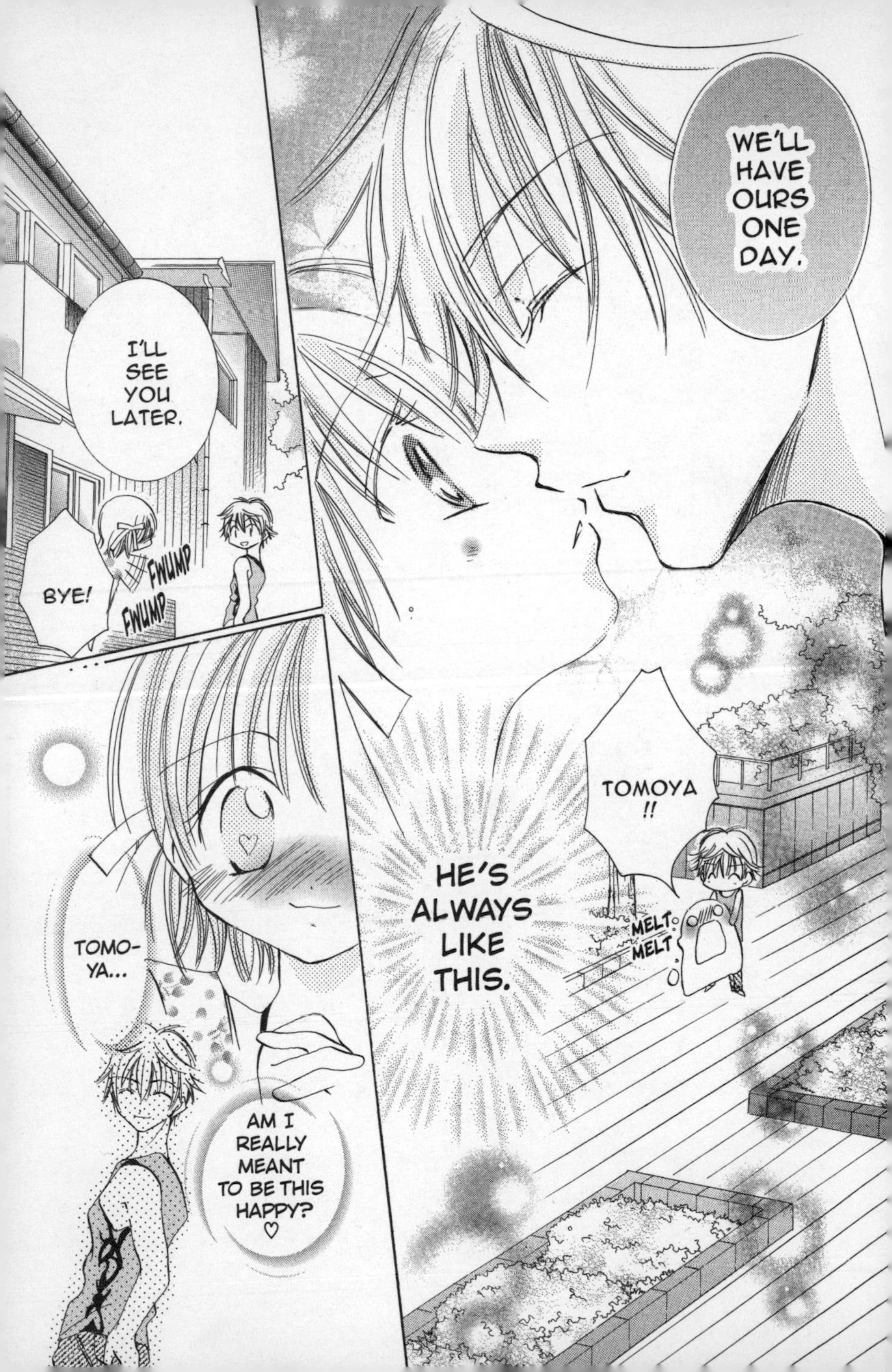

WE'LL HAVE OURS ONE DAY.
TOMOYA !!
MELT MELT
HE'S ALWAYS LIKE THIS.
I'LL SEE YOU LATER.
FWUMP FWUMP
BYE!
TOMO-YA...
AM I REALLY MEANT TO BE THIS HAPPY? ♡

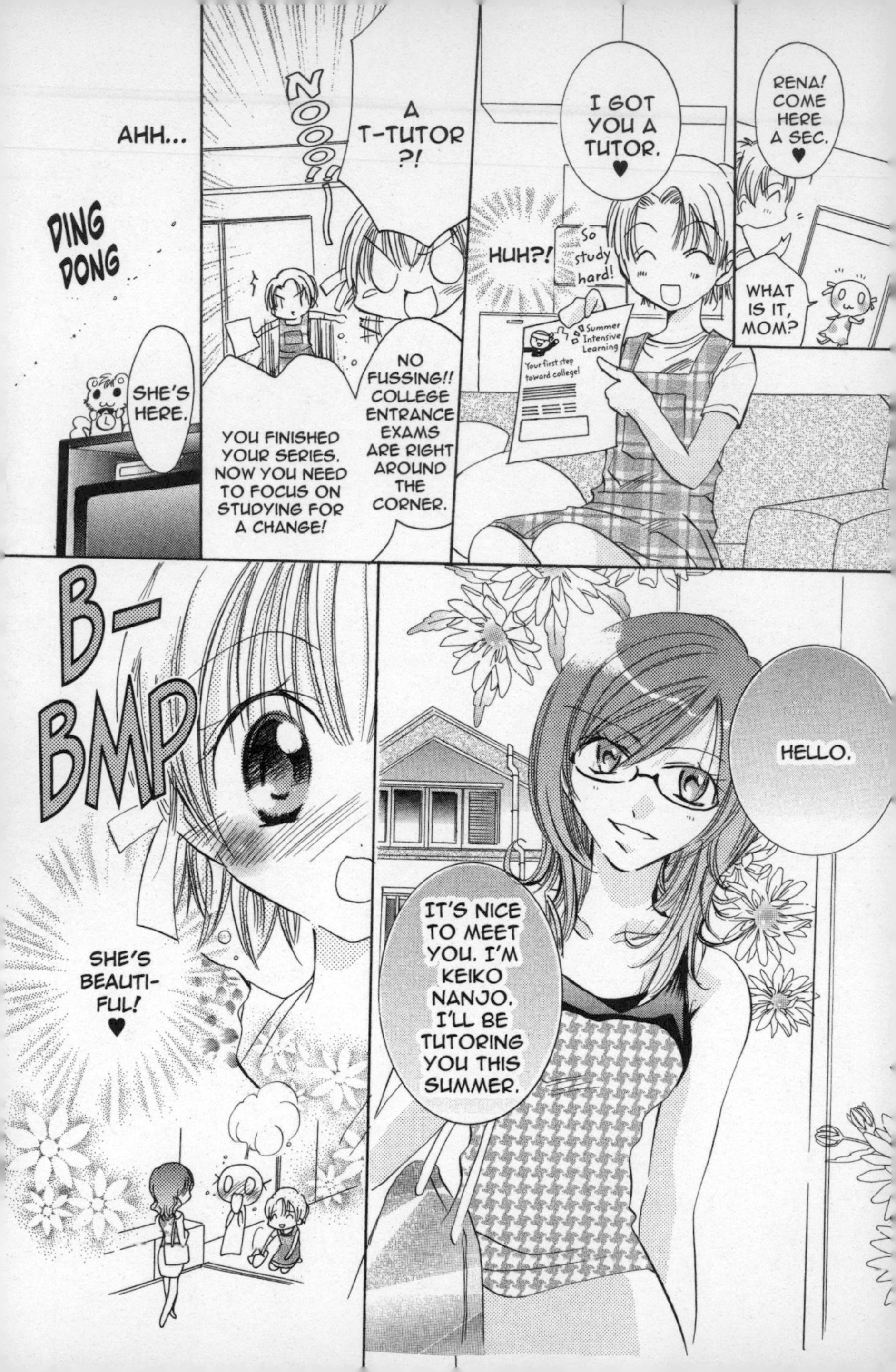
RENA! COME HERE A SEC. ♥
WHAT IS IT, MOM?
I GOT YOU A TUTOR. ♥
HUH?!
So study hard!
Summer Intensive Learning
Your first step toward college!
A T-TUTOR?!
NOOOO!!
NO FUSSING!! COLLEGE ENTRANCE EXAMS ARE RIGHT AROUND THE CORNER.
YOU FINISHED YOUR SERIES. NOW YOU NEED TO FOCUS ON STUDYING FOR A CHANGE!
AHH...
DING DONG
SHE'S HERE.
HELLO.
IT'S NICE TO MEET YOU. I'M KEIKO NANJO. I'LL BE TUTORING YOU THIS SUMMER.
B-BMP
SHE'S BEAUTI-FUL! ♥

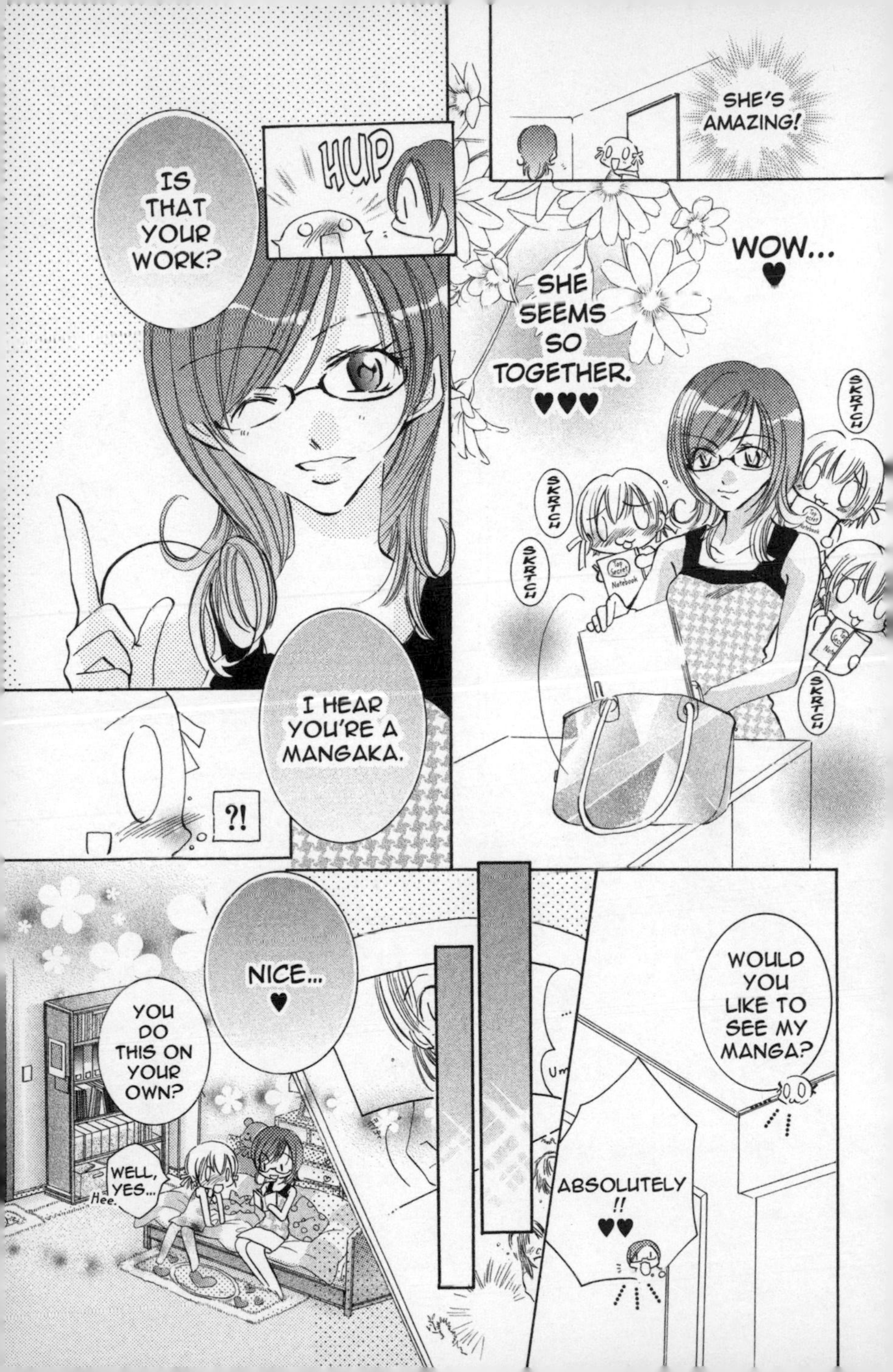
SHE'S AMAZING!
WOW... ♥
SHE SEEMS SO TOGETHER. ♥♥♥
SKRTCH
SKRTCH
SKRTCH
SKRTCH
HUP
IS THAT YOUR WORK?
I HEAR YOU'RE A MANGAKA.
?!
WOULD YOU LIKE TO SEE MY MANGA?
ABSOLUTELY!! ♥♥
...
Um
NICE... ♥
YOU DO THIS ON YOUR OWN?
WELL, YES...
Hee.

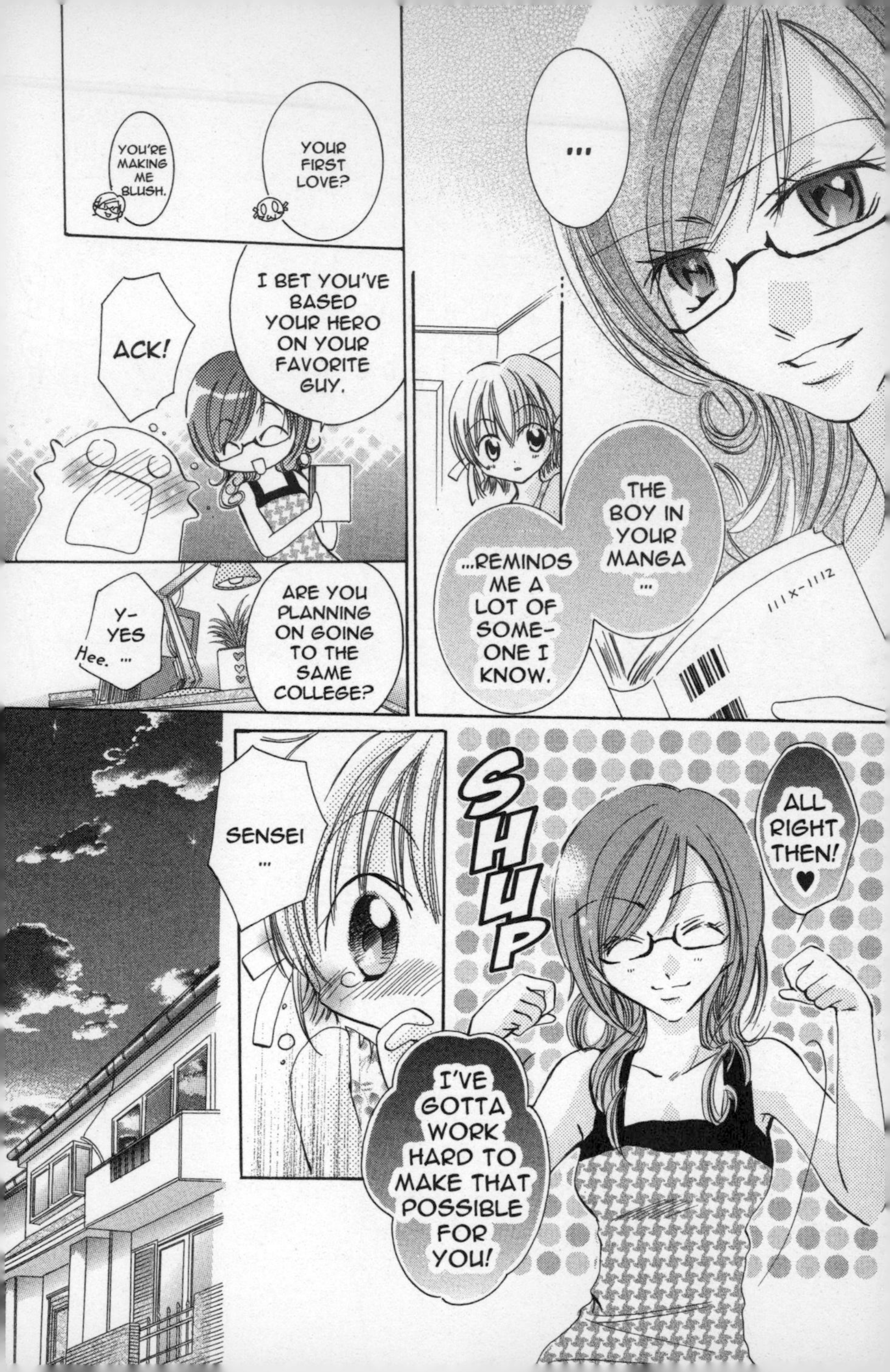
...
THE BOY IN YOUR MANGA ...
...REMINDS ME A LOT OF SOME-ONE I KNOW.
YOUR FIRST LOVE?
YOU'RE MAKING ME BLUSH.
I BET YOU'VE BASED YOUR HERO ON YOUR FAVORITE GUY.
ACK!
ARE YOU PLANNING ON GOING TO THE SAME COLLEGE?
Y-YES ...
Hee.
ALL RIGHT THEN! ♥
SHUP
I'VE GOTTA WORK HARD TO MAKE THAT POSSIBLE FOR YOU!
SENSEI ...

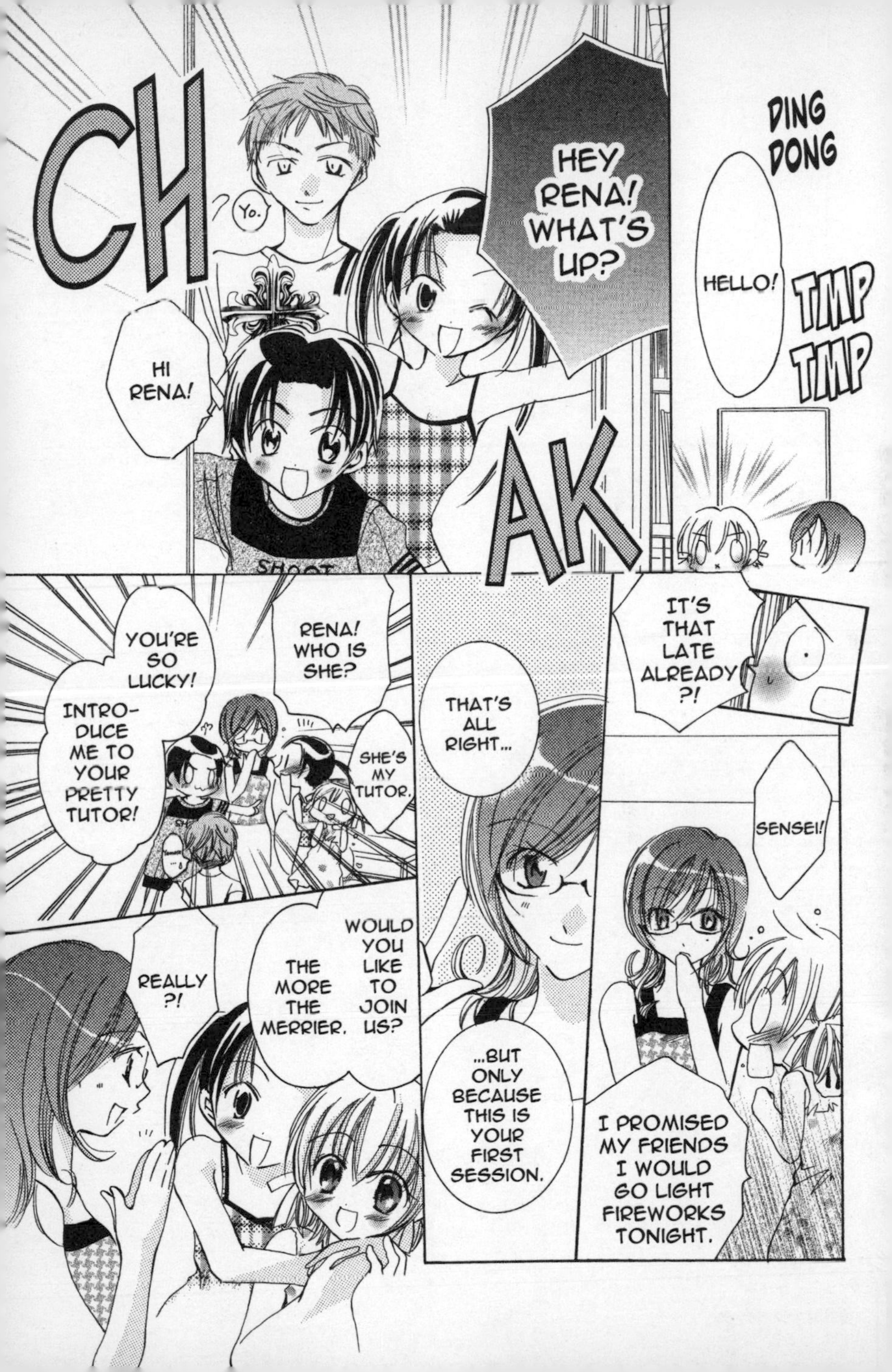
DING DONG
TMP TMP
HELLO!
CH
AK
HEY RENA! WHAT'S UP?
Yo.
HI RENA!
IT'S THAT LATE ALREADY?!
SENSEI!
I PROMISED MY FRIENDS I WOULD GO LIGHT FIREWORKS TONIGHT.
THAT'S ALL RIGHT...
...BUT ONLY BECAUSE THIS IS YOUR FIRST SESSION.
RENA! WHO IS SHE?
SHE'S MY TUTOR.
YOU'RE SO LUCKY!
INTRODUCE ME TO YOUR PRETTY TUTOR!
WOULD YOU LIKE TO JOIN US?
THE MORE THE MERRIER.
REALLY?!

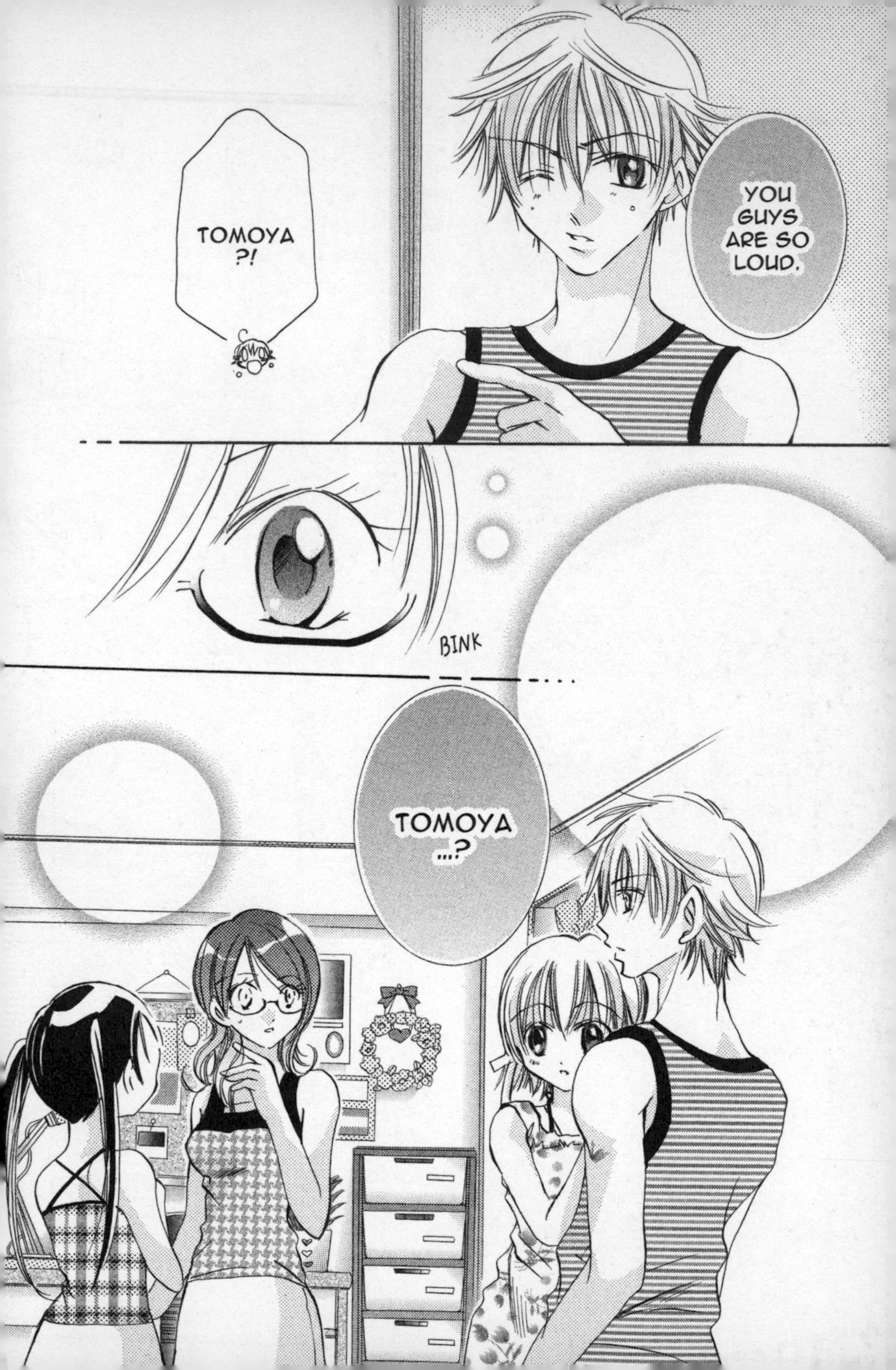
YOU GUYS ARE SO LOUD.
TOMOYA ?!
BINK
TOMOYA ...?

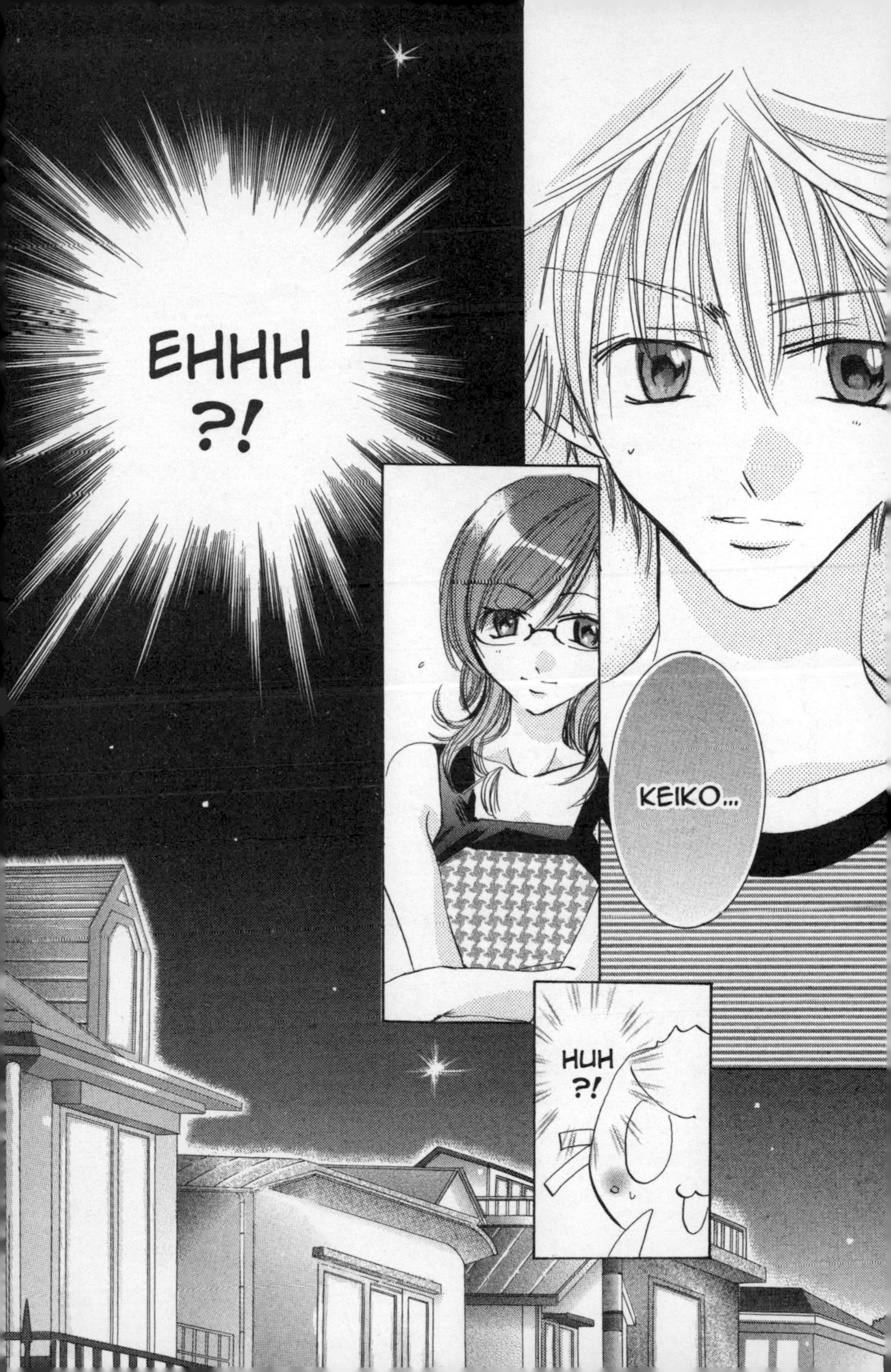
KEIKO...
HUH ?!
EHHH ?!

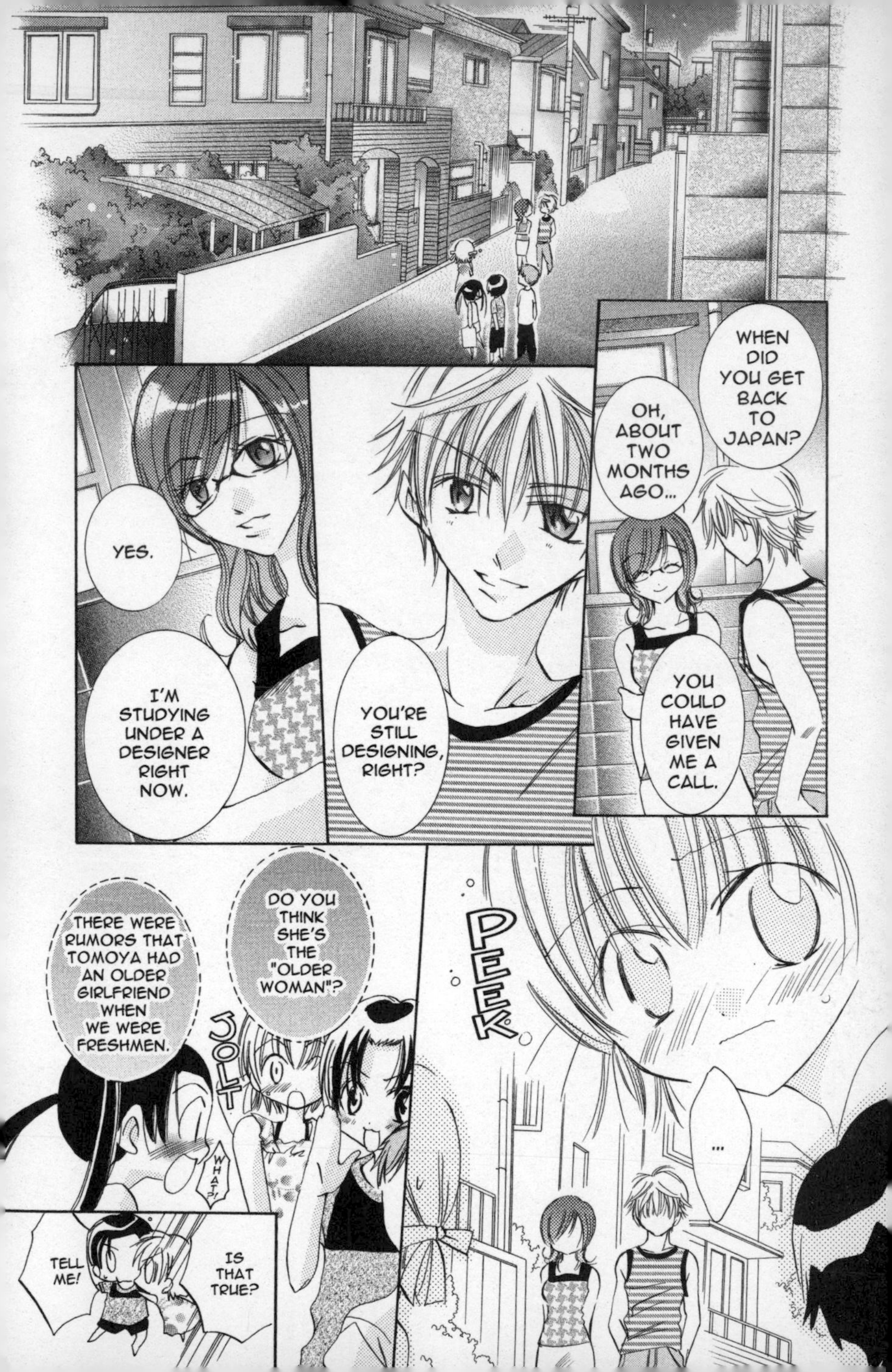
WHEN DID YOU GET BACK TO JAPAN?
OH, ABOUT TWO MONTHS AGO...
YOU COULD HAVE GIVEN ME A CALL.
YOU'RE STILL DESIGNING, RIGHT?
YES.
I'M STUDYING UNDER A DESIGNER RIGHT NOW.
PEEK
...
DO YOU THINK SHE'S THE "OLDER WOMAN"?
THERE WERE RUMORS THAT TOMOYA HAD AN OLDER GIRLFRIEND WHEN WE WERE FRESHMEN.
JOLT
WHAT?!
IS THAT TRUE?
TELL ME!

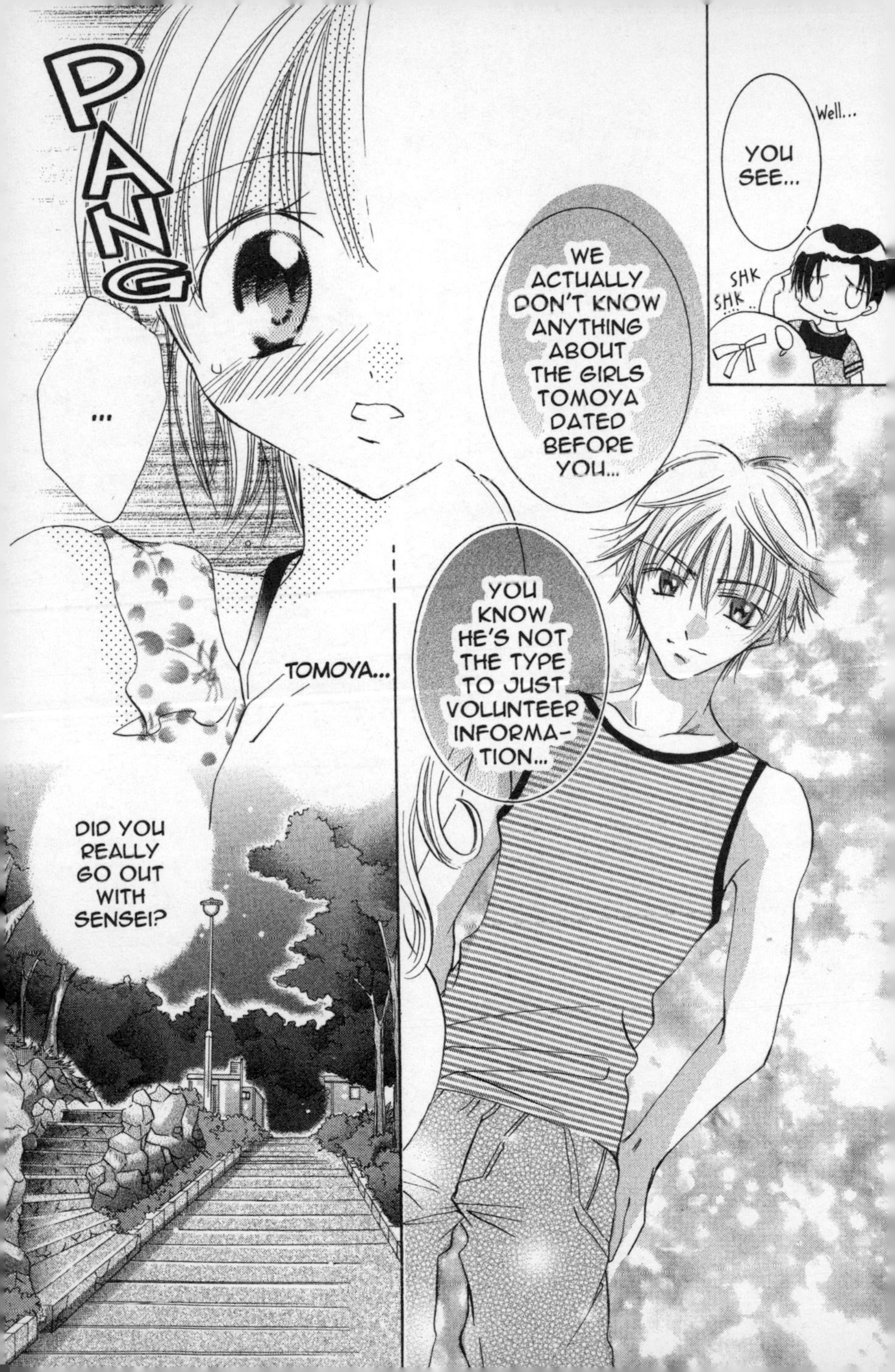
Well...
YOU SEE...
SHK SHK...
WE ACTUALLY DON'T KNOW ANYTHING ABOUT THE GIRLS TOMOYA DATED BEFORE YOU...
YOU KNOW HE'S NOT THE TYPE TO JUST VOLUNTEER INFORMA-TION...
PANG
...
TOMOYA...
DID YOU REALLY GO OUT WITH SENSEI?

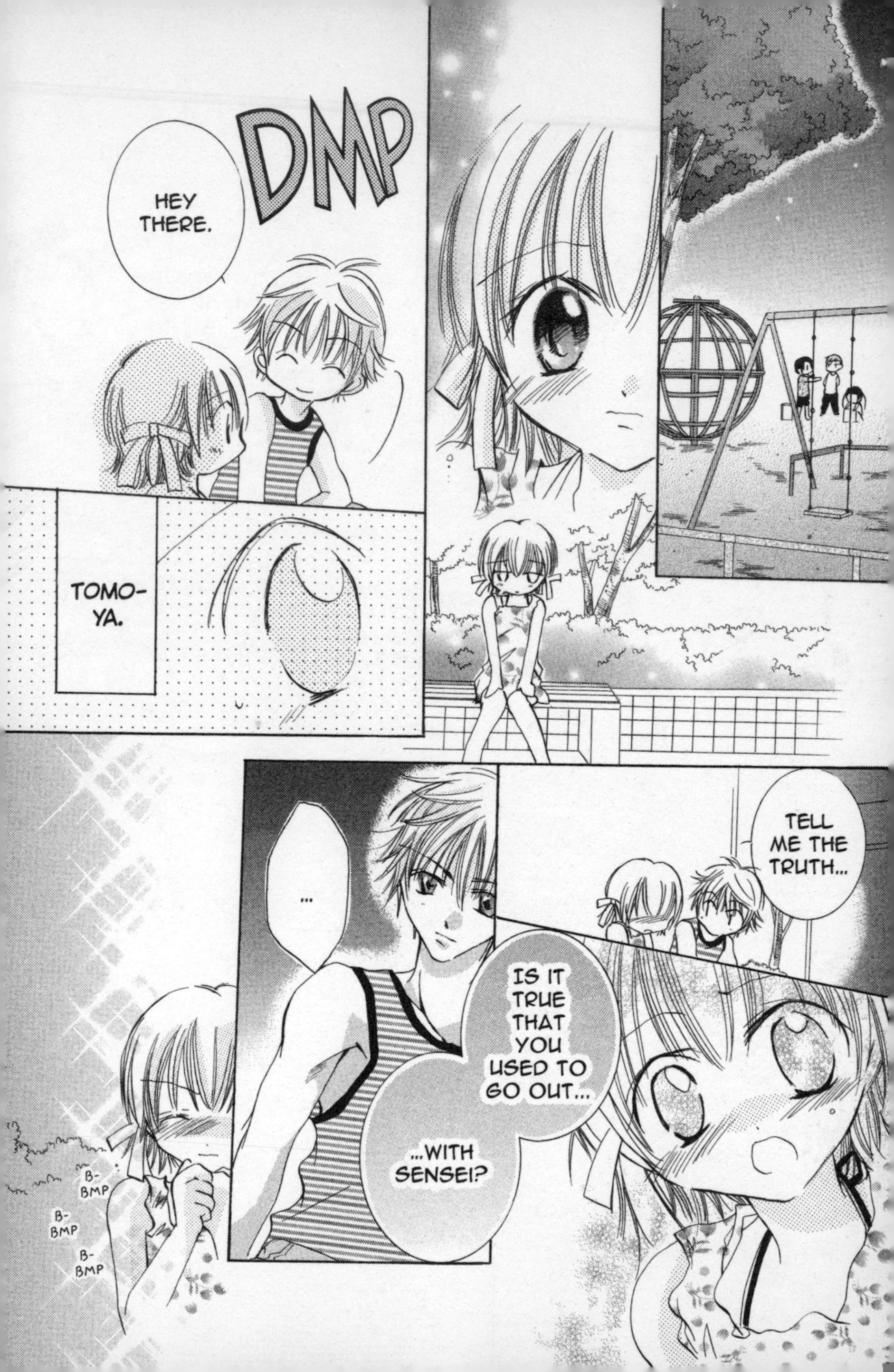
DMP
HEY THERE.
TOMO-YA.
TELL ME THE TRUTH...
IS IT TRUE THAT YOU USED TO GO OUT...
...WITH SENSEI?
...
B-BMP
B-BMP
B-BMP

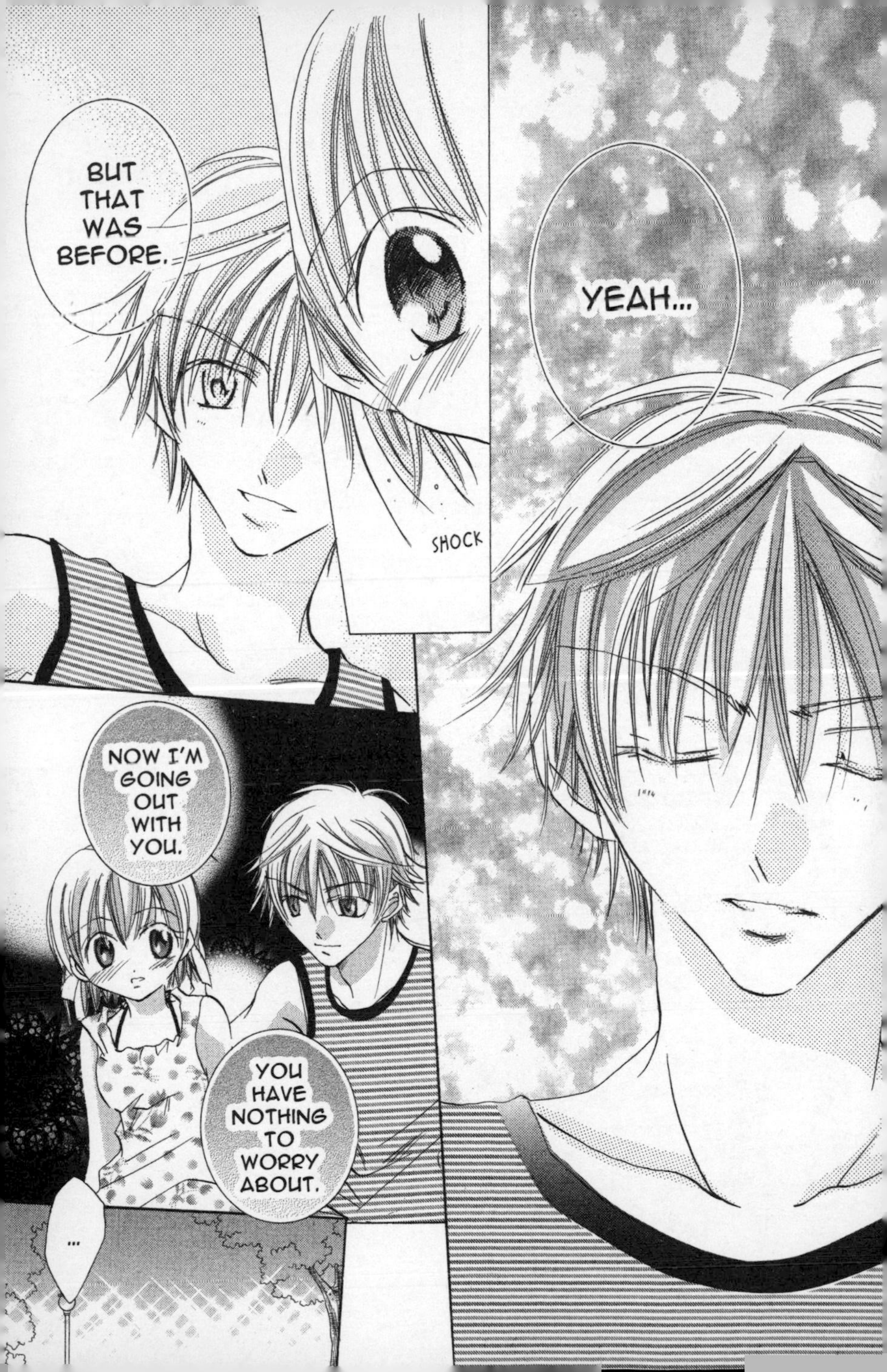
YEAH...
BUT THAT WAS BEFORE.
SHOCK
NOW I'M GOING OUT WITH YOU.
YOU HAVE NOTHING TO WORRY ABOUT.
...

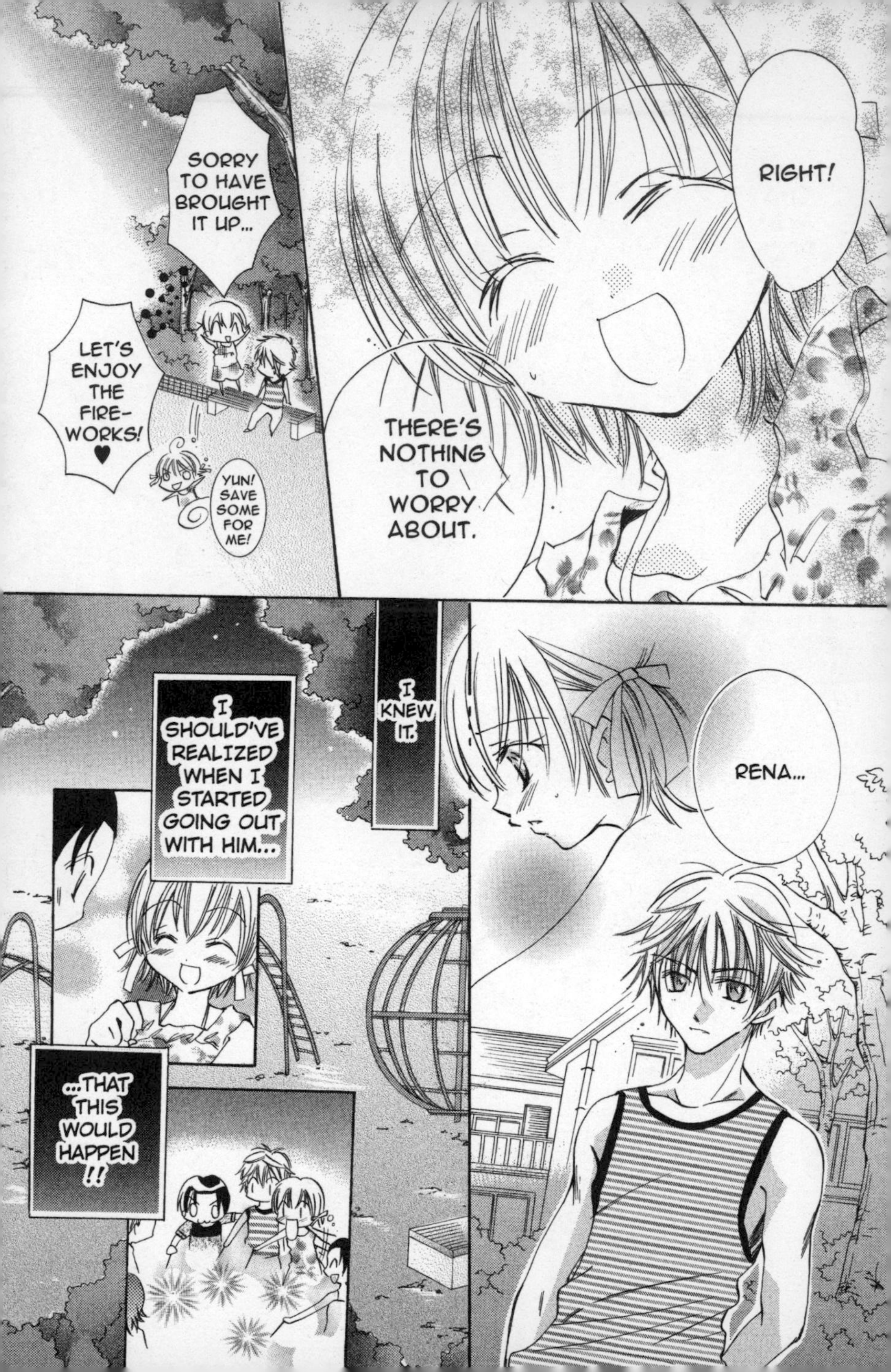
RIGHT!
THERE'S NOTHING TO WORRY ABOUT.
SORRY TO HAVE BROUGHT IT UP...
LET'S ENJOY THE FIRE-WORKS! ♥
YUN! SAVE SOME FOR ME!
RENA...
I KNEW IT.
I SHOULD'VE REALIZED WHEN I STARTED GOING OUT WITH HIM...
...THAT THIS WOULD HAPPEN!!

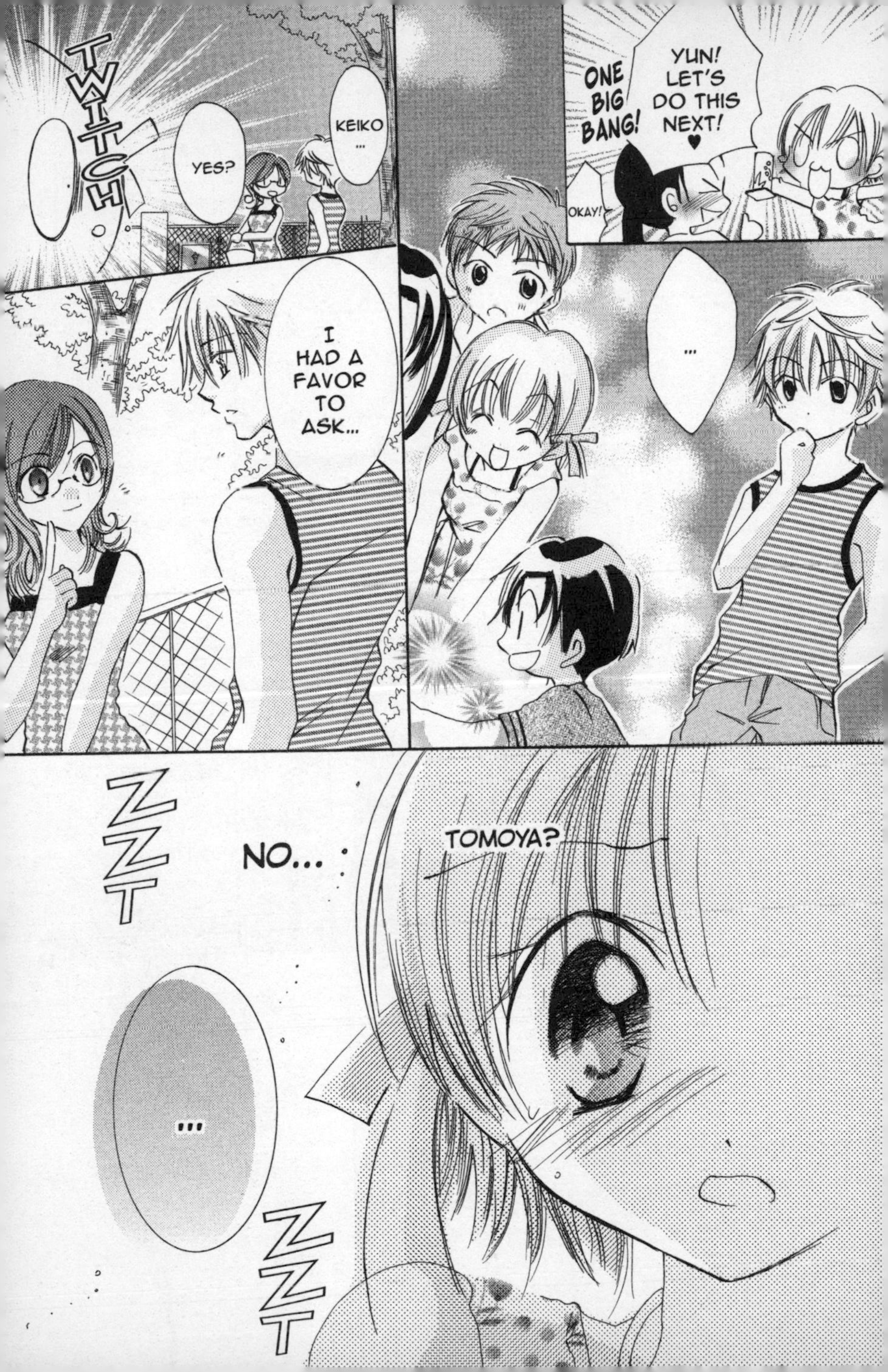
YUN! LET'S DO THIS NEXT! ♥
ONE BIG BANG!
OKAY!
...
KEIKO...
YES?
TWITCH
...
I HAD A FAVOR TO ASK...
TOMOYA?
NO...
ZZZ
...
ZZZ

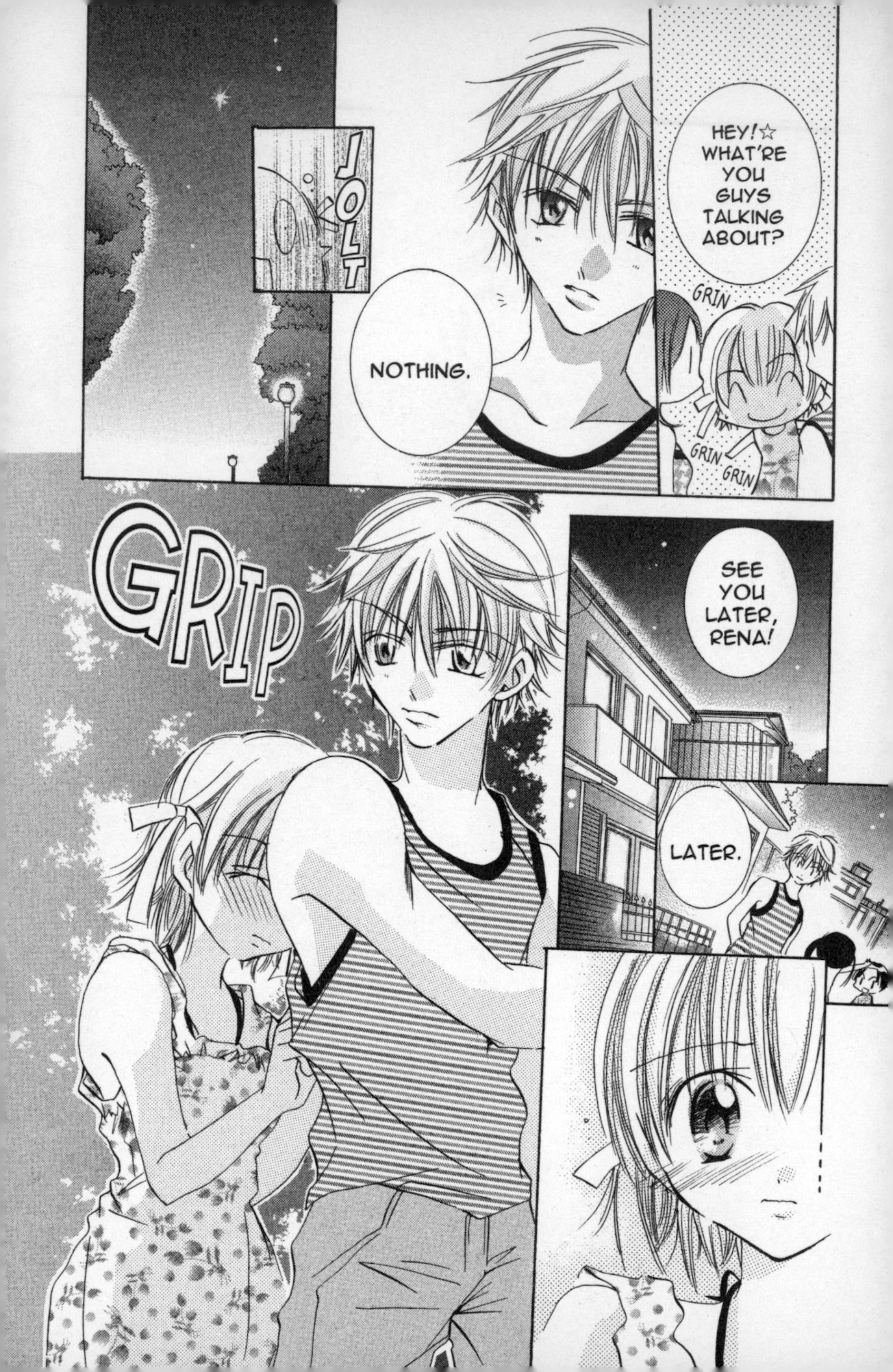
HEY!☆ WHAT'RE YOU GUYS TALKING ABOUT?
GRIN
GRIN
GRIN
NOTHING.
JOLT
SEE YOU LATER, RENA!
LATER.
GRIP

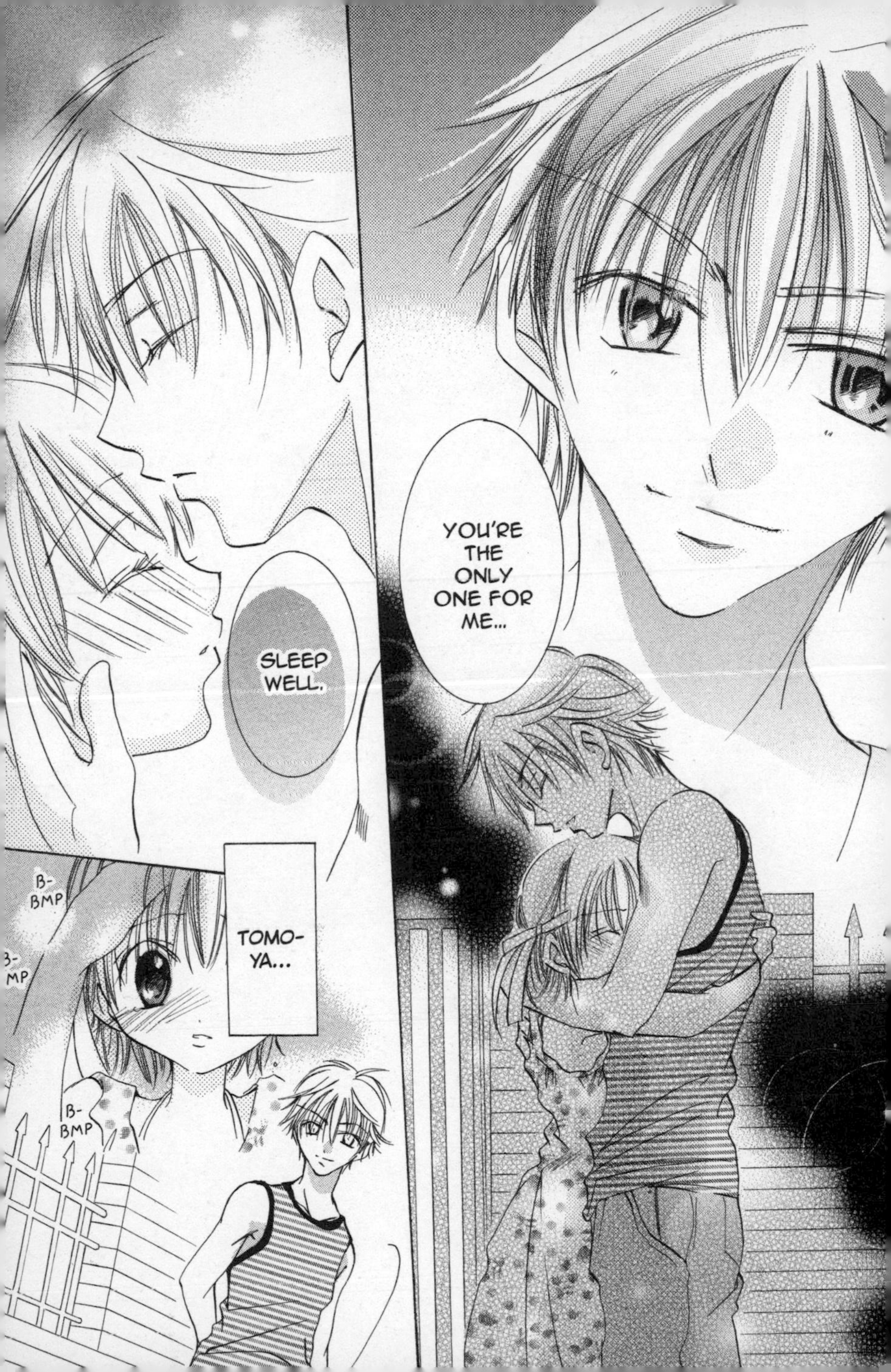
YOU'RE THE ONLY ONE FOR ME...
SLEEP WELL.
TOMO-YA...
B-BMP
B-BMP

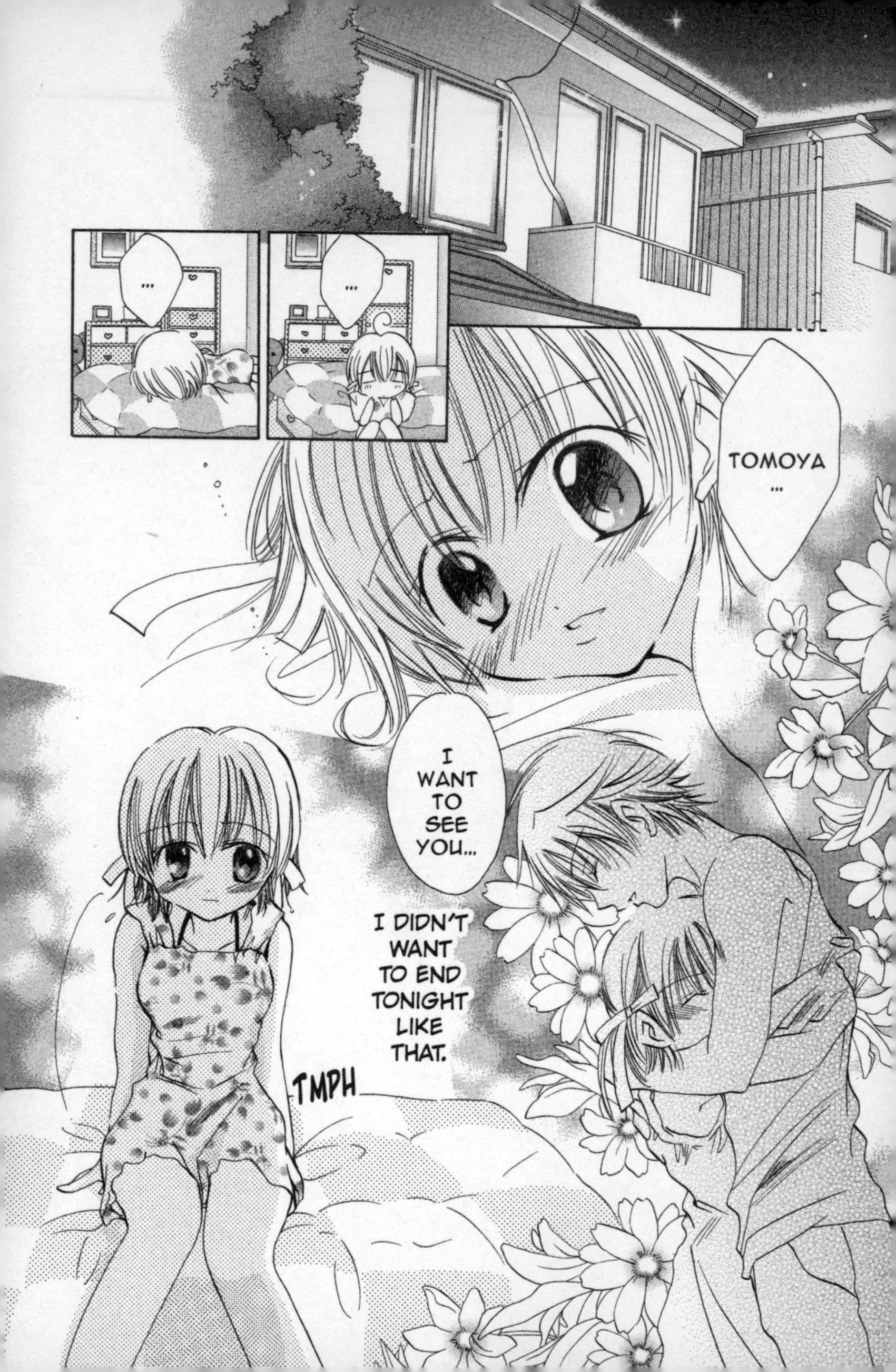
...
...
TOMOYA ...
I WANT TO SEE YOU...
I DIDN'T WANT TO END TONIGHT LIKE THAT.
TMPH

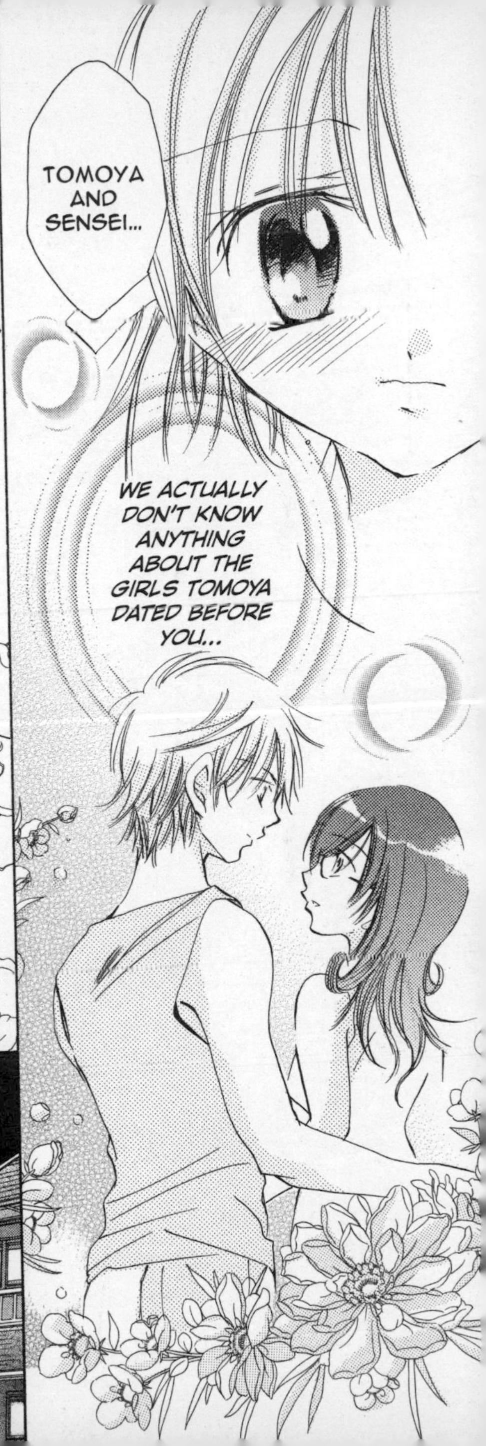
TOMOYA AND SENSEI...
WE ACTUALLY DON'T KNOW ANYTHING ABOUT THE GIRLS TOMOYA DATED BEFORE YOU...

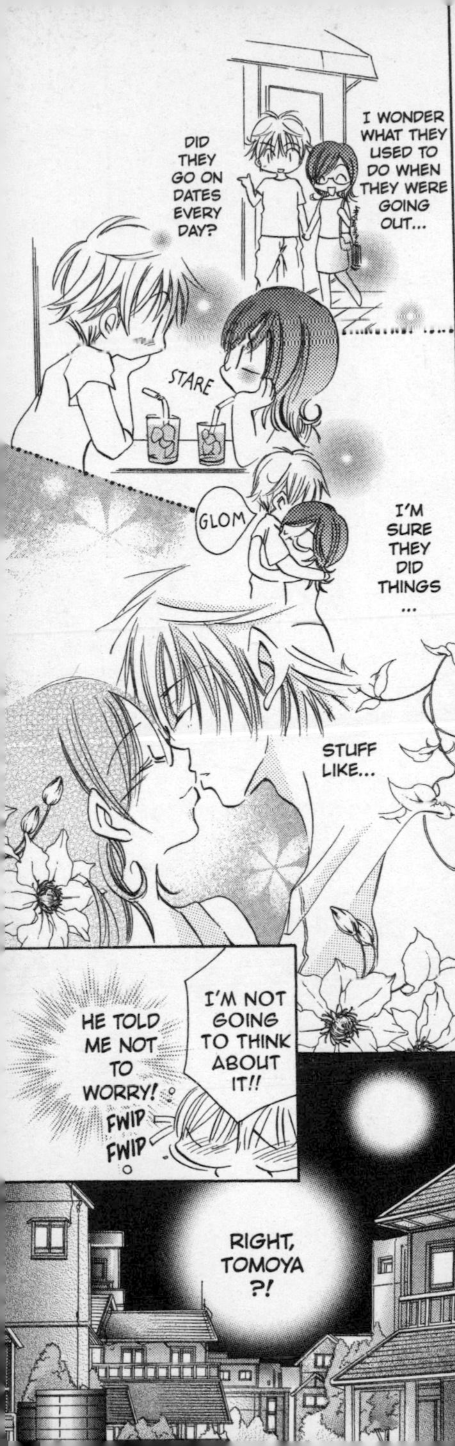
I WONDER WHAT THEY USED TO DO WHEN THEY WERE GOING OUT...
DID THEY GO ON DATES EVERY DAY?
STARE
I'M SURE THEY DID THINGS ...
GLOM
STUFF LIKE...
I'M NOT GOING TO THINK ABOUT IT!!
HE TOLD ME NOT TO WORRY!
FWIP FWIP
RIGHT, TOMOYA ?!

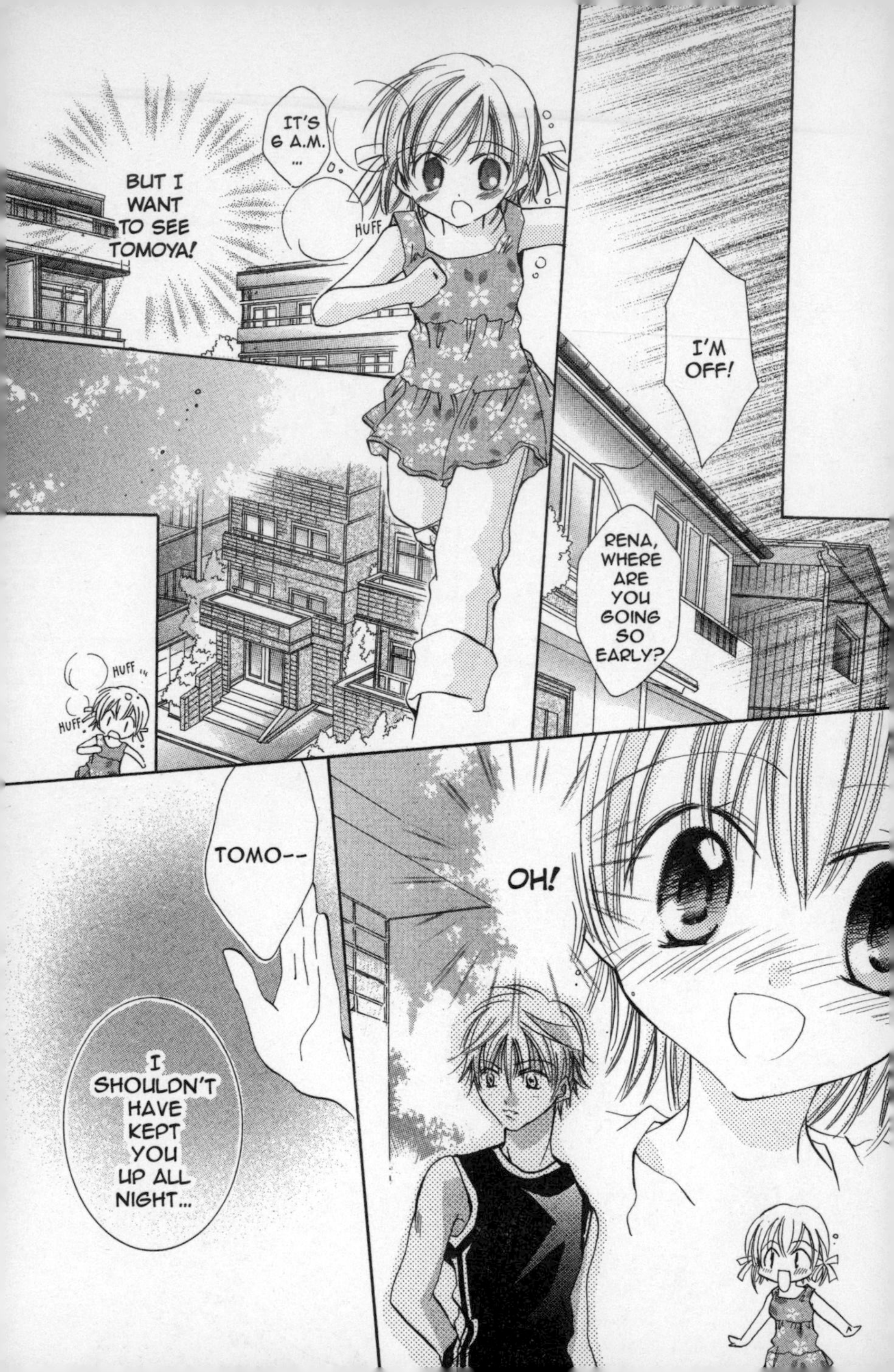
I'M OFF!
RENA, WHERE ARE YOU GOING SO EARLY?
IT'S 6 A.M. ...
BUT I WANT TO SEE TOMOYA!
HUFF
HUFF ...
HUFF
OH!
TOMO--
I SHOULDN'T HAVE KEPT YOU UP ALL NIGHT...

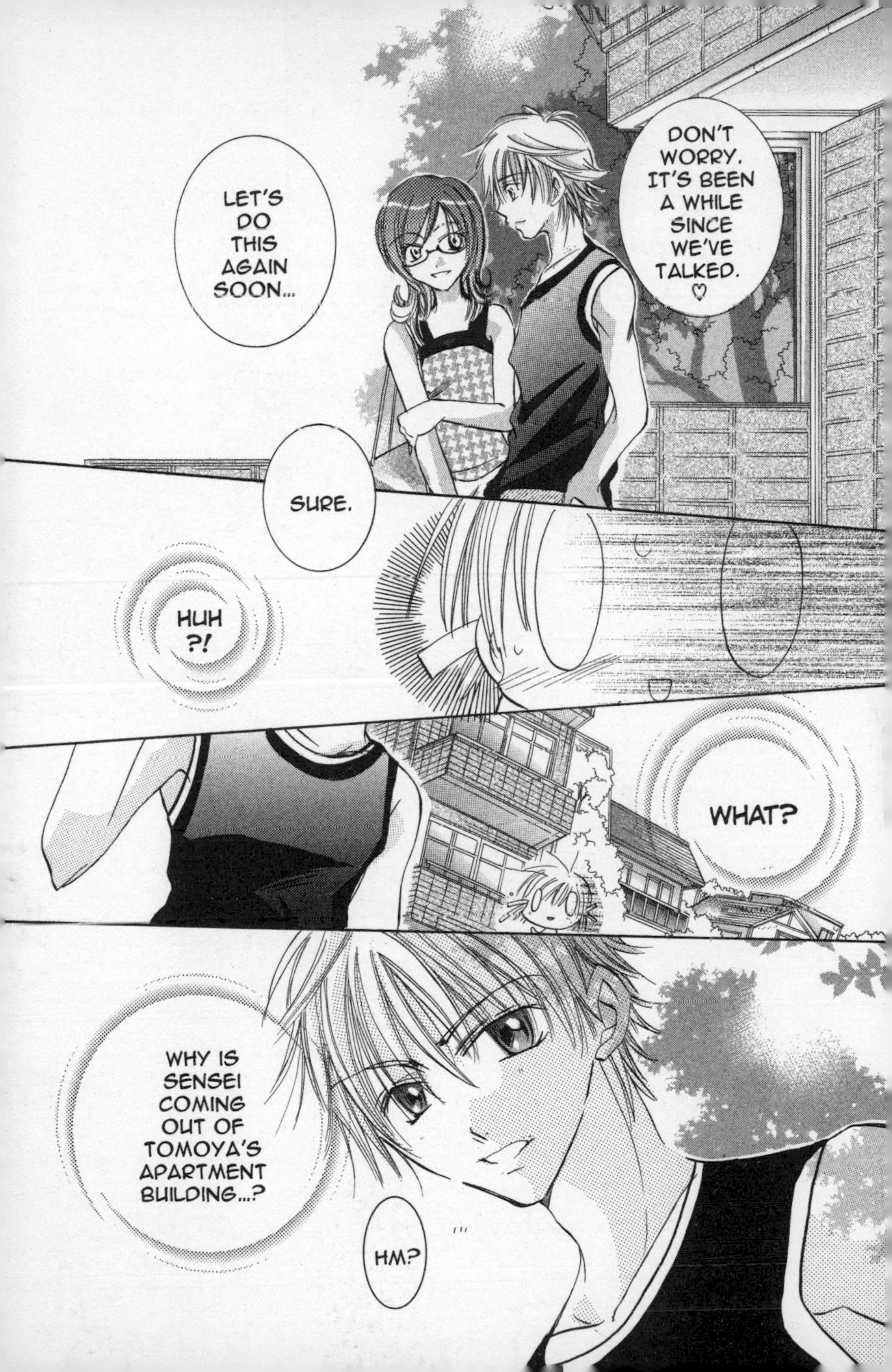
DON'T WORRY. IT'S BEEN A WHILE SINCE WE'VE TALKED. ♡
LET'S DO THIS AGAIN SOON...
SURE.
HUH ?!
WHAT?
WHY IS SENSEI COMING OUT OF TOMOYA'S APARTMENT BUILDING...?
HM?

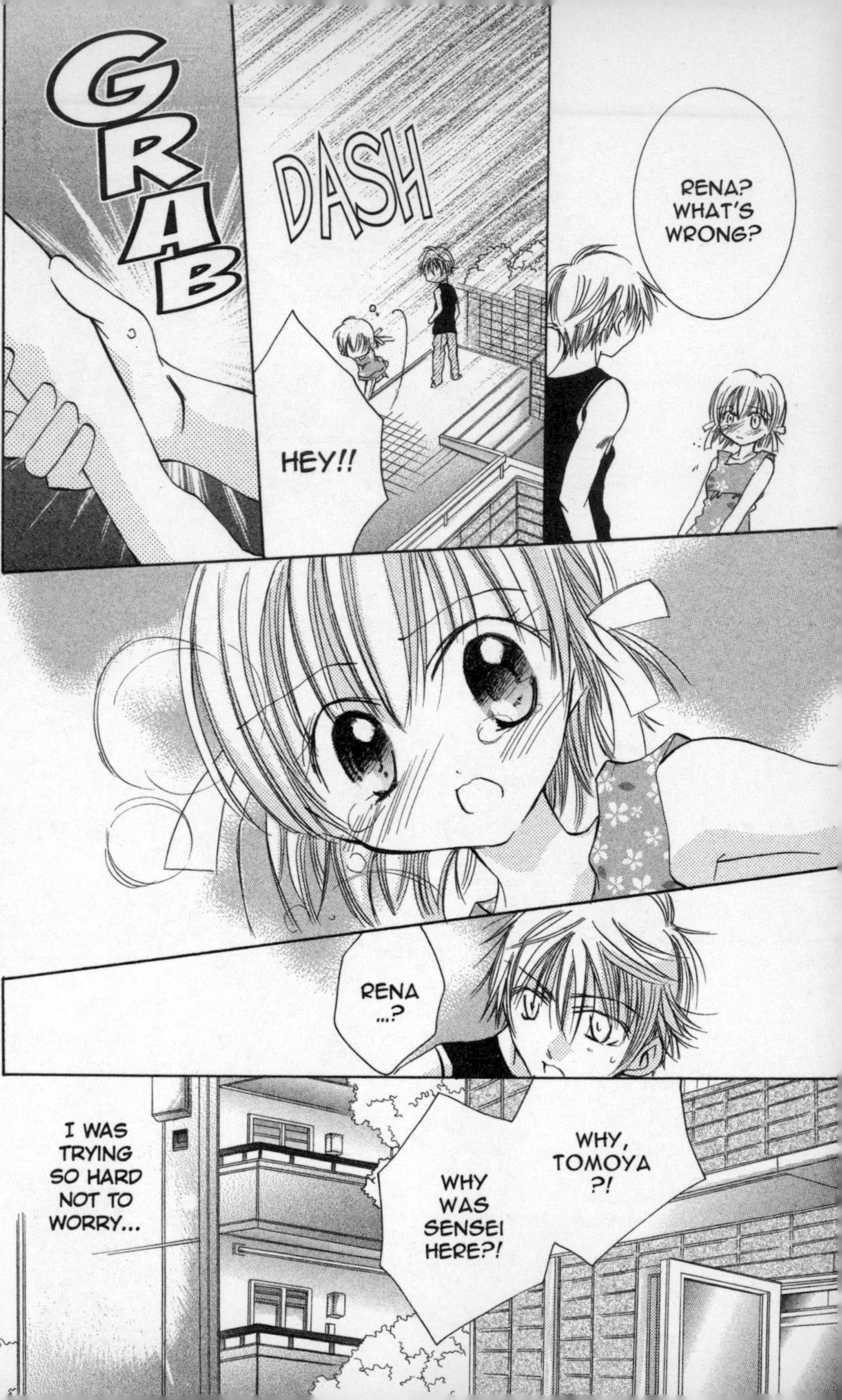
RENA? WHAT'S WRONG?
DASH
HEY!!
GRAB
RENA ...?
WHY, TOMOYA ?!
WHY WAS SENSEI HERE?!
I WAS TRYING SO HARD NOT TO WORRY...

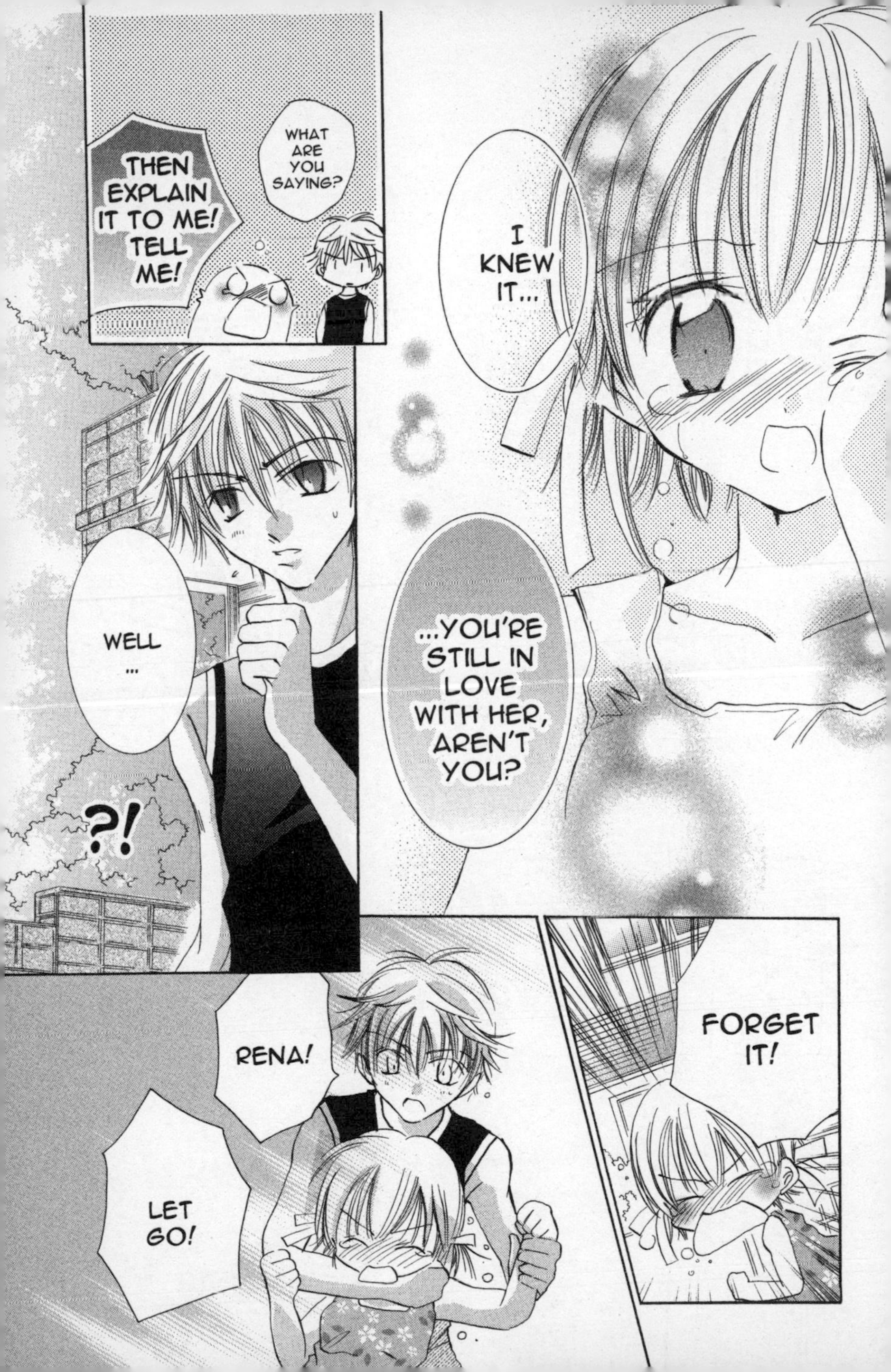
I KNEW IT...
...YOU'RE STILL IN LOVE WITH HER, AREN'T YOU?
WHAT ARE YOU SAYING?
THEN EXPLAIN IT TO ME! TELL ME!
WELL ...
?!
FORGET IT!
RENA!
LET GO!

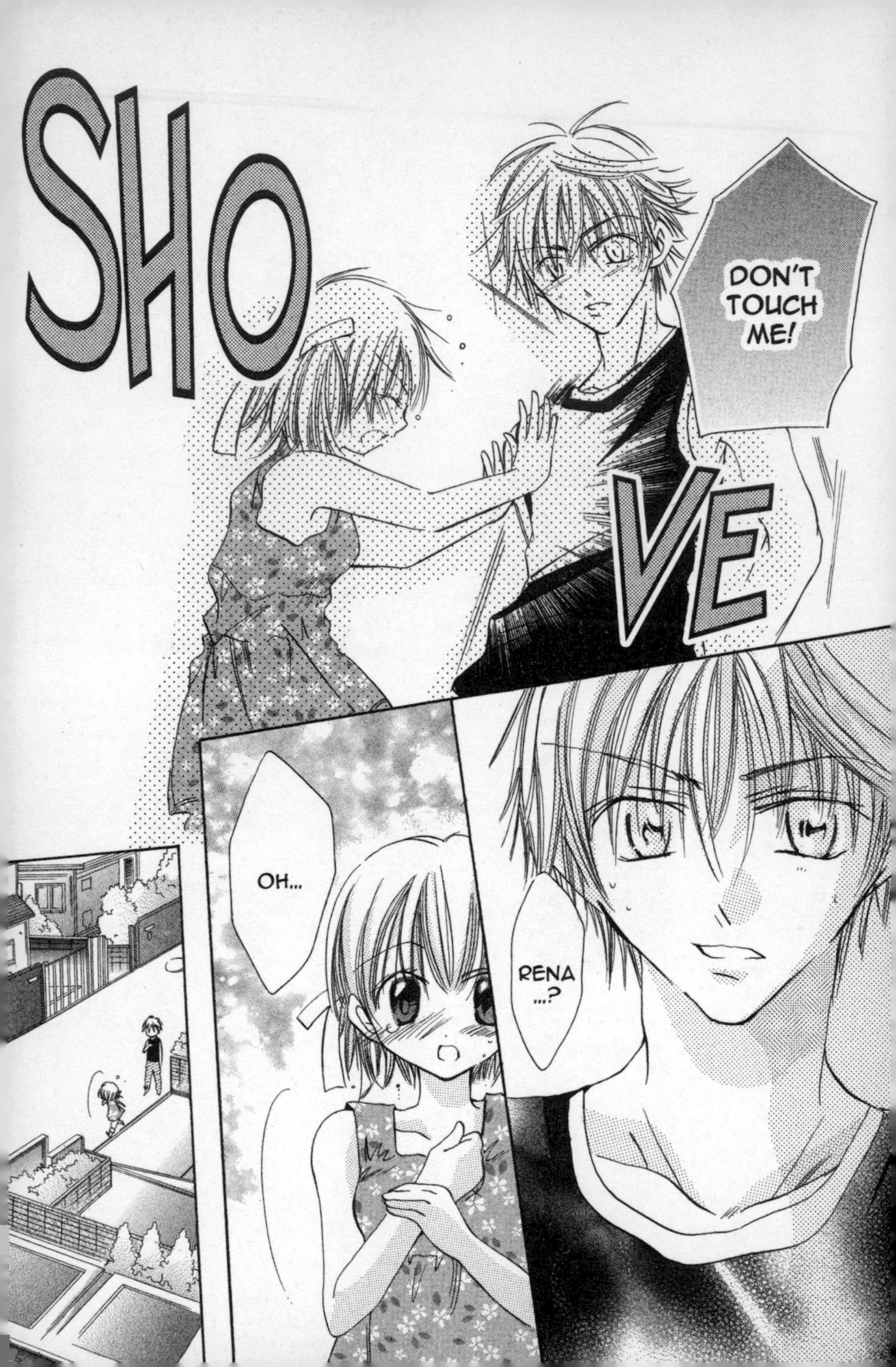
SHOVE
DON'T TOUCH ME!
RENA ...?
OH...

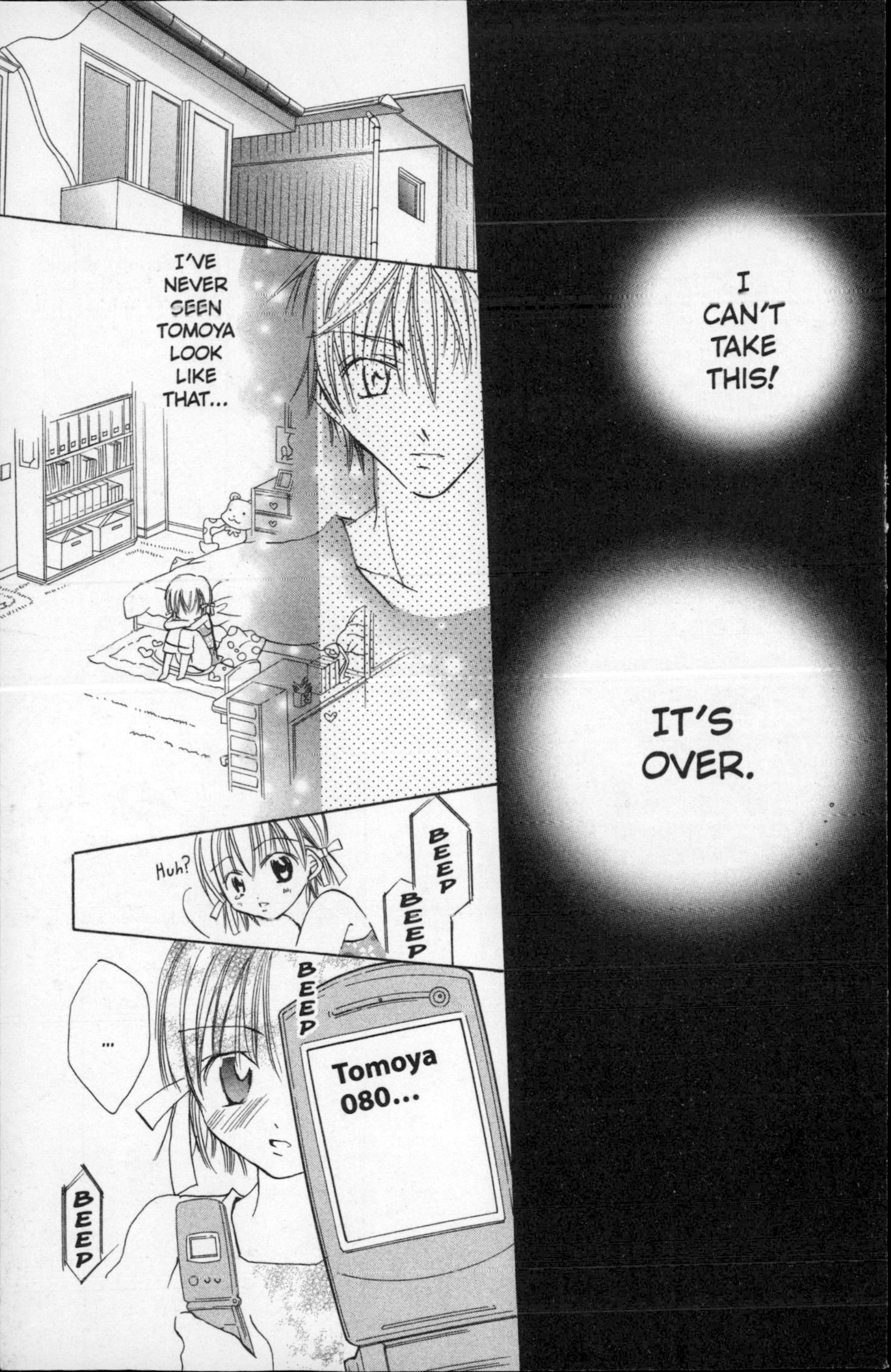
I CAN'T TAKE THIS!
IT'S OVER.
I'VE NEVER SEEN TOMOYA LOOK LIKE THAT...
BEEP
BEEP
Huh?
BEEP
...
Tomoya 080...
BEEP

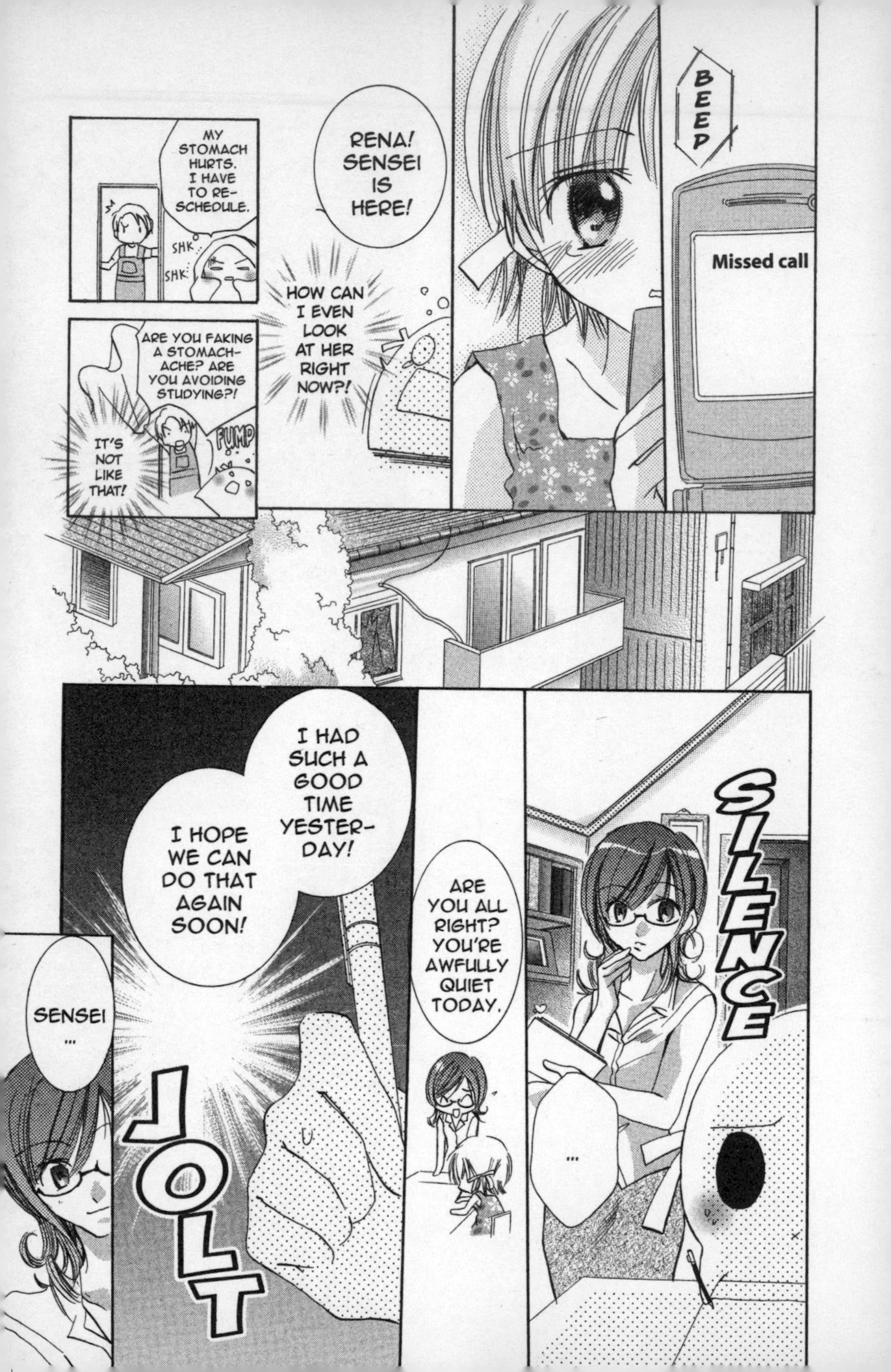
BEEP
Missed call
RENA! SENSEI IS HERE!
HOW CAN I EVEN LOOK AT HER RIGHT NOW?!
MY STOMACH HURTS. I HAVE TO RE-SCHEDULE.
SHK SHK
ARE YOU FAKING A STOMACH-ACHE? ARE YOU AVOIDING STUDYING?!
IT'S NOT LIKE THAT!
FUMP
SILENCE
ARE YOU ALL RIGHT? YOU'RE AWFULLY QUIET TODAY.
...
I HAD SUCH A GOOD TIME YESTER-DAY!
I HOPE WE CAN DO THAT AGAIN SOON!
JOLT
SENSEI ...

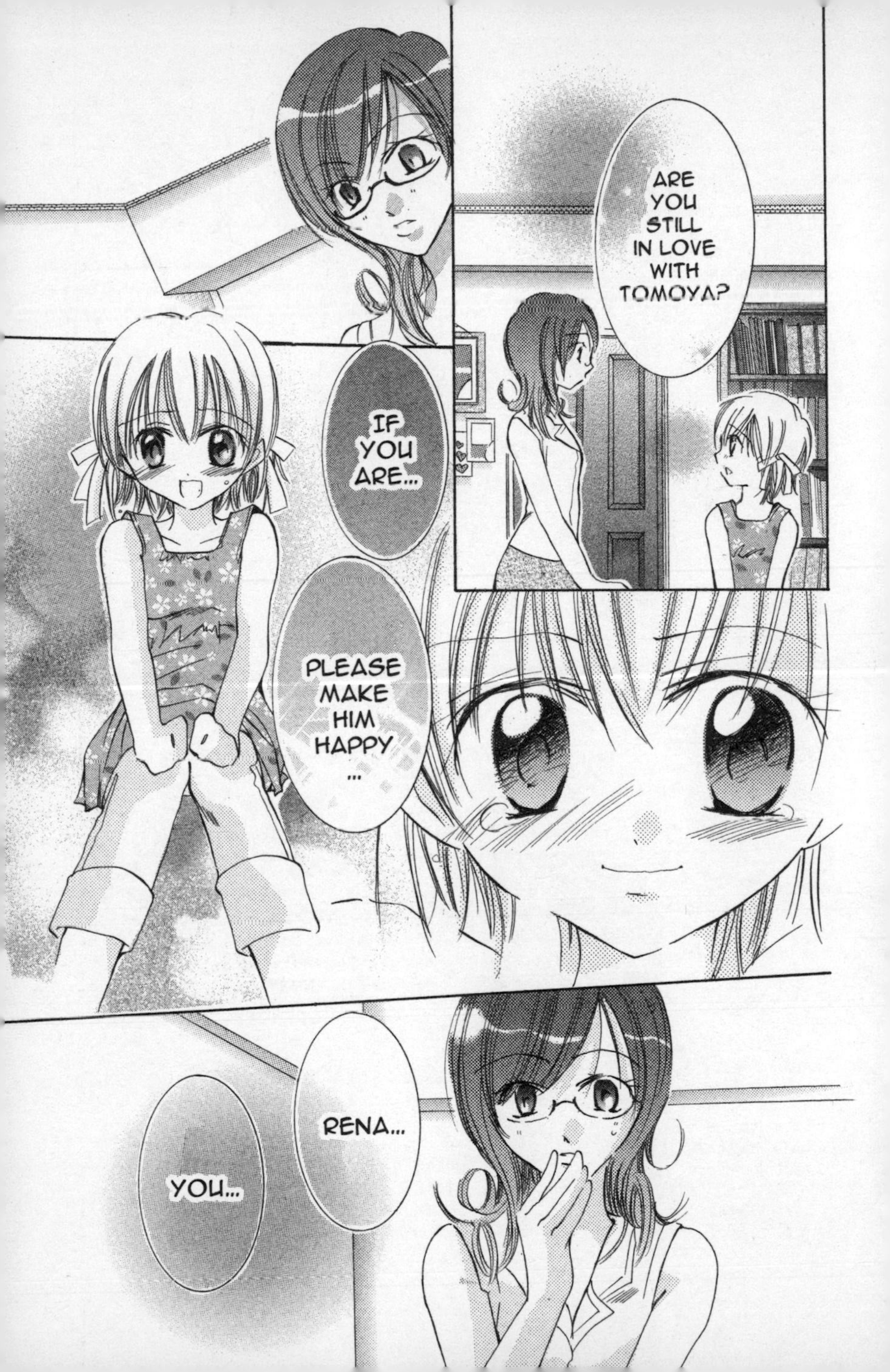
ARE YOU STILL IN LOVE WITH TOMOYA?
IF YOU ARE...
PLEASE MAKE HIM HAPPY ...
RENA...
YOU...

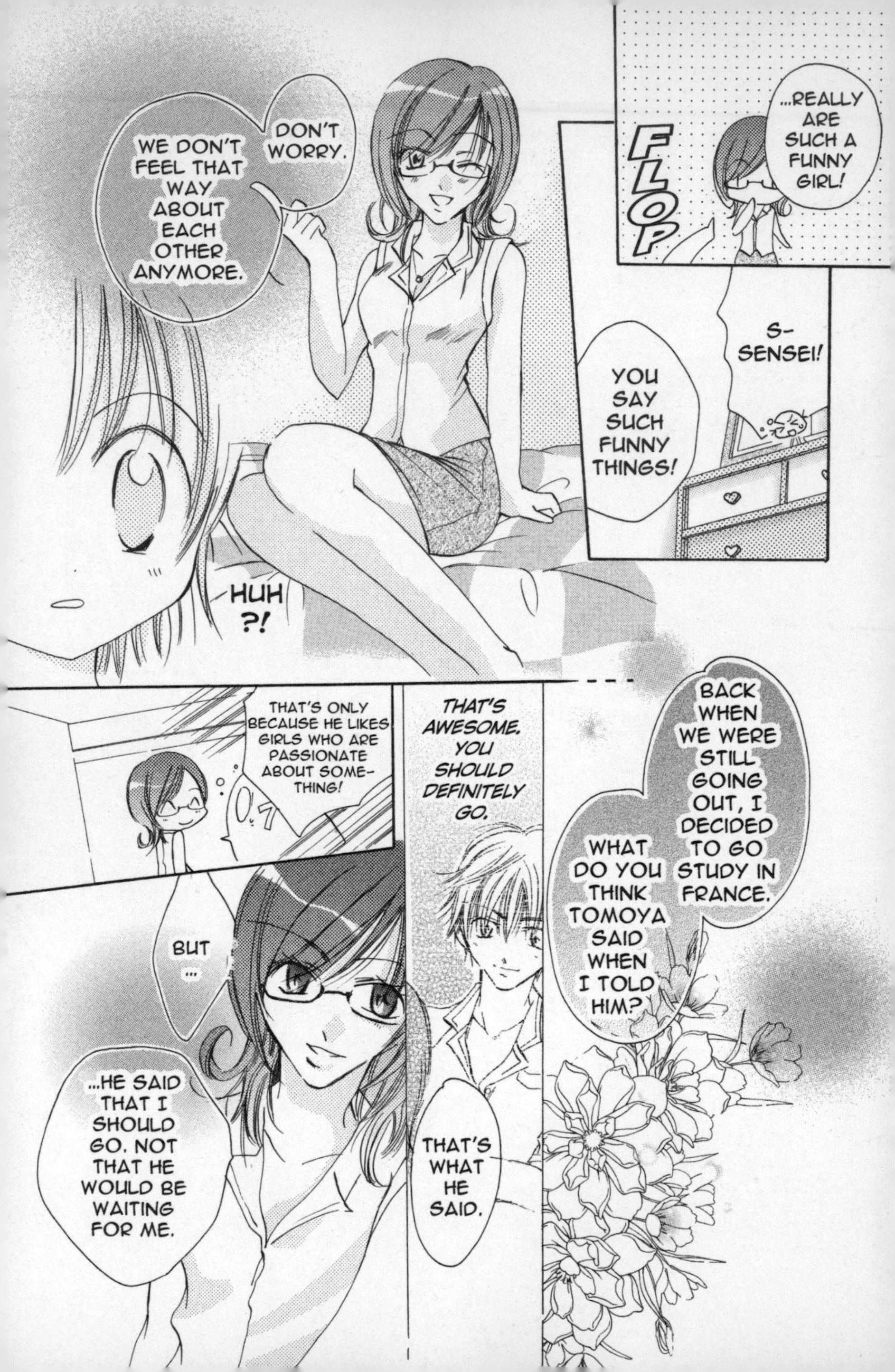
FLOP
...REALLY ARE SUCH A FUNNY GIRL!
S-SENSEI!
YOU SAY SUCH FUNNY THINGS!
DON'T WORRY.
WE DON'T FEEL THAT WAY ABOUT EACH OTHER ANYMORE.
HUH ?!
BACK WHEN WE WERE STILL GOING OUT, I DECIDED TO GO STUDY IN FRANCE.
WHAT DO YOU THINK TOMOYA SAID WHEN I TOLD HIM?
THAT'S AWESOME. YOU SHOULD DEFINITELY GO.
THAT'S WHAT HE SAID.
THAT'S ONLY BECAUSE HE LIKES GIRLS WHO ARE PASSIONATE ABOUT SOMETHING!
BUT ...
...HE SAID THAT I SHOULD GO. NOT THAT HE WOULD BE WAITING FOR ME.

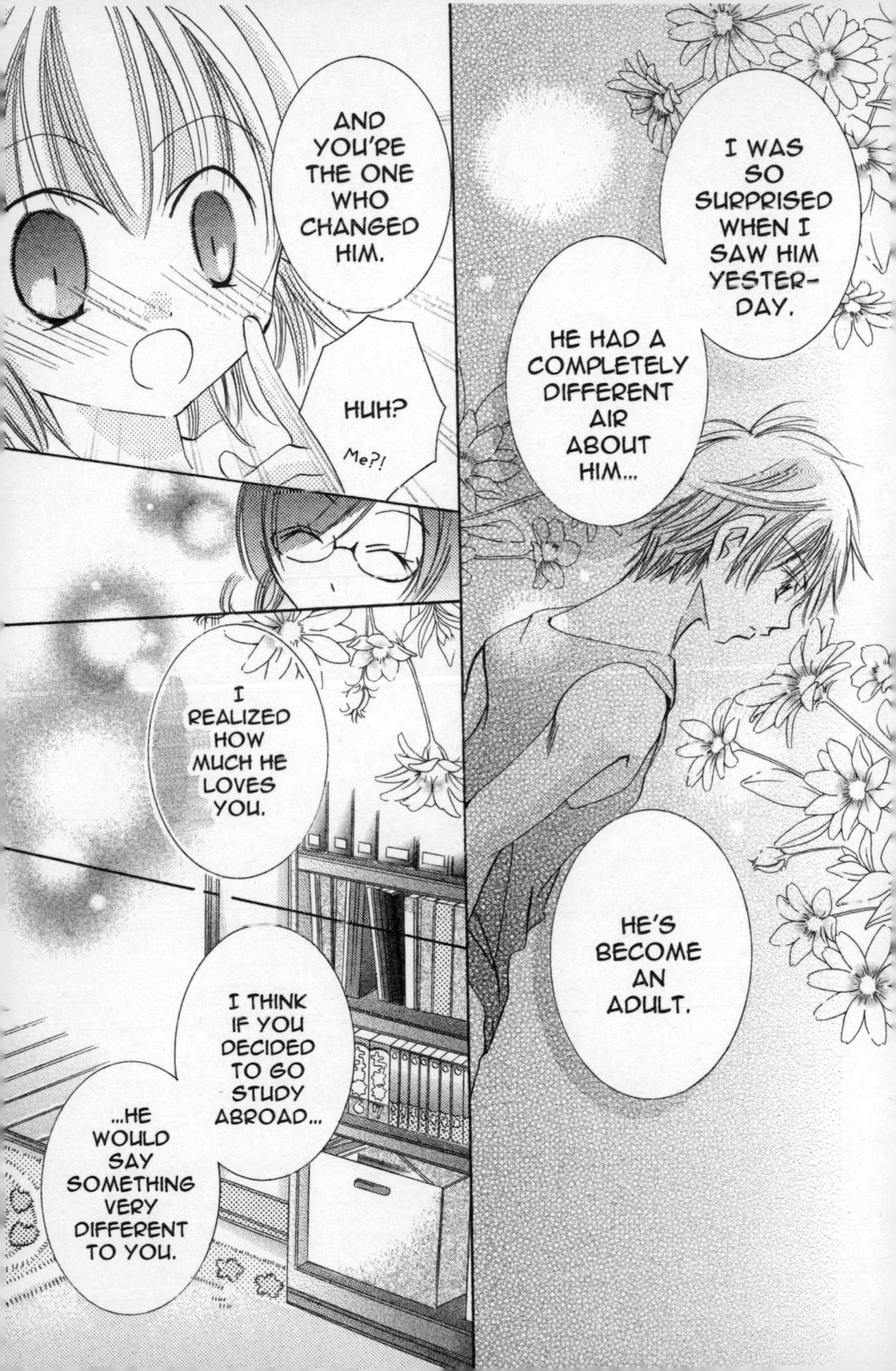
I WAS SO SURPRISED WHEN I SAW HIM YESTER-DAY.
HE HAD A COMPLETELY DIFFERENT AIR ABOUT HIM...
HE'S BECOME AN ADULT.
AND YOU'RE THE ONE WHO CHANGED HIM.
HUH?
Me?!
I REALIZED HOW MUCH HE LOVES YOU.
I THINK IF YOU DECIDED TO GO STUDY ABROAD...
...HE WOULD SAY SOMETHING VERY DIFFERENT TO YOU.

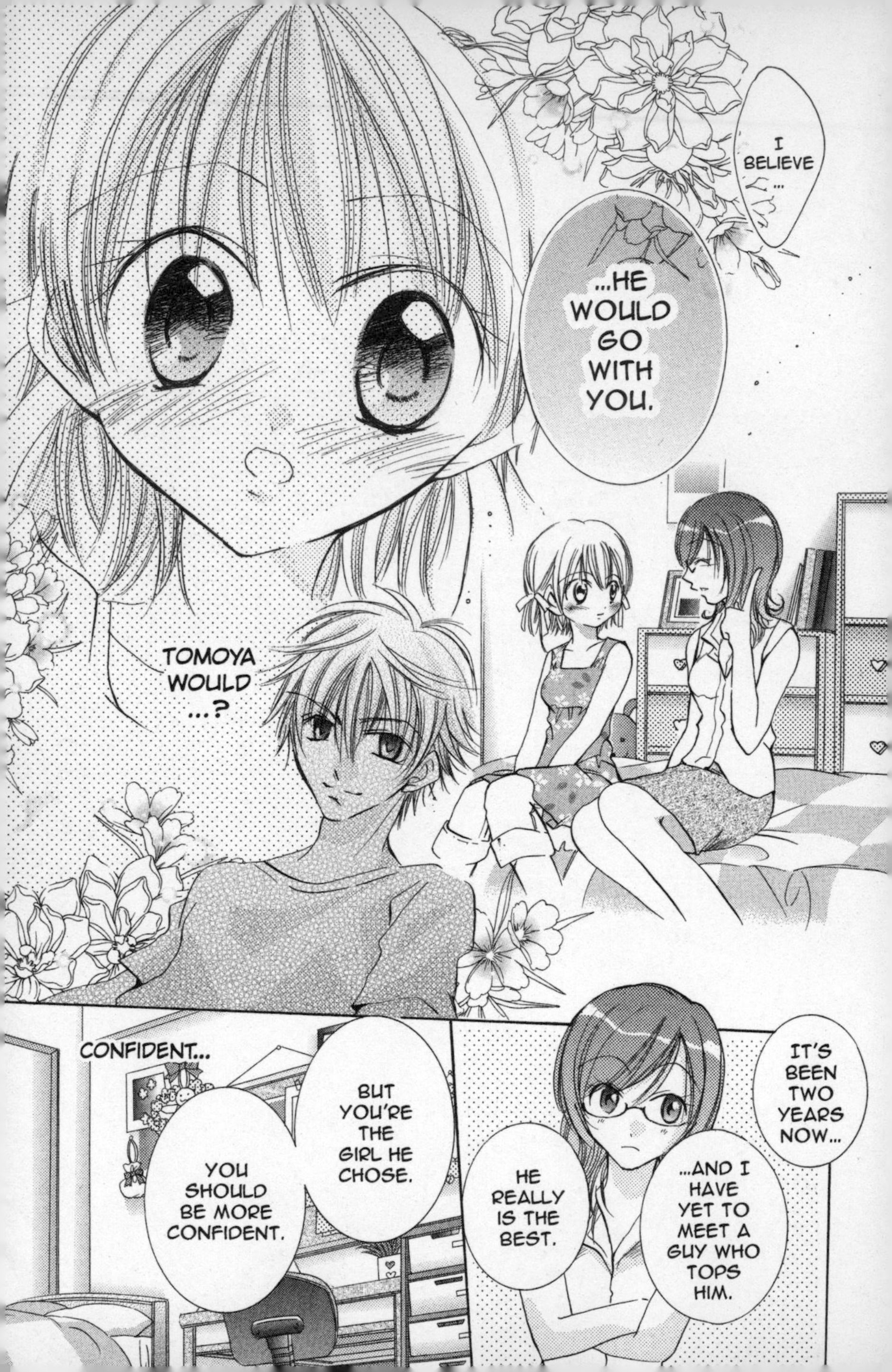
I BELIEVE...
...HE WOULD GO WITH YOU.
TOMOYA WOULD...?
IT'S BEEN TWO YEARS NOW...
...AND I HAVE YET TO MEET A GUY WHO TOPS HIM.
HE REALLY IS THE BEST.
BUT YOU'RE THE GIRL HE CHOSE.
YOU SHOULD BE MORE CONFIDENT.
CONFIDENT...

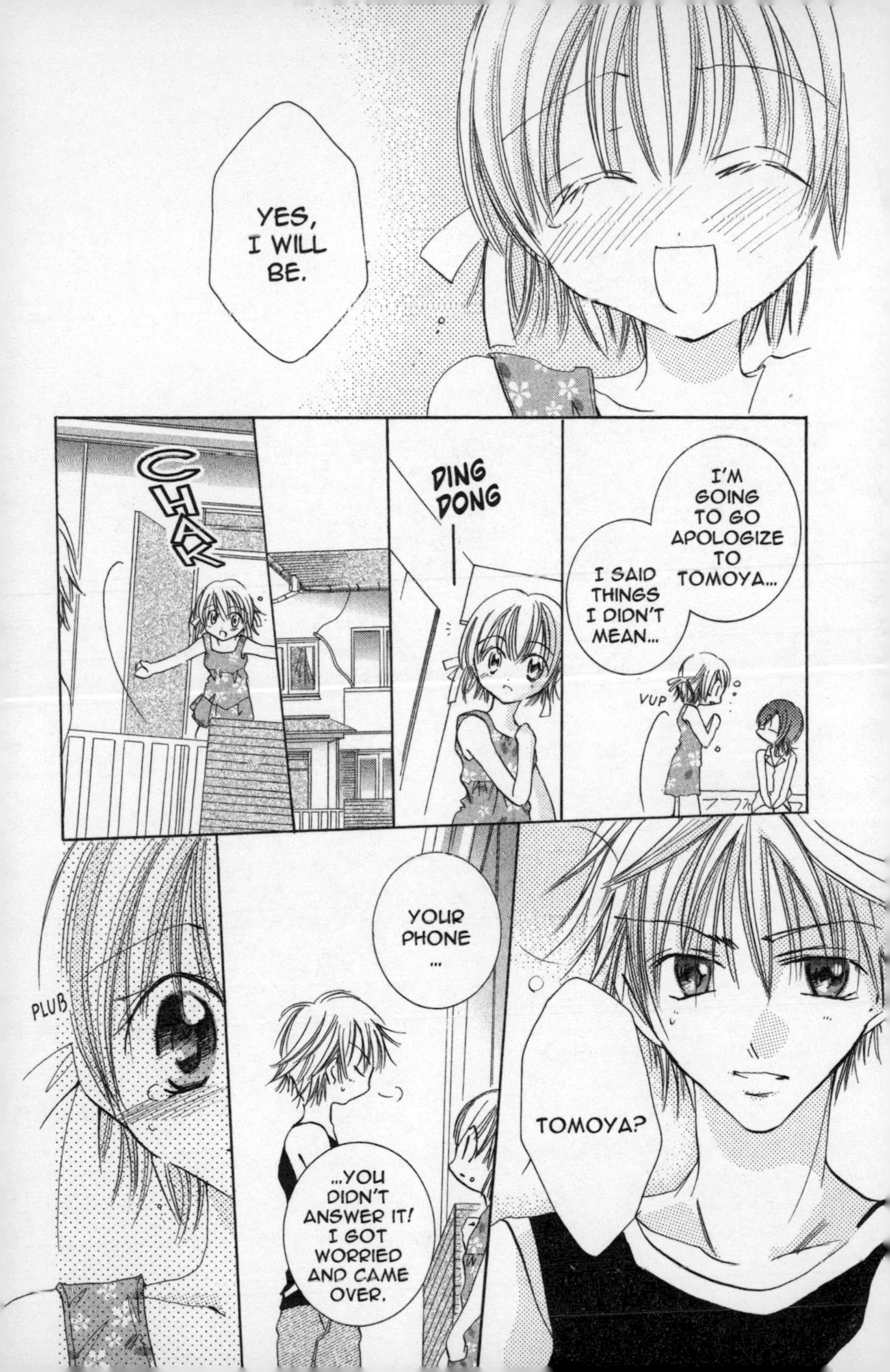
YES, I WILL BE.
I'M GOING TO GO APOLOGIZE TO TOMOYA...
I SAID THINGS I DIDN'T MEAN...
VUP
DING DONG
CHAR
TOMOYA?
YOUR PHONE ...
...YOU DIDN'T ANSWER IT! I GOT WORRIED AND CAME OVER.
PLUB

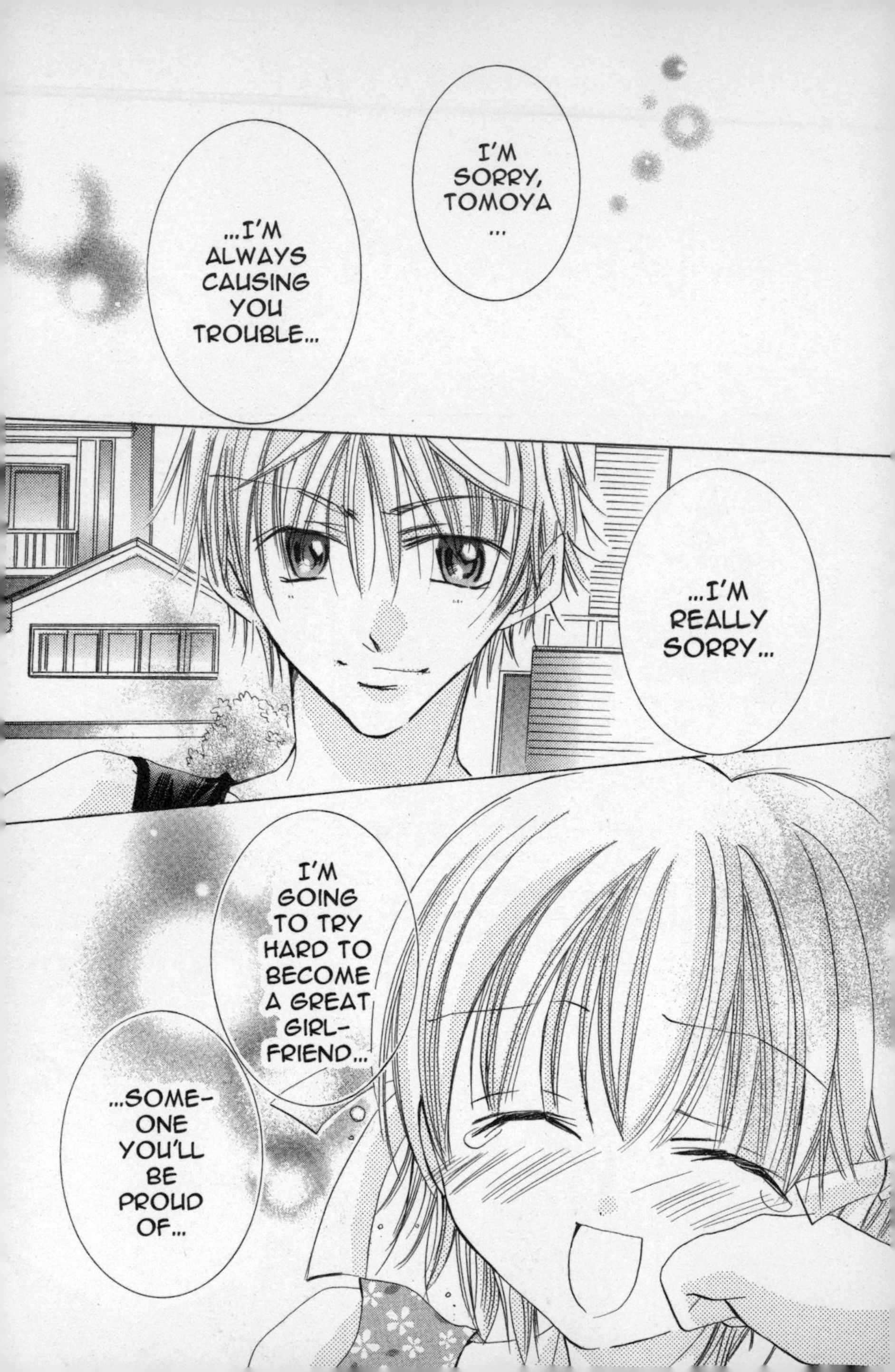
I'M SORRY, TOMOYA ...
...I'M ALWAYS CAUSING YOU TROUBLE...
...I'M REALLY SORRY...
I'M GOING TO TRY HARD TO BECOME A GREAT GIRL-FRIEND...
...SOME-ONE YOU'LL BE PROUD OF...

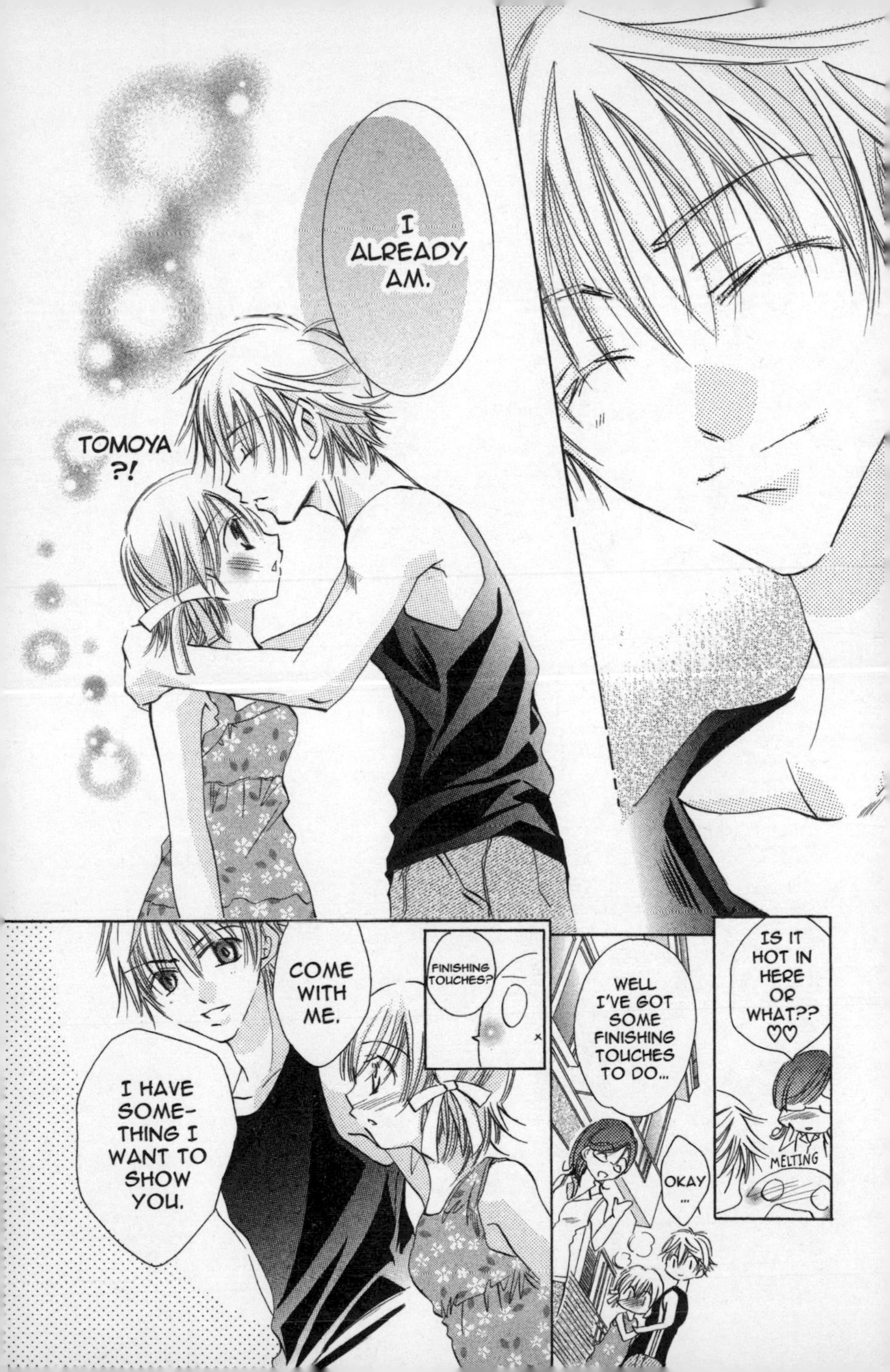
I ALREADY AM.
TOMOYA ?!
IS IT HOT IN HERE OR WHAT?? ♡♡
MELTING
WELL I'VE GOT SOME FINISHING TOUCHES TO DO...
OKAY ...
FINISHING TOUCHES?
COME WITH ME.
I HAVE SOME-THING I WANT TO SHOW YOU.

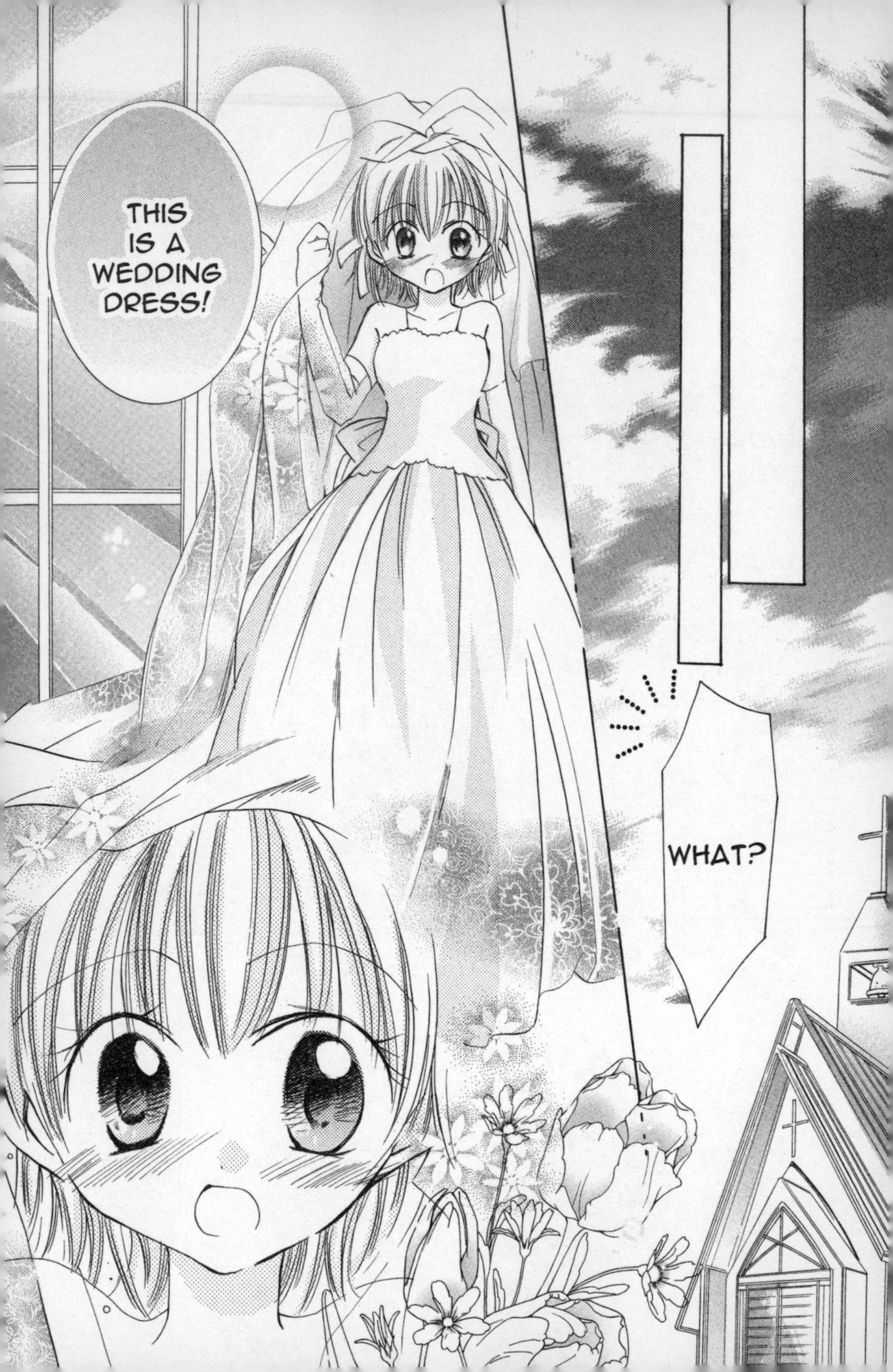
WHAT?
THIS IS A WEDDING DRESS!

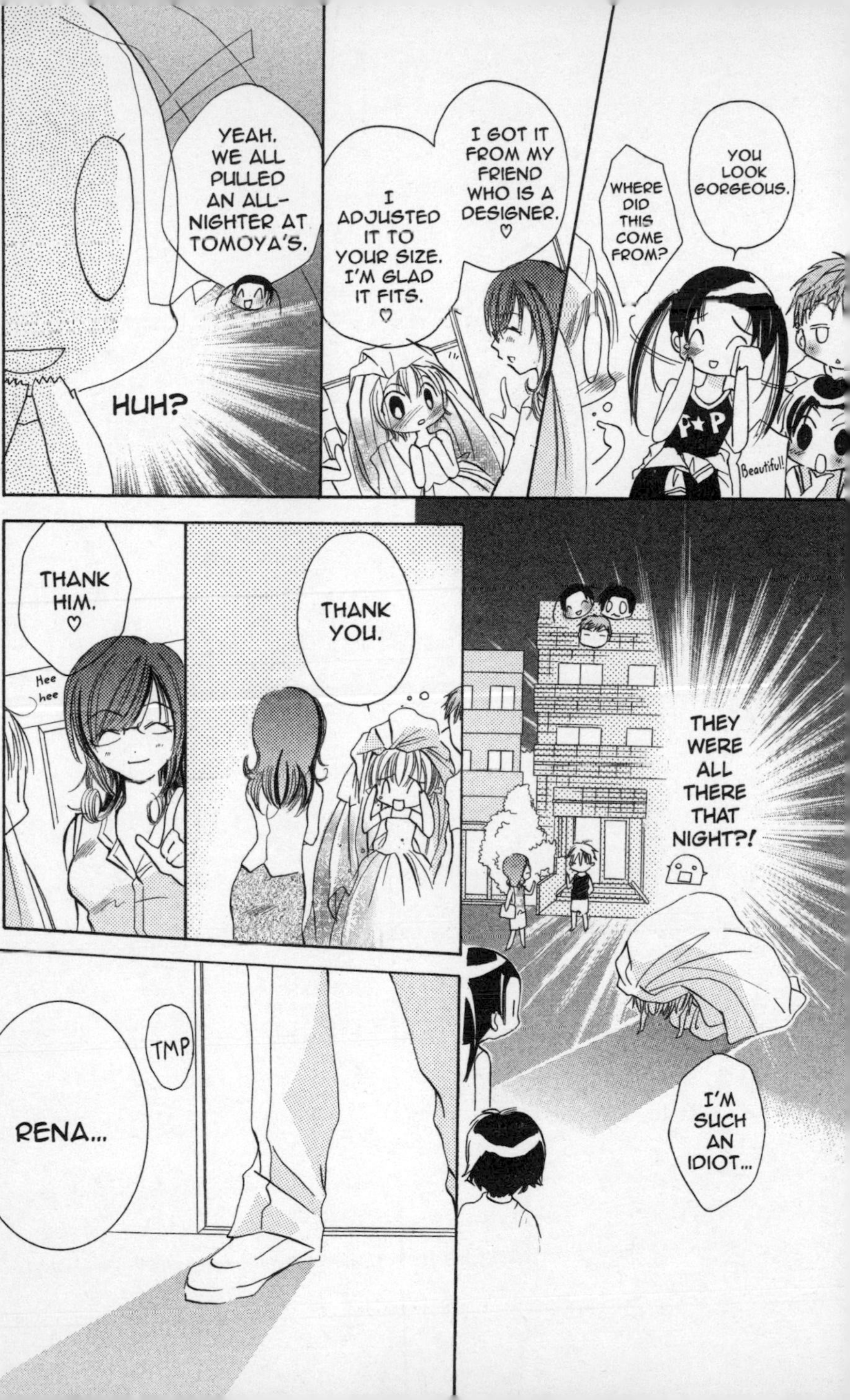
YOU LOOK GORGEOUS.
WHERE DID THIS COME FROM?
Beautiful!
I GOT IT FROM MY FRIEND WHO IS A DESIGNER. ♡
I ADJUSTED IT TO YOUR SIZE. I'M GLAD IT FITS. ♡
YEAH. WE ALL PULLED AN ALL-NIGHTER AT TOMOYA'S.
HUH?
THEY WERE ALL THERE THAT NIGHT?!
I'M SUCH AN IDIOT...
THANK YOU.
THANK HIM. ♡
Hee hee
TMP
RENA...

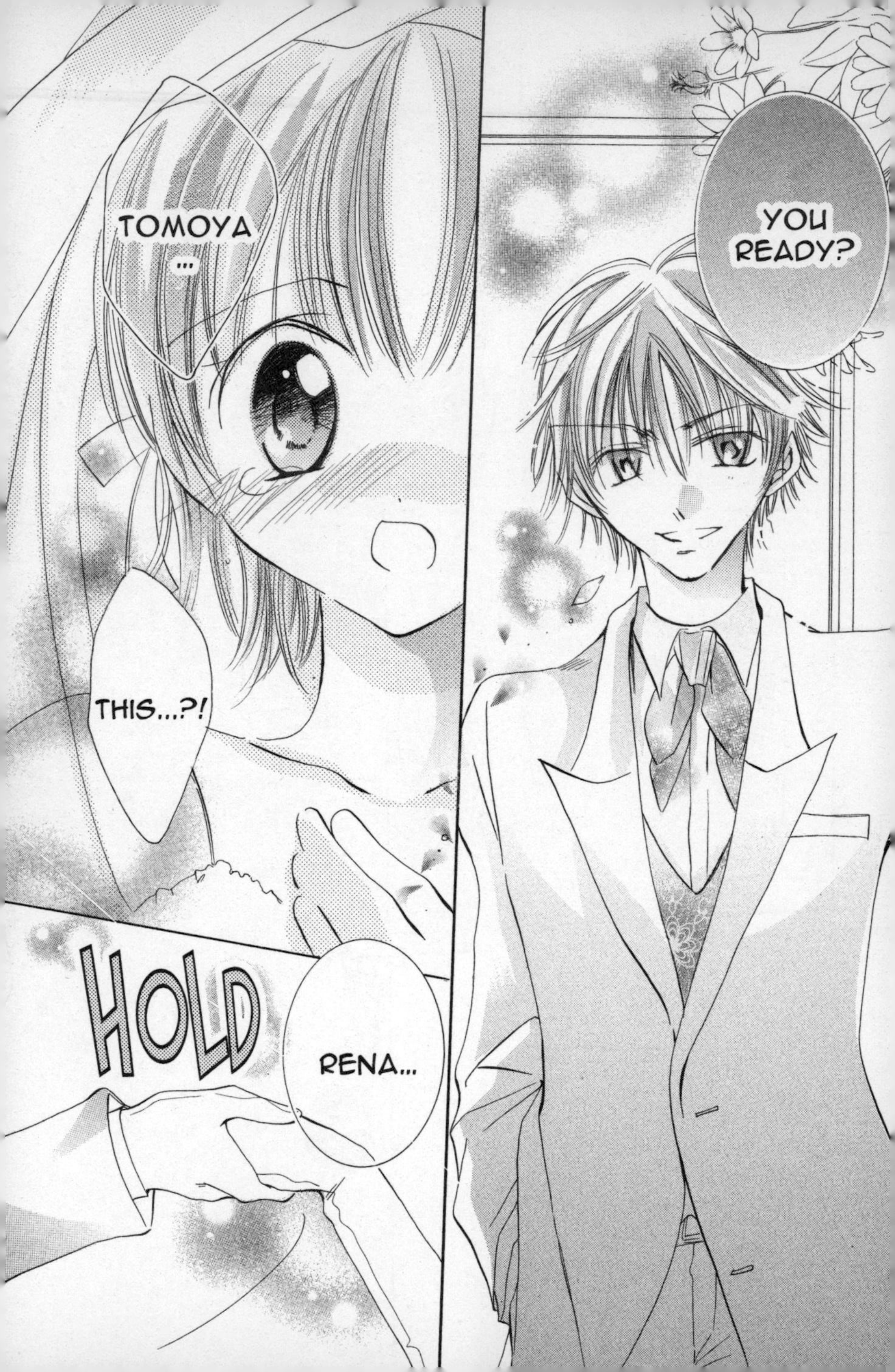
YOU READY?
TOMOYA ...
THIS...?!
RENA...
HOLD

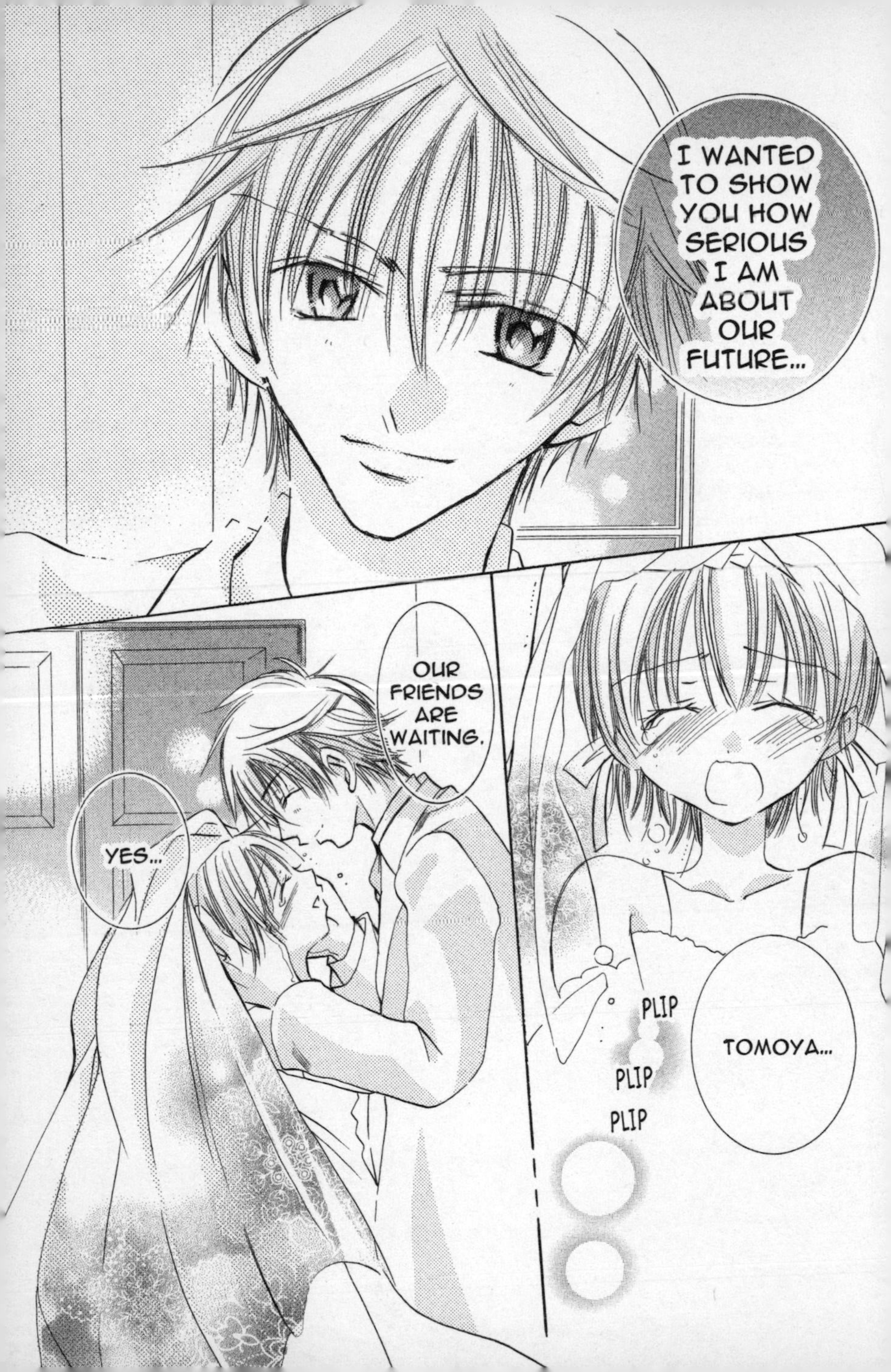
I WANTED TO SHOW YOU HOW SERIOUS I AM ABOUT OUR FUTURE...
TOMOYA...
PLIP
PLIP
PLIP
OUR FRIENDS ARE WAITING.
YES...

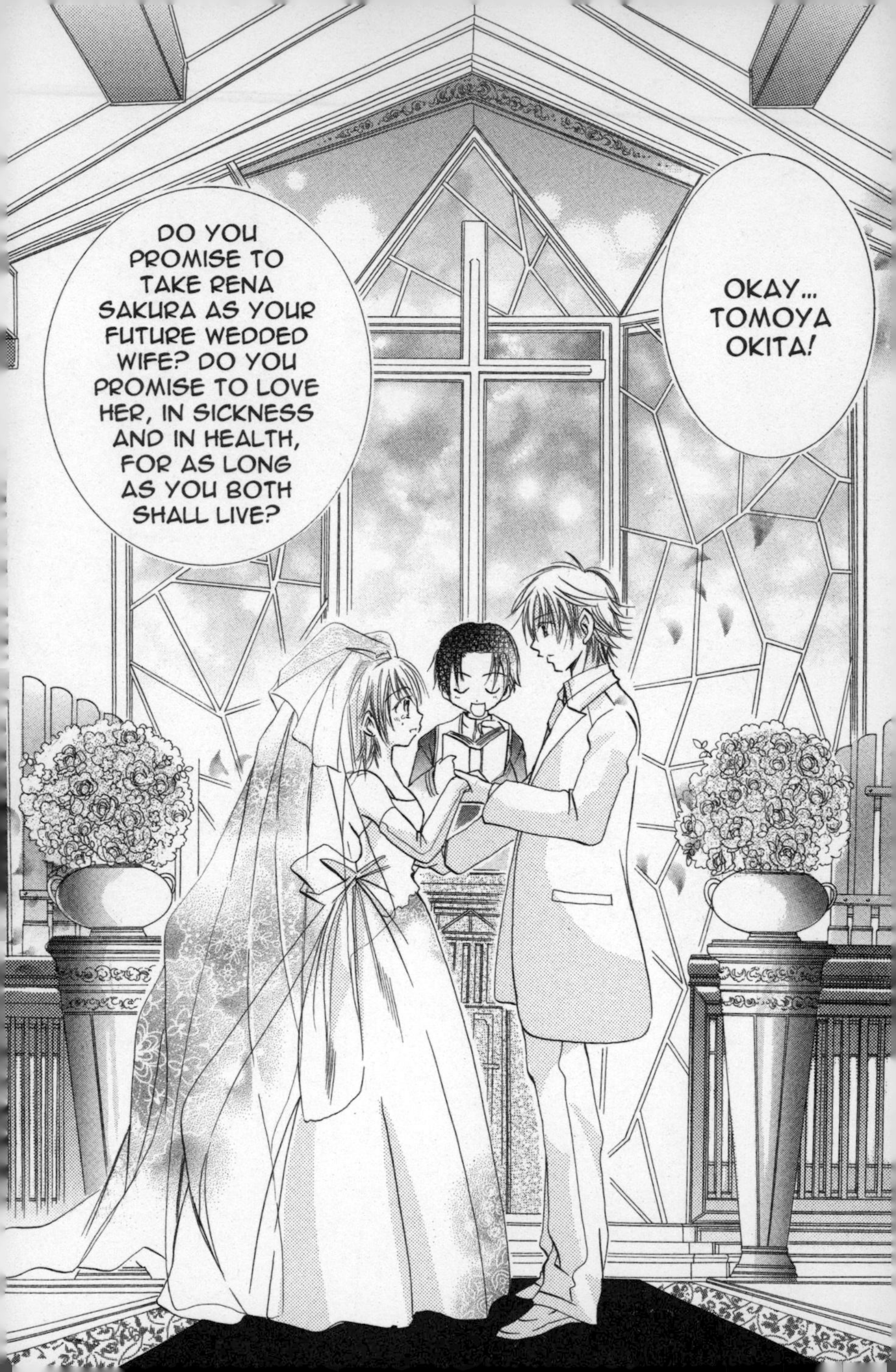
OKAY... TOMOYA OKITA!
DO YOU PROMISE TO TAKE RENA SAKURA AS YOUR FUTURE WEDDED WIFE? DO YOU PROMISE TO LOVE HER, IN SICKNESS AND IN HEALTH, FOR AS LONG AS YOU BOTH SHALL LIVE?

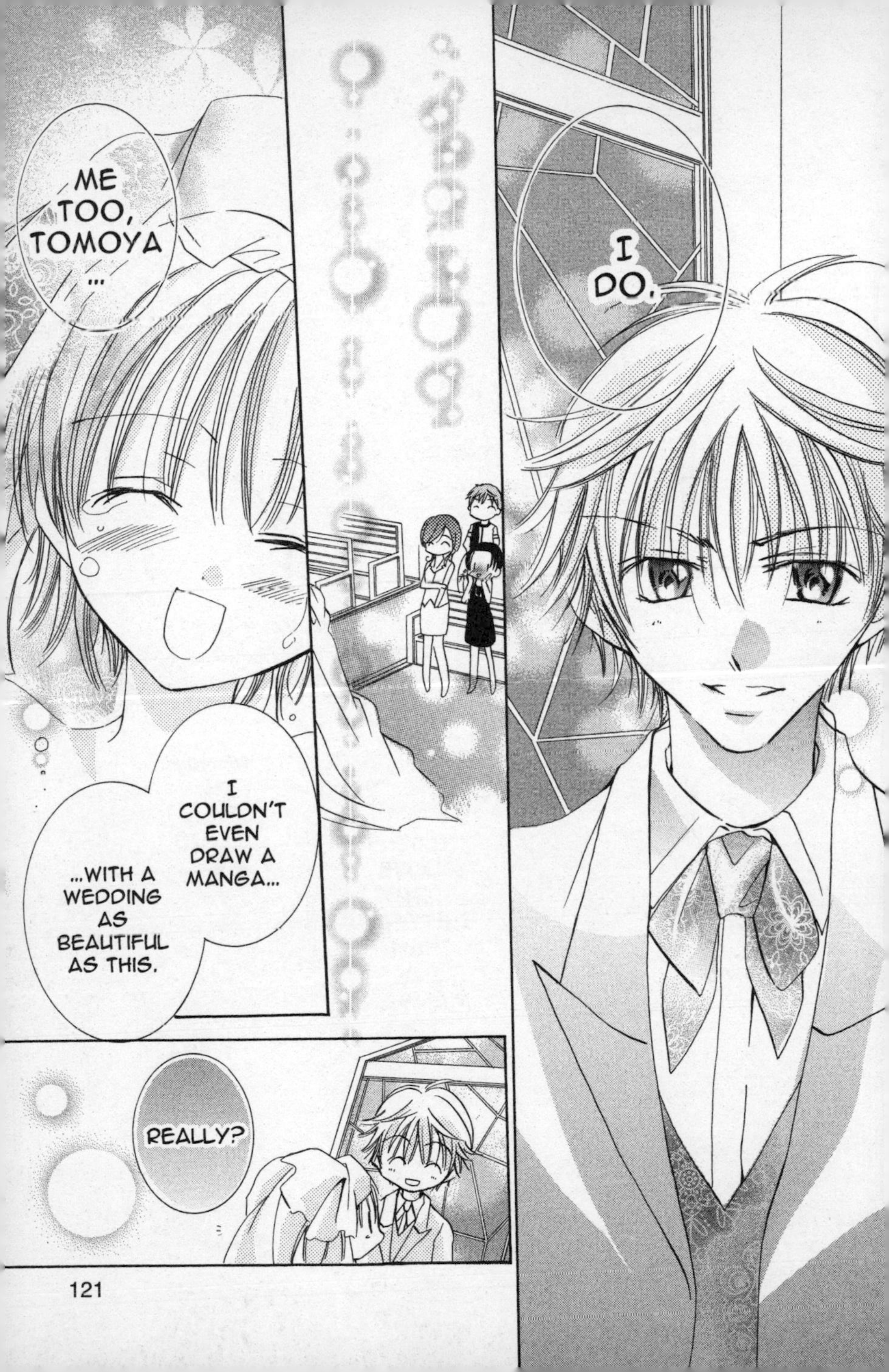
I DO.
ME TOO, TOMOYA...
I COULDN'T EVEN DRAW A MANGA...
...WITH A WEDDING AS BEAUTIFUL AS THIS.
REALLY?

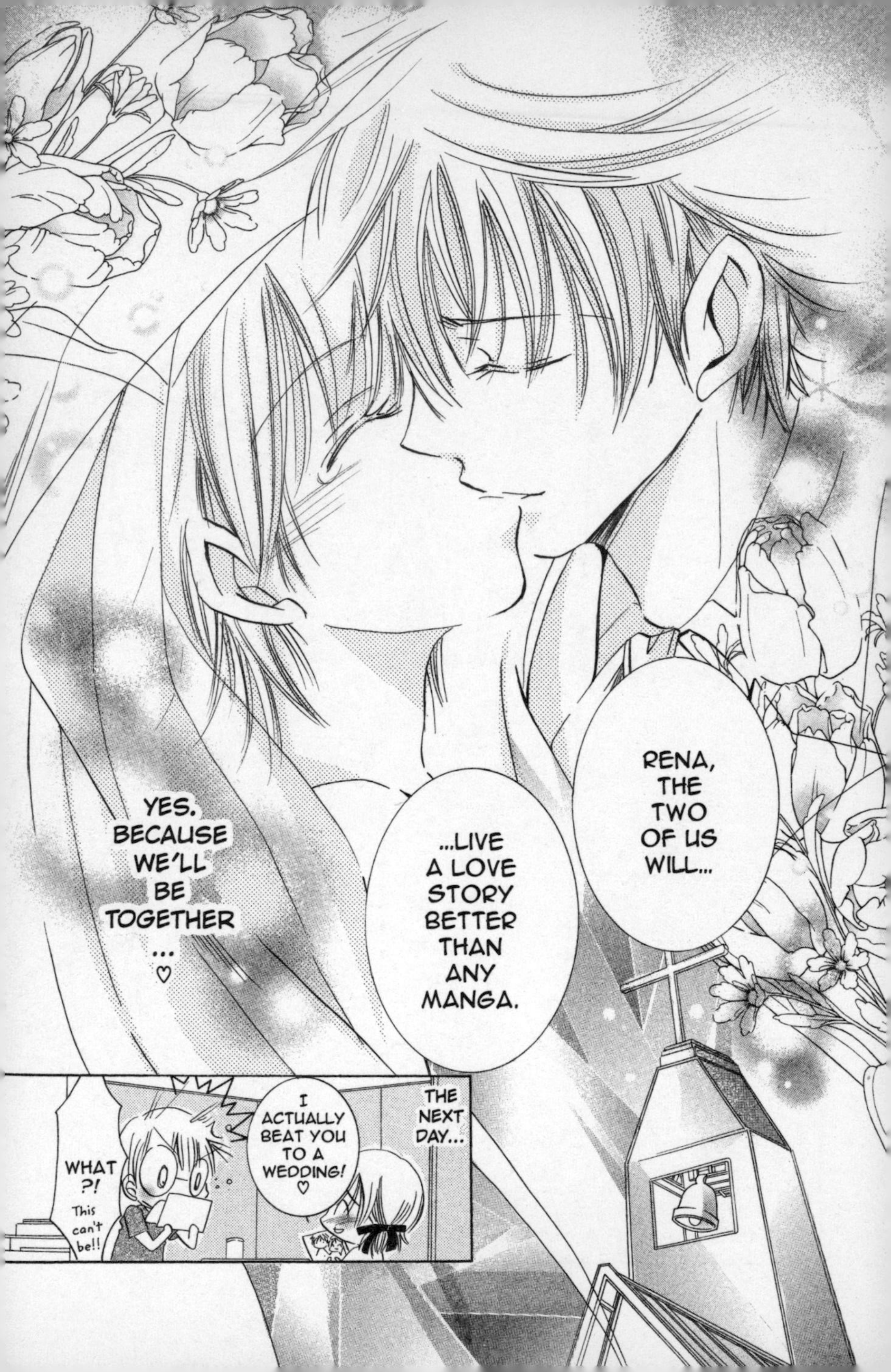
RENA, THE TWO OF US WILL...
...LIVE A LOVE STORY BETTER THAN ANY MANGA.
YES. BECAUSE WE'LL BE TOGETHER ... ♡
THE NEXT DAY...
I ACTUALLY BEAT YOU TO A WEDDING! ♡
WHAT?!
This can't be!!

★ Hello. This is Chitose Yagami. Thanks to all your support, I was able to publish the sequel to *Fall in Love Like a Comic!* I truly appreciate it. Thank you very much.

Fall in Love Like a Comic was my first series. I was then able to go on and keep adding new stories. Now I have the longest standing relationship with these characters. I can only hope that I've grown alongside Rena. *Urrrr.*
Although Rena and Tomoya have already had a wedding ceremony...But!!

They are dear characters to me whom I will never forget. I am truly grateful to them both. Thanks! Especially to Tomoya! I hope you continue to capture the hearts of the young *Ciao* magazine readers. (laugh)

 ※ I've added a bonus story about them in the future... I hope you enjoy that too. It was hard work!

★ I'd now like to comment on as many things I can possibly remember. (laugh)

Fall in Love Like a Comic: Heartthrob Vacation

This is a piece I wrote as a oneshot in the spring of 2003 for *ChuChu* magazine. I felt like I pushed the limits with this one... I had my heart racing during some of it. But I admit I like the story. I think it really embodied Rena and Tomoya. Plus I was able to sneak in a shower scene. *Hey there.*
I especially like Mr. Wakabayashi when he acts like Rena's guardian. (laugh) He's definitely got his hands full...
I think the Mr. Wakabayashi in this chapter is my favorite.

Fall in Love Like a Comic: Happy Ending

This is the last one. Tomoya's ex finally appears… I didn't want to make her evil because she was someone Tomoya used to date, but I still needed something to happen… (laugh)
I struggled on the name, but I was happy with the outcome. I think it was a good last chapter. What do you think? My favorite scene was the wedding at the church… of course. I'm wishing Tomoya and Rena the best. By the way… I struggled painfully with Tomoya's clothes. (laugh)
I spend a lot of time on the boys…
But I love Tomoya. I would gladly give my daughter away to Tomoya if I were a father.
Yep.

Fall in Love Like a Comic: A Small Crush

I was actually working on another series when I did this one, so I had a lot going on.
I wrote it for a summer extra in 2003. I had contemplated doing a horror story instead but when push came to shove, I stuck with what I knew. (laugh)

I got an email from a reader's mother who said that her daughter was excited because her name was Shiori as well (spelled with the same kanji). Apparently the other way of spelling it is the more common way. I think it's an adorable name either way.

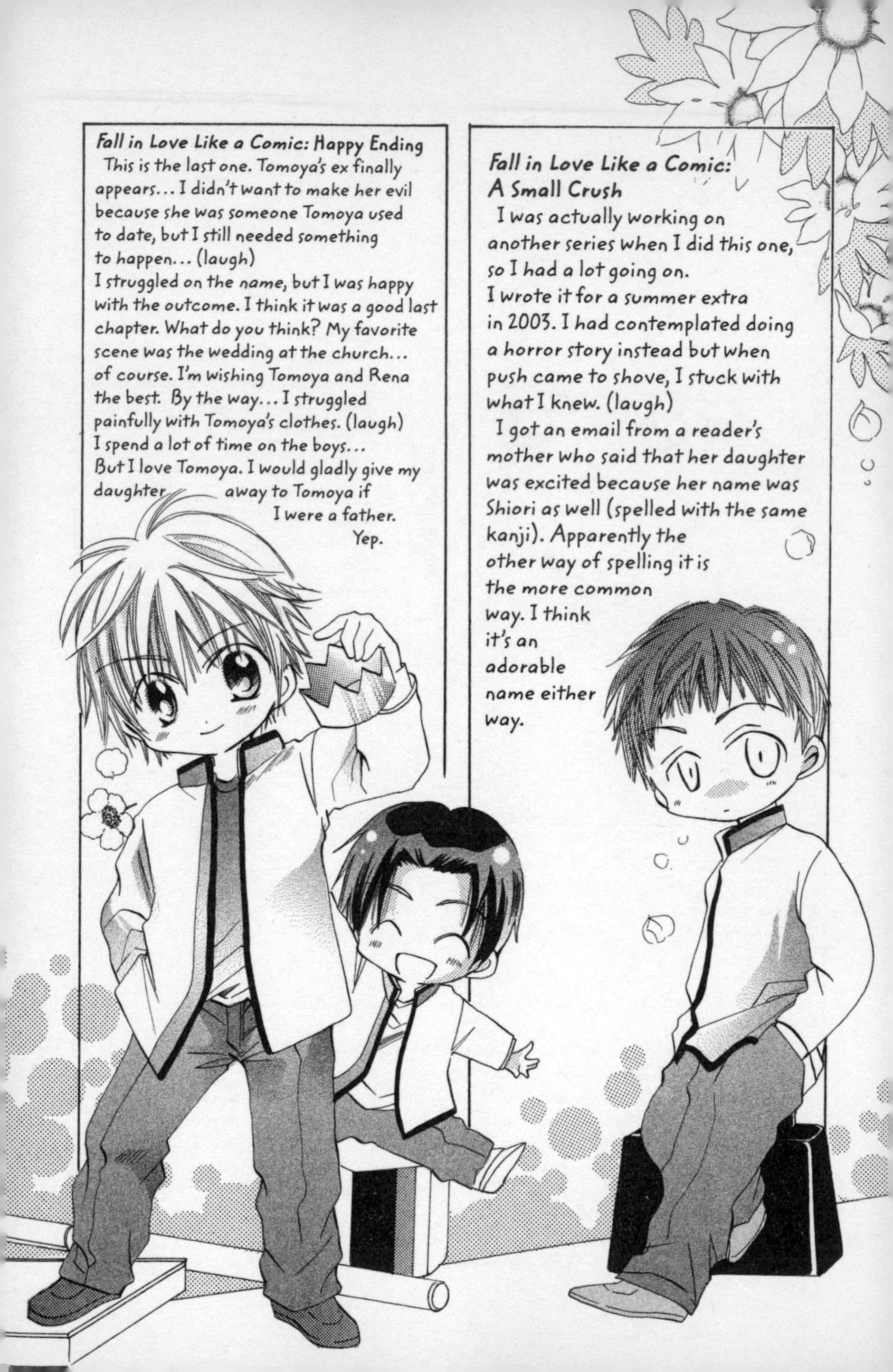

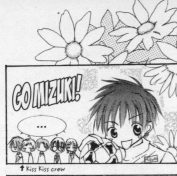

★ I am so grateful for all the feedback I've gotten, and not just for FLLC. I'm always so encouraged. Thank you.
I know all the regulars by name. I haven't had enough time to write back these days, but I'm hoping to be able to thank you again when I have the time.
I'm also grateful for the gifts that you sent to me, like souvenirs from trips. But please remember that it's not necessary. I'm just thankful to get a letter. That's all it really takes to get me going. Speaking of letters, I often find profile templates enclosed with my letters but haven't had the time to fill them out...
I know it's not the same, but I've included a personal profile.
(See page 186.)
I hope you'll continue to enjoy my manga. Hope to see you again in *Kiss Kiss* 1.

GO MIZUKI!
...
Mizuki
↑ Kiss Kiss crew

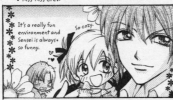

So cozy.
It's a really fun environment and Sensei is always so funny.

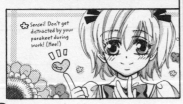

Sensei! Don't get distracted by your parakeet during work! (Hee!)

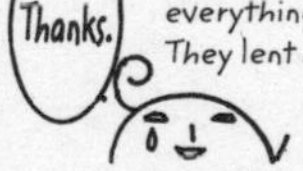

Thanks.

These are my assistants who make everything happy. Thank you so much. They lent me their help for "Happy Ending."

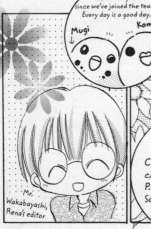

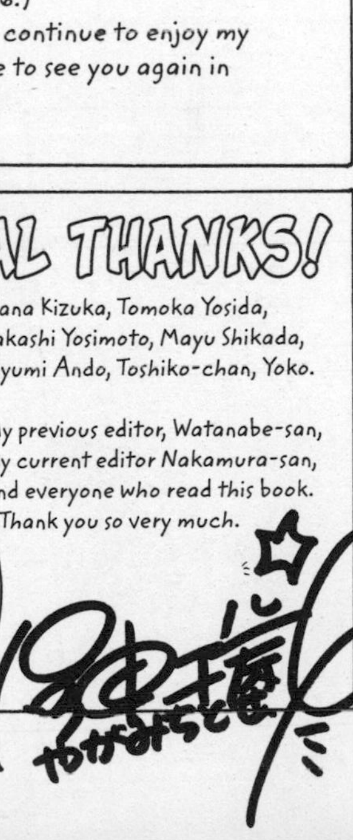

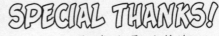

SPECIAL THANKS!

Nana Kizuka, Tomoka Yosida, Takashi Yosimoto, Mayu Shikada, Ayumi Ando, Toshiko-chan, Yoko.

My previous editor, Watanabe-san, my current editor Nakamura-san, and everyone who read this book. Thank you so very much.

It's been a year since we've joined the team. Every day is a good day.
Komugi
Mugi
Mr. Wakabayashi, Rena's editor

★ Fan letters:

Chitose Yagami
c/o Nancy Thistlethwaite
P.O. Box 77010
San Francisco, CA 94107

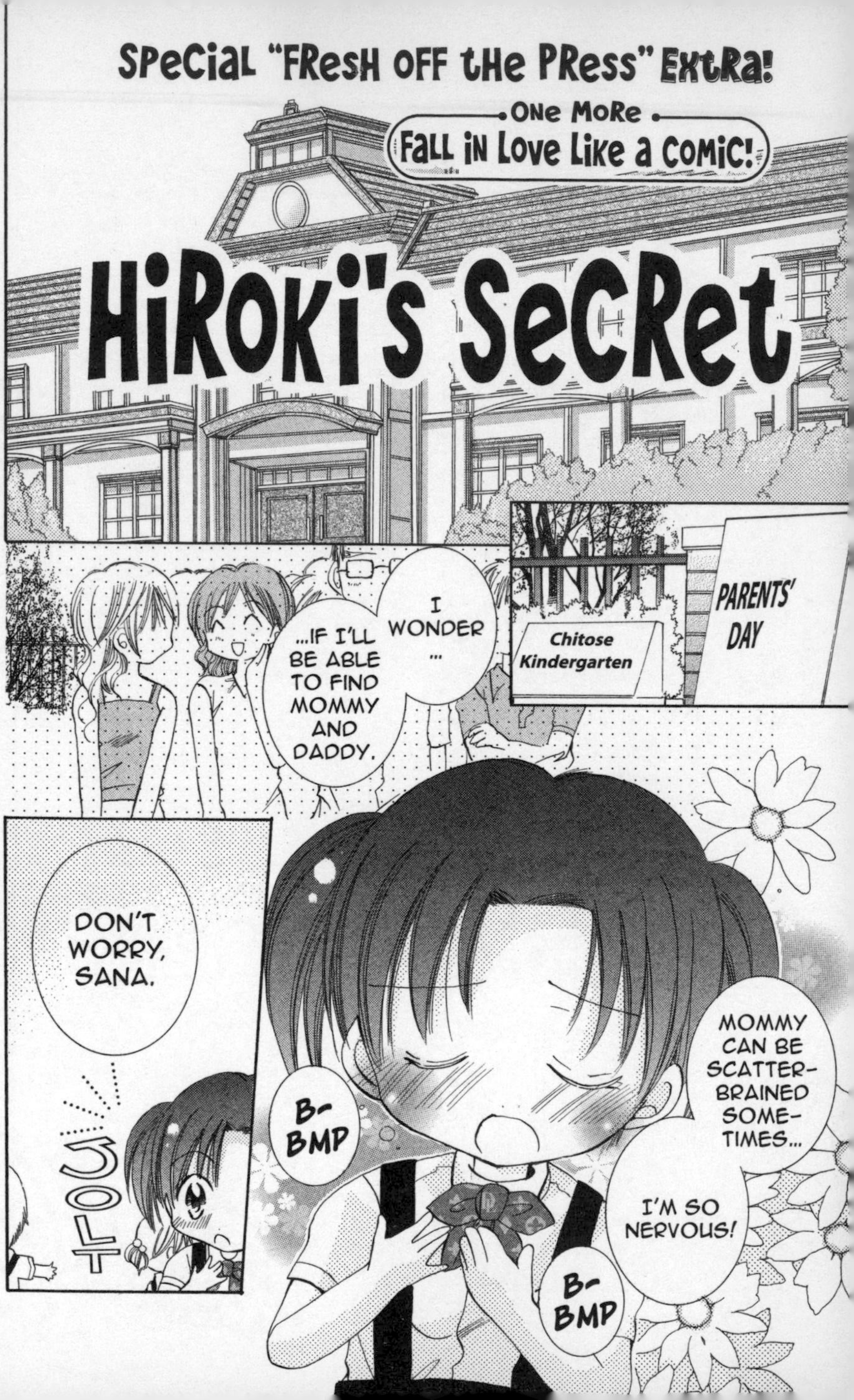
Special "Fresh off the Press" Extra!
One More
Fall in Love Like a Comic!
Hiroki's Secret
Chitose Kindergarten
PARENTS' DAY
I WONDER ...
...IF I'LL BE ABLE TO FIND MOMMY AND DADDY.
MOMMY CAN BE SCATTER-BRAINED SOME-TIMES...
B-BMP
I'M SO NERVOUS!
B-BMP
DON'T WORRY, SANA.
JOLT

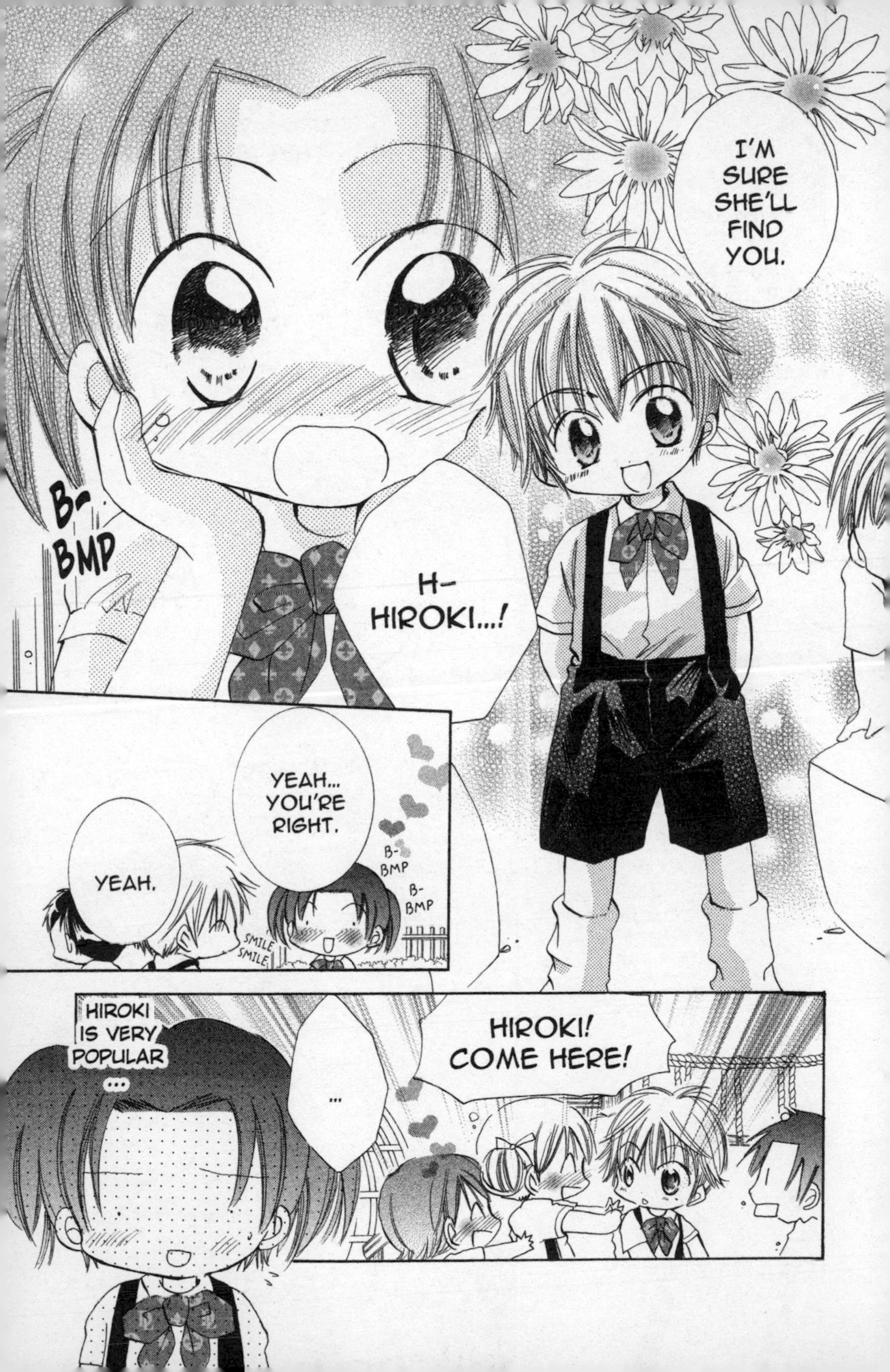
I'M SURE SHE'LL FIND YOU.
H-HIROKI...!
B-BMP
YEAH... YOU'RE RIGHT.
B-BMP
B-BMP
YEAH.
SMILE SMILE
HIROKI! COME HERE!
...
HIROKI IS VERY POPULAR ...

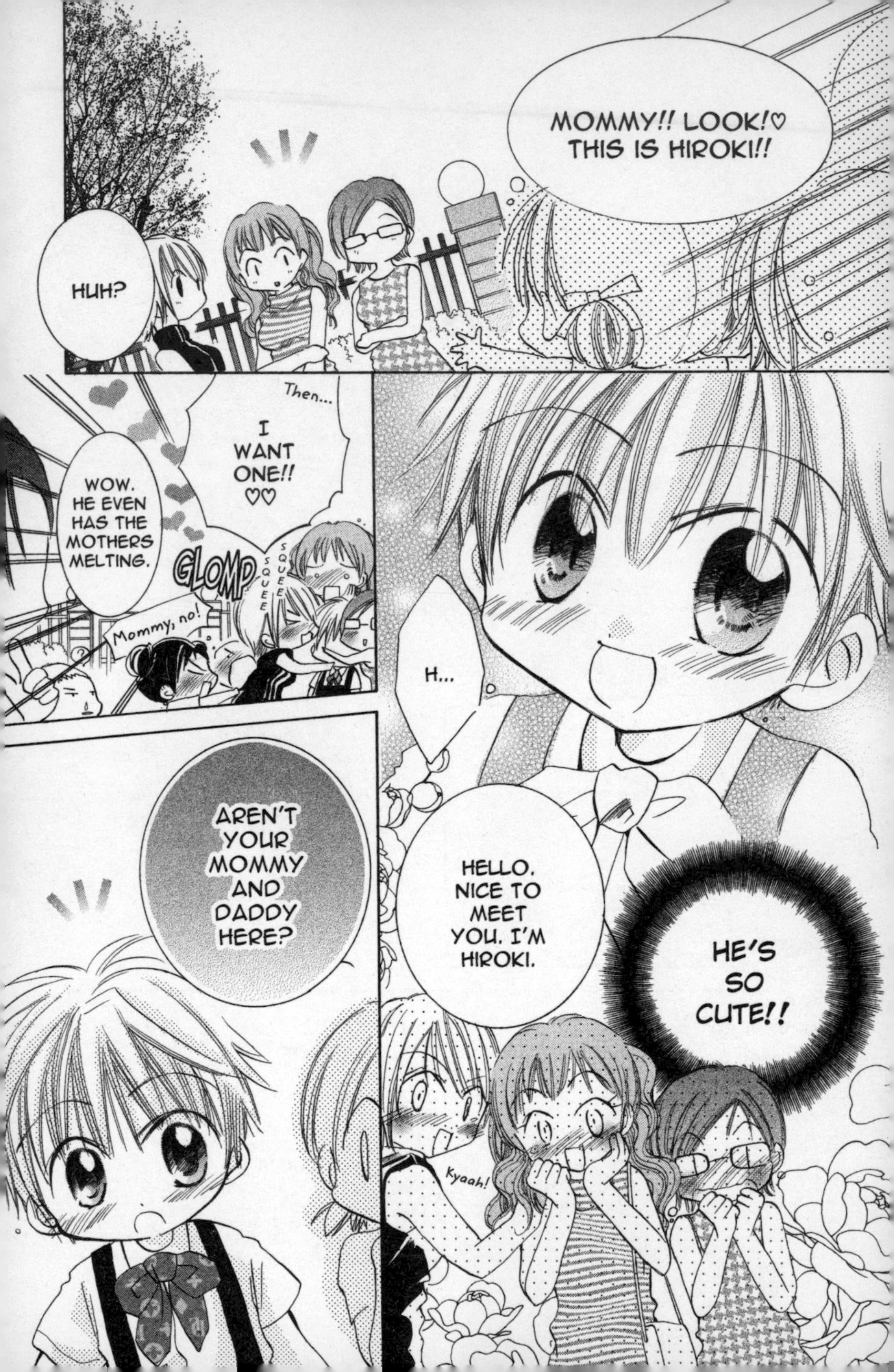
MOMMY!! LOOK!♡ THIS IS HIROKI!!
HUH?
H...
HELLO. NICE TO MEET YOU. I'M HIROKI.
HE'S SO CUTE!!
Kyaah!
Then...
I WANT ONE!! ♡♡
WOW. HE EVEN HAS THE MOTHERS MELTING.
GLOMP
SQUEE
SQUEE
Mommy, no!
AREN'T YOUR MOMMY AND DADDY HERE?

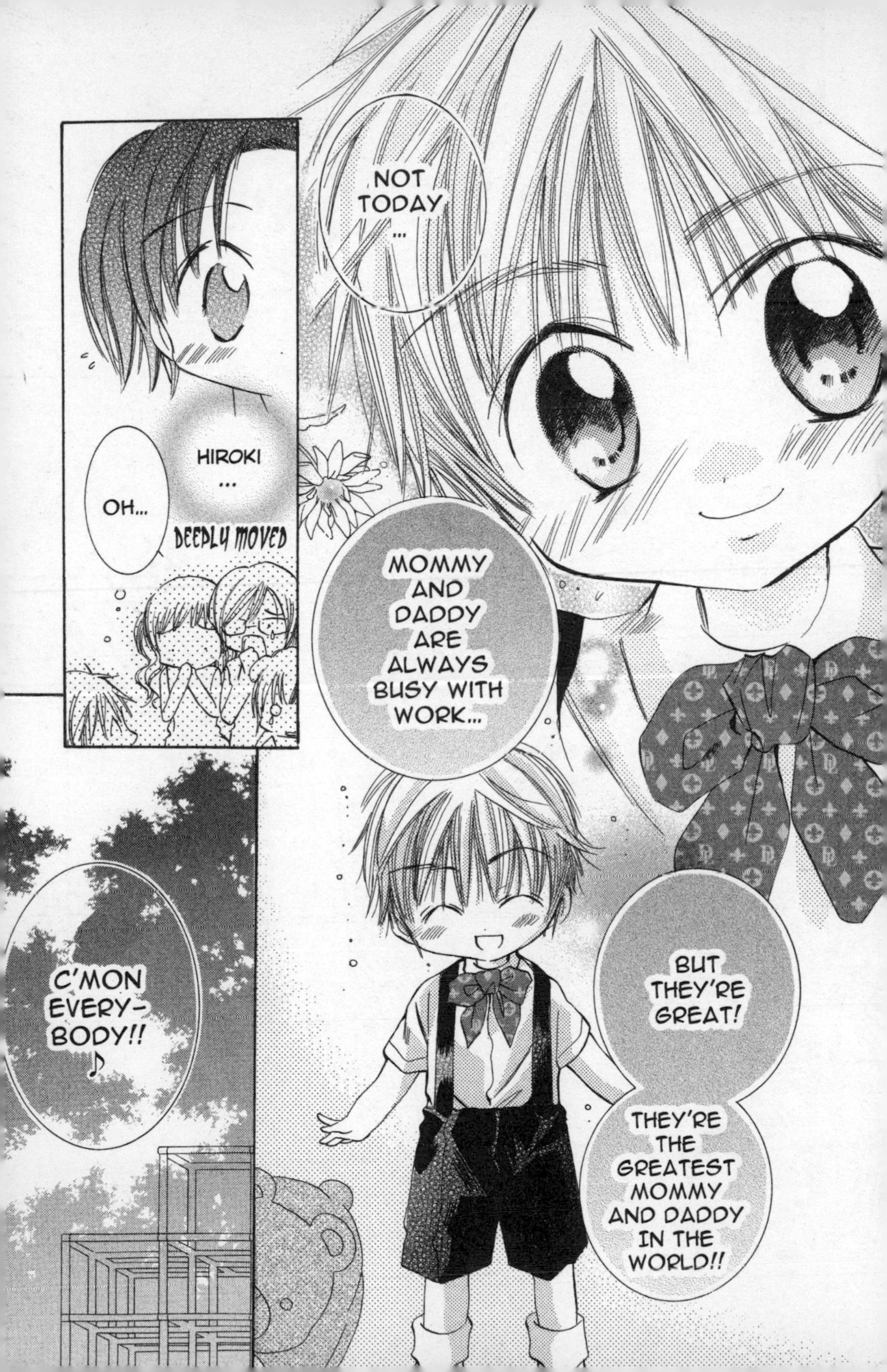
NOT TODAY ...
MOMMY AND DADDY ARE ALWAYS BUSY WITH WORK...
BUT THEY'RE GREAT!
THEY'RE THE GREATEST MOMMY AND DADDY IN THE WORLD!!
HIROKI ...
OH...
DEEPLY MOVED
C'MON EVERY-BODY!! ♪

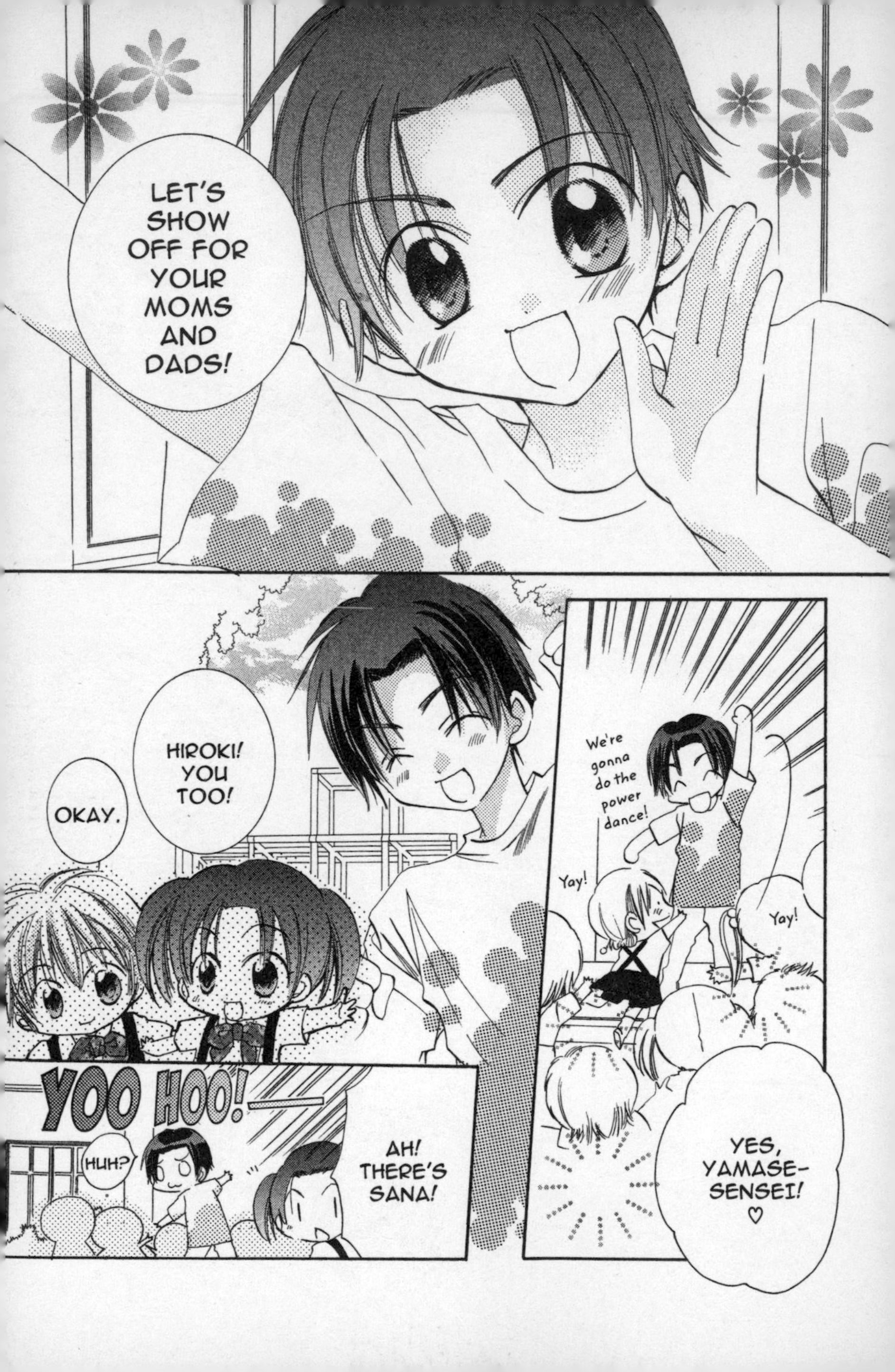
LET'S SHOW OFF FOR YOUR MOMS AND DADS!
We're gonna do the power dance!
Yay!
Yay!
YES, YAMASE-SENSEI! ♡
HIROKI! YOU TOO!
OKAY.
AH! THERE'S SANA!
YOO HOO!
HUH?

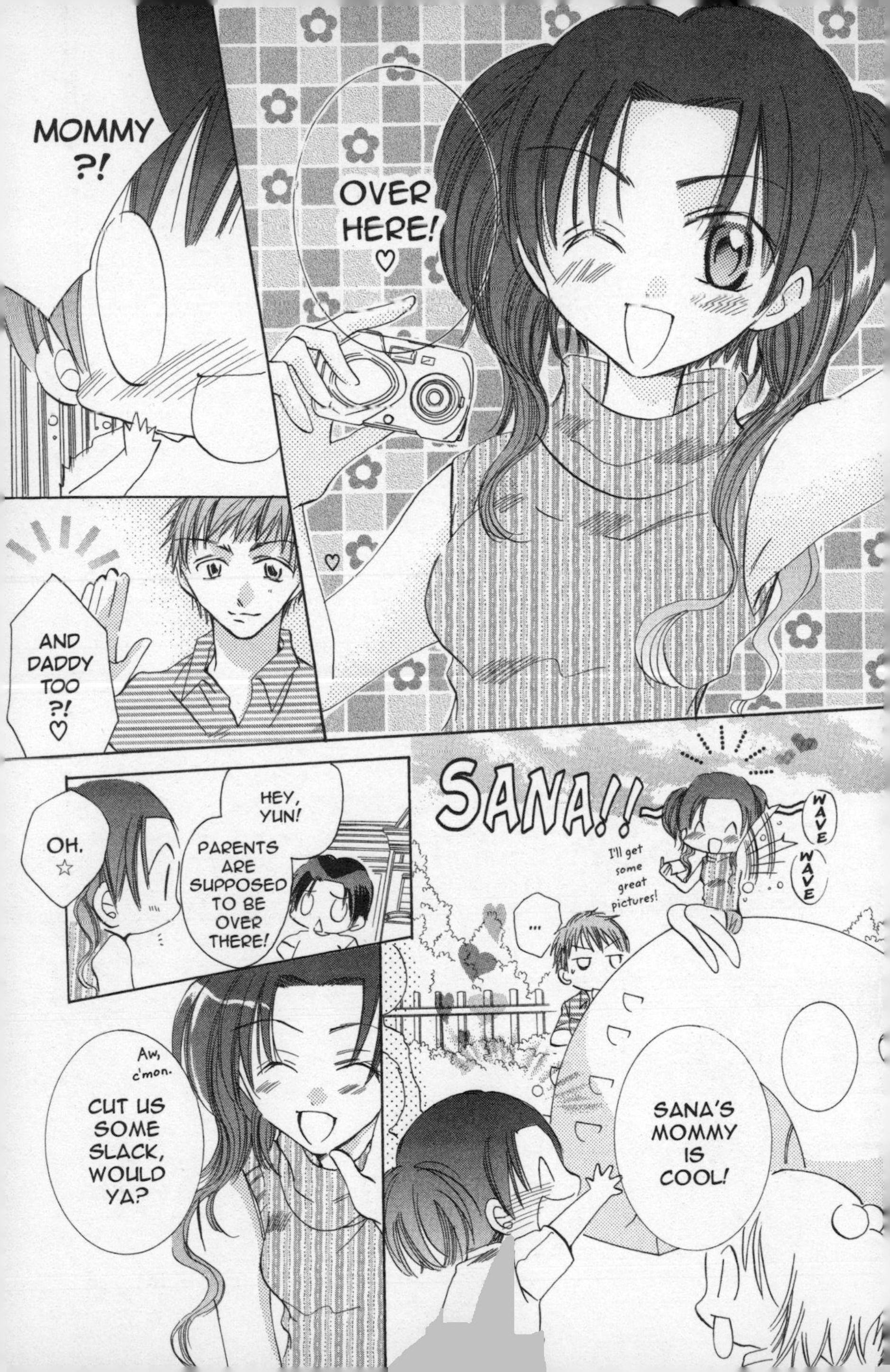
OVER HERE! ♡
MOMMY ?!
AND DADDY TOO ?! ♡
SANA!!
WAVE WAVE
I'll get some great pictures!
...
HEY, YUN!
PARENTS ARE SUPPOSED TO BE OVER THERE!
OH. ☆
Aw, c'mon.
CUT US SOME SLACK, WOULD YA?
SANA'S MOMMY IS COOL!

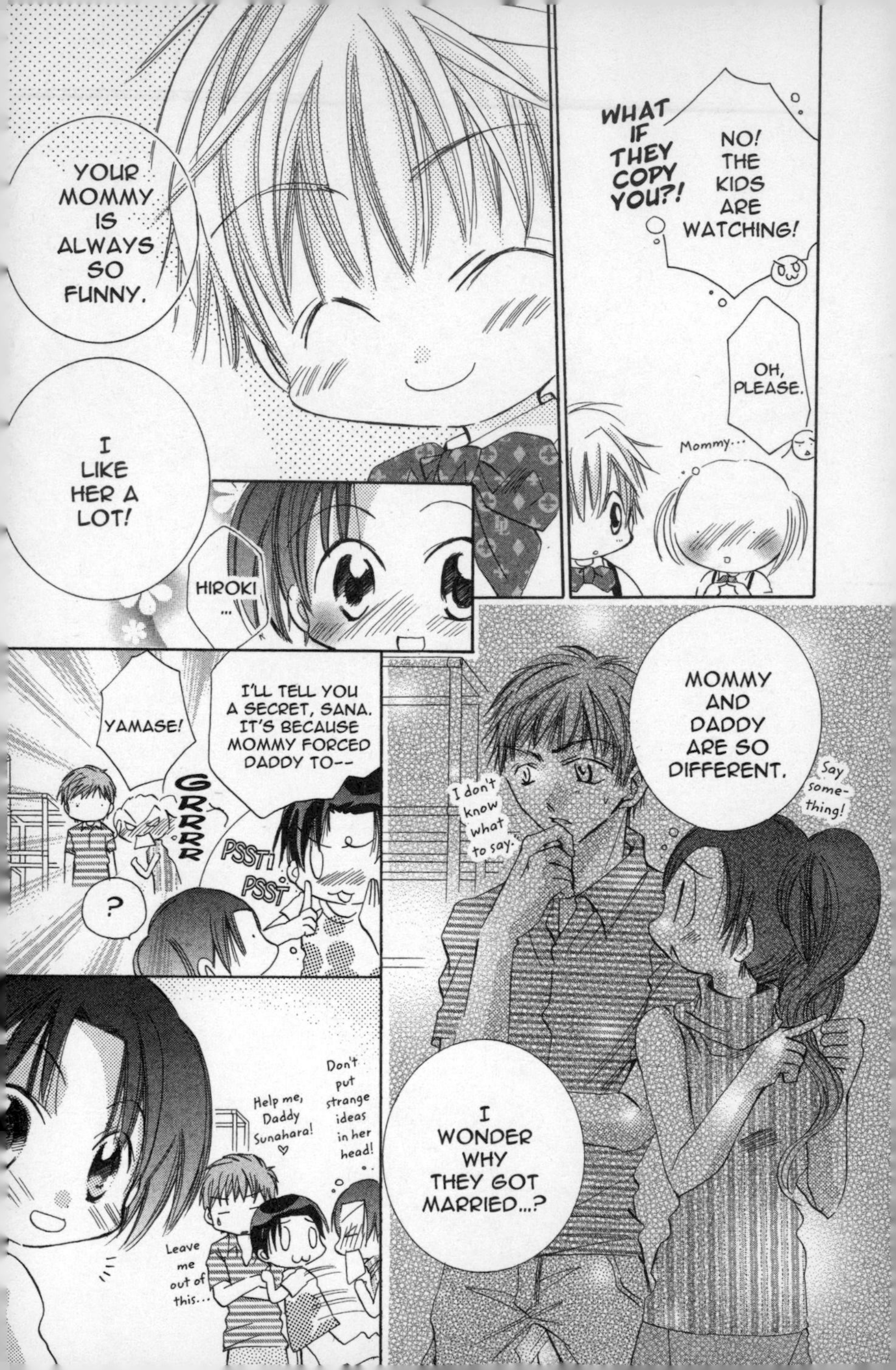
WHAT IF THEY COPY YOU?!
NO! THE KIDS ARE WATCHING!
OH, PLEASE.
Mommy...
YOUR MOMMY IS ALWAYS SO FUNNY.
I LIKE HER A LOT!
HIROKI...
MOMMY AND DADDY ARE SO DIFFERENT.
Say something!
I don't know what to say.
I WONDER WHY THEY GOT MARRIED...?
I'LL TELL YOU A SECRET, SANA. IT'S BECAUSE MOMMY FORCED DADDY TO--
YAMASE!
GRRRR
PSST! PSST
?
Don't put strange ideas in her head!
Help me, Daddy Sunahara! ♥
Leave me out of this...

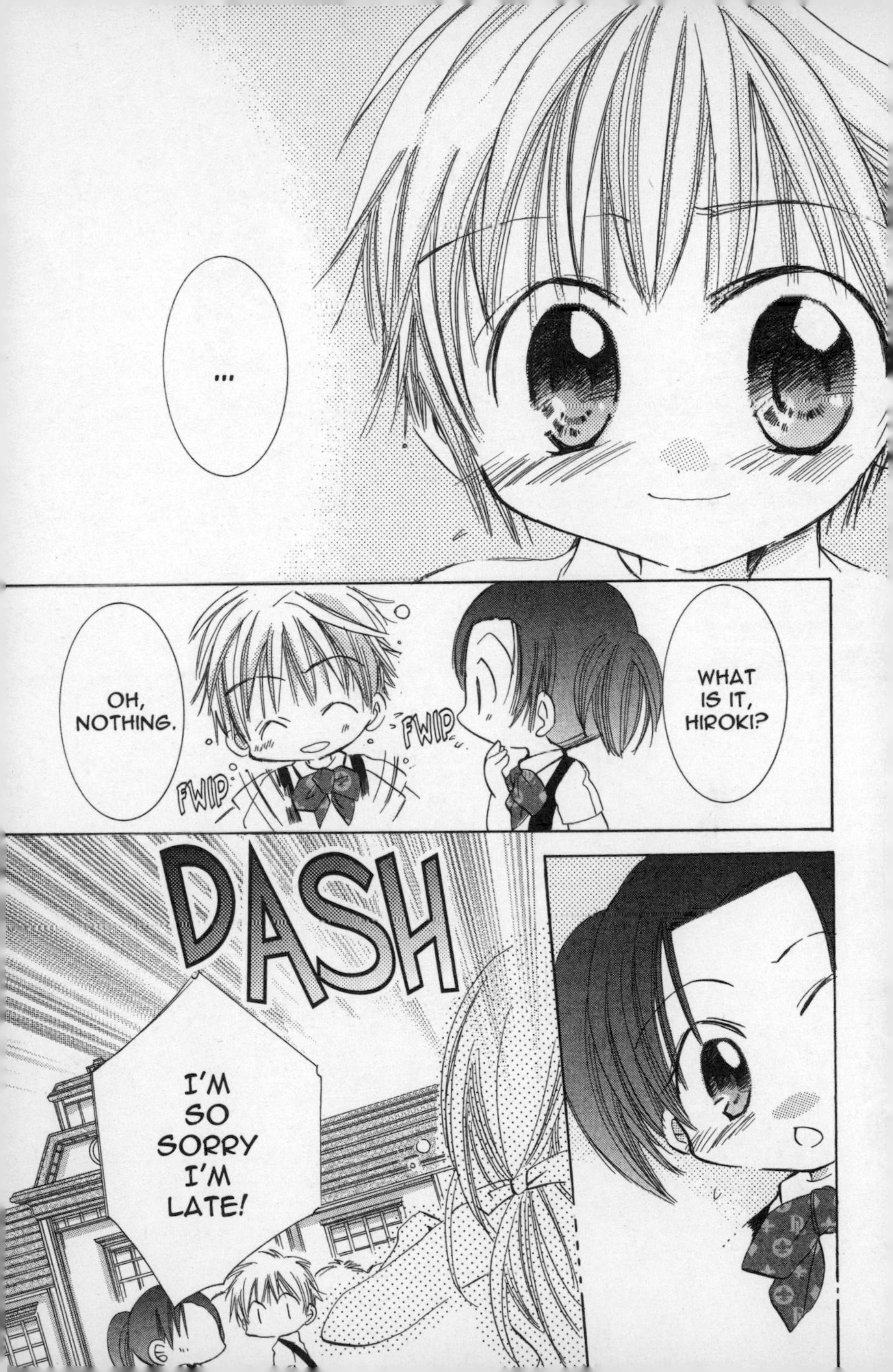
...
WHAT IS IT, HIROKI?
FWIP
OH, NOTHING.
FWIP
DASH
I'M SO SORRY I'M LATE!

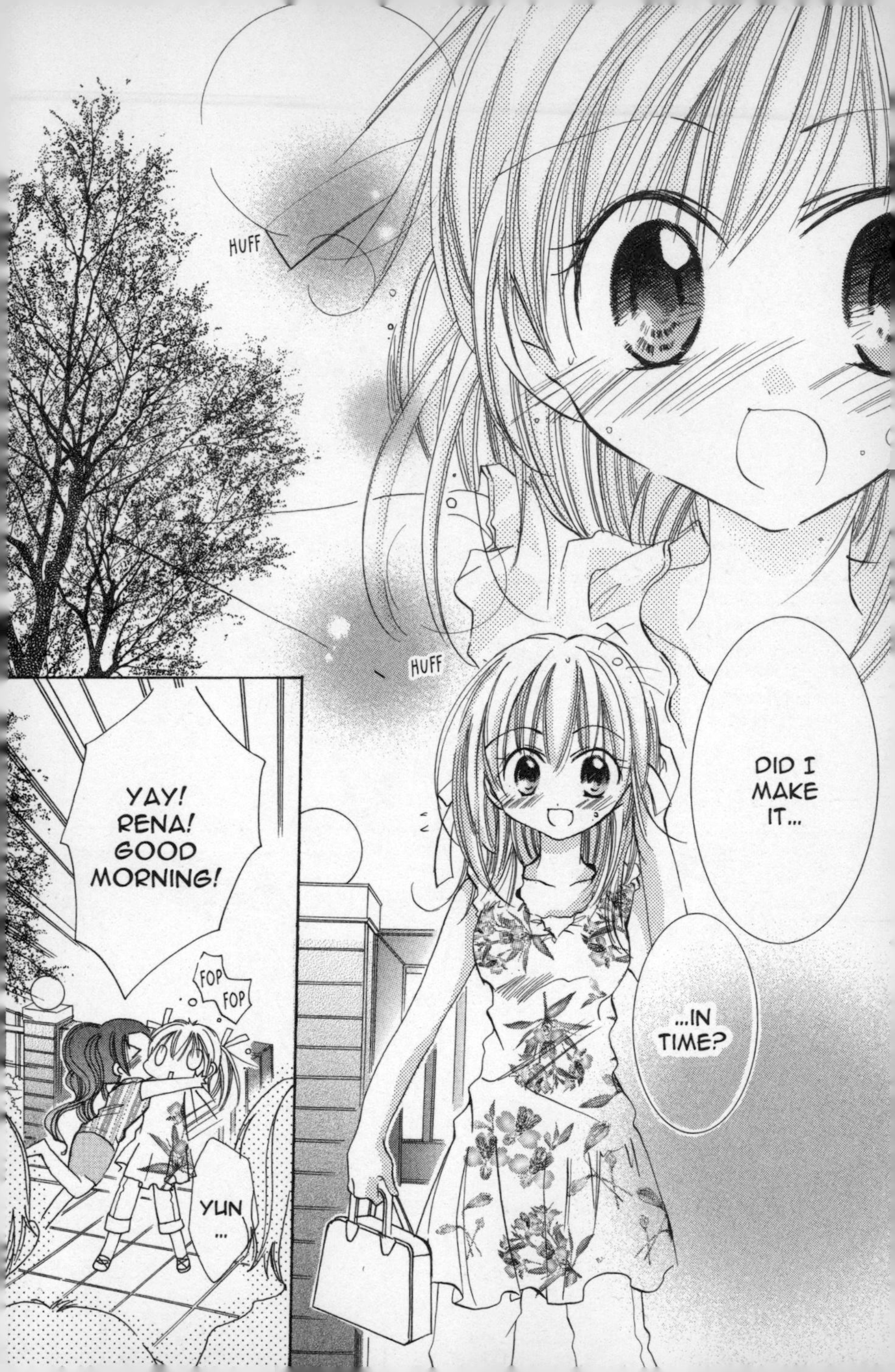
HUFF
HUFF
DID I MAKE IT...
...IN TIME?
YAY! RENA! GOOD MORNING!
FOP FOP
YUN ...

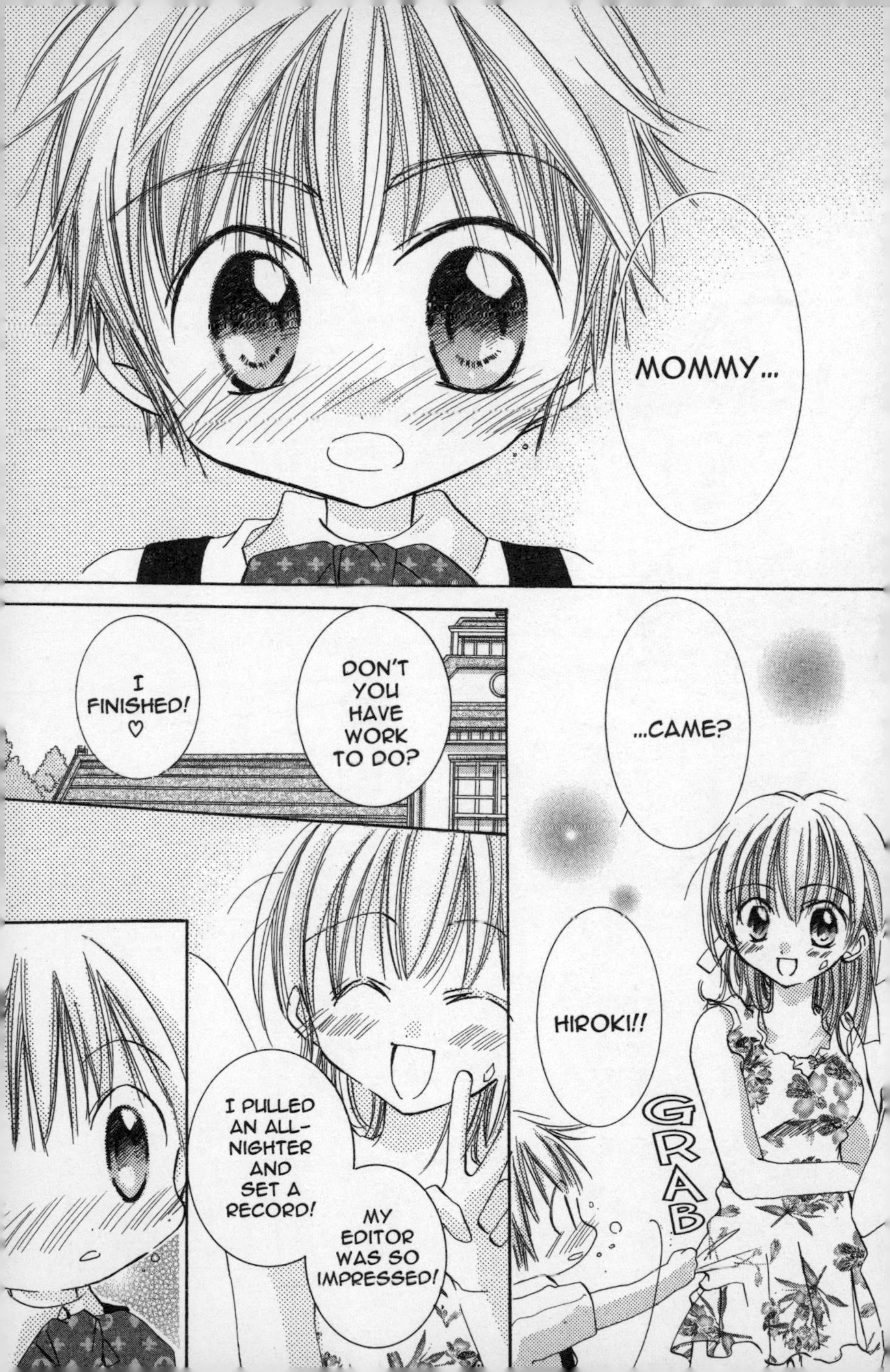
MOMMY...
...CAME?
HIROKI!!
GRAB
DON'T YOU HAVE WORK TO DO?
I FINISHED! ♡
I PULLED AN ALL-NIGHTER AND SET A RECORD!
MY EDITOR WAS SO IMPRESSED!

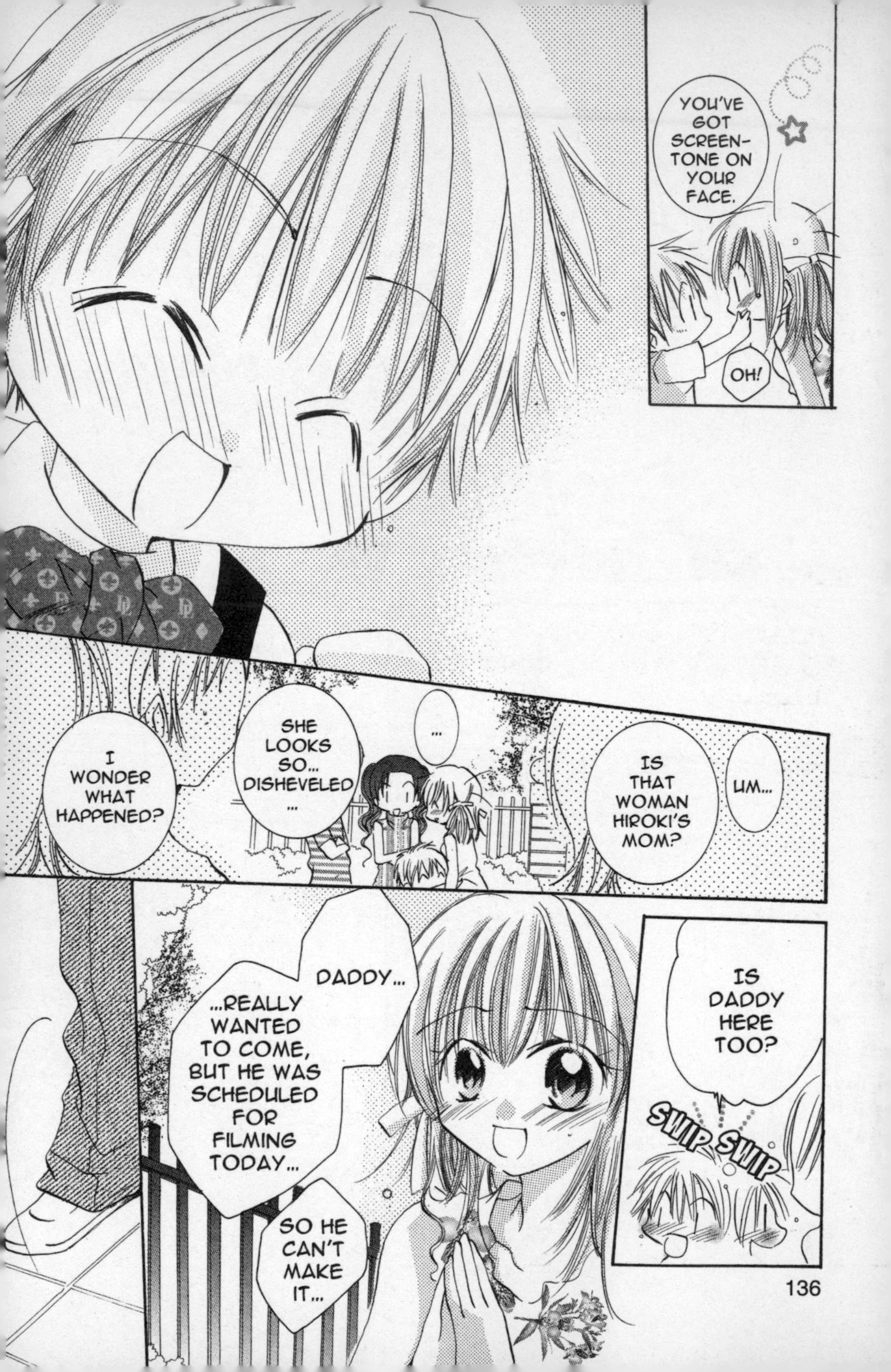

YOU'VE GOT SCREEN-TONE ON YOUR FACE.
OH!
UM...
IS THAT WOMAN HIROKI'S MOM?
...
SHE LOOKS SO... DISHEVELED...
I WONDER WHAT HAPPENED?
IS DADDY HERE TOO?
SWIP SWIP
DADDY...
...REALLY WANTED TO COME, BUT HE WAS SCHEDULED FOR FILMING TODAY...
SO HE CAN'T MAKE IT...

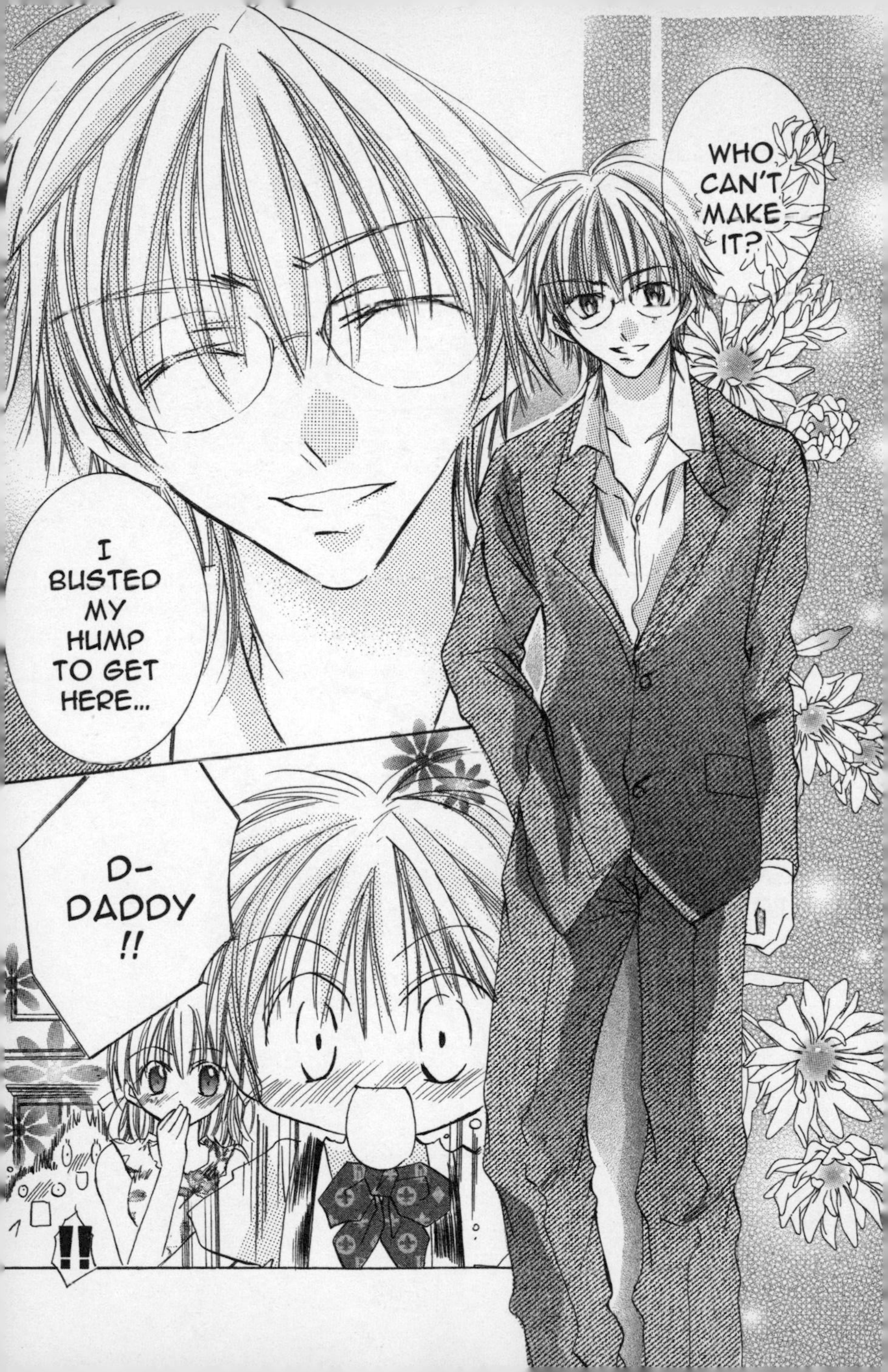
WHO CAN'T MAKE IT?
I BUSTED MY HUMP TO GET HERE...
D-DADDY !!
!!

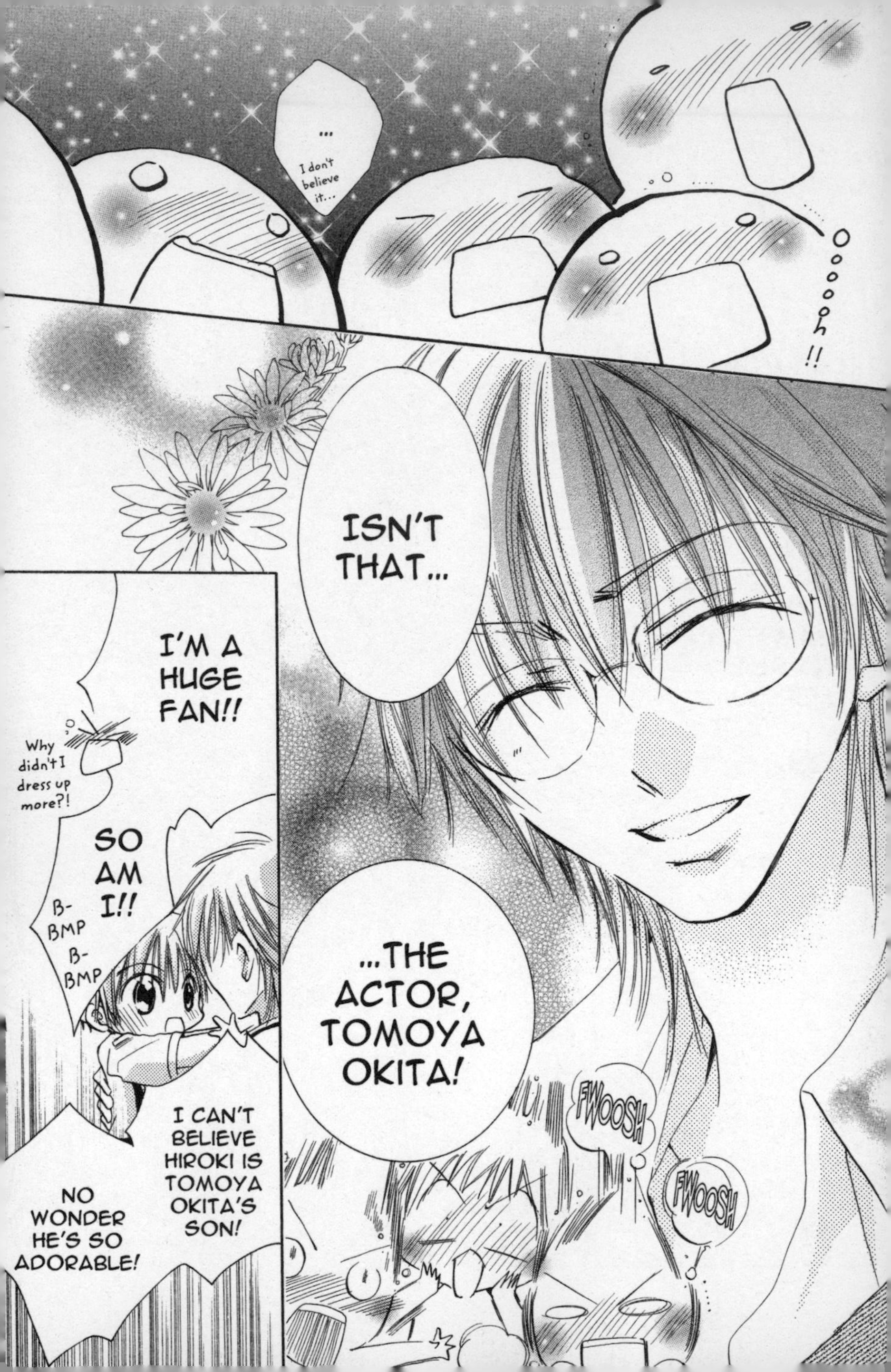
Ooooooh!!
...
I don't believe it...
ISN'T THAT...
...THE ACTOR, TOMOYA OKITA!
FWOOSH
FWOOSH
I'M A HUGE FAN!!
Why didn't I dress up more?!
SO AM I!!
B-BMP B-BMP
I CAN'T BELIEVE HIROKI IS TOMOYA OKITA'S SON!
NO WONDER HE'S SO ADORABLE!

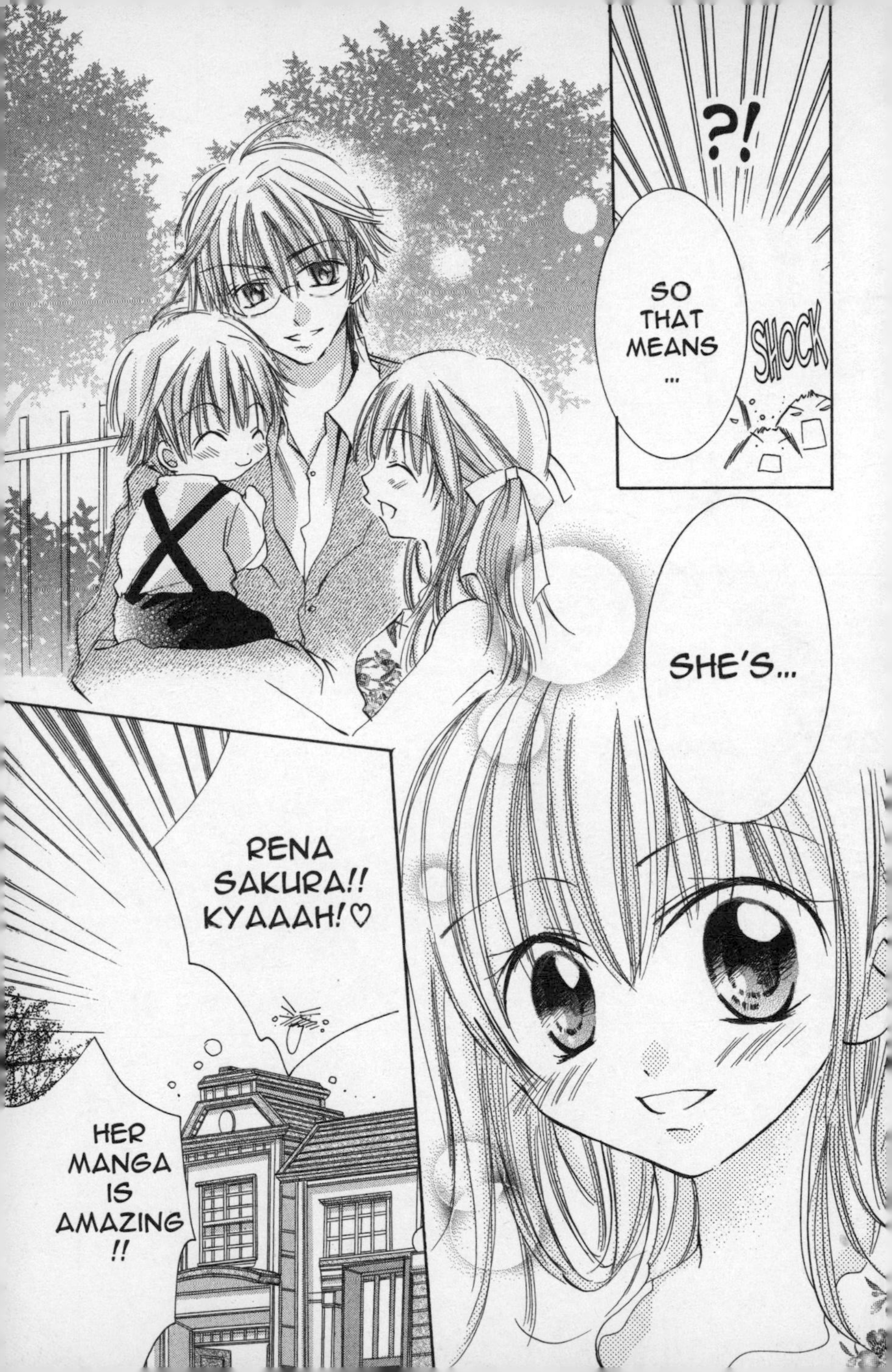
?!
SO THAT MEANS...
SHOCK
SHE'S...
RENA SAKURA!! KYAAAH!♡
HER MANGA IS AMAZING!!

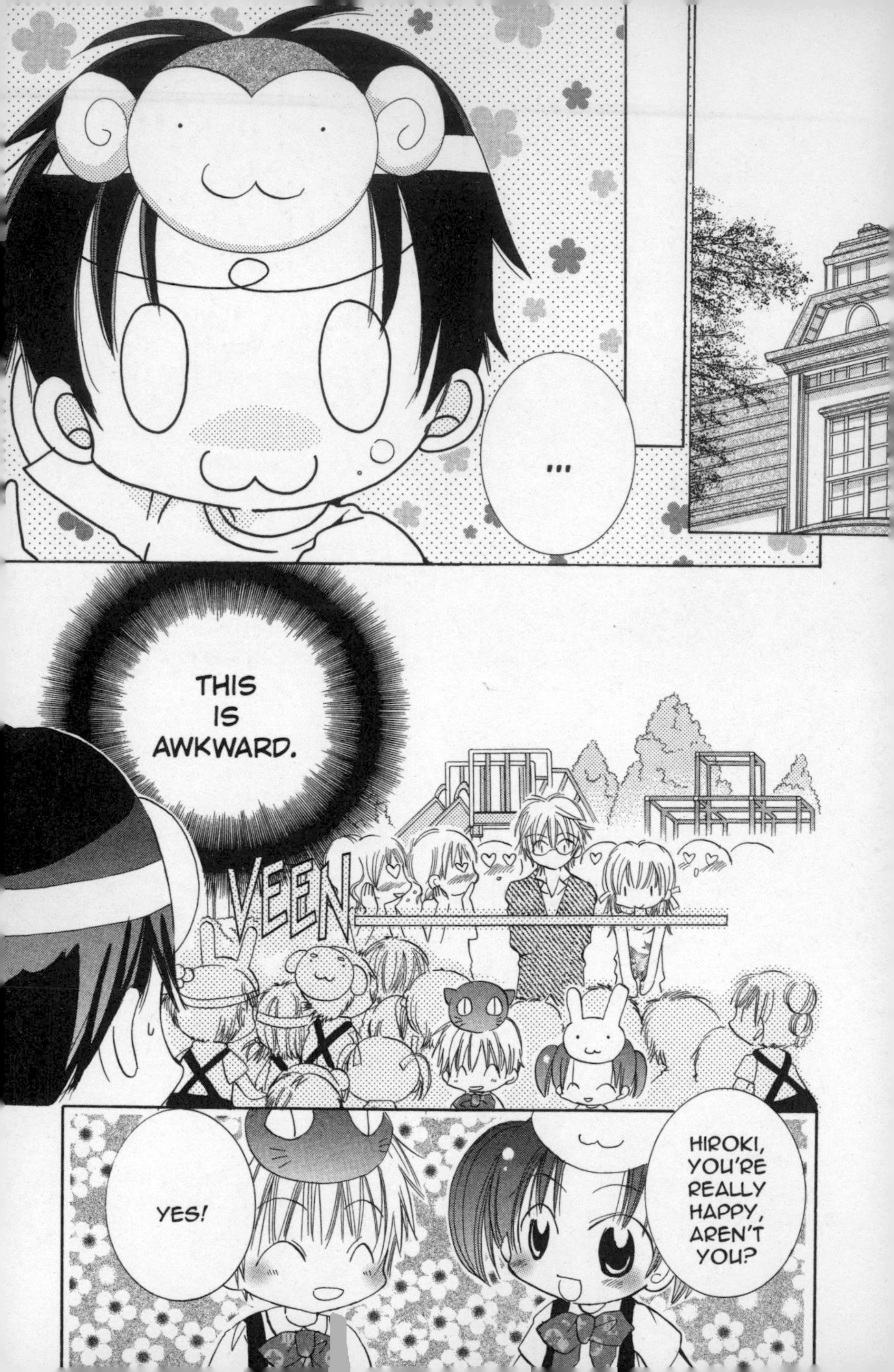
...
THIS IS AWKWARD.
VEEN
HIROKI, YOU'RE REALLY HAPPY, AREN'T YOU?
YES!

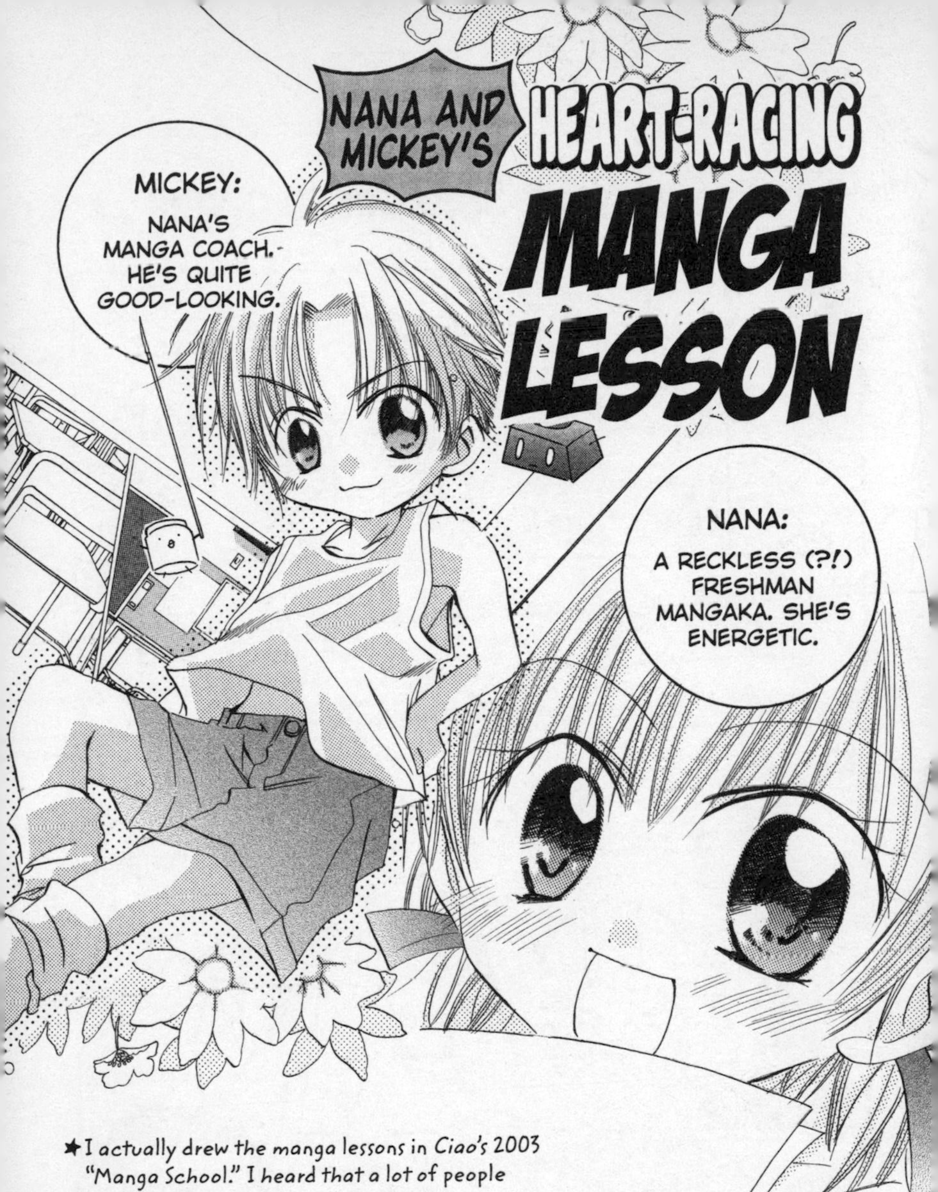
NANA AND MICKEY'S
HEART-RACING MANGA LESSON
NANA: A RECKLESS (?!) FRESHMAN MANGAKA. SHE'S ENERGETIC.
MICKEY: NANA'S MANGA COACH. HE'S QUITE GOOD-LOOKING.

★I actually drew the manga lessons in *Ciao's* 2003 "Manga School." I heard that a lot of people said they wanted to become mangaka, so I hope this helps. Let's get started then. Hope it's not too painful.

Yagami, 2004

☆Getting Your Supplies in Order☆

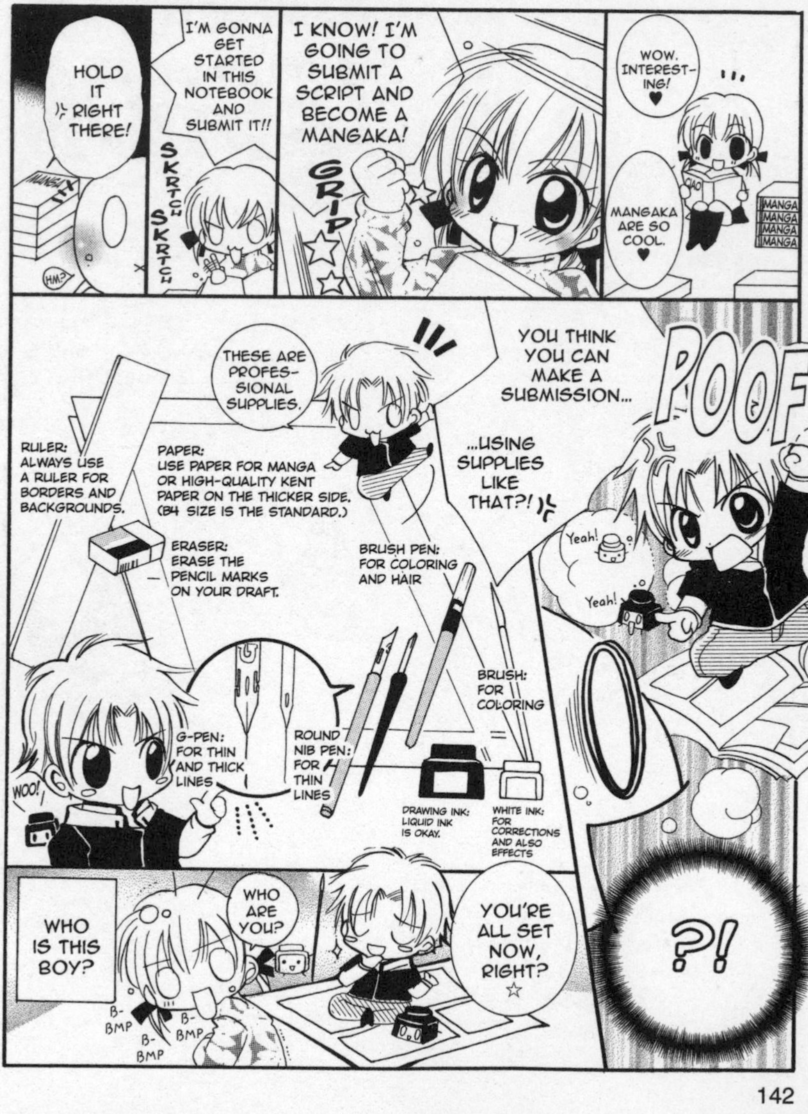
WOW. INTERESTING! ♥
MANGAKA ARE SO COOL. ♥
CIAO
MANGA
MANGA
MANGA
MANGA
I KNOW! I'M GOING TO SUBMIT A SCRIPT AND BECOME A MANGAKA!
GRIP
I'M GONNA GET STARTED IN THIS NOTEBOOK AND SUBMIT IT!!
SKRTCH
SKRTCH
HOLD IT RIGHT THERE!
MANGA
HM?
POOF
YOU THINK YOU CAN MAKE A SUBMISSION...
...USING SUPPLIES LIKE THAT?!
Yeah!
Yeah!
THESE ARE PROFESSIONAL SUPPLIES.
RULER: ALWAYS USE A RULER FOR BORDERS AND BACKGROUNDS.
PAPER: USE PAPER FOR MANGA OR HIGH-QUALITY KENT PAPER ON THE THICKER SIDE. (B4 SIZE IS THE STANDARD.)
ERASER: ERASE THE PENCIL MARKS ON YOUR DRAFT.
BRUSH PEN: FOR COLORING AND HAIR
BRUSH: FOR COLORING
G-PEN: FOR THIN AND THICK LINES
ROUND NIB PEN: FOR THIN LINES
DRAWING INK: LIQUID INK IS OKAY.
WHITE INK: FOR CORRECTIONS AND ALSO EFFECTS
WOO!
?!
YOU'RE ALL SET NOW, RIGHT? ☆
WHO ARE YOU?
WHO IS THIS BOY?
B-BMP
B-BMP
B-BMP

☆Creating the Characters☆

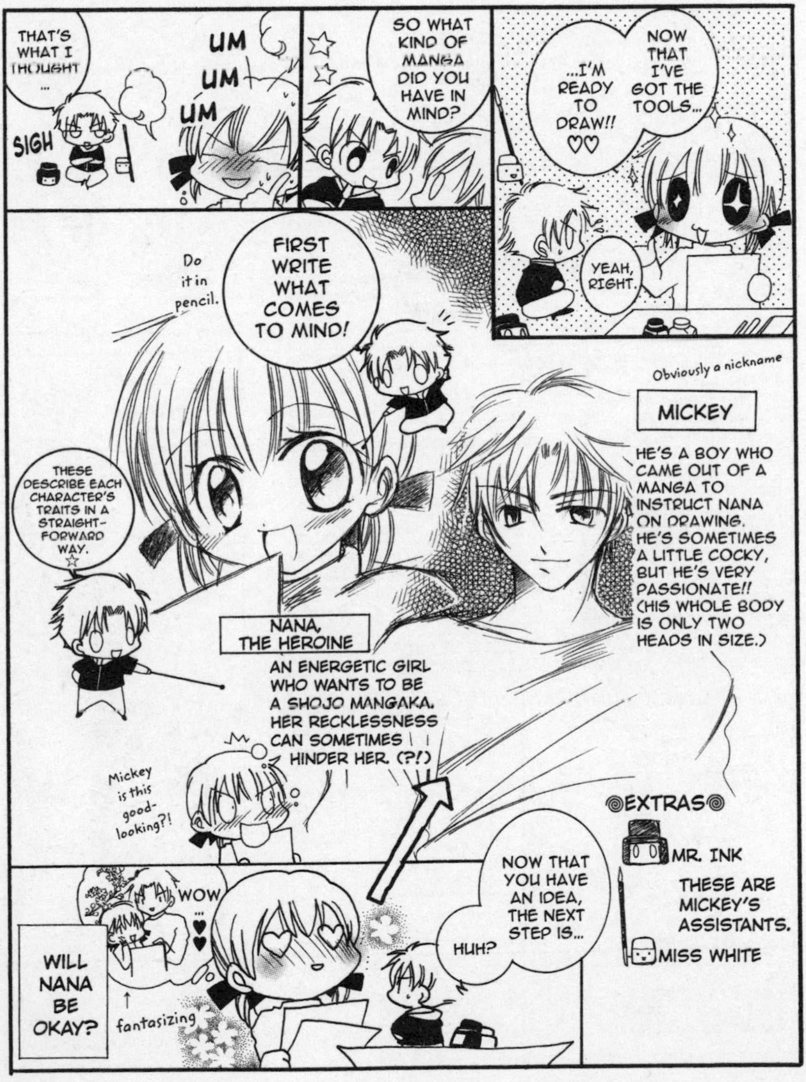
NOW THAT I'VE GOT THE TOOLS...
...I'M READY TO DRAW!! ♡♡
YEAH, RIGHT.
SO WHAT KIND OF MANGA DID YOU HAVE IN MIND?
UM
UM
UM
THAT'S WHAT I THOUGHT...
SIGH
FIRST WRITE WHAT COMES TO MIND!
Do it in pencil.
Obviously a nickname
MICKEY
HE'S A BOY WHO CAME OUT OF A MANGA TO INSTRUCT NANA ON DRAWING. HE'S SOMETIMES A LITTLE COCKY, BUT HE'S VERY PASSIONATE!! (HIS WHOLE BODY IS ONLY TWO HEADS IN SIZE.)
THESE DESCRIBE EACH CHARACTER'S TRAITS IN A STRAIGHT-FORWARD WAY. ☆
NANA, THE HEROINE
AN ENERGETIC GIRL WHO WANTS TO BE A SHOJO MANGAKA. HER RECKLESSNESS CAN SOMETIMES HINDER HER. (?!)
Mickey is this good-looking?!
EXTRAS
MR. INK
THESE ARE MICKEY'S ASSISTANTS.
MISS WHITE
NOW THAT YOU HAVE AN IDEA, THE NEXT STEP IS...
HUH?
WOW... ♥♥
↑ fantasizing
WILL NANA BE OKAY?

☆ Creating a Plot ☆

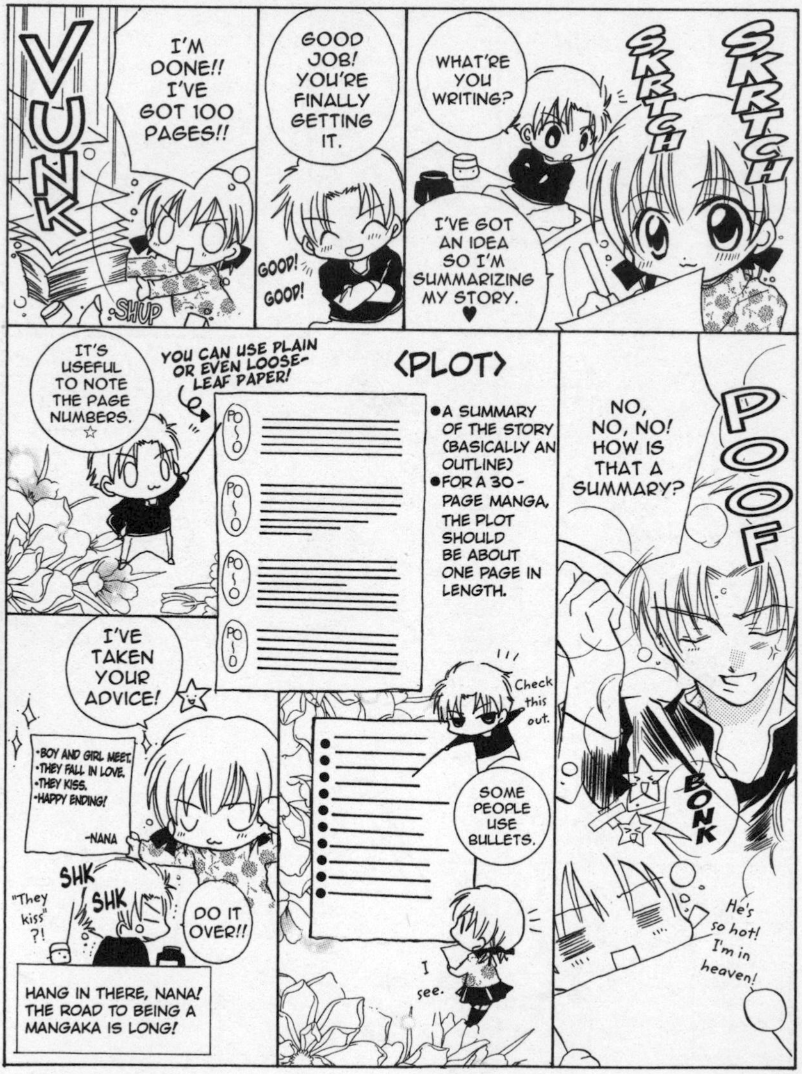
VUNK
I'M DONE!! I'VE GOT 100 PAGES!!
SHUP
GOOD JOB! YOU'RE FINALLY GETTING IT.
GOOD! GOOD!
WHAT'RE YOU WRITING?
I'VE GOT AN IDEA SO I'M SUMMARIZING MY STORY. ♥
SKRTCH SKRTCH
IT'S USEFUL TO NOTE THE PAGE NUMBERS. ☆
YOU CAN USE PLAIN OR EVEN LOOSE-LEAF PAPER!
PO ~ O
PO ~ O
PO ~ O
PO ~ O
<PLOT>
●A SUMMARY OF THE STORY (BASICALLY AN OUTLINE)
●FOR A 30-PAGE MANGA, THE PLOT SHOULD BE ABOUT ONE PAGE IN LENGTH.
I'VE TAKEN YOUR ADVICE!
•BOY AND GIRL MEET.
•THEY FALL IN LOVE.
•THEY KISS.
•HAPPY ENDING!
-NANA
SHK SHK
"They kiss" ?!
DO IT OVER!!
HANG IN THERE, NANA! THE ROAD TO BEING A MANGAKA IS LONG!
Check this out.
SOME PEOPLE USE BULLETS.
I see.
NO, NO, NO! HOW IS THAT A SUMMARY?
POOF
BONK
He's so hot! I'm in heaven!

☆What's a *NAME*?☆

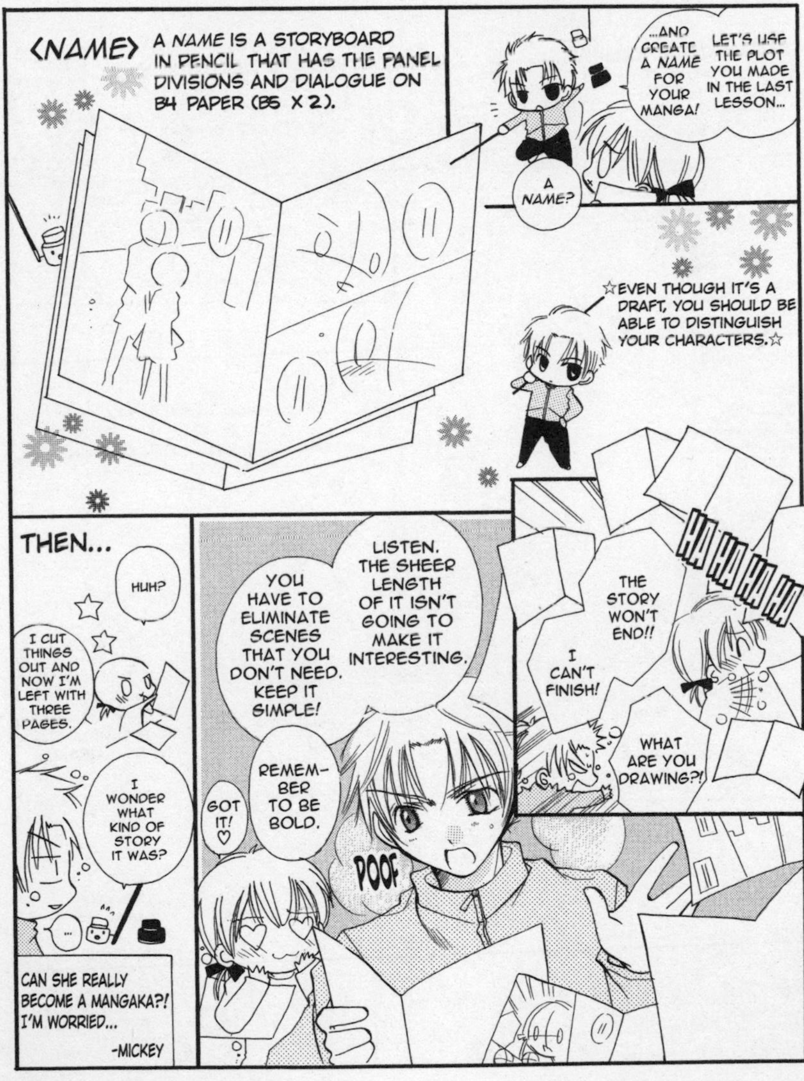
LET'S USE THE PLOT YOU MADE IN THE LAST LESSON...
...AND CREATE A *NAME* FOR YOUR MANGA!
A *NAME*?
☆EVEN THOUGH IT'S A DRAFT, YOU SHOULD BE ABLE TO DISTINGUISH YOUR CHARACTERS.☆
<NAME> A *NAME* IS A STORYBOARD IN PENCIL THAT HAS THE PANEL DIVISIONS AND DIALOGUE ON B4 PAPER (B5 X 2).
HA HA HA HA
THE STORY WON'T END!!
I CAN'T FINISH!
WHAT ARE YOU DRAWING?!
LISTEN. THE SHEER LENGTH OF IT ISN'T GOING TO MAKE IT INTERESTING.
YOU HAVE TO ELIMINATE SCENES THAT YOU DON'T NEED. KEEP IT SIMPLE!
REMEMBER TO BE BOLD.
GOT IT! ♡
POOF
THEN...
HUH?
I CUT THINGS OUT AND NOW I'M LEFT WITH THREE PAGES.
I WONDER WHAT KIND OF STORY IT WAS?
...
CAN SHE REALLY BECOME A MANGAKA?! I'M WORRIED...
-MICKEY

☆DRAWING TIPS☆

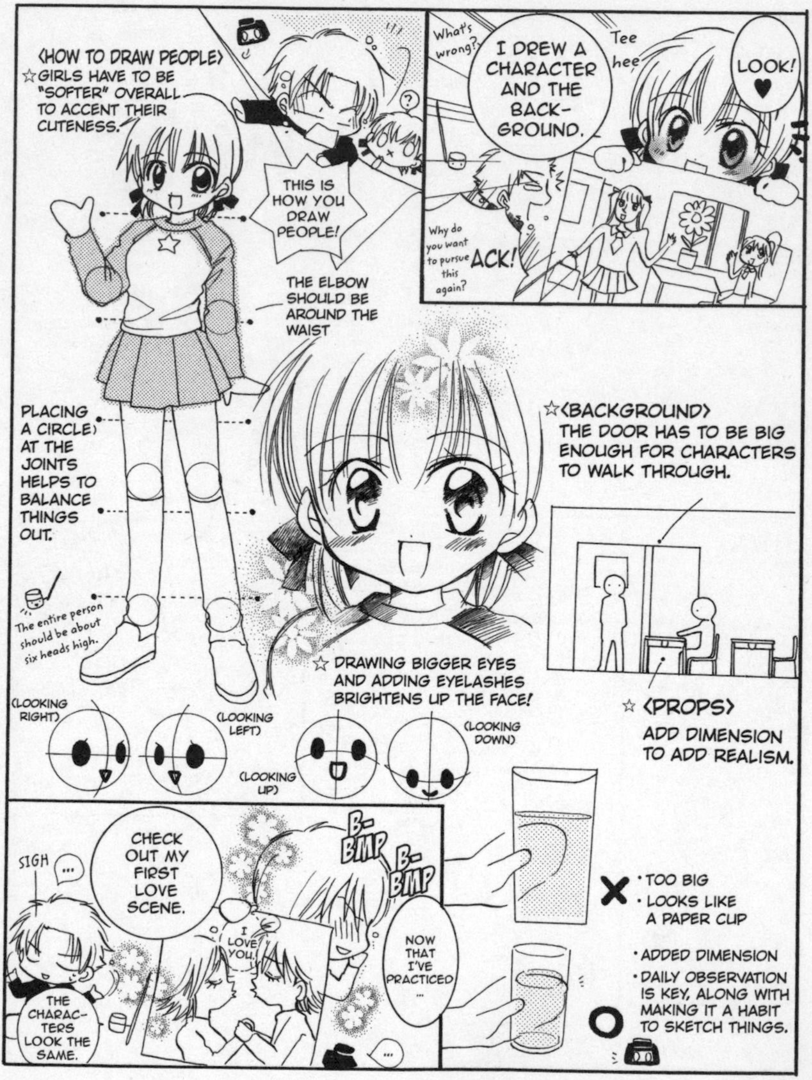
LOOK! ♥
Tee hee
I DREW A CHARACTER AND THE BACKGROUND.
What's wrong?
ACK!
Why do you want to pursue this again?
☆<BACKGROUND>
THE DOOR HAS TO BE BIG ENOUGH FOR CHARACTERS TO WALK THROUGH.
☆<PROPS>
ADD DIMENSION TO ADD REALISM.
X
• TOO BIG
• LOOKS LIKE A PAPER CUP
O
• ADDED DIMENSION
• DAILY OBSERVATION IS KEY, ALONG WITH MAKING IT A HABIT TO SKETCH THINGS.
THIS IS HOW YOU DRAW PEOPLE!
<HOW TO DRAW PEOPLE>
☆GIRLS HAVE TO BE "SOFTER" OVERALL TO ACCENT THEIR CUTENESS.
THE ELBOW SHOULD BE AROUND THE WAIST
PLACING A CIRCLE AT THE JOINTS HELPS TO BALANCE THINGS OUT.
The entire person should be about six heads high.
☆ DRAWING BIGGER EYES AND ADDING EYELASHES BRIGHTENS UP THE FACE!
(LOOKING DOWN)
(LOOKING UP)
(LOOKING LEFT)
(LOOKING RIGHT)
B-BMP
B-BMP
NOW THAT I'VE PRACTICED...
I LOVE YOU.
CHECK OUT MY FIRST LOVE SCENE.
SIGH
...
THE CHARACTERS LOOK THE SAME.
...

☆DRAWING BOYS AND GIRLS☆

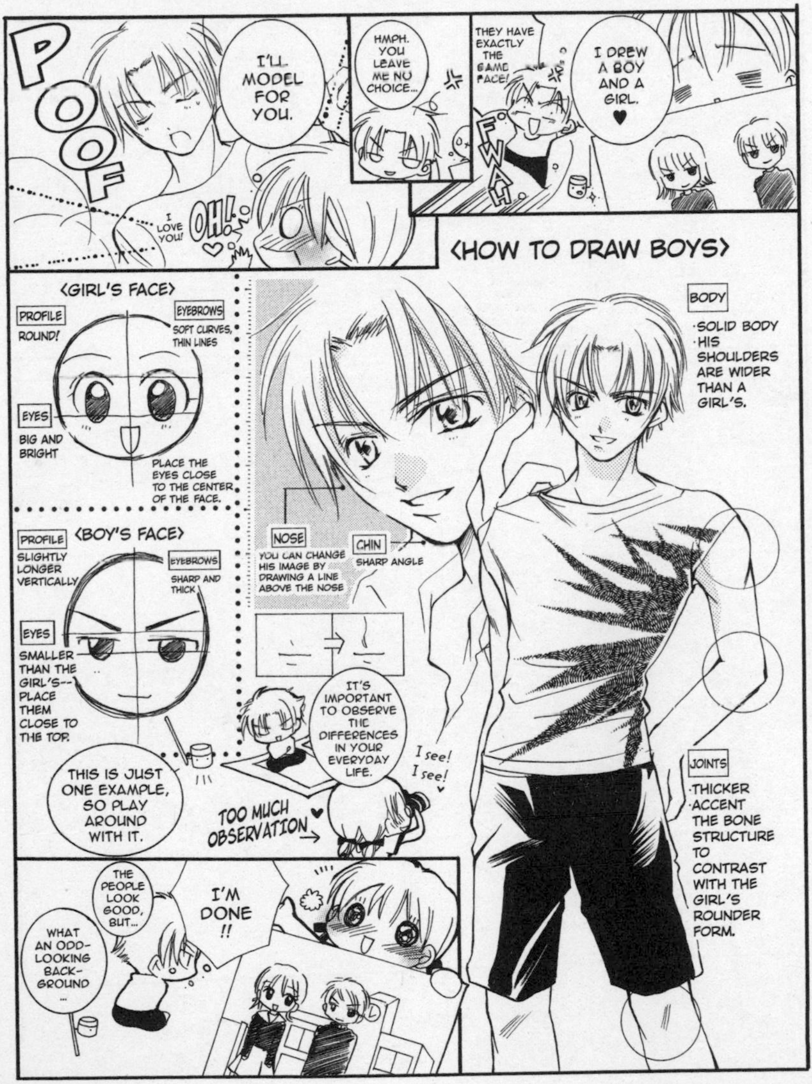
I DREW A BOY AND A GIRL. ♥
THEY HAVE EXACTLY THE SAME FACE!
FWAH
HMPH. YOU LEAVE ME NO CHOICE...
I'LL MODEL FOR YOU.
POOF
OH!
I LOVE YOU!
<HOW TO DRAW BOYS>
BODY
·SOLID BODY
·HIS SHOULDERS ARE WIDER THAN A GIRL'S.
NOSE
YOU CAN CHANGE HIS IMAGE BY DRAWING A LINE ABOVE THE NOSE
CHIN
SHARP ANGLE
JOINTS
·THICKER
·ACCENT THE BONE STRUCTURE TO CONTRAST WITH THE GIRL'S ROUNDER FORM.
<GIRL'S FACE>
PROFILE
ROUND!
EYEBROWS
SOFT CURVES, THIN LINES
EYES
BIG AND BRIGHT
PLACE THE EYES CLOSE TO THE CENTER OF THE FACE.
<BOY'S FACE>
PROFILE
SLIGHTLY LONGER VERTICALLY
EYEBROWS
SHARP AND THICK
EYES
SMALLER THAN THE GIRL'S--PLACE THEM CLOSE TO THE TOP.
IT'S IMPORTANT TO OBSERVE THE DIFFERENCES IN YOUR EVERYDAY LIFE.
I see! I see!
THIS IS JUST ONE EXAMPLE, SO PLAY AROUND WITH IT.
TOO MUCH OBSERVATION →
I'M DONE!!
THE PEOPLE LOOK GOOD, BUT...
WHAT AN ODD-LOOKING BACKGROUND...

✩ Spatial Effects (Parsing) ✩

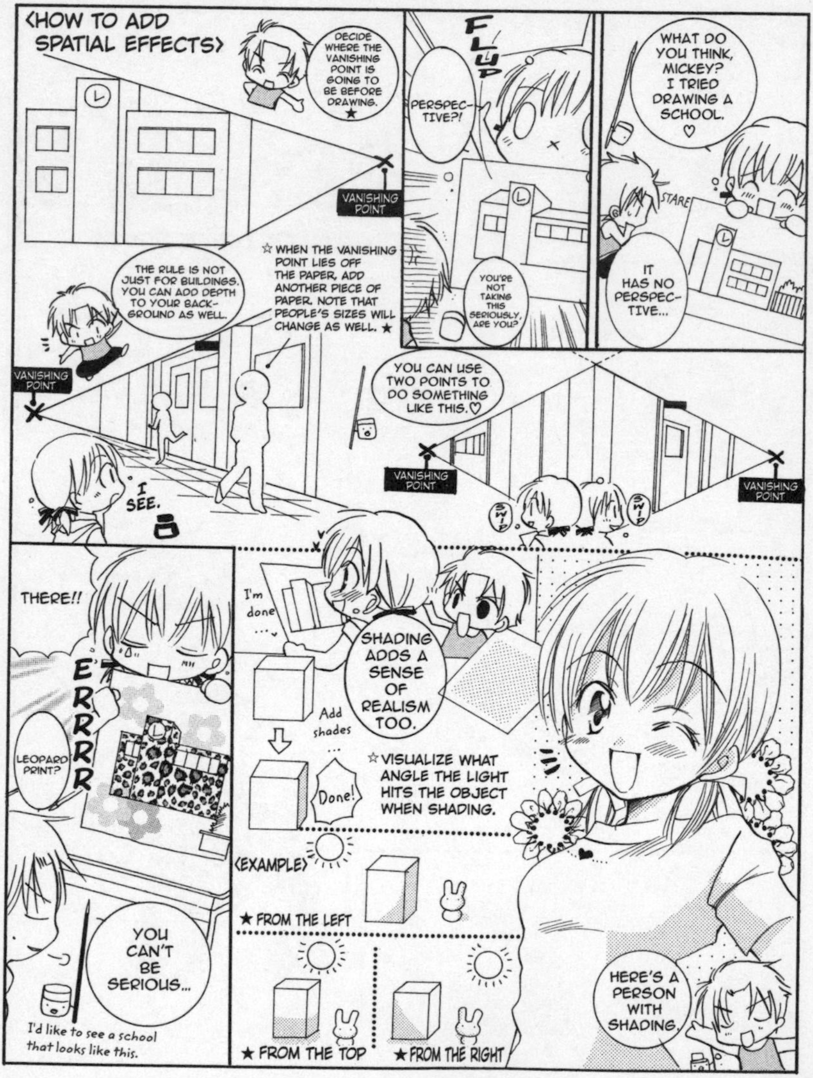
WHAT DO YOU THINK, MICKEY? I TRIED DRAWING A SCHOOL. ♡
STARE
IT HAS NO PERSPEC-TIVE...
FLUP
PERSPEC-TIVE?!
YOU'RE NOT TAKING THIS SERIOUSLY, ARE YOU?
<HOW TO ADD SPATIAL EFFECTS>
DECIDE WHERE THE VANISHING POINT IS GOING TO BE BEFORE DRAWING. ★
VANISHING POINT
☆ WHEN THE VANISHING POINT LIES OFF THE PAPER, ADD ANOTHER PIECE OF PAPER. NOTE THAT PEOPLE'S SIZES WILL CHANGE AS WELL. ★
THE RULE IS NOT JUST FOR BUILDINGS. YOU CAN ADD DEPTH TO YOUR BACK-GROUND AS WELL.
VANISHING POINT
I SEE.
YOU CAN USE TWO POINTS TO DO SOMETHING LIKE THIS.♡
VANISHING POINT
VANISHING POINT
SWIP
SWIP
SHADING ADDS A SENSE OF REALISM TOO.
I'm done ...
Add shades ...
Done!
☆ VISUALIZE WHAT ANGLE THE LIGHT HITS THE OBJECT WHEN SHADING.
<EXAMPLE>
★ FROM THE LEFT
★ FROM THE TOP
★ FROM THE RIGHT
HERE'S A PERSON WITH SHADING.
THERE!!
ERRRR
LEOPARD PRINT?
YOU CAN'T BE SERIOUS...
I'd like to see a school that looks like this.

☆ Using Screentones ☆

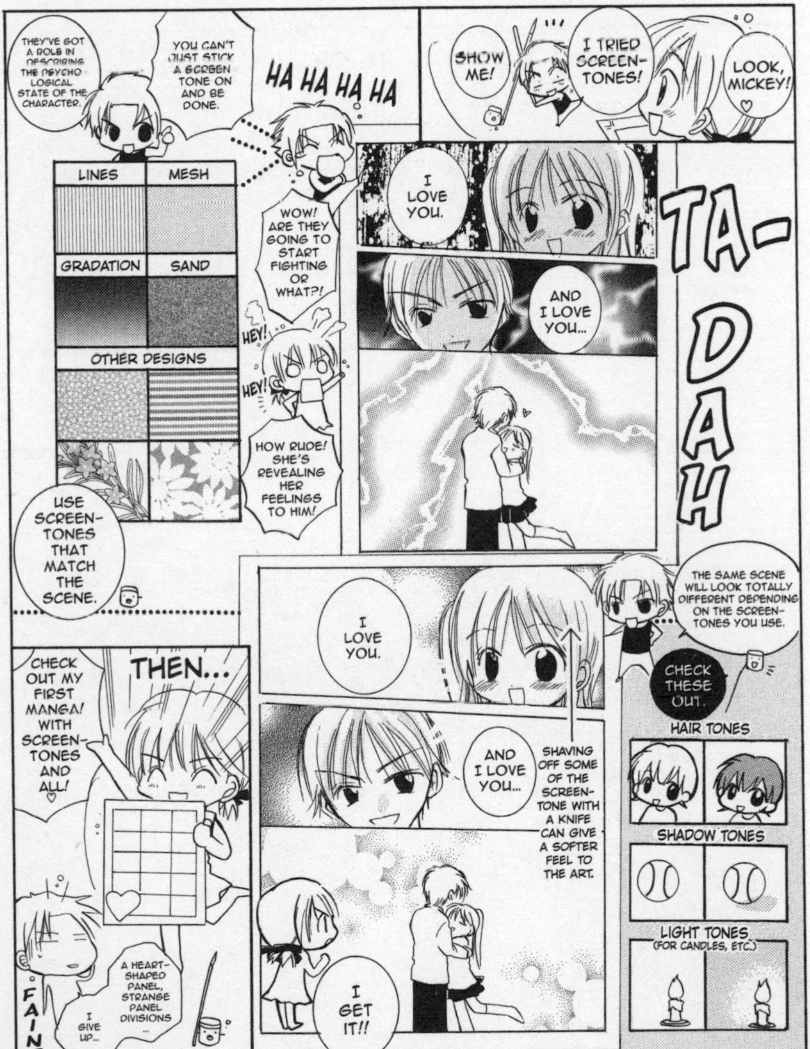

LOOK, MICKEY! ♡
I TRIED SCREENTONES!
SHOW ME!
HA HA HA HA
YOU CAN'T JUST STICK A SCREEN TONE ON AND BE DONE.
THEY'VE GOT A ROLE IN DESCRIBING THE PSYCHOLOGICAL STATE OF THE CHARACTER.
TA-DAH
I LOVE YOU.
AND I LOVE YOU...
WOW! ARE THEY GOING TO START FIGHTING OR WHAT?!
HEY!
HEY!
HOW RUDE! SHE'S REVEALING HER FEELINGS TO HIM!
LINES
MESH
GRADATION
SAND
OTHER DESIGNS
USE SCREENTONES THAT MATCH THE SCENE.
THE SAME SCENE WILL LOOK TOTALLY DIFFERENT DEPENDING ON THE SCREENTONES YOU USE.
CHECK THESE OUT.
HAIR TONES
SHADOW TONES
LIGHT TONES
(FOR CANDLES, ETC.)
I LOVE YOU.
AND I LOVE YOU...
SHAVING OFF SOME OF THE SCREENTONE WITH A KNIFE CAN GIVE A SOFTER FEEL TO THE ART.
I GET IT!!
THEN...
CHECK OUT MY FIRST MANGA! WITH SCREENTONES AND ALL! ♡
A HEART-SHAPED PANEL, STRANGE PANEL DIVISIONS ...
I GIVE UP...
FAINT

☆Panel Division☆

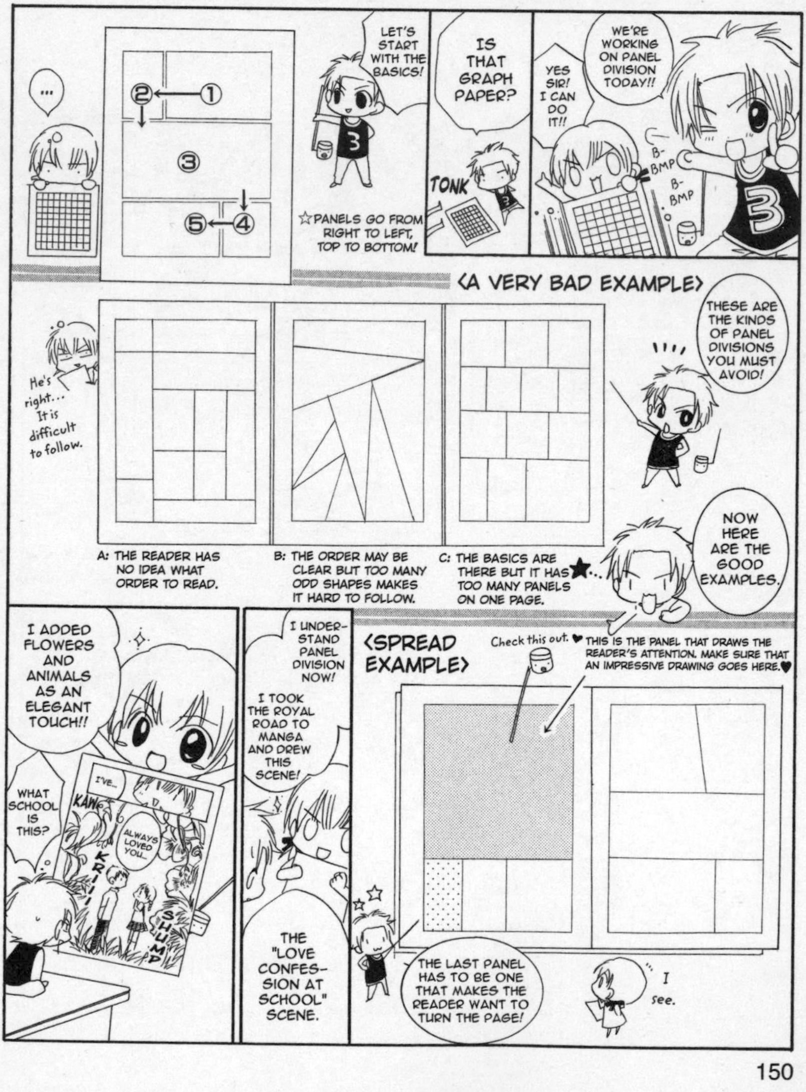
WE'RE WORKING ON PANEL DIVISION TODAY!!
YES SIR! I CAN DO IT!!
B-BMP
B-BMP
IS THAT GRAPH PAPER?
TONK
LET'S START WITH THE BASICS!
☆PANELS GO FROM RIGHT TO LEFT, TOP TO BOTTOM!
①
②
③
④
⑤
...
<A VERY BAD EXAMPLE>
THESE ARE THE KINDS OF PANEL DIVISIONS YOU MUST AVOID!
He's right... It is difficult to follow.
A: THE READER HAS NO IDEA WHAT ORDER TO READ.
B: THE ORDER MAY BE CLEAR BUT TOO MANY ODD SHAPES MAKES IT HARD TO FOLLOW.
C: THE BASICS ARE THERE BUT IT HAS TOO MANY PANELS ON ONE PAGE.
NOW HERE ARE THE GOOD EXAMPLES.
<SPREAD EXAMPLE>
Check this out.♥
THIS IS THE PANEL THAT DRAWS THE READER'S ATTENTION. MAKE SURE THAT AN IMPRESSIVE DRAWING GOES HERE.♥
THE LAST PANEL HAS TO BE ONE THAT MAKES THE READER WANT TO TURN THE PAGE!
I see.
I UNDERSTAND PANEL DIVISION NOW!
I TOOK THE ROYAL ROAD TO MANGA AND DREW THIS SCENE!
THE "LOVE CONFESSION AT SCHOOL" SCENE.
I ADDED FLOWERS AND ANIMALS AS AN ELEGANT TOUCH!!
WHAT SCHOOL IS THIS?
I'VE...
ALWAYS LOVED YOU...
KAW
KRII
SHUMP

☆DIFFERENT BALLOONS☆

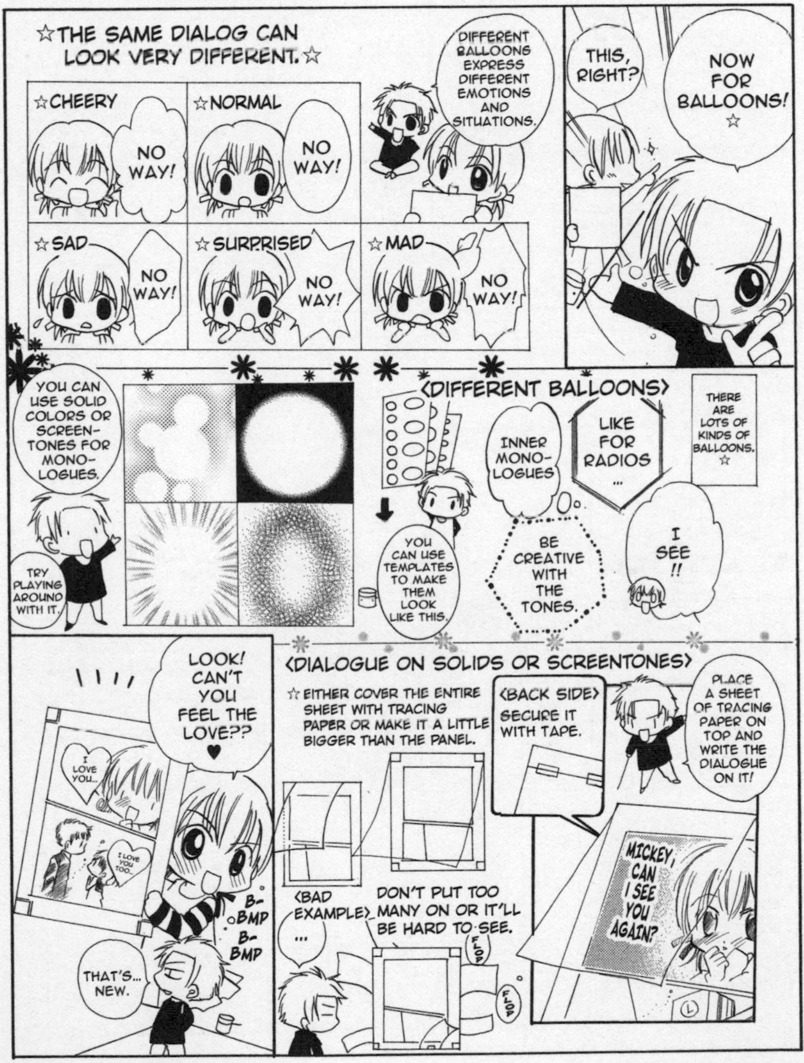

NOW FOR BALLOONS! ☆
THIS, RIGHT?
DIFFERENT BALLOONS EXPRESS DIFFERENT EMOTIONS AND SITUATIONS.
☆THE SAME DIALOG CAN LOOK VERY DIFFERENT.☆
☆NORMAL
NO WAY!
☆CHEERY
NO WAY!
☆MAD
NO WAY!
☆SURPRISED
NO WAY!
☆SAD
NO WAY!
THERE ARE LOTS OF KINDS OF BALLOONS. ☆
<DIFFERENT BALLOONS>
LIKE FOR RADIOS ...
INNER MONOLOGUES
I SEE !!
BE CREATIVE WITH THE TONES.
YOU CAN USE TEMPLATES TO MAKE THEM LOOK LIKE THIS.
YOU CAN USE SOLID COLORS OR SCREENTONES FOR MONOLOGUES.
TRY PLAYING AROUND WITH IT.
<DIALOGUE ON SOLIDS OR SCREENTONES>
PLACE A SHEET OF TRACING PAPER ON TOP AND WRITE THE DIALOGUE ON IT!
<BACK SIDE> SECURE IT WITH TAPE.
☆EITHER COVER THE ENTIRE SHEET WITH TRACING PAPER OR MAKE IT A LITTLE BIGGER THAN THE PANEL.
MICKEY, CAN I SEE YOU AGAIN?
DON'T PUT TOO MANY ON OR IT'LL BE HARD TO SEE.
<BAD EXAMPLE>
...
FLOP
FLOP
LOOK! CAN'T YOU FEEL THE LOVE?? ♥
I LOVE YOU...
I LOVE YOU TOO...
B-BMP B-BMP
THAT'S... NEW.

☆Finally Completing Your Script!☆

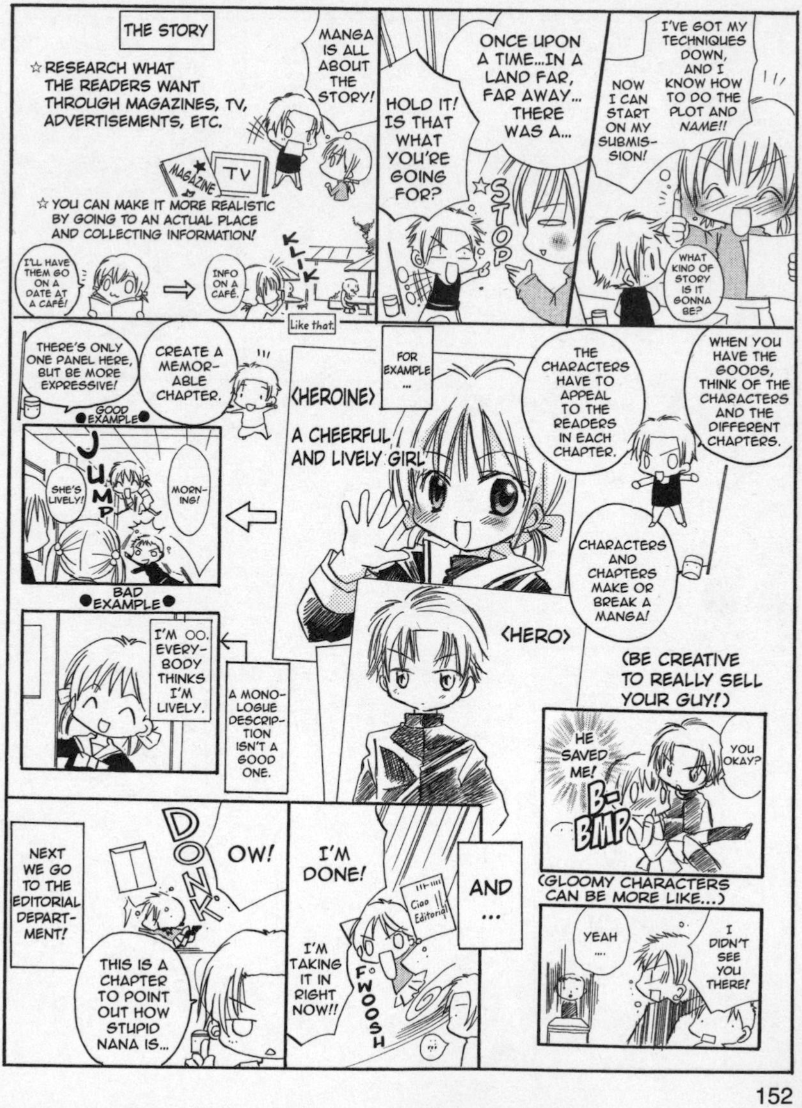

I'VE GOT MY TECHNIQUES DOWN, AND I KNOW HOW TO DO THE PLOT AND NAME!!
NOW I CAN START ON MY SUBMISSION!
WHAT KIND OF STORY IS IT GONNA BE?
ONCE UPON A TIME...IN A LAND FAR, FAR AWAY... THERE WAS A...
HOLD IT! IS THAT WHAT YOU'RE GOING FOR?
STOP
MANGA IS ALL ABOUT THE STORY!
THE STORY
☆RESEARCH WHAT THE READERS WANT THROUGH MAGAZINES, TV, ADVERTISEMENTS, ETC.
TV
MAGAZINE
☆YOU CAN MAKE IT MORE REALISTIC BY GOING TO AN ACTUAL PLACE AND COLLECTING INFORMATION!
KLIK
INFO ON A CAFÉ.
I'LL HAVE THEM GO ON A DATE AT A CAFÉ!
Like that.
WHEN YOU HAVE THE GOODS, THINK OF THE CHARACTERS AND THE DIFFERENT CHAPTERS.
THE CHARACTERS HAVE TO APPEAL TO THE READERS IN EACH CHAPTER.
CHARACTERS AND CHAPTERS MAKE OR BREAK A MANGA!
FOR EXAMPLE ...
〈HEROINE〉
A CHEERFUL AND LIVELY GIRL
〈HERO〉
(BE CREATIVE TO REALLY SELL YOUR GUY!)
YOU OKAY?
HE SAVED ME!
B-BMP
(GLOOMY CHARACTERS CAN BE MORE LIKE...)
I DIDN'T SEE YOU THERE!
YEAH ....
CREATE A MEMORABLE CHAPTER.
THERE'S ONLY ONE PANEL HERE, BUT BE MORE EXPRESSIVE!
●GOOD EXAMPLE●
MORNING!
JUMP
SHE'S LIVELY!
●BAD EXAMPLE●
I'M ○○. EVERYBODY THINKS I'M LIVELY.
A MONOLOGUE DESCRIPTION ISN'T A GOOD ONE.
AND ...
I'M DONE!
Ciao Editorial
I'M TAKING IT IN RIGHT NOW!!
FWOOSH
OW!
DONK
NEXT WE GO TO THE EDITORIAL DEPARTMENT!
THIS IS A CHAPTER TO POINT OUT HOW STUPID NANA IS...

☆The Final Step: Bringing the Script In☆

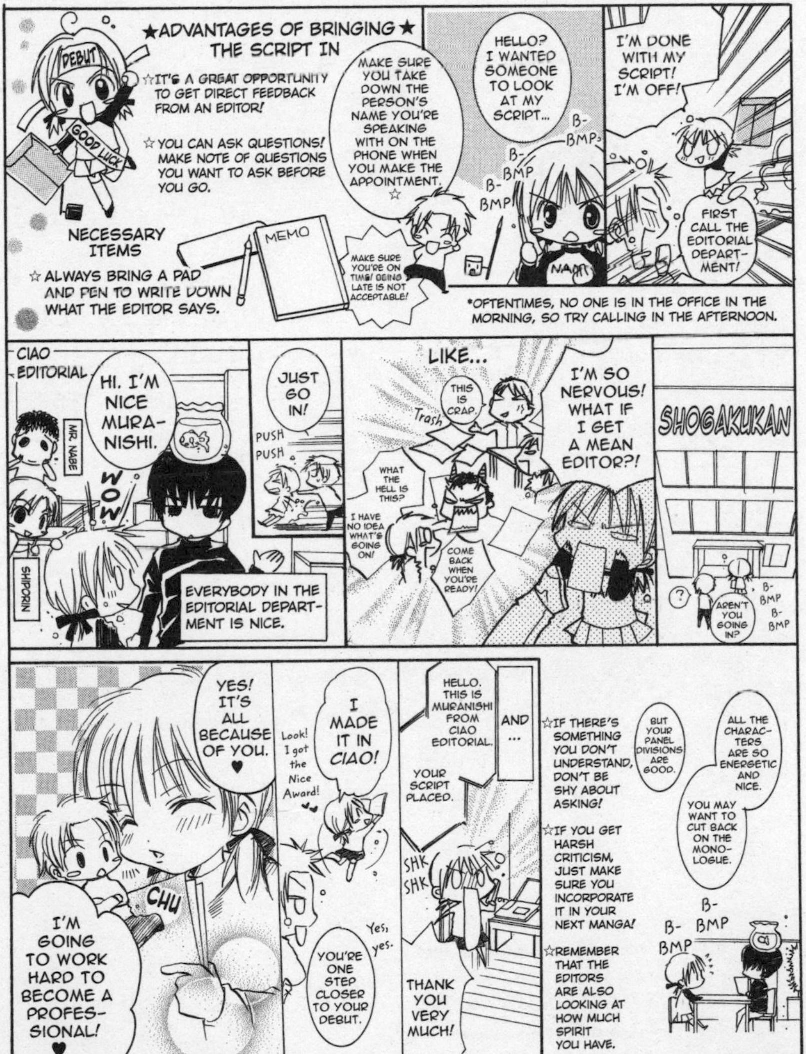
I'M DONE WITH MY SCRIPT! I'M OFF!
FIRST CALL THE EDITORIAL DEPART-MENT!
HELLO? I WANTED SOMEONE TO LOOK AT MY SCRIPT...
B-BMP B-BMP B-BMP
MAKE SURE YOU TAKE DOWN THE PERSON'S NAME YOU'RE SPEAKING WITH ON THE PHONE WHEN YOU MAKE THE APPOINTMENT. ☆
MAKE SURE YOU'RE ON TIME! BEING LATE IS NOT ACCEPTABLE!
MEMO
★ADVANTAGES OF BRINGING THE SCRIPT IN★
☆IT'S A GREAT OPPORTUNITY TO GET DIRECT FEEDBACK FROM AN EDITOR!
☆YOU CAN ASK QUESTIONS! MAKE NOTE OF QUESTIONS YOU WANT TO ASK BEFORE YOU GO.
DEBUT
GOOD LUCK
NECESSARY ITEMS
☆ALWAYS BRING A PAD AND PEN TO WRITE DOWN WHAT THE EDITOR SAYS.
*OFTENTIMES, NO ONE IS IN THE OFFICE IN THE MORNING, SO TRY CALLING IN THE AFTERNOON.
SHOGAKUKAN
B-BMP B-BMP
?
AREN'T YOU GOING IN?
I'M SO NERVOUS! WHAT IF I GET A MEAN EDITOR?!
LIKE...
THIS IS CRAP.
Trash
WHAT THE HELL IS THIS?
I HAVE NO IDEA WHAT'S GOING ON!
COME BACK WHEN YOU'RE READY!
JUST GO IN!
PUSH PUSH
CIAO EDITORIAL
HI. I'M NICE MURANISHI.
WOW
MR. NABE
SHIPORIN
EVERYBODY IN THE EDITORIAL DEPART-MENT IS NICE.
☆IF THERE'S SOMETHING YOU DON'T UNDERSTAND, DON'T BE SHY ABOUT ASKING!
☆IF YOU GET HARSH CRITICISM, JUST MAKE SURE YOU INCORPORATE IT IN YOUR NEXT MANGA!
☆REMEMBER THAT THE EDITORS ARE ALSO LOOKING AT HOW MUCH SPIRIT YOU HAVE.
BUT YOUR PANEL DIVISIONS ARE GOOD.
ALL THE CHARAC-TERS ARE SO ENERGETIC AND NICE.
YOU MAY WANT TO CUT BACK ON THE MONO-LOGUE.
B-BMP B-BMP
AND ...
HELLO. THIS IS MURANISHI FROM CIAO EDITORIAL.
YOUR SCRIPT PLACED.
SHK SHK
THANK YOU VERY MUCH!
I MADE IT IN CIAO!
Look! I got the Nice Award!
Yes, yes.
YOU'RE ONE STEP CLOSER TO YOUR DEBUT.
YES! IT'S ALL BECAUSE OF YOU. ♥
CHU
I'M GOING TO WORK HARD TO BECOME A PROFES-SIONAL! ♥

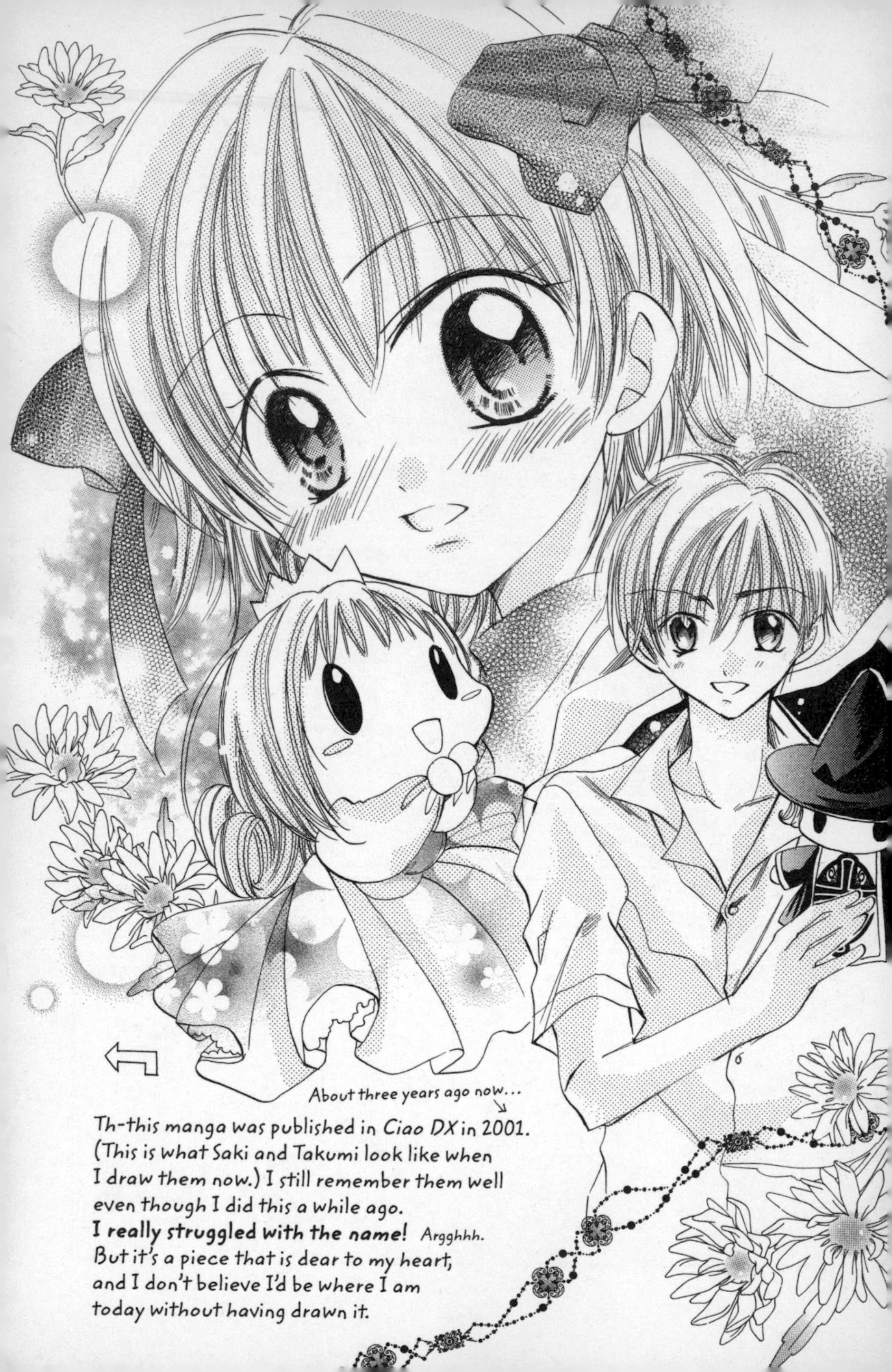

About three years ago now...

Th-this manga was published in *Ciao DX* in 2001. (This is what Saki and Takumi look like when I draw them now.) I still remember them well even though I did this a while ago. **I really struggled with the name!** Argghhh. But it's a piece that is dear to my heart, and I don't believe I'd be where I am today without having drawn it.

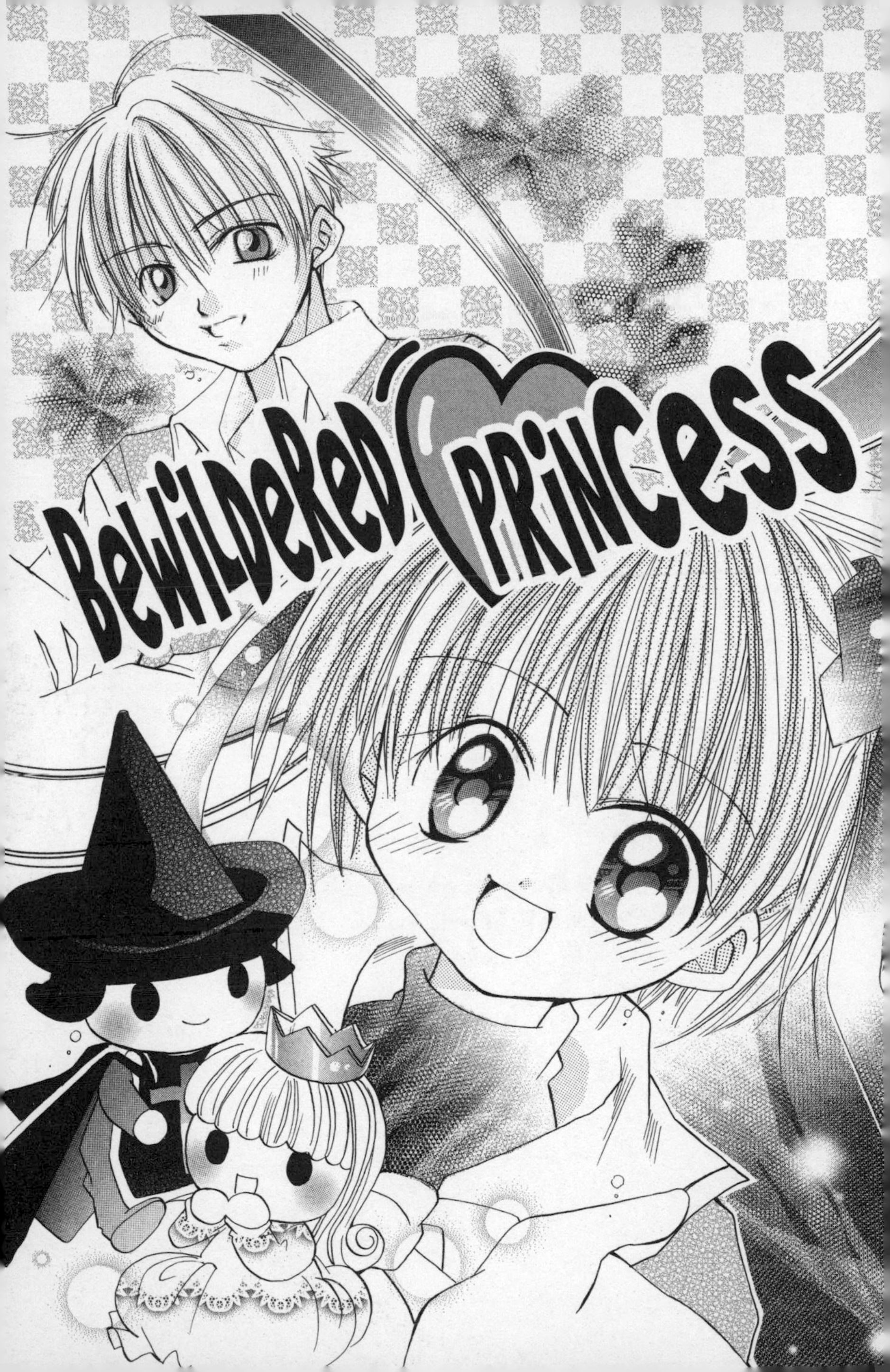
Bewildered Princess

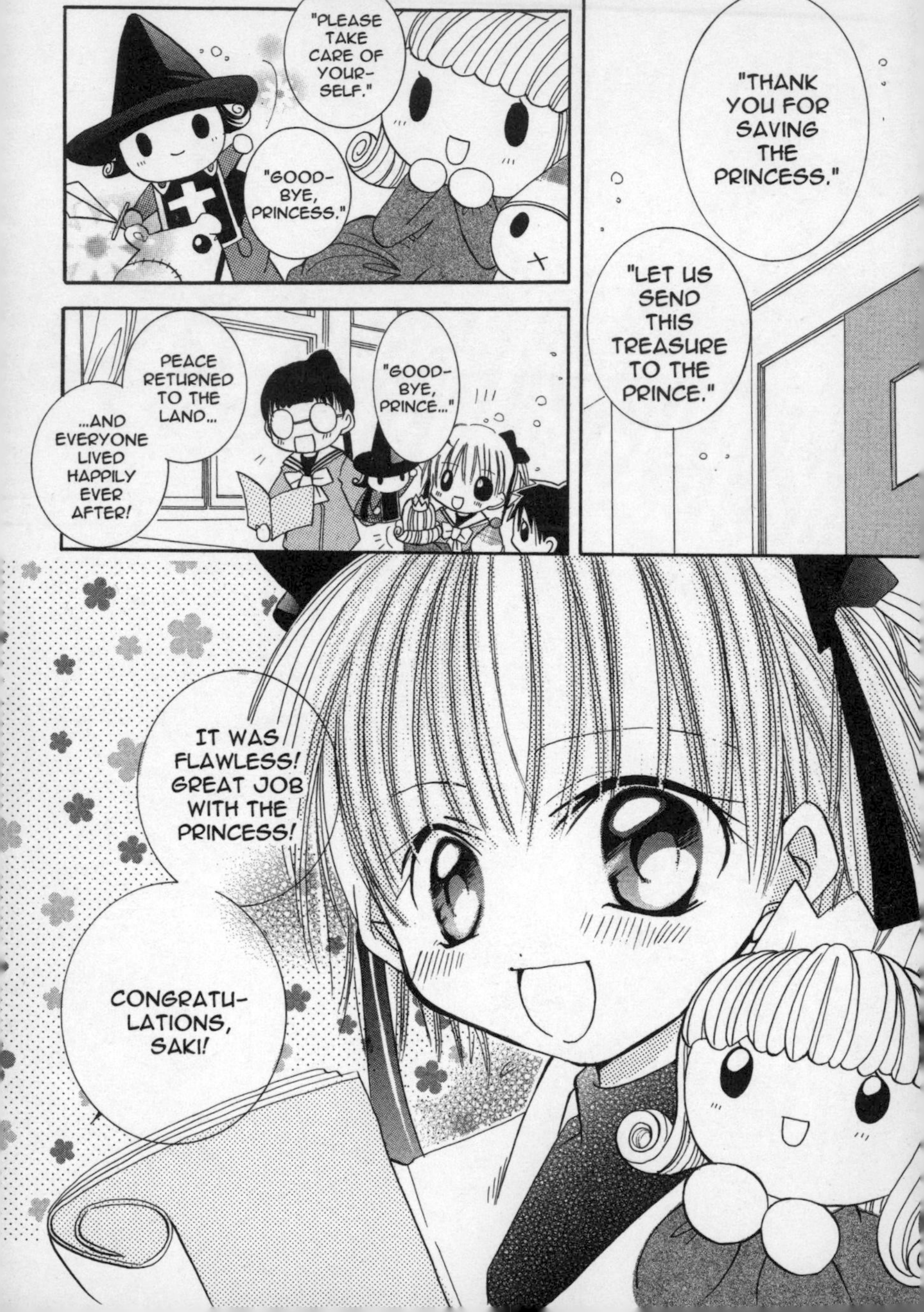
"THANK YOU FOR SAVING THE PRINCESS."
"LET US SEND THIS TREASURE TO THE PRINCE."
"PLEASE TAKE CARE OF YOUR-SELF."
"GOOD-BYE, PRINCESS."
"GOOD-BYE, PRINCE..."
PEACE RETURNED TO THE LAND...
...AND EVERYONE LIVED HAPPILY EVER AFTER!
IT WAS FLAWLESS! GREAT JOB WITH THE PRINCESS!
CONGRATU-LATIONS, SAKI!

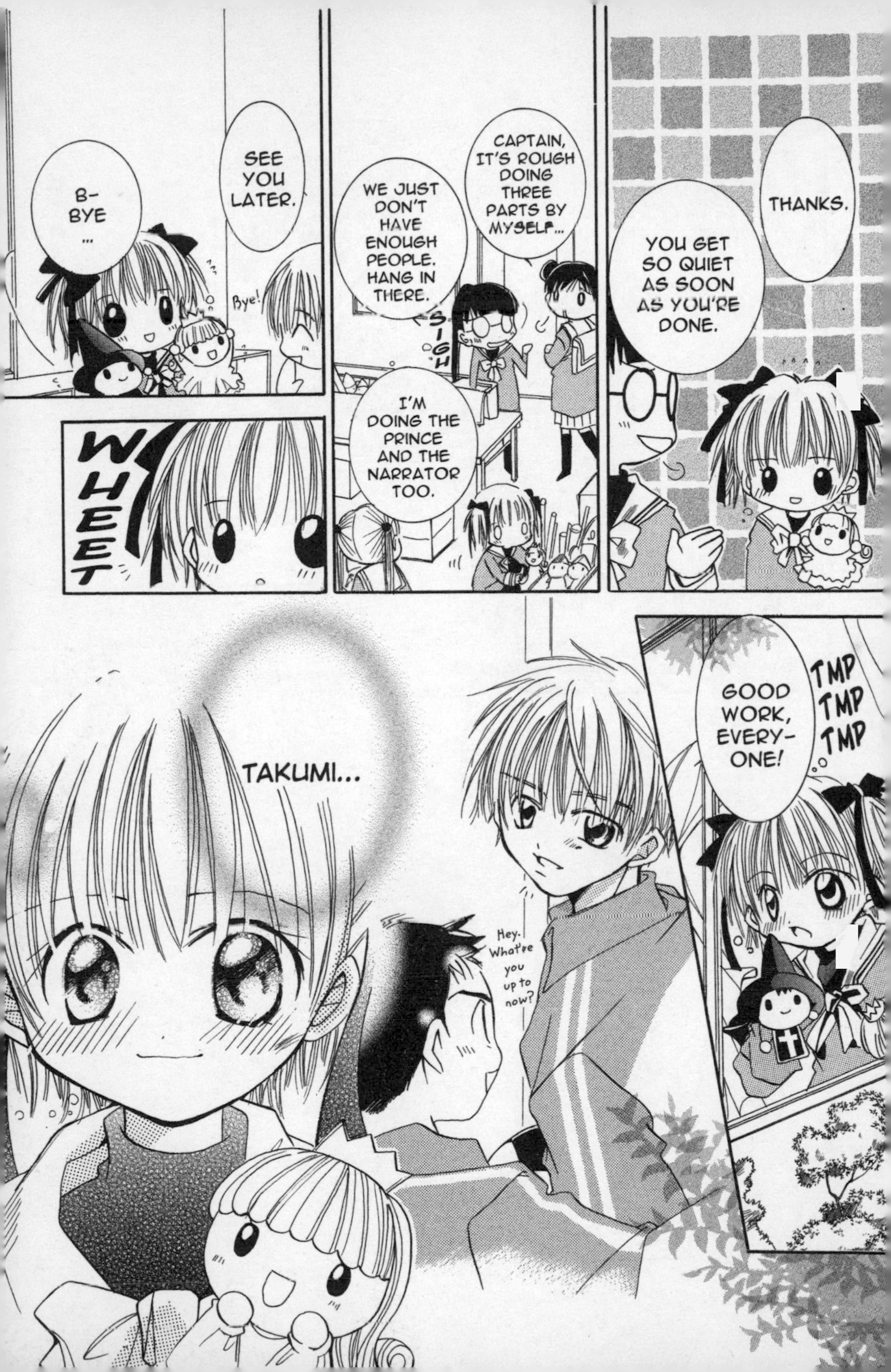
THANKS.
YOU GET SO QUIET AS SOON AS YOU'RE DONE.
CAPTAIN, IT'S ROUGH DOING THREE PARTS BY MYSELF...
WE JUST DON'T HAVE ENOUGH PEOPLE. HANG IN THERE.
SIGH
I'M DOING THE PRINCE AND THE NARRATOR TOO.
SEE YOU LATER.
Bye!
B-BYE...
WHEET
GOOD WORK, EVERY-ONE!
TMP TMP TMP
Hey. What're you up to now?
TAKUMI...

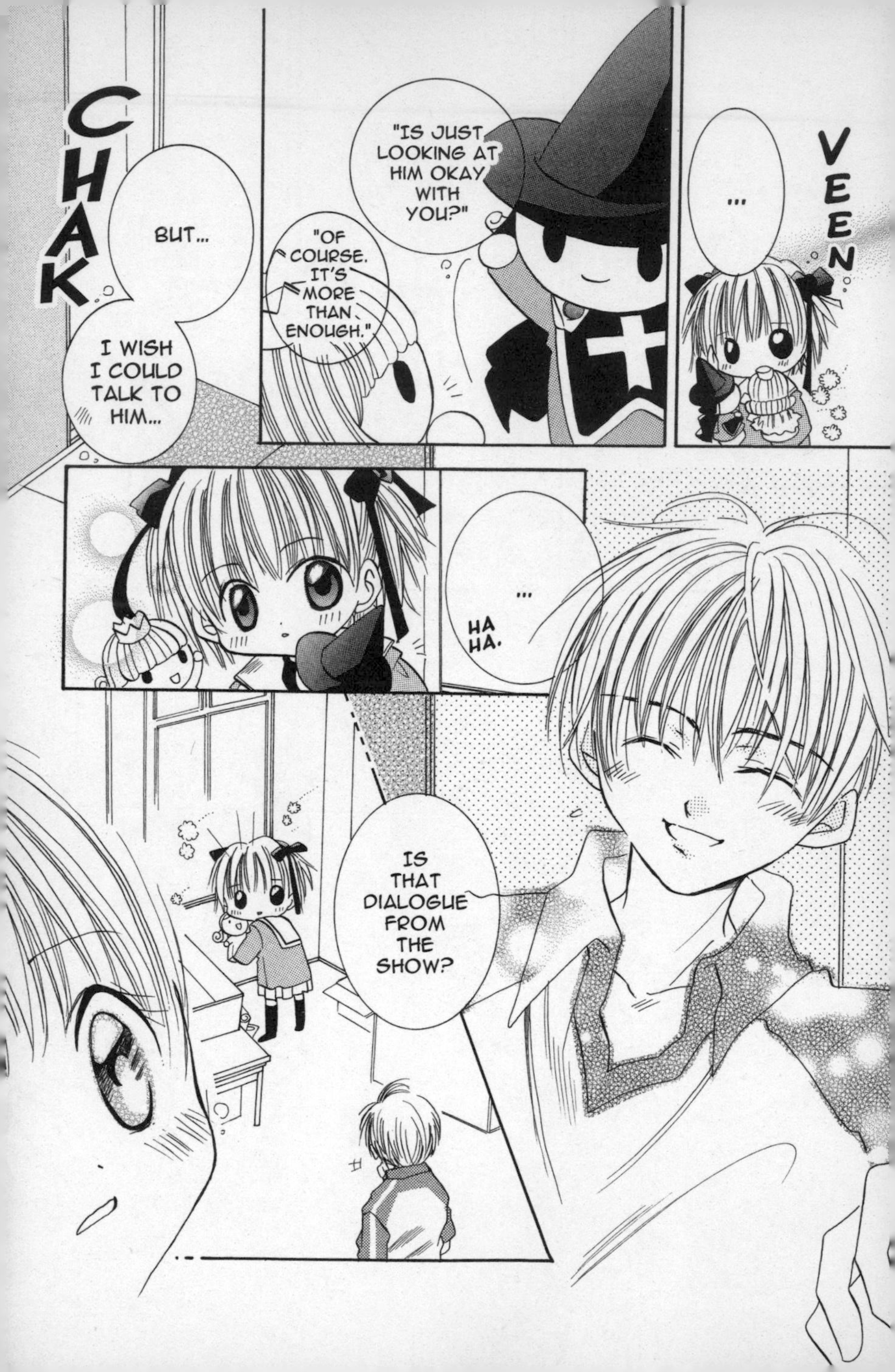
VEEN
...
"IS JUST LOOKING AT HIM OKAY WITH YOU?"
"OF COURSE. IT'S MORE THAN ENOUGH."
CHAK
BUT...
I WISH I COULD TALK TO HIM...
... HA HA.
IS THAT DIALOGUE FROM THE SHOW?

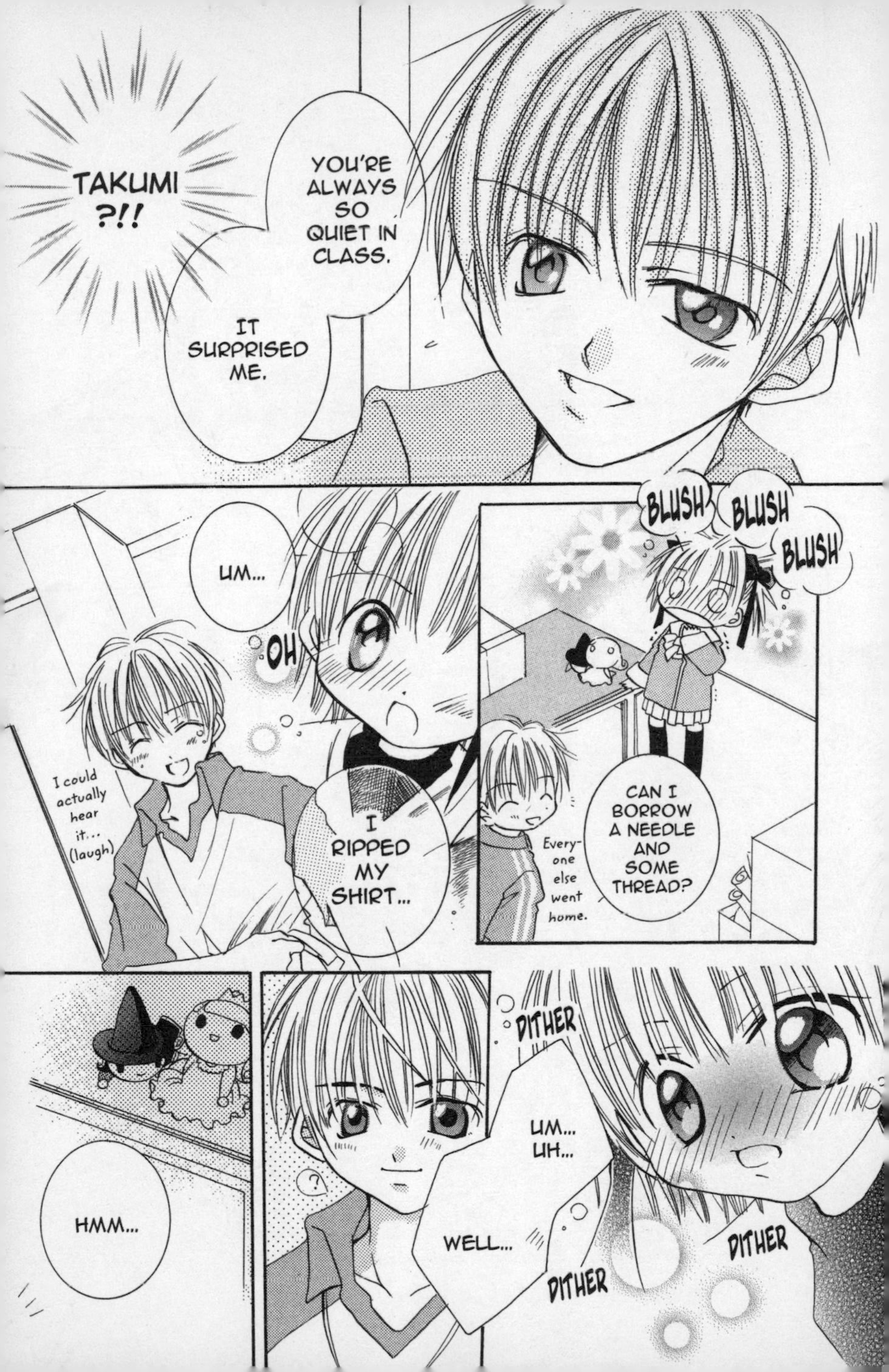

YOU'RE ALWAYS SO QUIET IN CLASS.
IT SURPRISED ME.
TAKUMI ?!!
BLUSH
BLUSH
BLUSH
CAN I BORROW A NEEDLE AND SOME THREAD?
Every-one else went home.
UM...
OH
I RIPPED MY SHIRT...
I could actually hear it... (laugh)
DITHER
UM... UH...
WELL...
DITHER
DITHER
HMM...

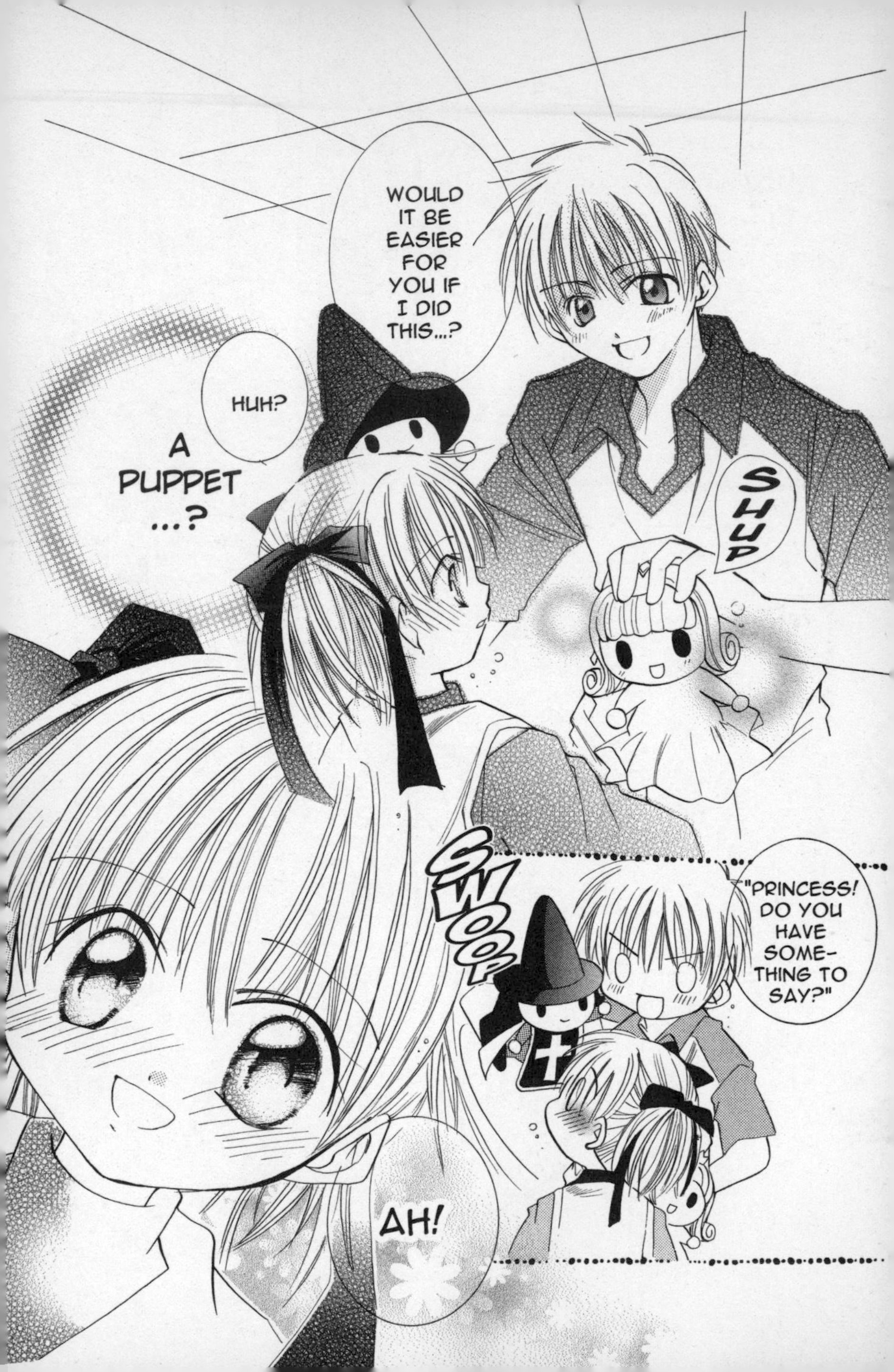
WOULD IT BE EASIER FOR YOU IF I DID THIS...?
HUH?
SHUP
A PUPPET ...?
"PRINCESS! DO YOU HAVE SOME-THING TO SAY?"
SWOOP
AH!

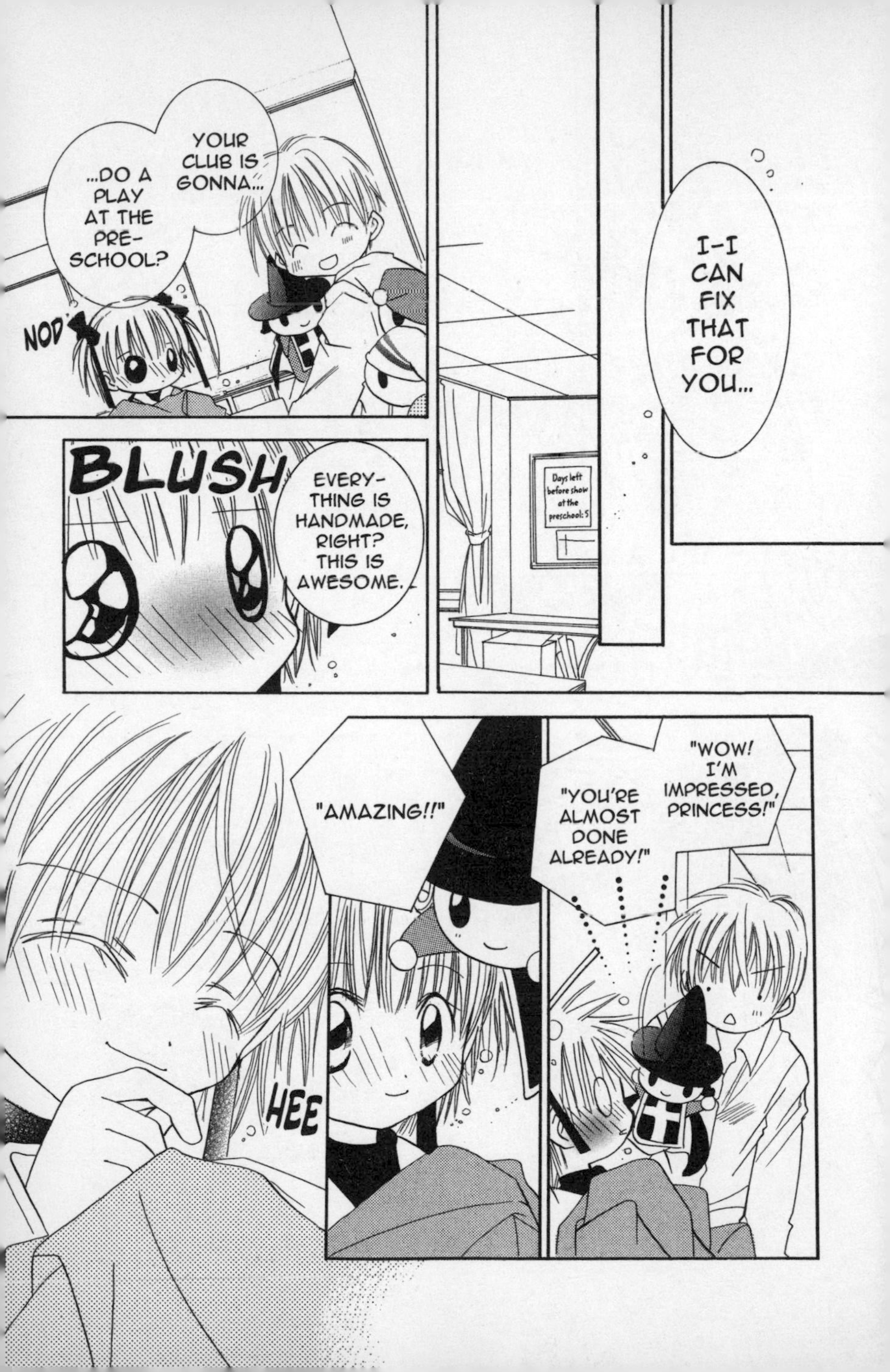
I-I CAN FIX THAT FOR YOU...
Days left before show at the preschool: 5
YOUR CLUB IS GONNA...
...DO A PLAY AT THE PRE-SCHOOL?
NOD
BLUSH
EVERY-THING IS HANDMADE, RIGHT? THIS IS AWESOME.
"WOW! I'M IMPRESSED, PRINCESS!"
"YOU'RE ALMOST DONE ALREADY!"
"AMAZING!!"
HEE

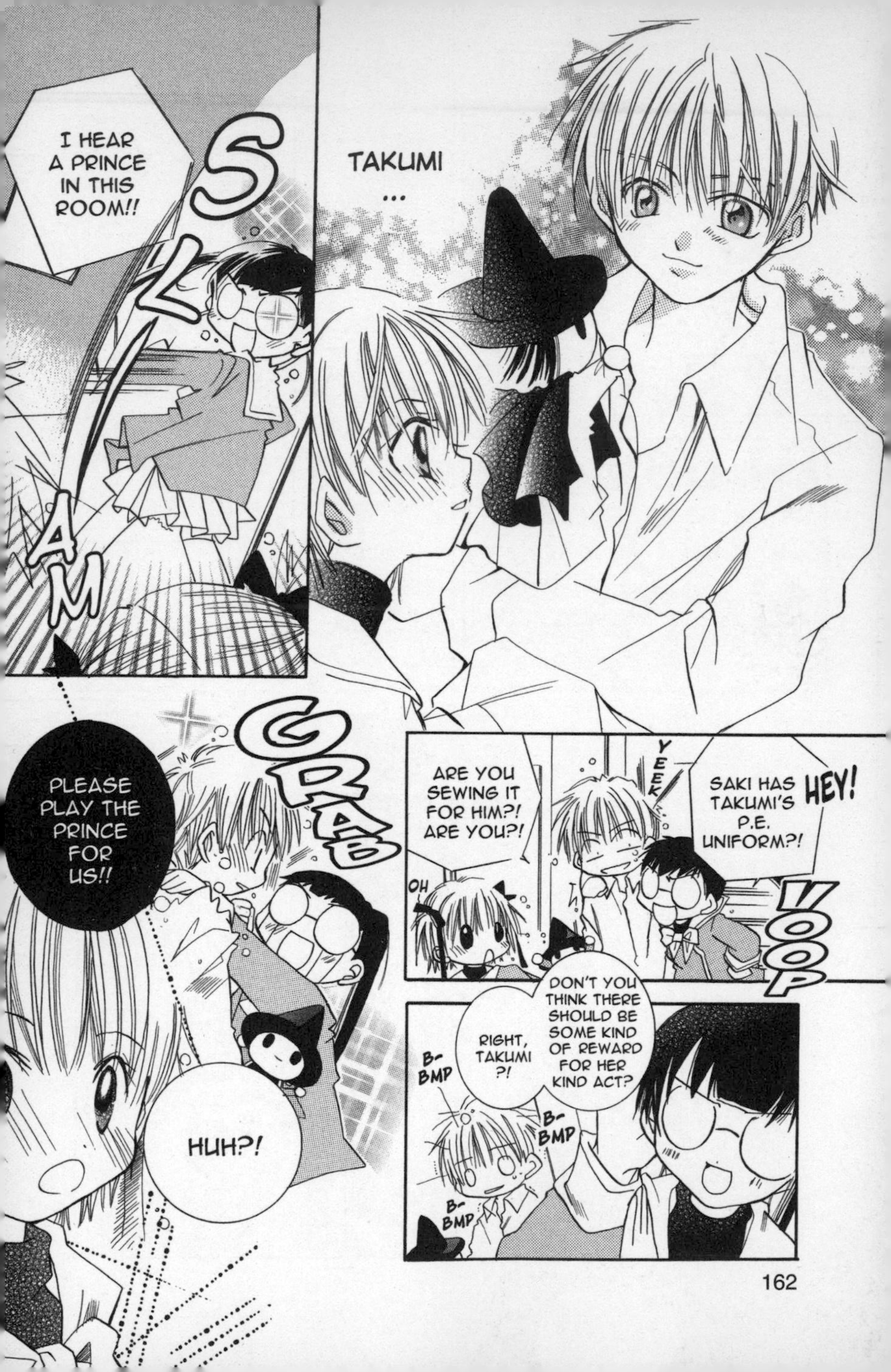

TAKUMI ...
I HEAR A PRINCE IN THIS ROOM!!
SLAM
HEY!
SAKI HAS TAKUMI'S P.E. UNIFORM?!
YEEK
ARE YOU SEWING IT FOR HIM?! ARE YOU?!
OH
VOOP
DON'T YOU THINK THERE SHOULD BE SOME KIND OF REWARD FOR HER KIND ACT?
RIGHT, TAKUMI?!
B-BMP
B-BMP
B-BMP
GRAB
PLEASE PLAY THE PRINCE FOR US!!
HUH?!

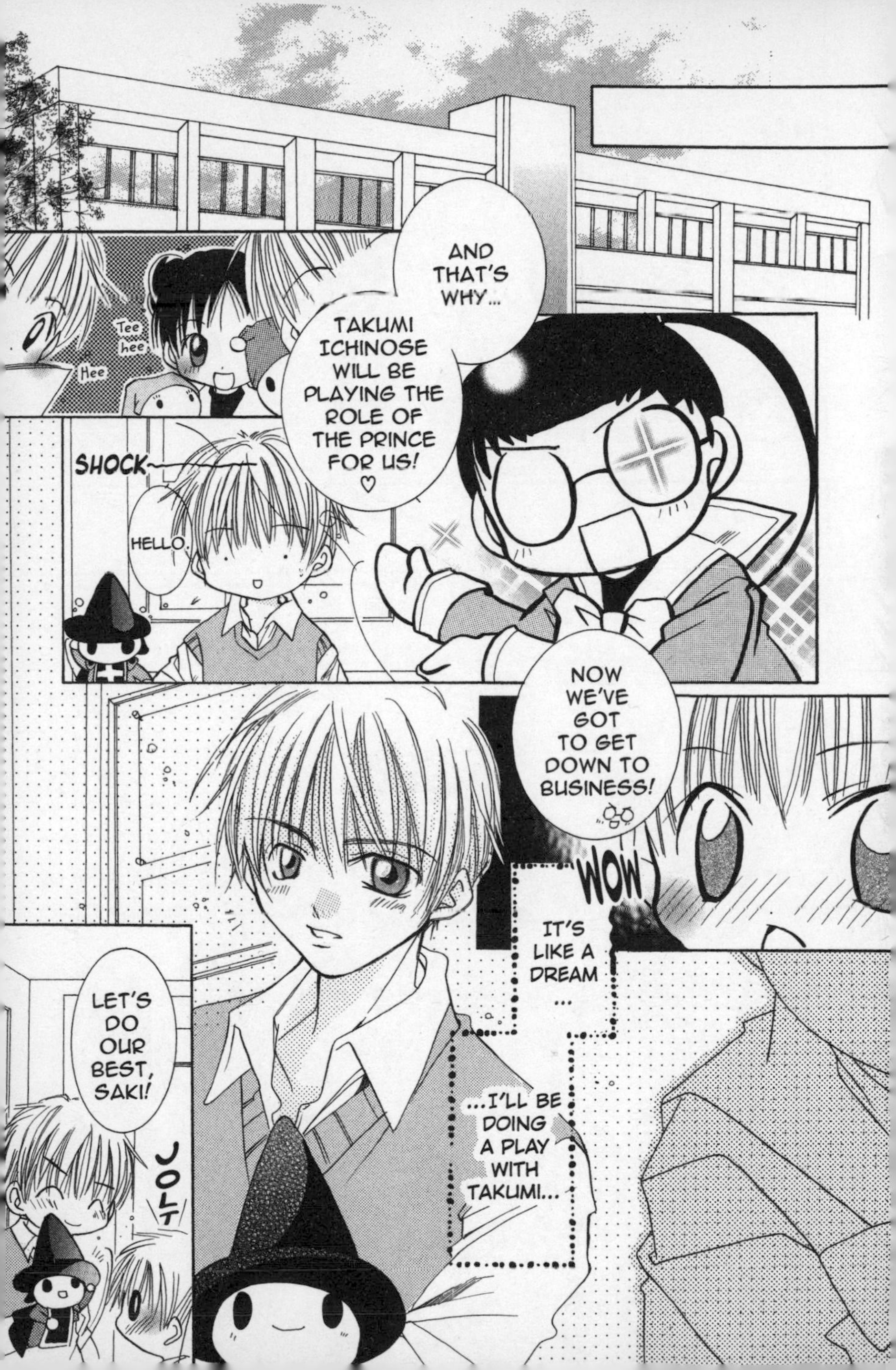
AND THAT'S WHY...
TAKUMI ICHINOSE WILL BE PLAYING THE ROLE OF THE PRINCE FOR US! ♡
Tee hee
Hee
SHOCK
HELLO.
NOW WE'VE GOT TO GET DOWN TO BUSINESS!
WOW
IT'S LIKE A DREAM...
...I'LL BE DOING A PLAY WITH TAKUMI...
LET'S DO OUR BEST, SAKI!
JOLT

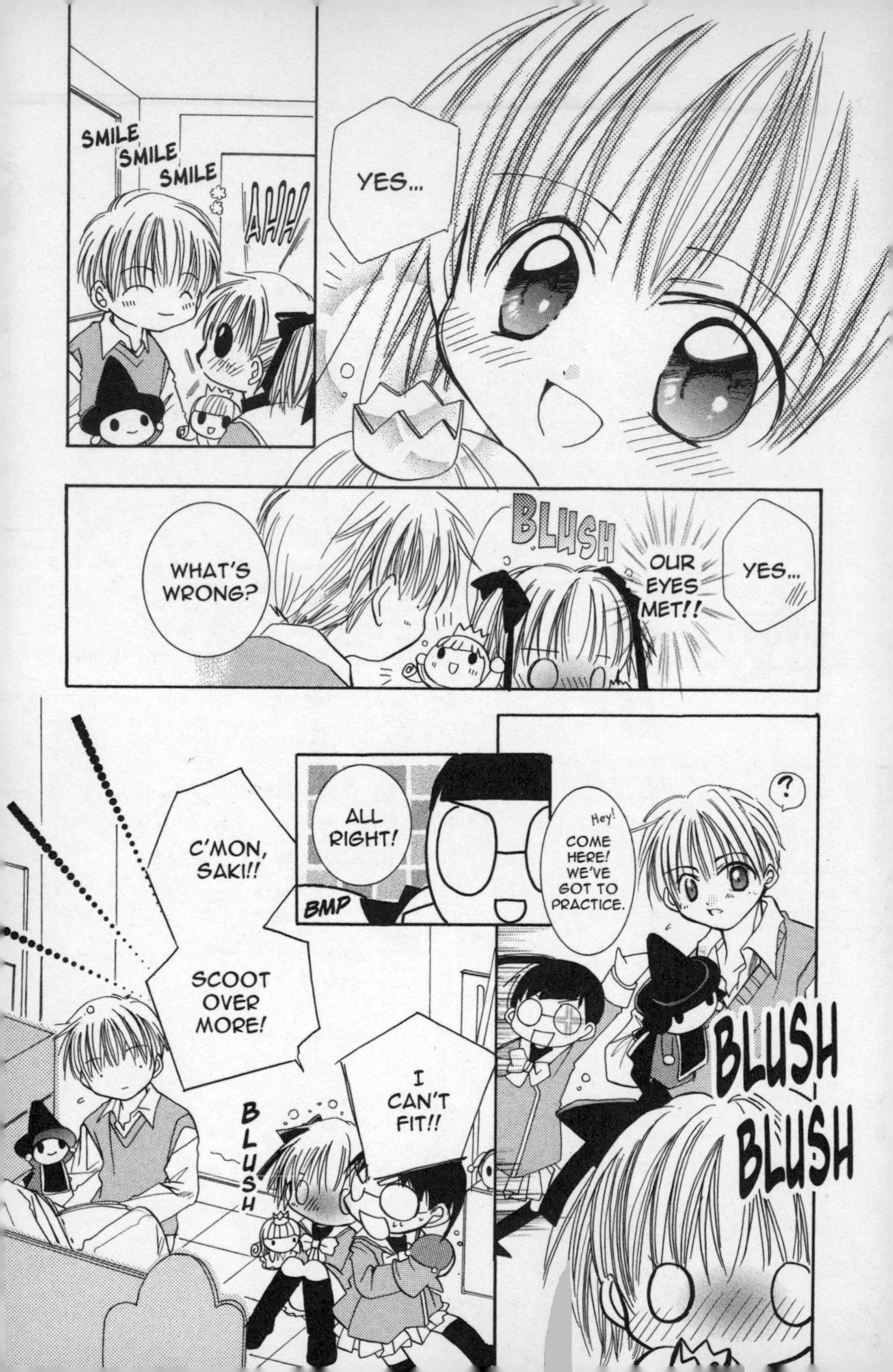
YES...
SMILE
SMILE
SMILE
AHH
YES...
OUR EYES MET!!
BLUSH
WHAT'S WRONG?
?
Hey! COME HERE! WE'VE GOT TO PRACTICE.
BLUSH
BLUSH
ALL RIGHT!
BMP
C'MON, SAKI!!
SCOOT OVER MORE!
I CAN'T FIT!!
BLUSH

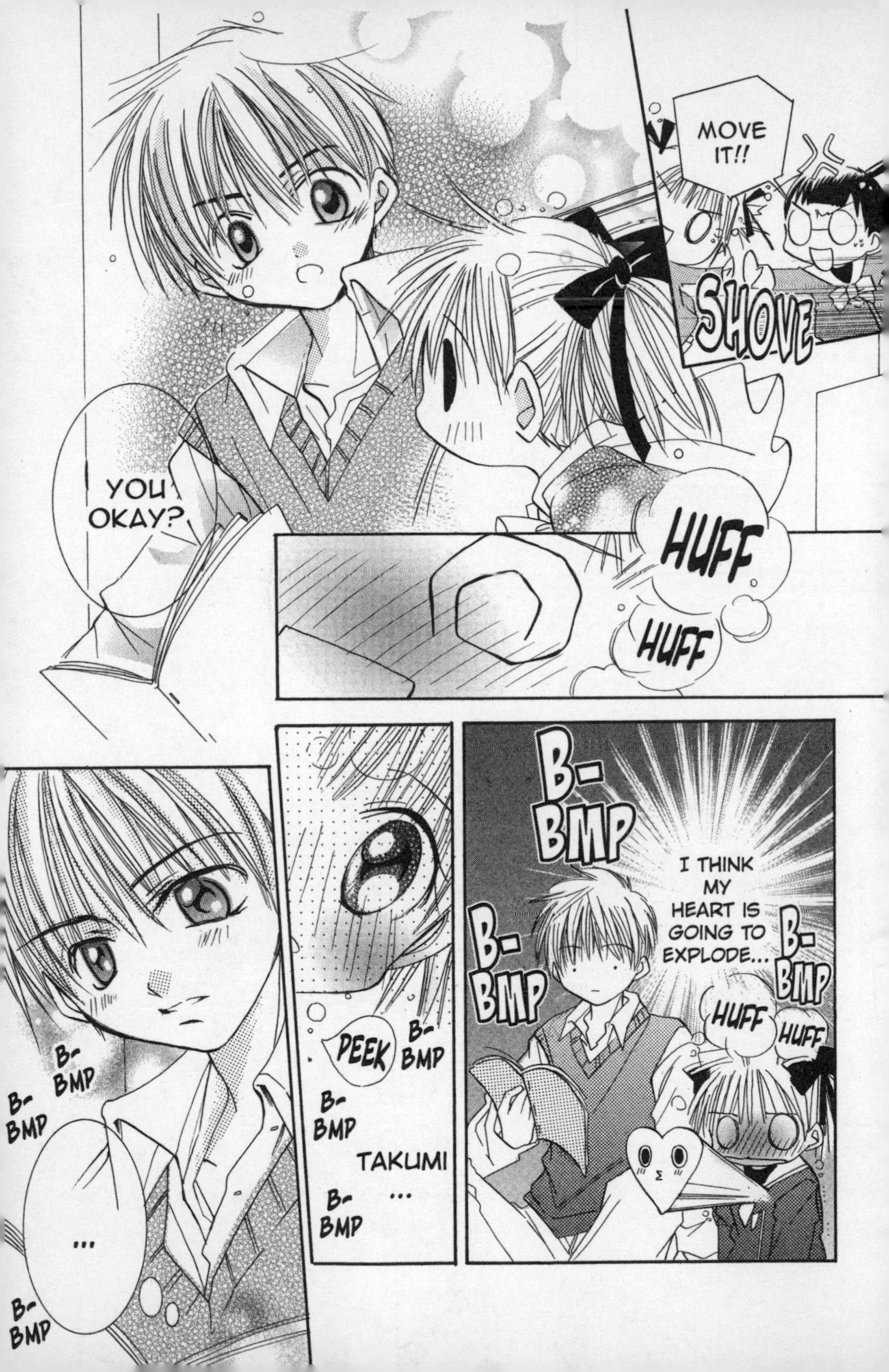
MOVE IT!!
SHOVE
HUFF
HUFF
YOU OKAY?
B-BMP
I THINK MY HEART IS GOING TO EXPLODE...
B-BMP
B-BMP
HUFF
HUFF
PEEK
B-BMP
B-BMP
TAKUMI ...
B-BMP
B-BMP
B-BMP
...
B-BMP

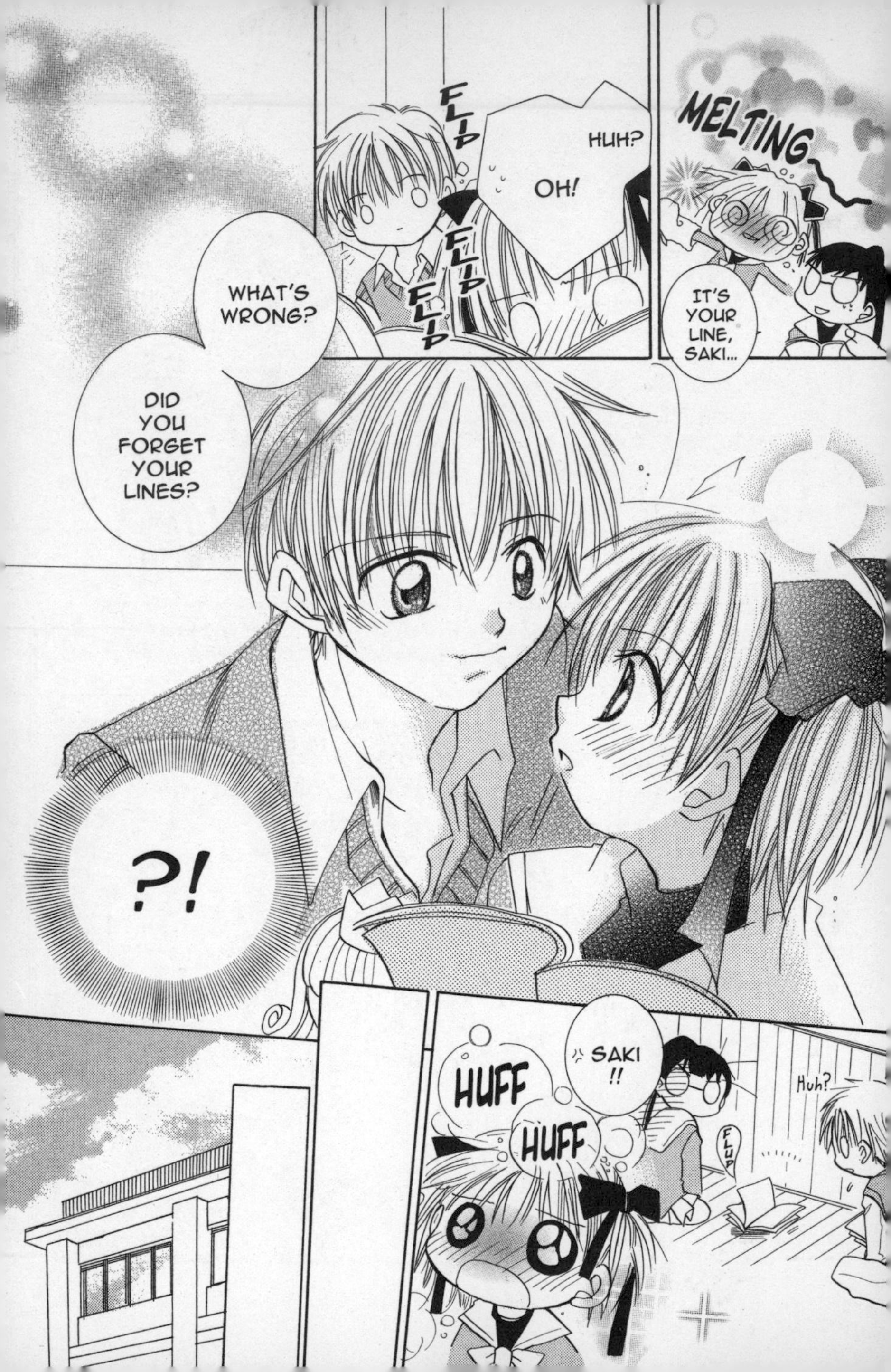
MELTING
IT'S YOUR LINE, SAKI...
FLIP
HUH?
OH!
FLIP
FLIP
FLIP
WHAT'S WRONG?
DID YOU FORGET YOUR LINES?
?!
SAKI !!
HUFF
HUFF
Huh?
FLUP

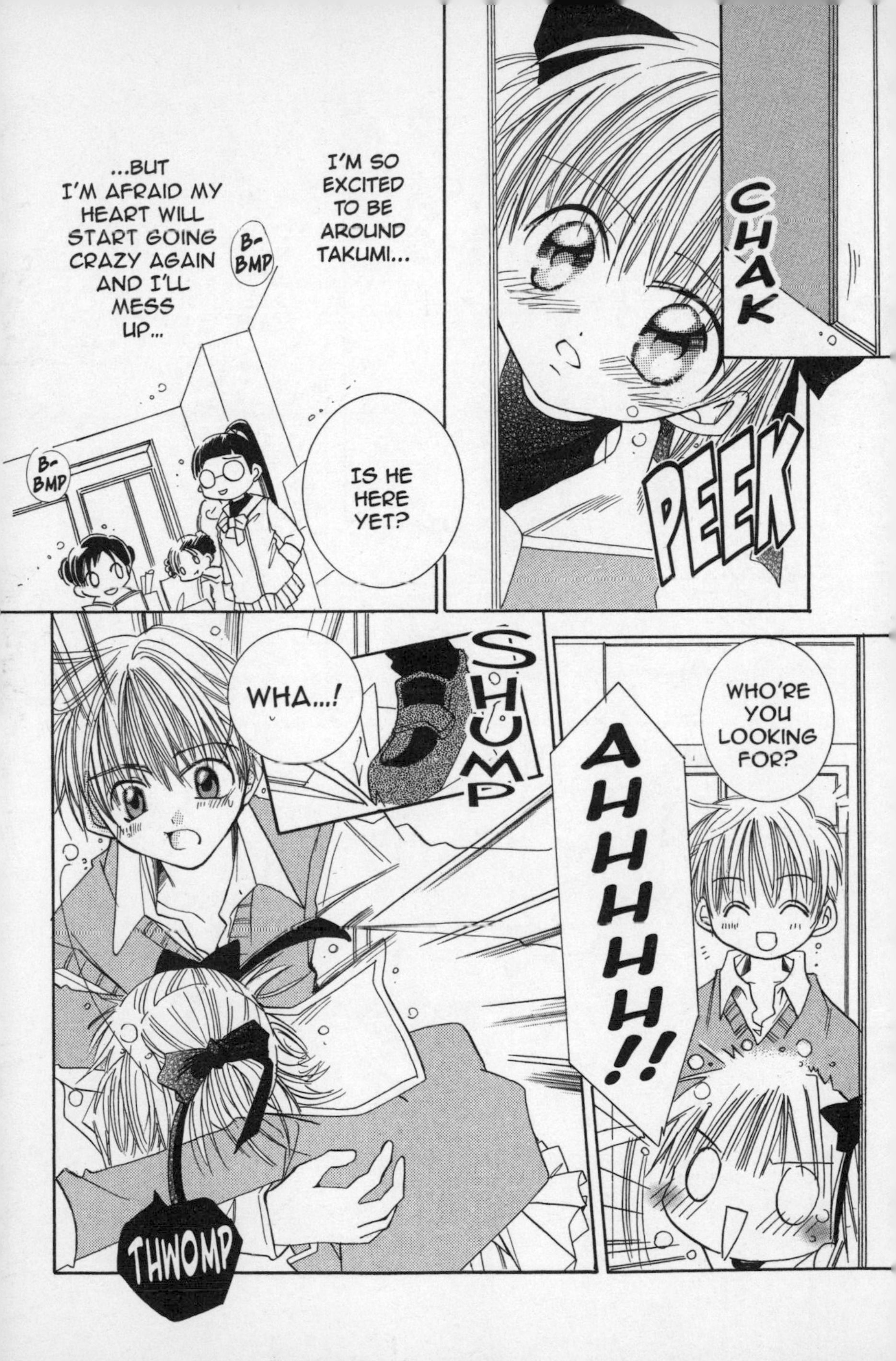
CHAK
PEEK
I'M SO EXCITED TO BE AROUND TAKUMI...
B-BMP
...BUT I'M AFRAID MY HEART WILL START GOING CRAZY AGAIN AND I'LL MESS UP...
IS HE HERE YET?
B-BMP
WHO'RE YOU LOOKING FOR?
AHHHHHH!!
SHUMP
WHA...!
THWOMP

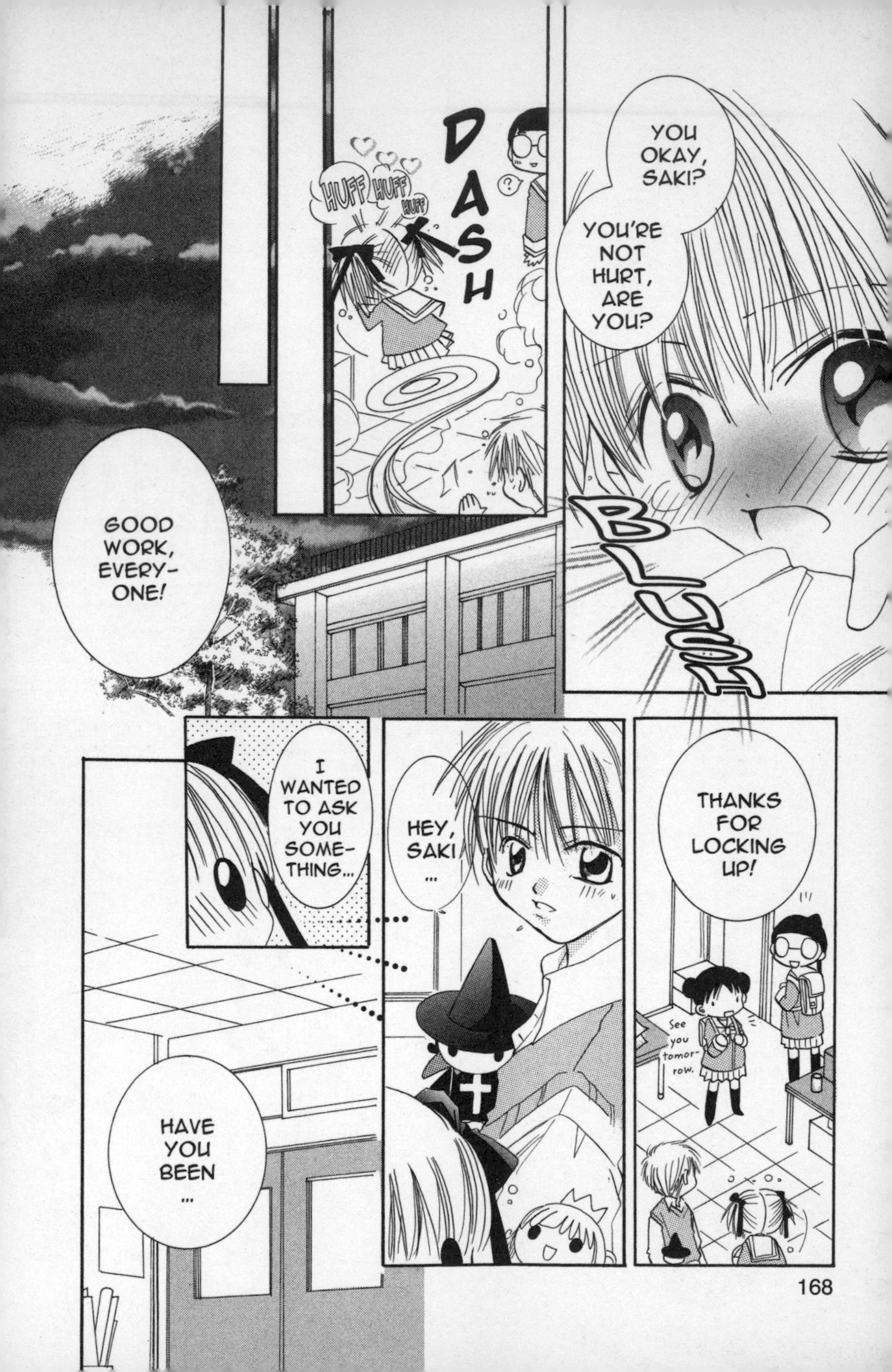

YOU OKAY, SAKI?
YOU'RE NOT HURT, ARE YOU?
BLUSH
DASH
HUFF HUFF HUFF
GOOD WORK, EVERY-ONE!
THANKS FOR LOCKING UP!
See you tomor-row.
HEY, SAKI ...
I WANTED TO ASK YOU SOME-THING...
HAVE YOU BEEN ...

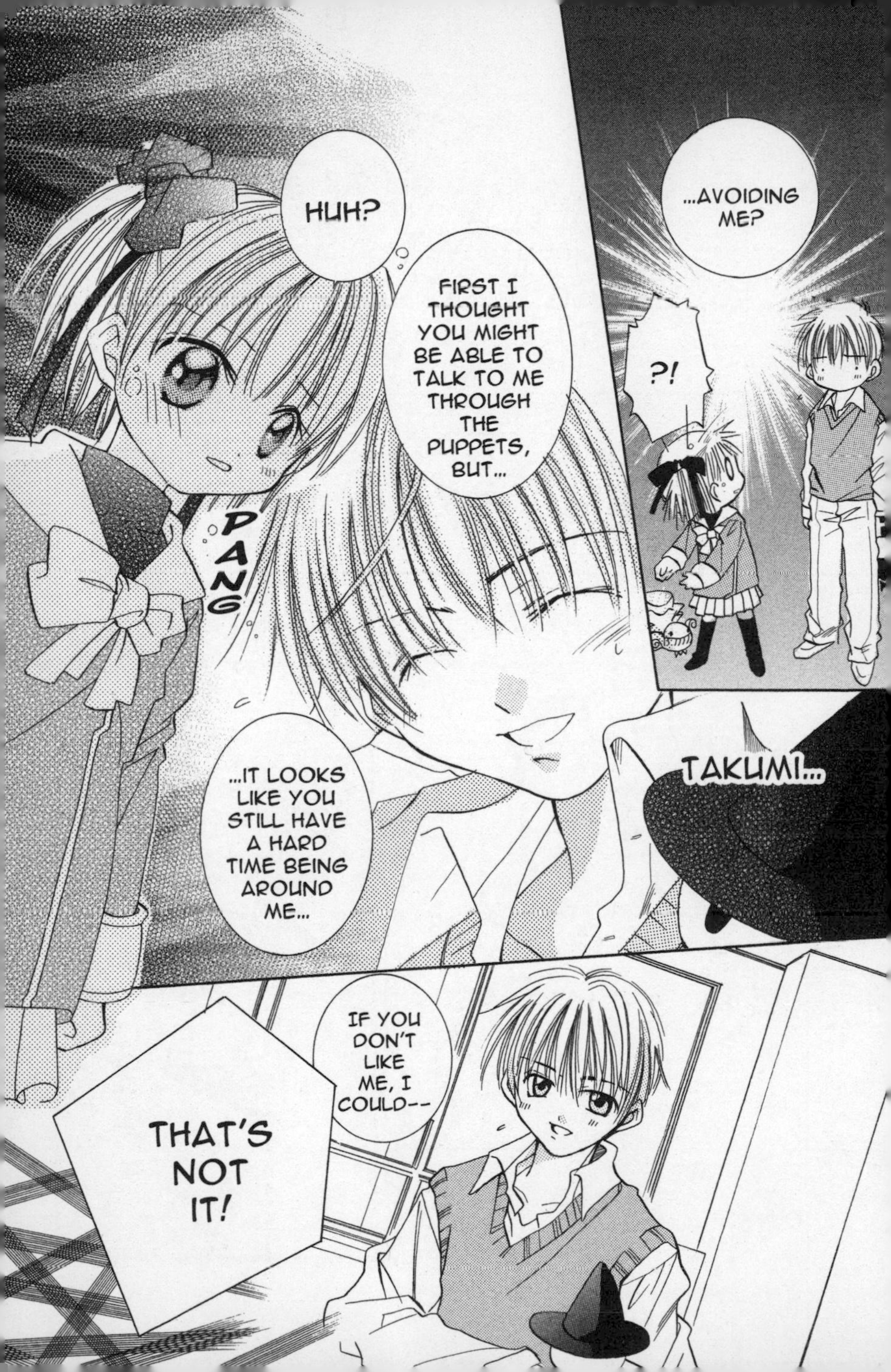
...AVOIDING ME?
?!
TAKUMI...
HUH?
FIRST I THOUGHT YOU MIGHT BE ABLE TO TALK TO ME THROUGH THE PUPPETS, BUT...
PANG
...IT LOOKS LIKE YOU STILL HAVE A HARD TIME BEING AROUND ME...
IF YOU DON'T LIKE ME, I COULD--
THAT'S NOT IT!

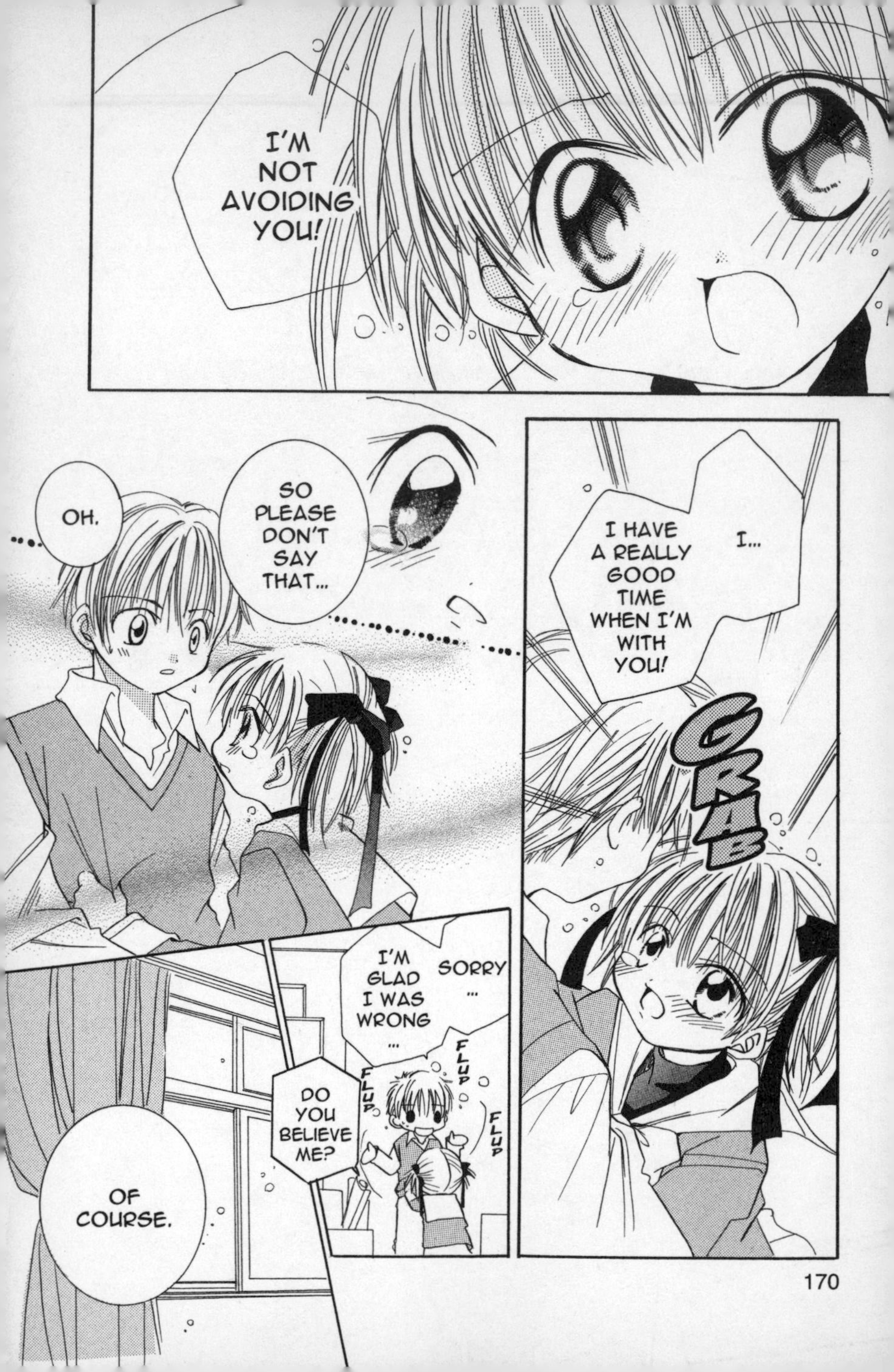
I'M NOT AVOIDING YOU!
I...
I HAVE A REALLY GOOD TIME WHEN I'M WITH YOU!
GRAB
SO PLEASE DON'T SAY THAT...
OH.
SORRY...
I'M GLAD I WAS WRONG...
FLUP
FLUP
FLUP
DO YOU BELIEVE ME?
OF COURSE.

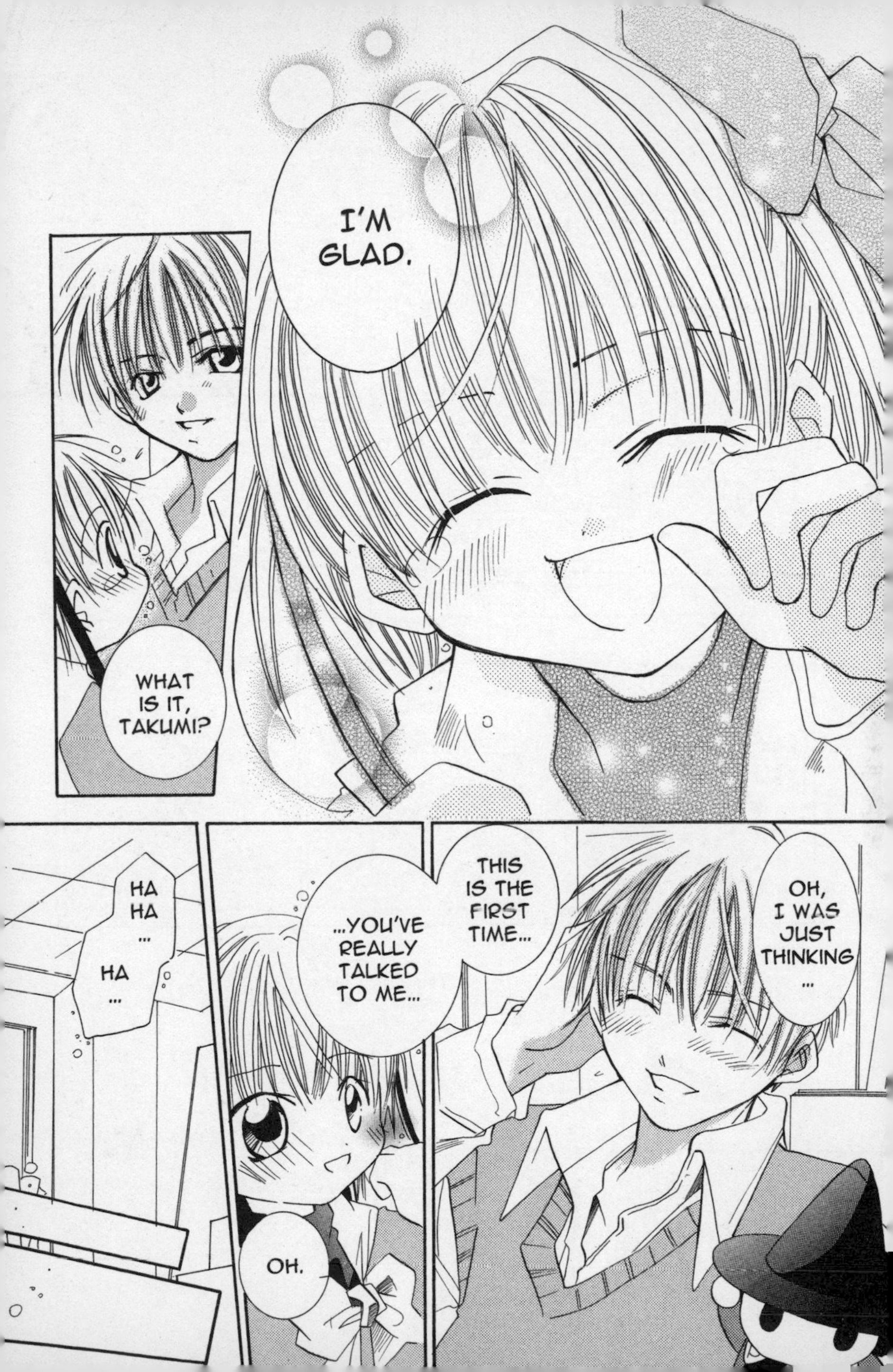
I'M GLAD.
WHAT IS IT, TAKUMI?
OH, I WAS JUST THINKING ...
THIS IS THE FIRST TIME...
...YOU'VE REALLY TALKED TO ME...
OH.
HA HA ... HA ...

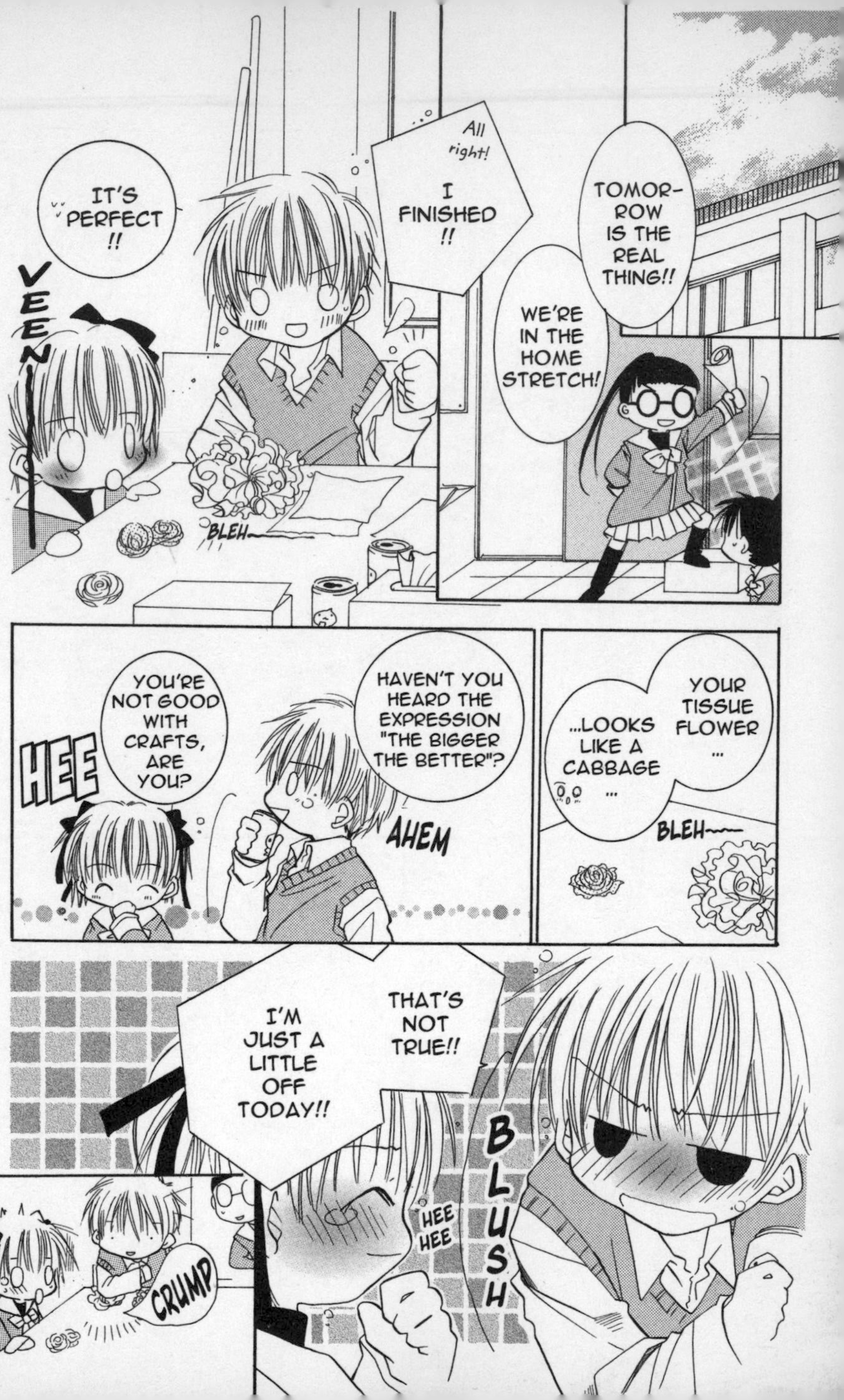
TOMORROW IS THE REAL THING!!
WE'RE IN THE HOME STRETCH!
All right!
I FINISHED!!
IT'S PERFECT!!
VEEN
BLEH
YOUR TISSUE FLOWER...
...LOOKS LIKE A CABBAGE...
BLEH
HAVEN'T YOU HEARD THE EXPRESSION "THE BIGGER THE BETTER"?
AHEM
YOU'RE NOT GOOD WITH CRAFTS, ARE YOU?
HEE
THAT'S NOT TRUE!!
I'M JUST A LITTLE OFF TODAY!!
BLUSH
HEE HEE
CRUMP

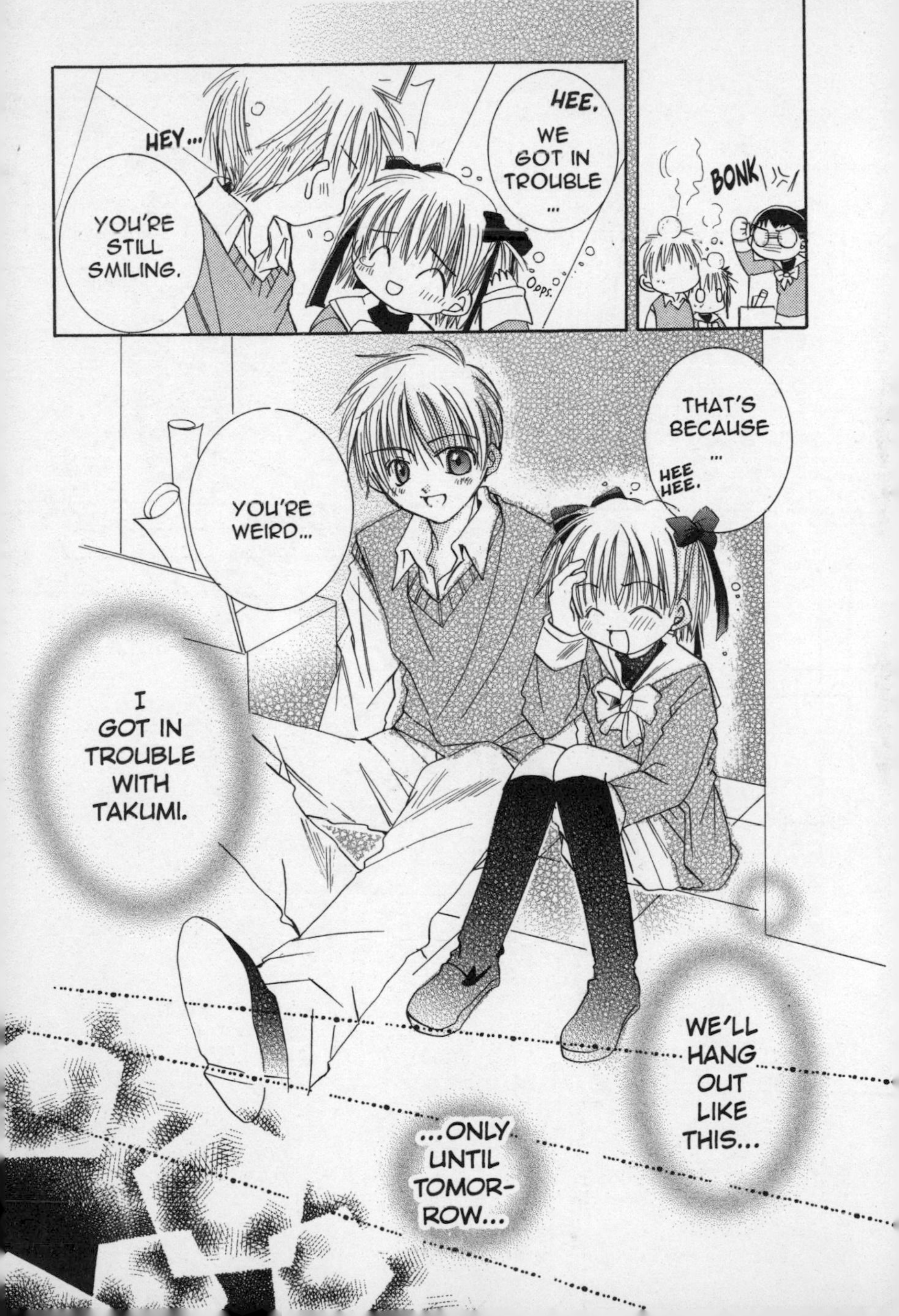
BONK
HEE. WE GOT IN TROUBLE ...
HEY...
YOU'RE STILL SMILING.
Opps.
THAT'S BECAUSE ...
HEE HEE.
YOU'RE WEIRD...
I GOT IN TROUBLE WITH TAKUMI.
WE'LL HANG OUT LIKE THIS...
...ONLY UNTIL TOMOR-ROW...

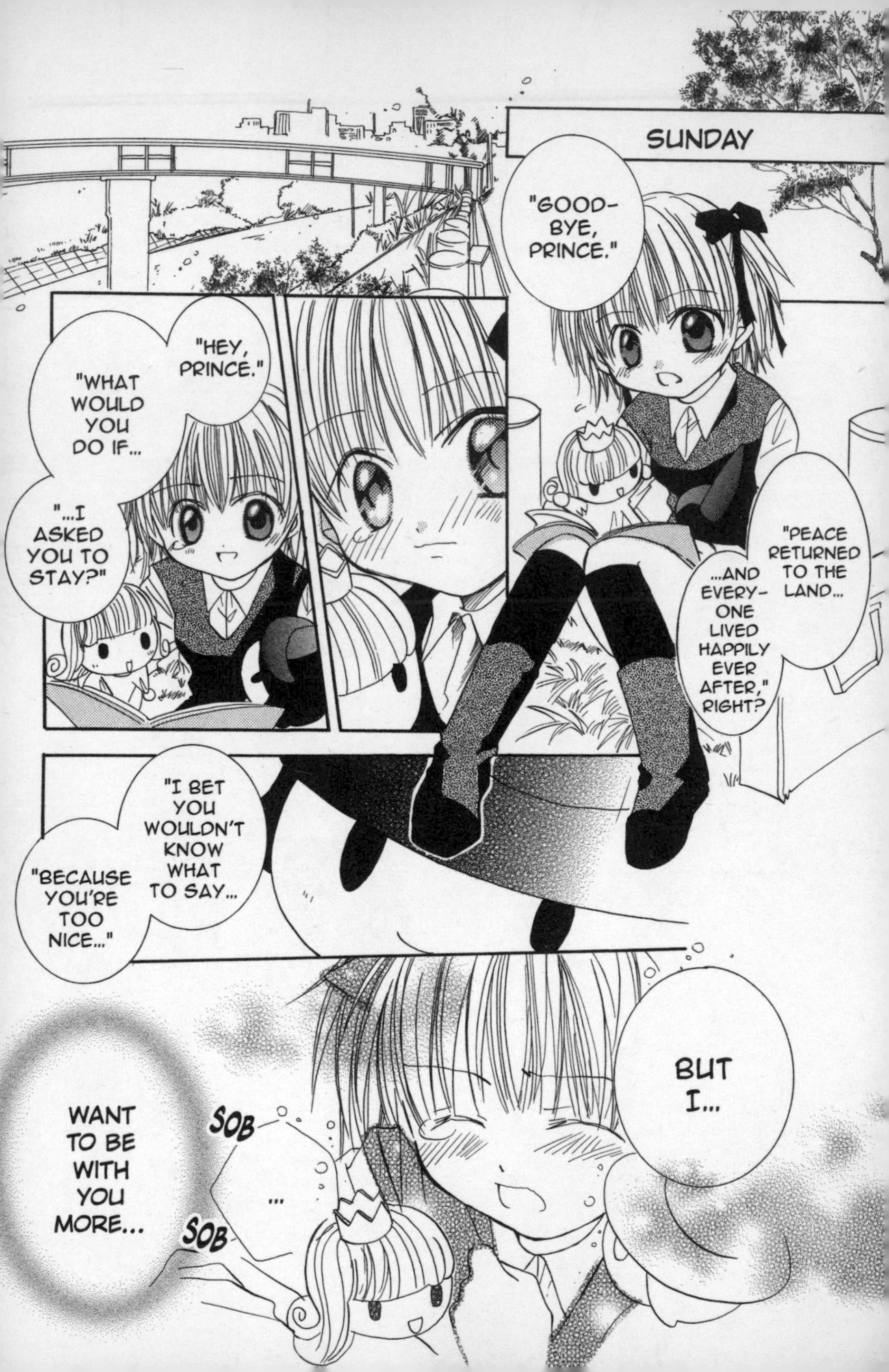

SUNDAY
"GOOD-BYE, PRINCE."
"PEACE RETURNED TO THE LAND...
...AND EVERYONE LIVED HAPPILY EVER AFTER," RIGHT?
"HEY, PRINCE."
"WHAT WOULD YOU DO IF...
"...I ASKED YOU TO STAY?"
"I BET YOU WOULDN'T KNOW WHAT TO SAY...
"BECAUSE YOU'RE TOO NICE..."
BUT I...
SOB
...
SOB
WANT TO BE WITH YOU MORE...

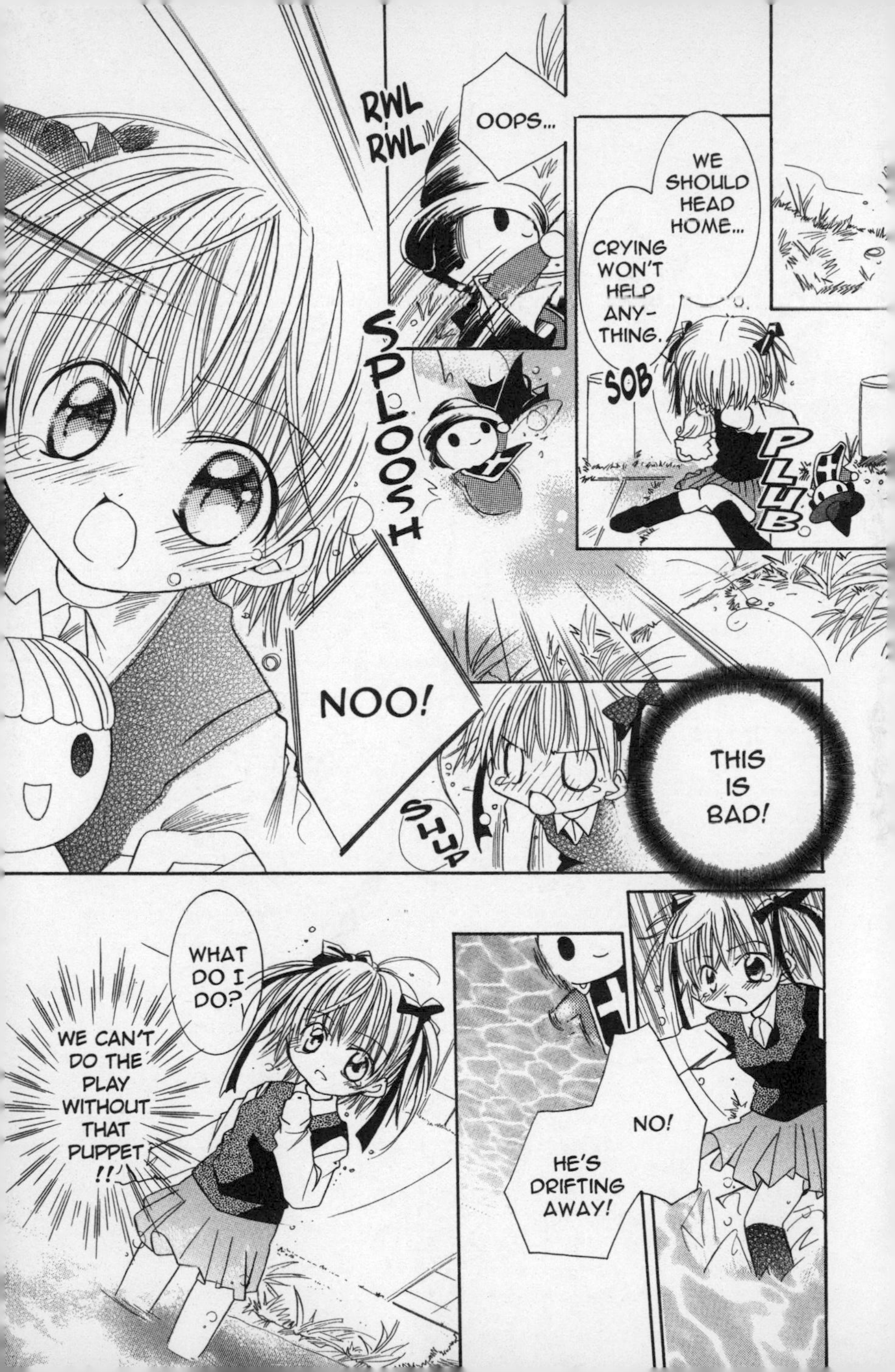
WE SHOULD HEAD HOME...
CRYING WON'T HELP ANYTHING.
SOB
PLUB
RWL RWL
OOPS...
SPLOOSH
THIS IS BAD!
SHUP
NOO!
NO!
HE'S DRIFTING AWAY!
WHAT DO I DO?
WE CAN'T DO THE PLAY WITHOUT THAT PUPPET!!

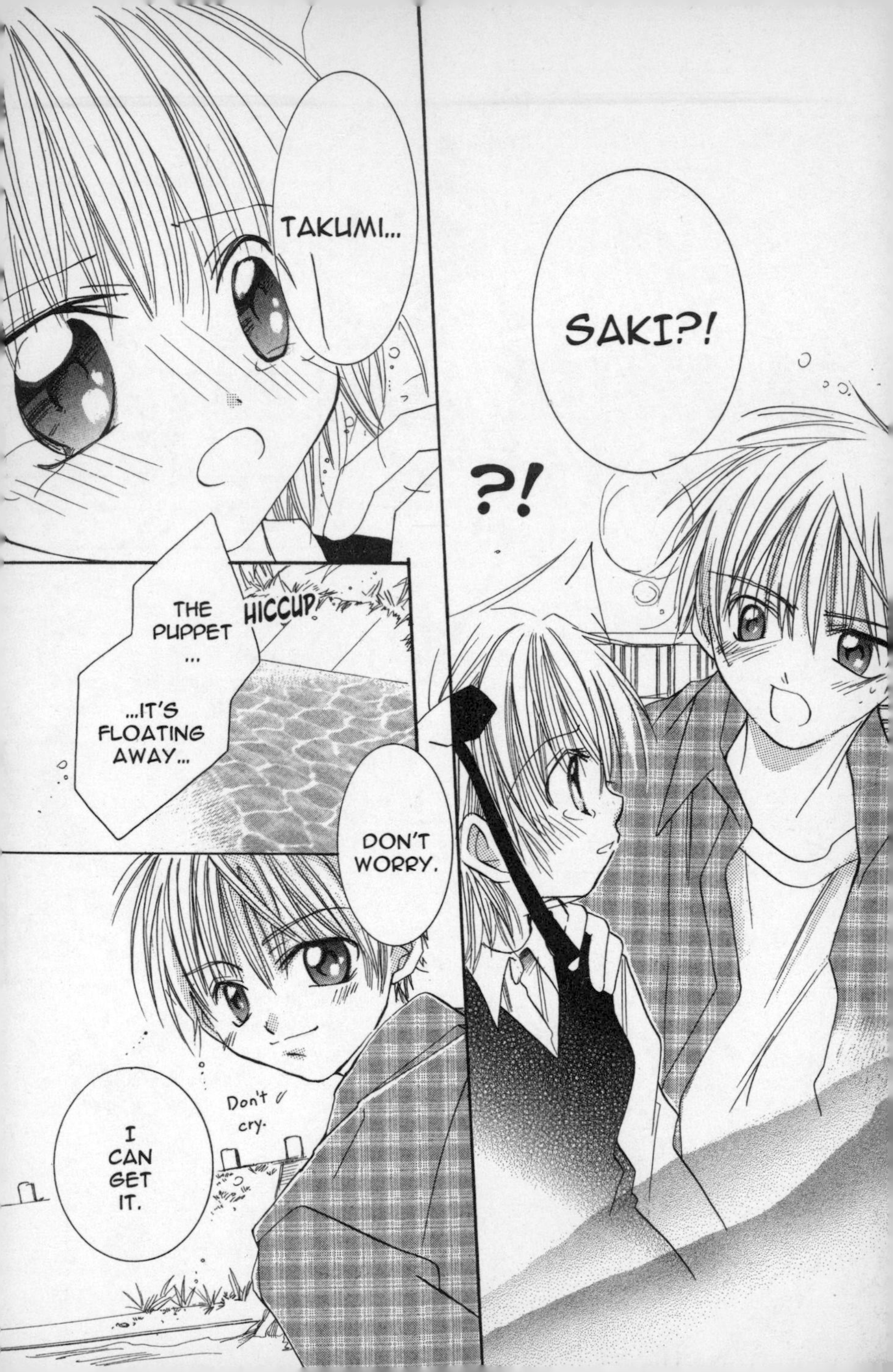
SAKI?!
?!
TAKUMI...
HICCUP
THE PUPPET ...
...IT'S FLOATING AWAY...
DON'T WORRY.
Don't cry.
I CAN GET IT.

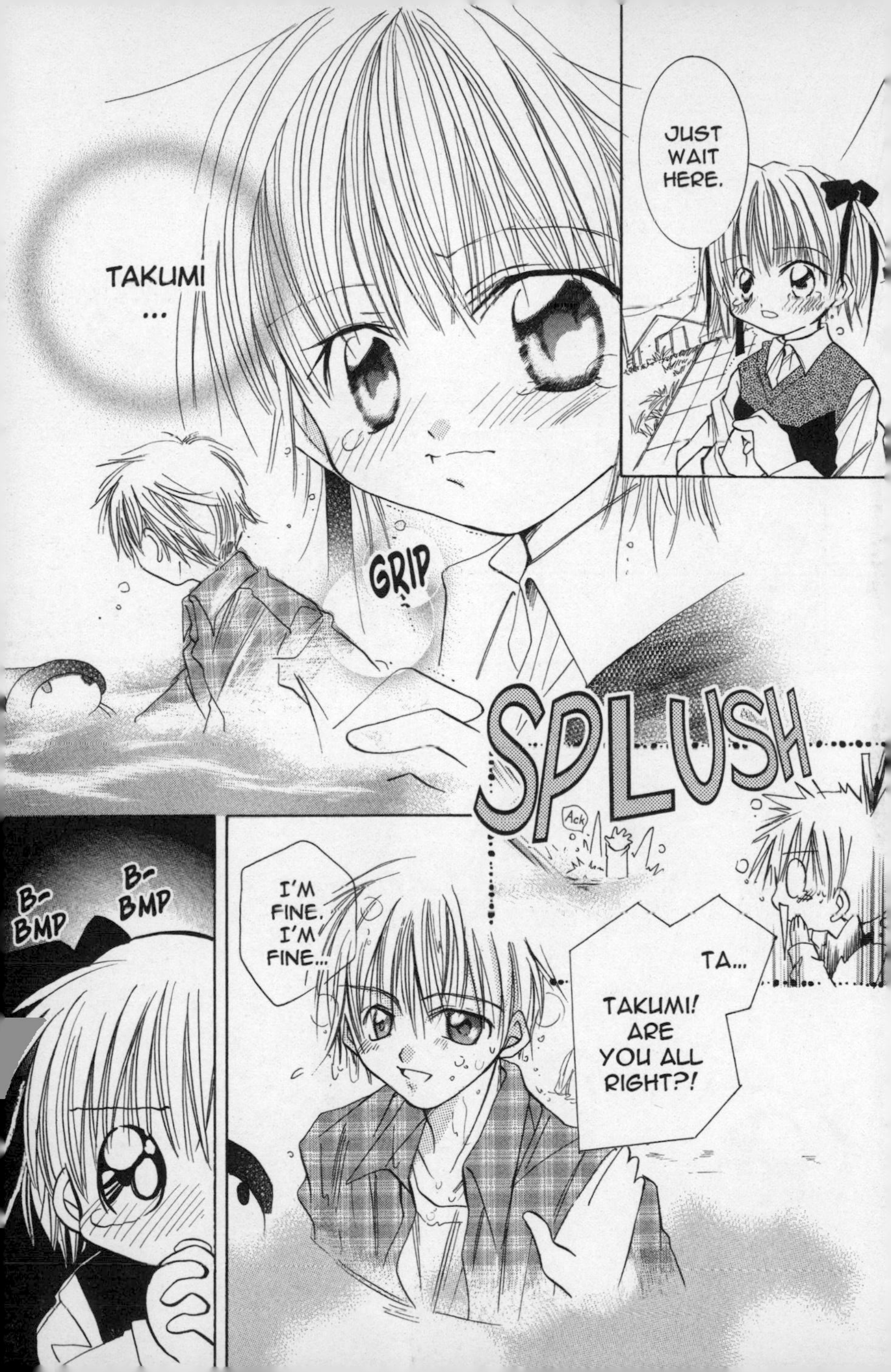
JUST WAIT HERE.
TAKUMI ...
GRIP
SPLUSH
Ack
TA...
TAKUMI! ARE YOU ALL RIGHT?!
I'M FINE. I'M FINE...
B-BMP
B-BMP

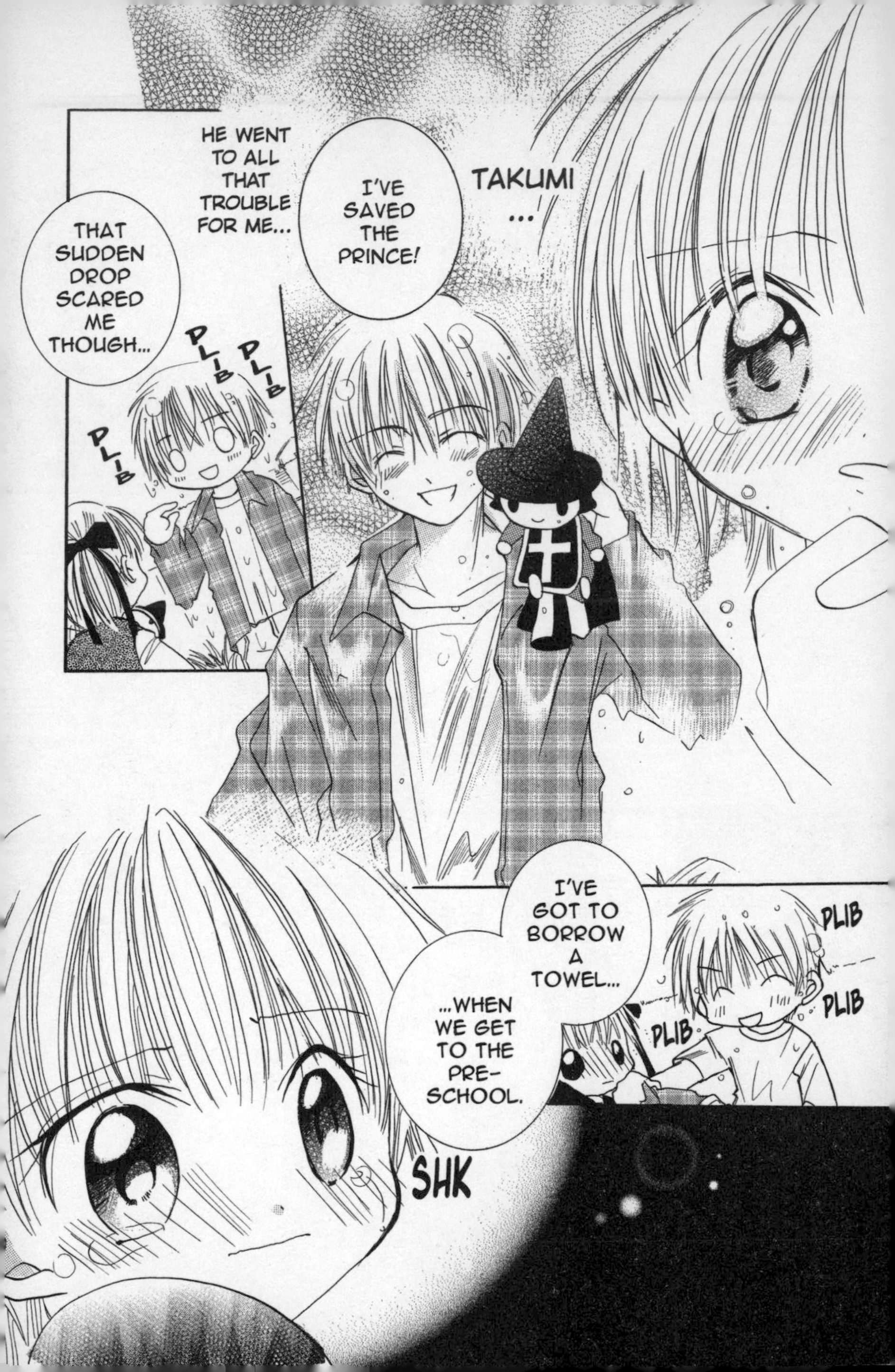

TAKUMI ...
I'VE SAVED THE PRINCE!
HE WENT TO ALL THAT TROUBLE FOR ME...
PLIB PLIB
PLIB
THAT SUDDEN DROP SCARED ME THOUGH...
PLIB
PLIB
PLIB
I'VE GOT TO BORROW A TOWEL...
...WHEN WE GET TO THE PRE-SCHOOL.
SHK

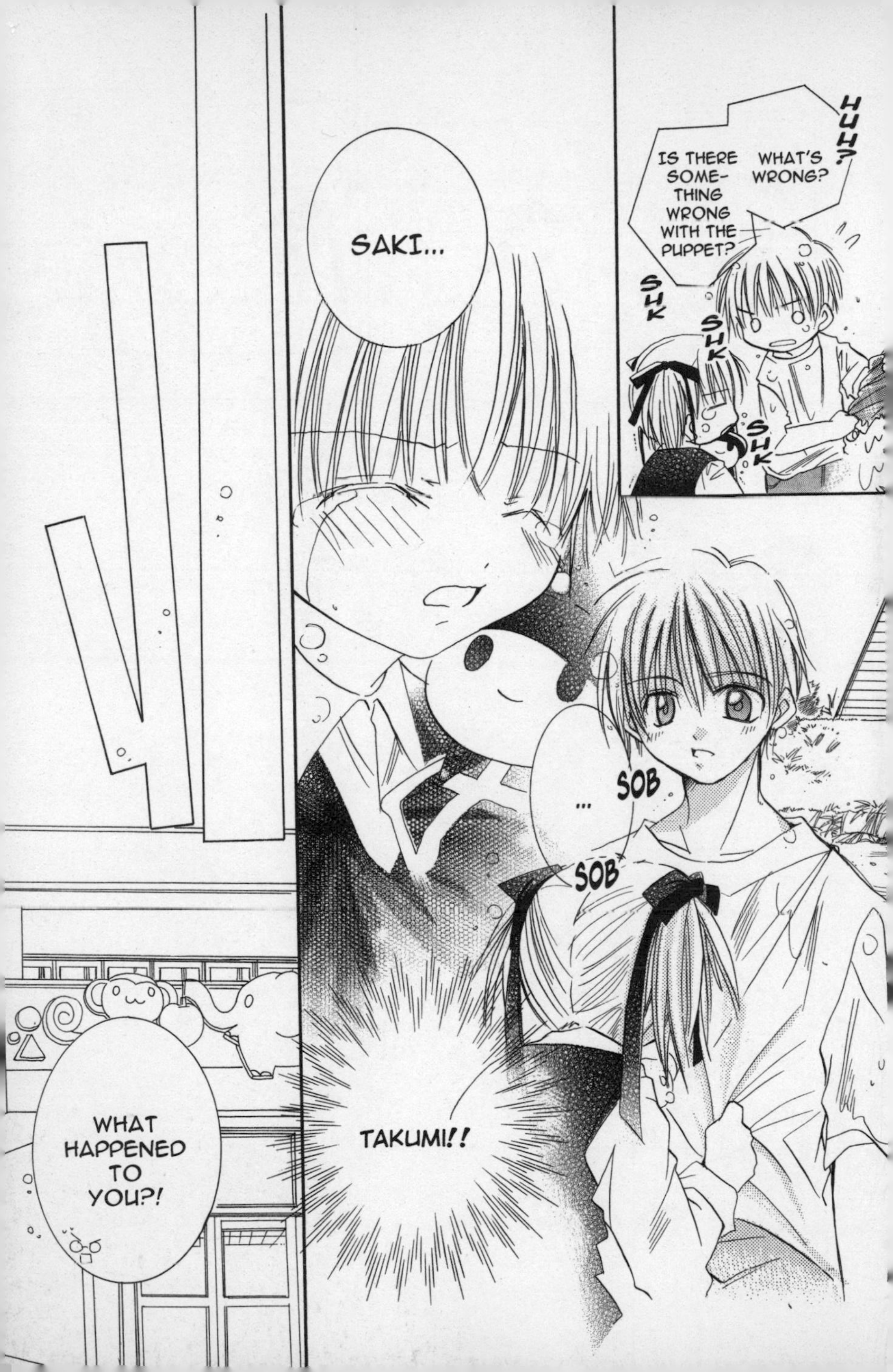
HUH?
WHAT'S WRONG?
IS THERE SOMETHING WRONG WITH THE PUPPET?
SHK
SHK
SHK
...
SOB
SOB
SAKI...
TAKUMI!!
WHAT HAPPENED TO YOU?!

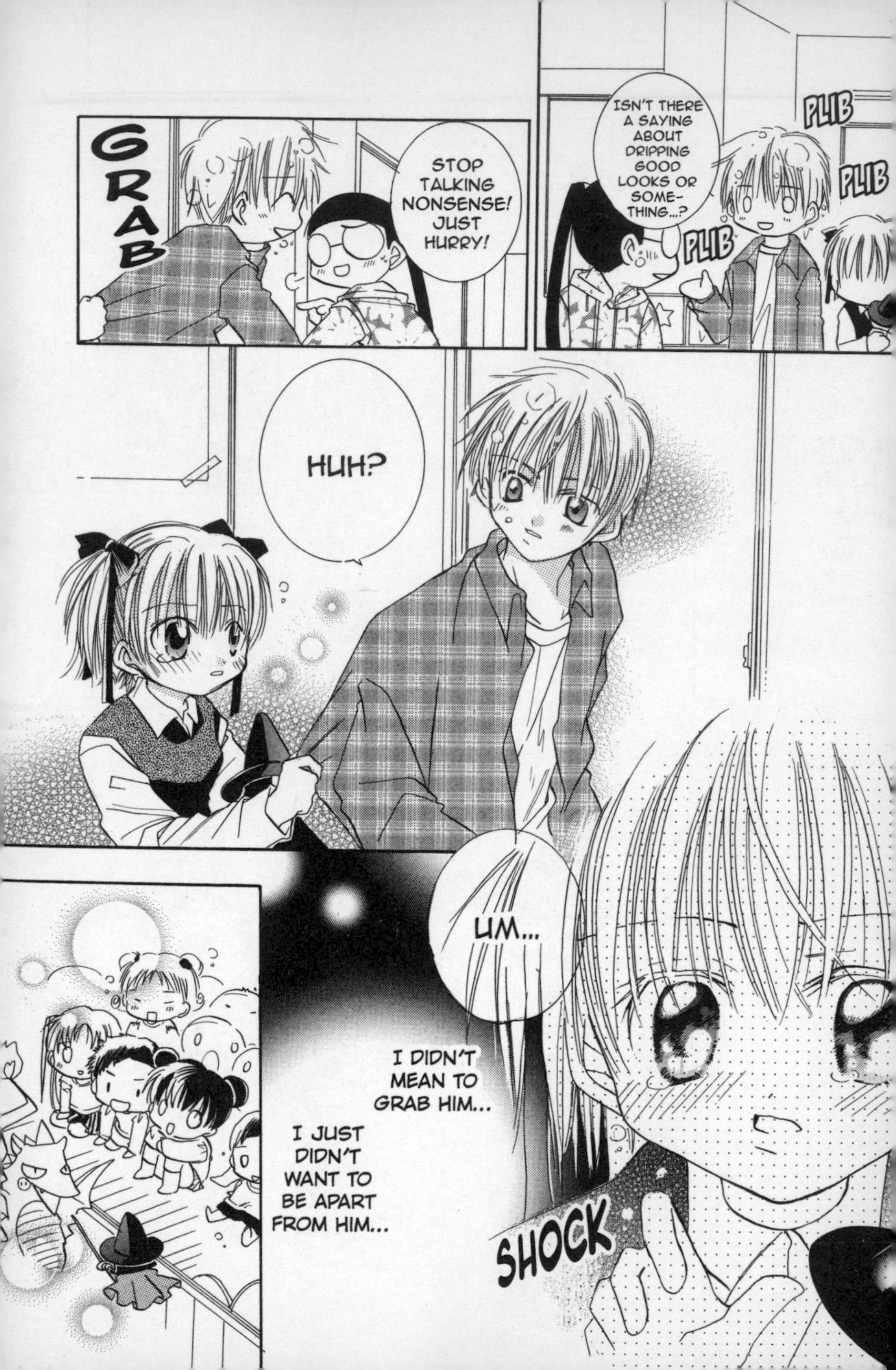
ISN'T THERE A SAYING ABOUT DRIPPING GOOD LOOKS OR SOME-THING...?
PLIB
PLIB
PLIB
GRAB
STOP TALKING NONSENSE! JUST HURRY!
HUH?
UM...
SHOCK
I DIDN'T MEAN TO GRAB HIM...
I JUST DIDN'T WANT TO BE APART FROM HIM...

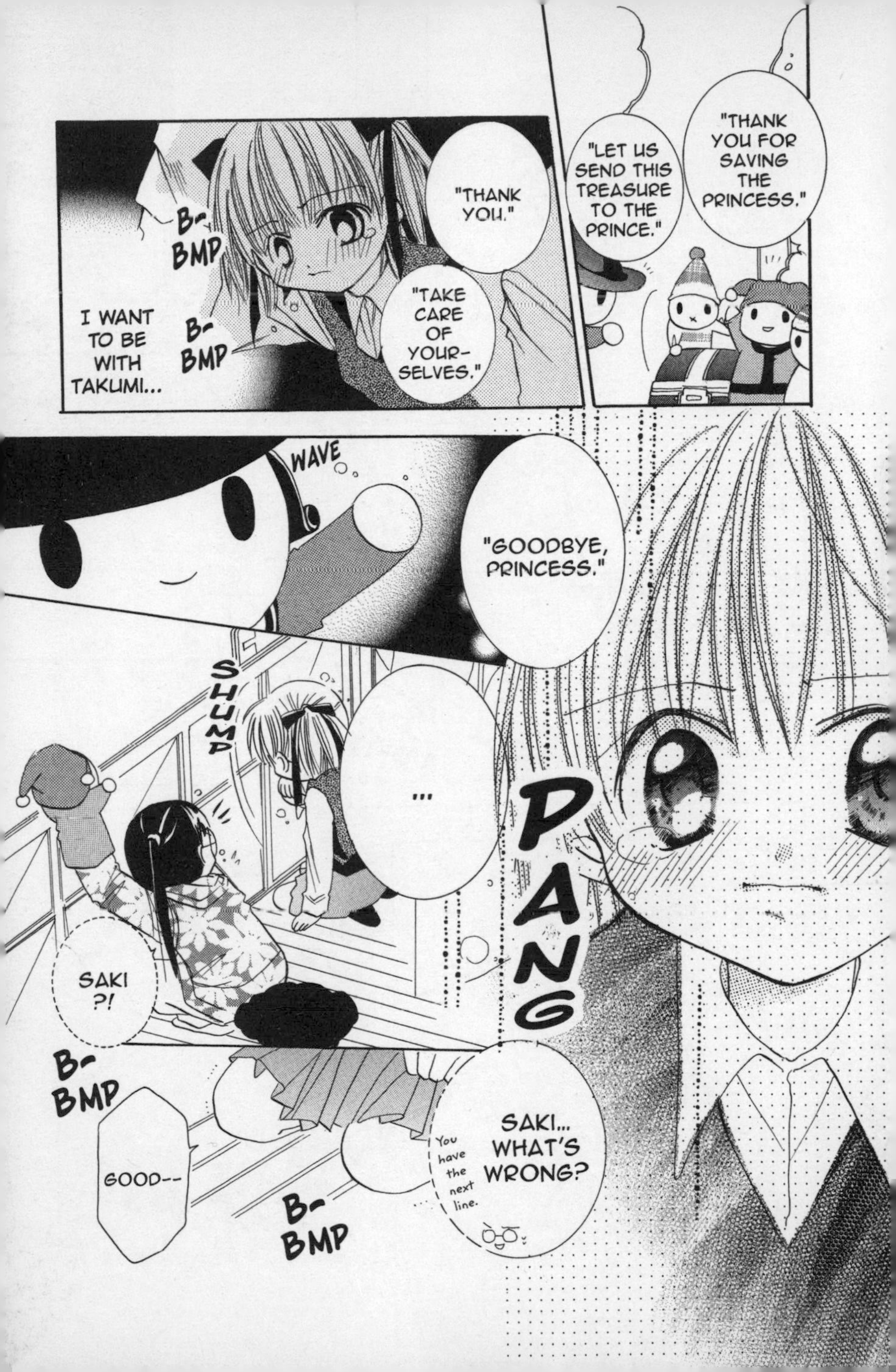

"THANK YOU FOR SAVING THE PRINCESS."
"LET US SEND THIS TREASURE TO THE PRINCE."
"THANK YOU."
B-BMP
"TAKE CARE OF YOURSELVES."
B-BMP
I WANT TO BE WITH TAKUMI...
WAVE
"GOODBYE, PRINCESS."
SHUMP
...
SAKI ?!
PANG
SAKI... WHAT'S WRONG?
You have the next line.
B-BMP
GOOD--
B-BMP

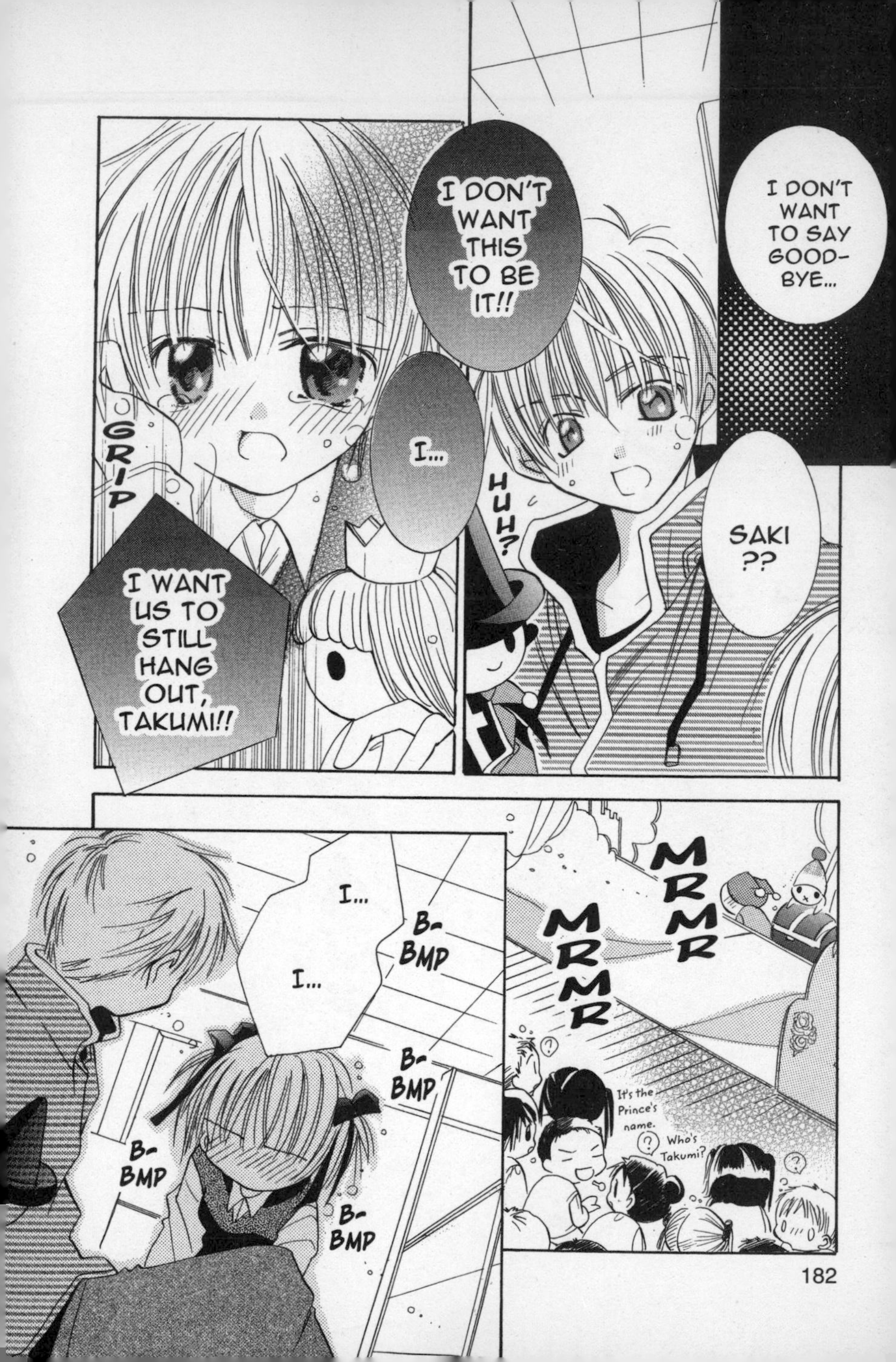
I DON'T WANT TO SAY GOOD-BYE...
I DON'T WANT THIS TO BE IT!!
I...
GRIP
I WANT US TO STILL HANG OUT, TAKUMI!!
HUH?
SAKI ??
MRMR
MRMR
It's the Prince's name.
Who's Takumi?
I...
B-BMP
I...
B-BMP
B-BMP
B-BMP

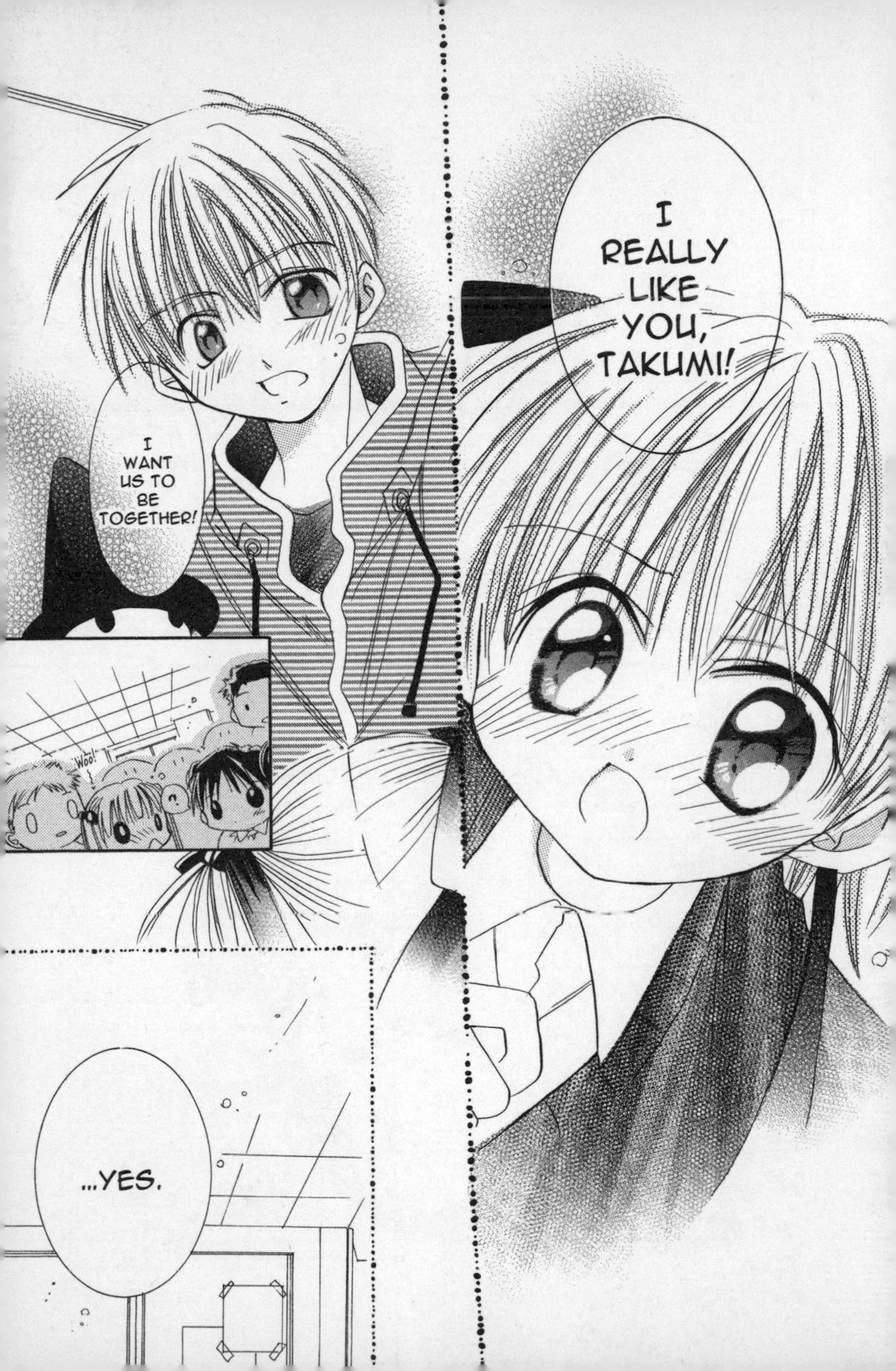
I REALLY LIKE YOU, TAKUMI!
I WANT US TO BE TOGETHER!
Woo!
...YES.

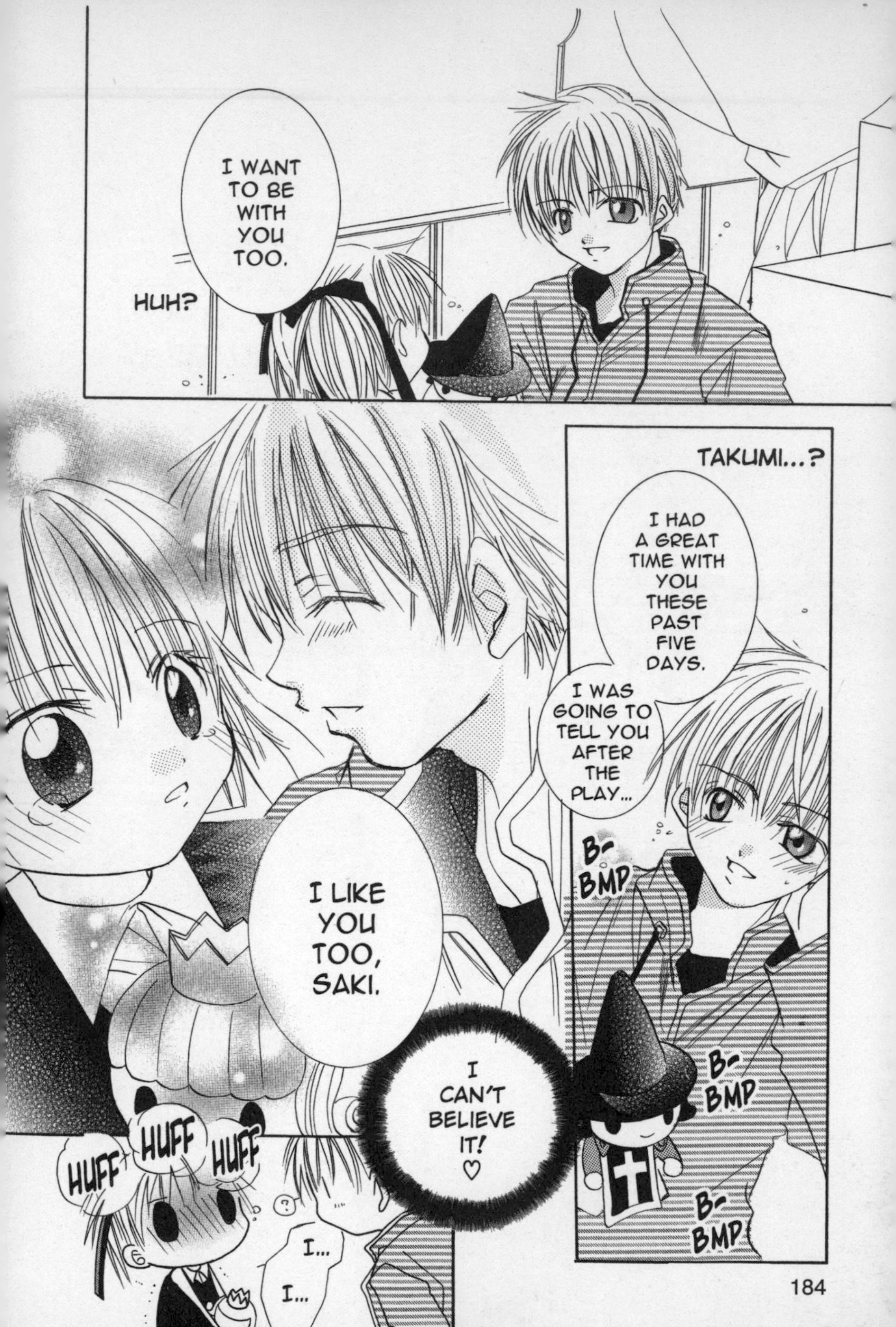
I WANT TO BE WITH YOU TOO.
HUH?
TAKUMI...?
I HAD A GREAT TIME WITH YOU THESE PAST FIVE DAYS.
I WAS GOING TO TELL YOU AFTER THE PLAY...
B-BMP
B-BMP
B-BMP
I LIKE YOU TOO, SAKI.
I CAN'T BELIEVE IT! ♡
HUFF
HUFF
HUFF
I...
I...

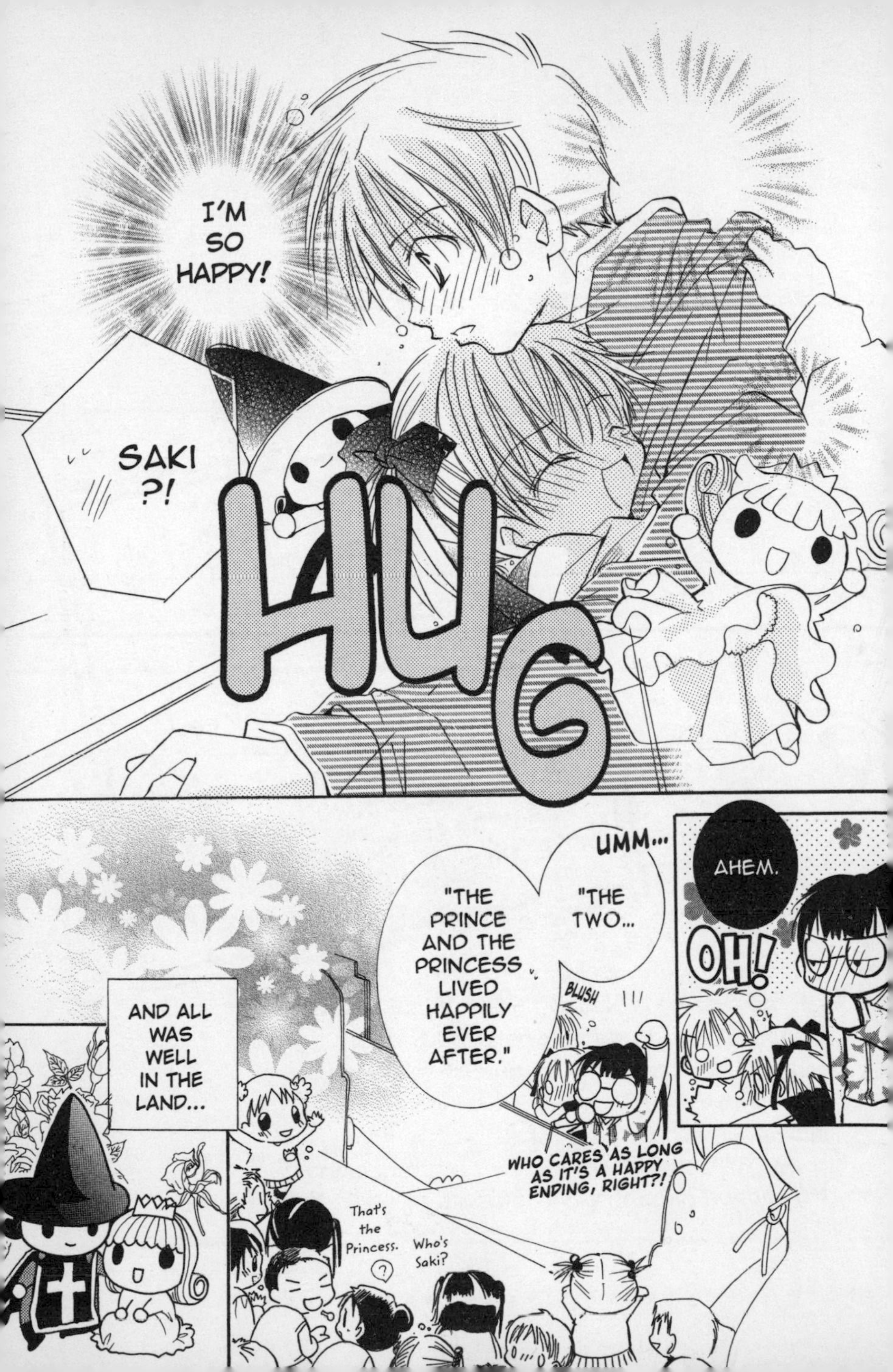
I'M SO HAPPY!
SAKI ?!
HUG
AHEM.
OH!
UMM...
"THE TWO...
"THE PRINCE AND THE PRINCESS LIVED HAPPILY EVER AFTER."
BLUSH
WHO CARES AS LONG AS IT'S A HAPPY ENDING, RIGHT?!
That's the Princess.
Who's Saki?
AND ALL WAS WELL IN THE LAND...

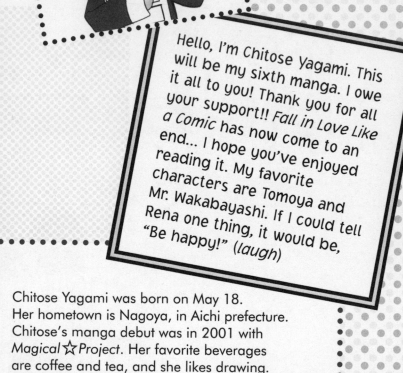

Hello, I'm Chitose Yagami. This will be my sixth manga. I owe it all to you! Thank you for all your support!! *Fall in Love Like a Comic* has now come to an end... I hope you've enjoyed reading it. My favorite characters are Tomoya and Mr. Wakabayashi. If I could tell Rena one thing, it would be, "Be happy!" *(laugh)*

Chitose Yagami was born on May 18. Her hometown is Nagoya, in Aichi prefecture. Chitose's manga debut was in 2001 with *Magical ☆ Project*. Her favorite beverages are coffee and tea, and she likes drawing. Her other works include *Boku no Platinum Lady* (My Platinum Lady), *Kiss Kiss*, and *Ikenai Navigation* (Naughty Navigation).

Fall in Love Like a Comic

Vol. 2

The Shojo Beat Manga Edition

STORY & ART BY

CHITOSE YAGAMI

Translation & Adaptaton/Mai Ihara
Touch-up Art & Lettering/Walden Wong
Design/Izumi Hirayama
Editor/Nancy Thistlethwaite

Editor in Chief, Books/Alvin Lu
Editor in Chief, Magazines/Marc Weidenbaum
VP of Publishing Licensing/Rika Inouye
VP of Sales/Gonzalo Ferreyra
Sr. VP of Marketing/Liza Coppola
Publisher/Hyoe Narita

Printed in Canada

Published by VIZ Media, LLC
P.O. Box 77064
San Francisco, CA 94107

Shojo Beat Manga Edition
10 9 8 7 6 5 4 3 2 1
First printing, January 2008

www.viz.com

store.viz.com

PARENTAL ADVISORY

FALL IN LOVE LIKE A COMIC is rated T+ for Older Teen and is recommended for ages 16 and up. This volume contains sexual themes.

RATED T+ FOR OLDER TEEN

ratings.viz.com

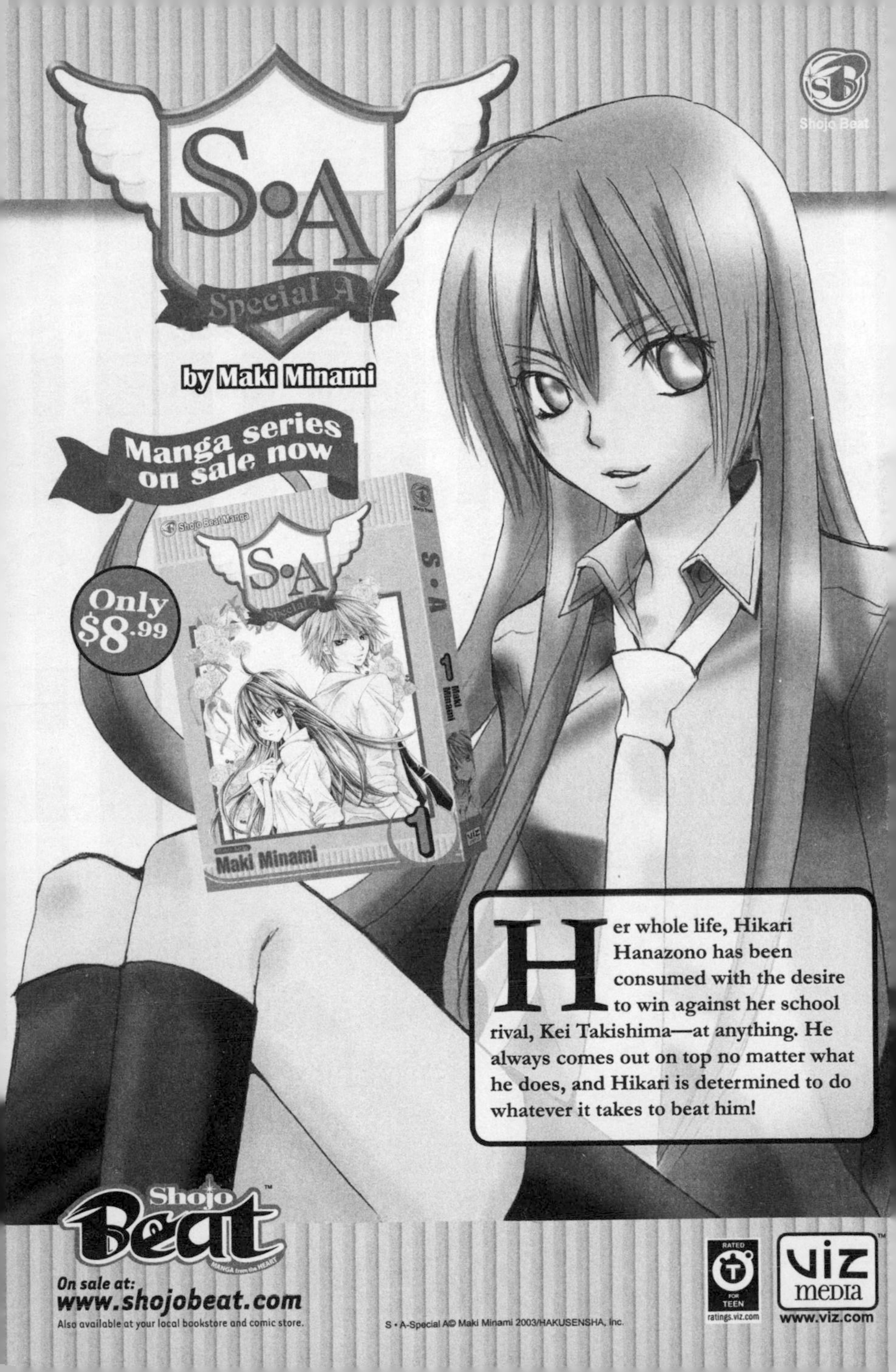

S•A
Special A
by Maki Minami
Manga series on sale now
Only $8.99
Shojo Beat Manga
S•A
Special A
1
Maki Minami
Her whole life, Hikari Hanazono has been consumed with the desire to win against her school rival, Kei Takishima—at anything. He always comes out on top no matter what he does, and Hikari is determined to do whatever it takes to beat him!
Shojo Beat
Shojo Beat™
MANGA from the HEART
On sale at:
www.shojobeat.com
Also available at your local bookstore and comic store.
S • A-Special A© Maki Minami 2003/HAKUSENSHA, Inc.
RATED T FOR TEEN
ratings.viz.com
VIZ media™
www.viz.com

Tell us what you think about Shojo Beat Manga!

Our survey is now available online. Go to:

shojobeat.com/mangasurvey

Help us make our product offerings better!